Landmark Essays

Landmark Essays

on
Voice and Writing

Edited by Peter Elbow

Hermagoras Press
1994

Landmark Essays Volume Four

Cover design by Kathi Zamminer

Originally published 1994 by Hermagoras Press,
now an Imprint of Lawrence Erlbaum Associates, Inc.

Lawrence Erlbaum Associates, Inc., Publishers
10 Industrial Avenue
Mahwah, New Jersey 07430

ISBN 1-880393-07-7

Books published by Lawrence Erlbaum Associates are printed
on acid-free paper, and their bindings are chosen
for strength and durability.

Printed in the United States of America

10 9 8 7 6 5 4 3 2 1

Dedication

For Estelle Jones. Whose remarkable voice I've heard longer than any other.

Acknowledgements

I'm grateful to the many many colleagues and students with whom I've talked, wrestled, and fussed about voice over the years. I've benefited from a lot of slow-motion collaboration.

I'm grateful to Jerry Murphy for the idea of this book and the chance to do it. I've found it an exciting and illuminating project. He's been tactful, supportive, wise—and a resourceful publisher.

I'm grateful for the chance to have worked during this same period with Kathleen Yancey on her collection of new essays about voice (cited in my bibliography). I benefited from working with her and some of the other contributors on an annotated bibliography for that volume. I'm also grateful for permission from her and from NCTE to use Randall Freisinger's essay from that collection here, and to cannibalize much of what I wrote in my essay there for my introduction here.

I'm grateful to the University of Massachusetts for some time released from teaching under a Graduate Office "Conti" fellowship that has made it possible for me to work on this book.

About the Editor

Peter Elbow is Professor of English at the University of Massachusetts at Amherst. He has written three books about writing: *Writing Without Teachers* (Oxford), *Writing with Power: Techniques for Mastering the Writing Process* (Oxford), and *A Community of Writers*, (McGraw Hill—this last a textbook co-authored with Pat Belanoff). He is author of a book of essays about learning and teaching: *Embracing Contraries* (Oxford). He has also written *Oppositions in Chaucer* (Wesleyan), as well as numerous essays about writing and teaching. His most recent book, *What is English?* (MLA and also NCTE), explores current issues in the profession of English.

His chapters on voice in *Writing With Power* have been frequently referred to in subsequent debates about voice in writing. His essay "The Shifting Relationships Between Speech and Writing" won the Richard Braddock award and was published in *College Composition and Communication* in October, 1985. With Pat Belanoff, he initiated the use of collaboratiave program-wide portfolio evaluation of writing, and many of his recent essays have been about assessment (e.g., "Ranking, Evaluating, Liking: Exploring Three Evaluative Responses," *College English* in February 1993.)

He has taught at M.I.T., Franconia College, Evergreen State College, and SUNY Stony Brook—where for five years he directed the Writing Program. He served for four years on the Executive Council of the Modern Language Association, and is now a member of the Executive Committee of the Conference on College Composition and Communication. He has given talks and workshops at many colleges and universities.

Table of Contents

Introduction

Section 2: Two Recent Views

Introduction

About Voice and Writing
by Peter Elbow

I'm setting out on a long path in this introduction so I'd better start with a quick overview of the terrain. In the first section (Part I) I describe three major debates about voice. These debates involve large, ideological questions about the nature of self or identity and about the relation of the text to the writer. These debates are all the more troublesome and unresolvable because they tend to be cast in binary, either/or terms.

In the longer second section (Part II), I respond to these debates by trying to show that we don't need to resolve them in either/or terms. Instead we can look carefully at the term *voice* and see that it has some fairly noncontroversial meanings when applied to writing. Thus I devote most of Part II to an extended exploration of a family of five meanings for the term *voice* in writing—meanings that make the concept of voice solid and usable apart from the theoretical debates.

I'm not saying that the two theoretical debates never come up. But they only come up in relatively circumscribed arenas and so don't muddy most uses of the concept of voice in writing. In short, my hope is that I can make descriptive *claims* about the meanings of voice in writing that people from various ideological camps will be able to agree on.

In the course of my introduction I will make brief references to the essays I have gathered into this anthology in order to suggest a bit of context or perspective on them. At the end of Part I, I risk a tentative grouping of these essays in terms of their theoretical orientation.

PART I

1. *The overarching debate:*
discourse as text vs. discourse as voice

Imagine the following mini-history of music: Once upon a time people just sang and played on drums, flutes, and strings. Then they learned to write down music on paper. Music was always performed, yet composers and editors often wrote it down so as to preserve it and to help with performing. A few composers and performers came to be able to look at the scores and "hear" the music. Slowly, slowly, over a long period of time, more and more people learned to read and enjoy music silently off the page and to write down music out of their heads. Finally it came to pass that reading and writing music on paper were as normal as singing, playing, or listening. It seemed self-evident that anyone who didn't write music or read it off the page for mental listening was seriously flawed and not a full member of society.

As a history of music, this is fantasy. But it *is* the history of language. In our highly literate culture, at least, writing simply *is* as "primary" and "natural" and "foundational" a medium as speech. I treasure many of Ong's insights about orality and literacy, but when he declares that writing is "thoroughly artificial and essentially defective," I have to throw up my hands in dismay.[1] When Saussure claims that writing is unnatural and corrupt, how can Derrida not make a fuss (in *On Grammatology*).

Such excesses as these by Ong and Saussure might tempt us to flop over to the other extreme and declare that *writing* is prior, or more foundational, or essential. But that would be wrong too. Even Derrida (as far as I can tell) is not claiming that writing is metaphysically real while voice is not. I take it that he's simply fighting the opposite claim or assumption that *voice* is metaphysically real while writing is not. If I am right about this, Derrida's "grammatology" is simply the study of discourse *as* "writing."

Even Barthes, declaring the "Death of the Author" (1968) and celebrating discourse not as "work" but as "text"—not as an authored or fathered work but as a free orphan we can play with as we please—text as plural, slippery, and a site for the play of myriad interpretations: even Barthes isn't saying that all discourse *is* text, not even all written discourse. He's saying that we can choose which lens to look through.

In short, we now have a *choice* about how to think about discourse: as semiotic text or as voiced utterance. Yes, virtually everyone learns to speak before learning to write, and most people remain more comfortable in speech than writing. But we live in a text world just as much as we live in an oral world. In some ways I feel *more* comfortable writing and reading than I do speaking and listening—and this condition is not really so uncommon. Furthermore, the burgeoning electronic media of networked computers and E-mail and Internet are making more and more people feel as easy and fluid with text as with speech. In our culture, then, both speech and writing can be seen as equally grounded and natural—neither more authentic or real than the other.

There is no problem with either the voice lens or the text lens. There is only a problem when people try to outlaw one and insist that this isn't a matter of two lenses for discourse, two "terministic screens," but rather an either/or debate between right and wrong. The fact is, we need both lenses. Each one shows us things the other hides.

Insofar as we consider discourse as text or semiosis, it is pure disembodied language; no one is speaking to anyone. The paradigm cases are mathematics and logic. Mathematics is language—and in many ways the best one we've got. An equation is seldom a case of someone saying something to

---

[1] Walter Ong, "From Mimesis to Irony: Writing and Print as Integuments of Voice," *Interfaces of the Word: Studies in the Evolution of Consciousness and Culture* (Ithaca: Cornell UP, 1977), 280.

anyone else. It's usually just a set of things-standing-for-things or semiosis. The symbols mainly proclaim a relationship: that something is the case, or means something, or equals something.

If we look at natural language through this lens of text or semiosis, we see important things about it. We strip away the people, the historical drama, the body, the actual person trying to do something to someone else. So stripped, we can see better those root, bare meanings and relationships. The people, the body, the historical drama, and the fact that someone has designs on us when they speak or write these words—all these things muddy the water and often make us confused or mistaken in our reading or analysis of the signs as pure semiosis. (Most of us can probably remember examples of trying to listen to mathematics when the voice or embodiment or human relationship got in the way. Perhaps we were so mad at someone that we couldn't understand the train of thought they were explaining. Perhaps we were trying to listen to a math teacher who thought we were dumb. We could have heard the math better from a machine.)

I may be going against the current emphasis on the historical and subjective dimension of all discourse (the rhetorical emphasis) in saying that it can be useful to look at even natural language as pure disembodied meaning. But there's no doubting how much we have learned from this approach in our era. The New Critics made us better readers by teaching us to look at literature not as authors talking to us but as well wrought urns existing out of time.[2] Semiotics, sign theory, and structuralism in linguistics and literary criticism also changed our reading forever by showing us how to see highly abstract, geometricized, impersonal patterns in any myth or piece of literature or discourse at all. "Text" and "sign" became the preferred word not just for language but for anything that carries meaning (e.g., the textuality of clothing or the semiotics of driving). Poststructuralists carried on with this powerful project of helping us not be "fooled" by the writer's character or the music of his language.

But of course it's become obvious in recent years how helpful it is to use the *other* lens and see discourse as always historically situated and always coming from persons and addressed to others—that is, to fight free of the stripping-away lens. But in taking what could be called this rhetorical point of view, not so many people use the voice metaphor. The tendency is always to talk in terms of "text" or "discourse" as issuing from historically situated persons—not "utterance" or "voice." It is this fear and avoidance of the term *voice* that I hope to remove.

After all, Bakhtin—admired on all fronts—insists on voice as the central

---

[2] In telling a simple, stripped down story, I pass over some interesting complications. For example, when New Critics insist that the text is *not* an author or real person talking to us as persons, the word or metaphor they latch onto is "*speaker*." They insist that every text involves a speaker and they ask us to sharpen our ears and hear "all language as a drama—as an act of defining a particular voice. . . ." (Gibson's words—from the essay in this volume).

term (even while acknowledging that discourse *can* be analyzed as disembodied language). Here's one passage:

> Where linguistic analysis sees only words and the interrelations of their abstract factors (phonetic, morphological, syntactic, and so on), there, for living artistic perception and for concrete sociological analysis, relations among *people* stand revealed, relations merely reflected and fixed in verbal material. Verbal discourse is the skeleton that takes on living flesh only in the process of creative perception—consequently, only in the process of living social communication.[3]

Bakhtin describes all discourse in terms of "voices" and "speakers" and "listeners." All discourse is part of a "Speech Chain" (the title of one of his essays). "For Bakhtin, words cannot be conceived apart from the voices who speak them."[4]

For of course it can even be helpful to look at mathematical discourse through this voice lens. *In a sense* (we need this phrase that Aristotle loved, since he saw that understanding depends on the ability to look at something first through one lens and then through another), a set of equations doesn't just sit as a semantic relationship, it can also be seen as someone responding to someone else who wrote different equations.

In short, the *textuality* metaphor highlights how discourse issues from other discourse (seeing all texts as "intertextual"), while the *voice* metaphor highlights how discourse issues from individual persons and from physical bodies. The text metaphor highlights the visual and spatial features of language and emphasizes language as an abstract, universal system; the voice metaphor highlights sound and hearing rather than vision, and it emphasizes the way all linguistic meaning moves historically through time rather than existing simultaneously in space. The textuality metaphor calls attention to the commonalities between one person's discourse and that of others and of the culture; the voice metaphor calls attention to the differences from one person to another. (The same discourse in two human settings is not the same. Even two people's "cat" are similar as text, but they sound very different as spoken or voiced.) We benefit from both metaphors or lenses and lose out if either is outlawed. I openly celebrate the discourse-as-voice lens and the dimension of sound because of my own interests and because it is a kind of underdog in the scholarly world; but I'm not trying to get rid of the discourse-as-text lens or the visual metaphor.

But when we turn from theory and reading to *writing* and teaching

---

[3] From the essay printed in this volume ("Discourse in Life and Discourse in Art"), but from a passage that occurs in a later part of the essay (109) that is not included here.

[4] Caryl Emerson, "The Outer Word and Inner Speech: Bakhtin, Vygotsky, and the Internalization of Language," *Critical Inquiry* 10 (December 1983): 24. Deborah Brandt argues in an important book that texts are sites of interaction between people, and that in a text we don't just have persona and implied author but the real presence of actual writer and reader (see *Literacy as Involvement*, Southern Illinois UP, 1990, e.g., 71). Speech act theory is another approach to language that insist on the centrality of who is speaking to whom for what purpose (agent, act, motive) for the analysis of discourse.

writing, it might seem hard to keep up this benign, tolerant approach. In writing it seems as though we are forced to make an either/or choice: should we try to use our voice to *speak* and *utter* on paper? Or should we try to deploy textuality to *construct* written discourse? In teaching, we see a similar debate: on one side, people argue that we should heighten the difference between orality and writing; that the very weakness in weak writers is their tendency to be too oral.[5] Brandt (note 4) and others would disagree.

Yet even here we can avoid the either/or trap. That is, I find myself benefiting at certain moments in my writing from just playing with meanings or structures—as though I'm doing pure math or playing disembodied games or trying to get musical shapes right—and not trying to respond to anyone or *address* my words to anyone. This is especially true during private, exploratory freewriting. At other moments (sometimes also in freewriting), it helps me to experience myself as embodied and trying to reach out palpably with my words toward other embodied readers. And it helps me to move back and forth between these text and voice modalities. (However, even when I'm in a text modality and just playing with meanings, not with people, I always find it more helpful to let myself as it were *speak* my words onto paper.)

It's my belief, then, that even in the processes of writing and teaching writing, we do better not to try to declare a winner in the voice/text debate, but instead to make use of both approaches or lenses.[6]

2. *The traditional debate in rhetoric: ethos as real virtue in the real person vs ethos as the appearance of virtue*

It's worth taking a few pages to show how far back the debate goes between whether we hear the actual author through his or her language—or just hear an adopted role. In an important essay about the history of rhetoric, Nan Johnson writes: "The status of *ethos* in the hierarchy of rhetorical principles has fluctuated as rhetoricians in different eras have tended to define rhetoric in terms of either idealistic aims or pragmatic skills" (105).[7] She shows that Plato and Aristotle stand at the head of this traditional debate:

> [For Plato] the reality of the speaker's virtue is presented as a prerequisite to effective speaking. In contrast, Aristotle's *Rhetoric*

---

[5] See Reed Way Dasenbrock, "Becoming Aware of the Myth of Presence." *Journal of Advanced Composition* 8 (1988): 1-11; Thomas J. Farrell, "IQ and Standard English," *College Composition and Communication* 34 (December 1983): 470-84; Andrea Lunsford, "The Content of Basic Writers' Essays," *College Composition and Communication* 31 (October 1980): 278-90; David R. Olson, "The Languages of Instruction: The Literate Bias of Schooling," in R. C. Anderson, R. J. Siro, and W. E. Montague (eds.), *Schooling and the Acquisition of Knowledge* (Hillsdale, NJ: Lawrence Erlbaum, 1977).
[6] For more about treating writing as both "text" and "speech," see my "Shifting Relationships Between Speech and Writing," *College Composition and Communication* 36 (1985): 283-303. For more about ignoring audience, see my "Closing My Eyes as I Speak: An Argument For Ignoring Audience," *College English* 49.1 (Jan, 1987): 50-69. For a defense against kneejerk critiques of any binary categories, see my "The Uses of Binary Thinking," *Journal of Advanced Composition* 12.1 (Winter, 1993).
[7] Nan Johnson, "Ethos and the Aims of Rhetoric," in *Essays on Classical Rhetoric and Modern Discourse*, ed. Robert J. Connors, Lisa Ede and Andrea Lunsford (Carbondale: Southern Illinois UP: 1984), 98-114.

presents rhetoric as a strategic art which facilitates decisions in civil
matters and accepts the appearance of goodness as sufficient to inspire
conviction in hearers. (99)

> The contrasting views of Cicero and Quintilian about the aims of
> rhetoric and the function of ethos are reminiscent of Plato's and
> Aristotle's differences of opinion about whether or not moral virtue in
> the speaker is intrinsic and prerequisite or selected and strategically
> presented. . . . (105)

She goes on to trace these two traditions of ethos in the history of rhetoric.
For example in the medieval period, the *ars dictaminis* or letter writing
followed the strategic or pragmatic tradition of Aristotle and Cicero; the *ars
praedicandi* or preaching or ecclesiastic rhetoric followed the more idealistic
tradition of Plato and Quintilian. "A focus on the 'opinion' of the hearers is
typical in pragmatic definitions of ethos; the emphasis is placed much more
on the speaker's need to be aware of audience needs than on the disposition
of the intrinsic virtue of the orator. Ecclesiastical rhetoric, however,
emphasizes the importance of the reality rather than the appearance of virtue"
(108).

As these traditions appear in 18th and 19th century rhetoric, she notes that
the pragmatic tradition is more belletristic—and is represented by Whately;
the idealistic tradition is essentially epistemological—and is represented by
Channing (109). Thus Channing writes:

> It would not be going too far to say that it is not in all the graces
> of address, or sweetness and variety of tones, or beauty of
> illustration—in all the outward and artificial accomplishments of the
> orator, to equal or even approach the power conferred by a good
> character. Its still eloquence is felt in the commonest transactions of
> life. (Quoted in Johnson 110).

Blair and Campbell, she says, try to do justice to both the pragmatic,
belletristic tradition *and* the idealistic, epistemological one—according to
whether they are dealing with secular or religious situations.

Matthew Hope, writing in the mid nineteenth century, brings in a term
that has become a center of modern dispute. "Hope regards the character of
the speaker as potentially having great persuasive force, a force Hope defines
as 'presence.' Presence, he explains, is 'due to intellectual force, somewhat to
strength of will or purpose or character, somewhat to the spiritual qualities of
the man'" (111).

Johnson describes contemporary rhetoric as dominated by the pragmatic
or strategic tradition (noting Richard Weaver and Wayne Booth as
exceptions):

> The marked tendency of modern rhetorical texts to present
> strategic definitions of ethos seems to proceed from a widely held
> Aristotelian-Ciceronian view that rhetoric is an art of inventional,
> compositional, and communicative competence. . . . Explanations and

guidelines for the use of ethos repeat traditional pragmatic advice that writers must create the appearance of sincerity in order to persuade. The concept of ethos rarely appears in current texts by name. Rather, it is discussed under such varied stylistic headings as "tone," "writer's voice," "personal appeal," "attitude," "persona," and "credibility." [She goes on to quote a typical textbook example:] "When you write you create an identity for yourself. Using only words—no make-up, no costumes, no scenery, no music—you have to present yourself to an audience and get its attention and its confidence. You can . . . by using imagination and trying to develop a sense of tone, learn to present yourself in various ways . . . you ask, 'how can I use language to make my audience believe in this character?' (51)"

Modern texts advise students to correlate 'persona' with assessments of the reader and the writing situation. Such advice presents ethos as a skill of stylistic adaptability to mode and audience, and typically eschews moral implications (112-13).

This ancient and venerable debate about ethos and virtue leads to, and in a sense even contains, the modern debate about the relationship between voice and identity. That is, if persuasion depends on genuine virtue in the speaker, not just on virtuous-seeming words, then the implication is clear: Plato, Quintilian, Channing and the others in that tradition believe that listeners and readers get a sense of the real speaker and his or her real virtue (or the absence of it) through the words on the page.

3. *The modern debate: voice as self vs. voice as role*

Johnson suggests, then, that modern rhetorical studies are dominated by a "strategic" or "pragmatic" stance on voice: that "we create an identity for ourselves" when we write, that our written voice is a linguistic creation rather than any reflection of some "real self," and that in discussions or explorations of textual voice there's no use bringing in talk about the actual character of the writer. This continuation of Johnson's "pragmatic" tradition becomes in our times what I think of as the sophisticated, ironic, critical view on voice. In this view, either there is *no* "real self"—"self" consisting of nothing but the succession of voices or selves that we create in language; or perhaps there *is* a real self but it's completely invisible and unavailable to readers, so the only thing worth talking about is the created self on paper.

But there have always been staunch defenders of the opposite view about the relationship between voice and identity: a view that people do have some kind of identity that exists apart from the language they use, and that it's worth trying to talk about whether or not that identity shows in a textual voice. There are various versions of this view—some seeming more naive than others: that everyone has a unique and special self or that only special geniuses do; that the self is single and unchanging or developing and multiform; that it is rare and difficult to express or embody this identity in words or that it's easy if only you speak or write naturally and sincerely instead of artificially. In any event, the phrase "finding one's own voice" became common and remains so—and not just among self-obsessed sophomores, not just among naive members of the general public, but across a wide spectrum of critics, scholars, creative and imaginative writers, and teachers of writing. Here is Helen Vendler talking about Sylvia Plath: she "had early mastered certain coarse sound effects," but in her later poetry, "she has given up on a bald imitation of Thomas and has found her own voice." Here is John Simon (anything but loose about language) talking about Ingmar Bergman: "With Barktok and Stravinsky, Braque and Picasso, Rilke and Valéry, Borges and Proust, among others, he is one of the fertile and seminal masters, an artist of many modes and one, unique voice."[8]

Here are two classic or grandfather formulations of this kind of thinking about voice and identity, one by Tolstoy (in "What is Art?") and the other by Yeats (in *Autobiographies*):

> I have mentioned three conditions of contagion in art, but they may be all summed up into one, the last, sincerity; that is, that the artist should be impelled by an inner need to express his feelings. . . . if the artist is sincere he will express the feeling as he experienced it. And as each man is different, from every one else, his feeling will be individual for everyone else; and the more individual it is—the more the artist has drawn it from the depths of his nature—the more sympathetic and sincere it will be.
>
> We should write our own thoughts in as nearly as possible the language we thought them in, as though in a letter to an intimate friend. We should not disguise them in any way; for our lives give them force as the lives of people in plays give force to their words. . . . I tried from then on to write out my emotions exactly as they came to me in life, not changing them to make them more beautiful. 'If I can be sincere and make my language natural, and without becoming discursive, like a novelist, and so indiscreet and prosaic,' I said to myself, 'I should, if good luck or bad luck make my life interesting, be a great poet; for it will be no longer a matter of literature at all.'

Views like these almost cry out for sophisticated critiques—and critiques are not hard to find. New Critics talk of the intentional fallacy and say that we are in no position to talk about sincerity or the real person who wrote the text. Marxist and cultural critics say that "the subject is itself a social construct that emerges through the linguistically-circumscribed interaction of the individual, the community, and the material world."[9] Poststructural and deconstructive critics cut loose the text from the author yet again. Plenty of influential critics and sociologists say that the "self" is nothing but a

---

[8] Helen Vendler, "An Intractable Metal," *New Yorker* (15 Feb 1982): 131. John Simon, Rev. of *Images: My Life in Film* by Ingmar Bergman, *New York Times Book Review* (30 Jan 1994): 7-8.
[9] James A. Berlin, "Rhetoric and Ideology in the Writing Class," *College English* 50.5 (Sept 1988): 489.

collection of roles. And plenty of writing teachers—even if they have conventional views of the self and of sincerity—nevertheless say, in effect, "Sure, sincerity is a virtue in writing, but only a minor one. The major virtues are careful thinking, coherent structure, clear syntax. Let's not kid students into thinking they can get very far with sincerity or self in writing. What needs to show through in writing is not the self but the craft."

It's worth calling attention to an interesting site of this sophisticated, ironic view of the self as continually created anew from language: the Amherst College first year English course inaugurated and directed by Theodore Baird from 1938 to 1966. Walker Gibson and William Coles (with essays in this volume) both worked in that course, and there is a remarkable list of others who also taught in it or can be argued to have been influenced by it: Rueben Brower, Richard Poirer, Roger Sale, Neil Hertz, David Bartholomae, Gordon Pradl. Robert Frost, with his interest in voice, lurked in the background of this course. Baird and the others who taught in the course were interested in voice and had some of the best ears around for noticing its nuances. They engaged in what Pritchard called "ear training." They were very interested in the self—but a self continually being re-made by language.[10]

This large dispute about the relationship between voice and identity, then, is the issue of greatest contention in "voice" discussions in composition. Indeed, with Derrida's focus on what he calls the metaphysics of voice and presence, this issue of voice/discourse/identity has become one of the main critical issues in all of English studies, cultural studies, and critical theory. It is certainly the main issue of contention among the essays I have gathered for this volume.

At first glance the debate seems to be between a naive credulity about the power of sincere presence in texts and a sophisticated, ironic critique—especially when we look at it from our present cultural moment. But I hope this book will encourage readers not to define the debate in such simplistic terms. On the one hand, what I'm calling the sophisticated position can take many forms, and I find the Amherst version represented by Gibson and Coles to be subtle and nuanced. On the other hand (and of course I tend to lean toward this hand), the allegedly naive position can be seen as not so naive. In some formulations it functions as a kind of sophisticated (but not ironic) critique of the sophisticated critique. I see this kind of complexity in Park's and Freisinger's essays (in this volume). Similarly, when Gilligan, hooks, and

---

[10]On this course, see Robin Varnum, *English 1-2 at Amherst College, 1938-66* (Urbana IL: NCTE, in press). Also Joseph Harris, "Voice" in *Contested Terms*, Unpublished MS; and William Pritchard, "Ear Training," in *Teaching What We Do* (Amherst MA: Amherst College P, 1991). The passages from Tolstoy and Yeats, above, came from one of the assignment series for that course—a semester long series of assignments on the topic of masks. Stanford University was another interesting site of rich experimentation on voice and writing. See John Hawkes, "The Voice Project: An Idea for Innovation in the Teaching of Writing," in *Writers as Teachers: Teachers as Writers* (New York: Holt Rinehart and Winston, 1970), 89-144. (Hawkes described the project at greater length in *Voice Project, Final Report*, Stanford: Stanford U, 1967, ERIC ED 018 44.) The project was influenced by *The Personal Voice*, a text/reader by Albert Guerard, John Hawkes, and Claire Rosenfield.

Jordan (also gathered here) speak as women and/or African Americans, they are not fighting for a single, unchanging, unsocial voice, but they *are* insisting that if your habitual or accustomed or home voice has been devalued or silenced, there is something important and political at stake in being able to use a voice that you experience as *yours*. In short, they are rejecting the ironic, sophisticated view that says, "All voices are just roles, and the relation between your textual voice and who you really are is irrelevant." The experience of feeling that one's habitual voice is considered illegitimate makes you want to insist that a piece of one's identity is at stake in one's textual voice.

In this volume I have arranged the essays in the order of their publication, but perhaps it might useful for me to risk here a brief and arguable grouping of them in terms of their orientation to this debate about discourse and identity. The following authors can probably be said to take the more sophisticated or ironic stance—criticizing the idea that we can talk about the real person in the textual voice: Gibson, Coles, Derrida/Johnson, Hashimoto, Faigley. In contrast, the following writers in one way or another defend or celebrate the value of attending to the relationship of the text to the actual writer: Ong, hooks, Jordan, Park, Freisinger, Gilligan. And the following authors don't seem so much to argue for one side or the other but rather to *analyze* some of the terms and concepts that are involved in exploring the relationship between voice and writing: Bakhtin, Cherry, Palacas, Fulwiler.

PART II[11]

The best way to deal with these three debates about voice and writing is to distinguish between *different senses* of voice. We don't have to figure out winners or losers in these binary and ideological disputes if we apply the term with more care and discrimination. In this longer part of my introduction I will first explore some of the features of literal, physical voice, and then describe five meanings of voice as applied to writing: (1) audible voice or intonation (the sounds in a text); (2) dramatic voice (the character or implied author in a text); (3) recognizable or distinctive voice; (4) voice with authority; (5) resonant voice or presence. By making these distinctions I think I can confine the ideological dispute to that fifth meaning—the only meaning that requires a link between the known text and the unknown actual author. That is, I think I can show that the first four senses of voice in writing are sturdy, useful, and relatively noncontroversial.

Literal Voice: Observations About the Human Voice

When people refer to voice in writing or to someone "achieving voice" (for example in Belenky et al, in *Women's Ways of Knowing*), they are using a

---

[11]In this part, I draw heavily on my essay, "What Do We Mean When We Talk about Voice in Writing?" in *Voices on Voice: A (Written) Discussion*, ed. Kathleen Blake Yancey (NCTE, 1994).

metaphor. This metaphor is so common that perhaps it will one day become literal—as "leg of the table" has become a literal phrase. Once you start listening for the word *voice*, it's amazing how often you find it in books and articles and reviews—especially in titles. Sometimes the writer is consciously using the term to make some point about writing or psychology, but more often the term is just used in a loosely honorific, poetic way. When there is so much metaphorical talk about voice, I find it intellectually cleansing to remind myself that it *is* a metaphor and to acquaint myself better with the literal term—and even try to immerse myself better in the experience of the literal thing itself, the human voice. If this were a workshop, it would be good to do some talking, reciting, singing, and other exercises in orality—and stop and see what we notice.

Let me put down here, then, some literal facts about the human voice. These are not quite "innocent facts" since I want them to show why voice has become such a suggestive and resonant term. But I hope you will agree that they are "true facts."

- Voice is produced by the body. To talk about voice in writing is to import connotations of the body into the discussion—and by implication, to be interested in the role of the body in writing.

- Almost always, people learn to speak before they learn to write. Normally we learn speech at such an early age that we are not aware of the learning process. Speech habits are laid down at a deep level. Also, speaking comes before writing in the development of cultures.

- We identify and recognize people by their voices—usually even when they have a cold or over a bad phone connection. We usually recognize people by voice even after a number of years. Something constant persists despite the change. Of course there are exceptions—such as when some boys go through adolescence.

- People have demonstrably unique voices: "voice prints" are evidently as certain as fingerprints for identification. This might suggest the analogy of our bodies being genetically unique, but our voice prints are less dependent upon genes than our bodies.

- For we can distinguish two dimensions to someone's voice: the *sound* of their voice and the *manner* or style with which they speak. The first is the quality of noise they make based as it were on the physical "instrument" they are "playing"; and the second is the kind of "tunes, rhythms, and styles" they play on their instrument.

- Despite the unique and recognizable quality of an individual's voice, we all usually display enormous variation in how we speak from occasion to occasion. Sometimes we speak in monotone, sometimes with lots of intonation. And we use different "tones" of voice at different times, e.g., excited, scared, angry, sad. Furthermore we sometimes speak self-consciously or "artificially," but more often we speak with no attention or even awareness of how we are speaking. The distinction between a "natural" and "artificial" way of talking is theoretically vexed, but in fact listeners and speakers often agree in judgments as to whether someone was speaking naturally or artificially on a given occasion.

- Our speech often gives a naked or candid picture of how we're feeling—as when our voice quavers with fear or unhappiness or lilts with elation or goes flat with depression. People sometimes detect our mood after hearing nothing but our "hello" on the phone. Our moods often show through in our writing too—at least to sensitive readers; but it's easier to hide how we're feeling in our writing. We can ponder and revise the words we put down. Speaking is harder to control, usually less self conscious, closer to autonomic behavior. Cicero says the voice is a picture of the mind. People commonly identify someone's voice with *who* he or she is—with their character—just as it is common to identify one's self with one's body. (The word "person" means both body and self—and it suggests a link between the person and the sound of the voice. "Persona" was the word for the mask that Greek actors wore to amplify their voices [per + sona].)

- Audience has a big effect on voice. Partly it's a matter of *imitating* how those around us talk. Partly it's a matter of *responding* to those around us. That is, our voice tends to change as we speak to different people—often without awareness. We tend to speak differently to a child, to a buddy, to someone we are afraid of. My wife says she can hear when I'm speaking to a woman on the phone. Some listeners seem to bring out more intonation in our speech (see Bakhtin on "choral support" in his essay here).

- There are good actors, on and off the stage, who can convincingly make their voices seem to show whatever feeling or character they want.

- People can become just as comfortable in writing as in speaking; indeed we are sometimes deeply awkward, tangled, and even blocked in our speaking.

- Though voice is produced by the body, it is produced out of *air* or *breath*: something that is not the body and which is shared or common to us all—but which issues from inside us and is a sign of life. This may partly explain why so many people have been tempted to invest voice with deep or even spiritual connotations.

- Voice involves sound, hearing and time; writing or text involves sight and space. The differences between these modalities are profound and interesting. (To try to characterize these modalities, however, as Ong and Ihde do at length, is speculative so I must resort briefly to parentheses here. Sight seems to tell us more about the outsides of things, sound more about the insides of things. Evolutionarily, sight is the most recent sense modality to become dominant in humans—and is dealt with in the largest and most recent parts of the human brain. Sight seems to be most linked to rationality—in our brain and our metaphors—e.g., "Do you see?" But there are crucial dangers in going along with Ong and others in making such firm and neat associations between certain *mentalities* and orality and literacy—especially for the teaching of writing.[12]

---

[12]For Ong's analysis see his works listed in the bibliography of this volume; also those by Ihde, Havelock, and Goody. For a warning about linking mentallty with orality and literacy see Brandt, Tannen, and my "Shifting Relations Between Speech and Writing"—all also in the bibliography.)

- Spoken language has more semiotic channels than writing. That is, speech contains more channels for carrying meaning, more room for the play of difference. The list of channels is impressive. For example, there is volume (loud and soft), pitch (high and low), speed (fast and slow), accent (present or absent), intensity (relaxed and tense). And note that these are not just binary items, for in each case there is a full range of subtle *degrees* all the way between extremes. In addition there are many patterned sequences: for example tune is a pattern of pitches; rhythm is a pattern of slow and fast and accent. Furthermore there is a wide spectrum of timbres (breathy, shrill, nasal, &c); there are glides and jumps; there are pauses of varying lengths. Combinations of *all* of these factors make the possibilities dizzying. And *all* these factors carry meaning. Consider the subtle or not so subtle pauses we make as we speak, the little intensity or lengthening of a syllable—and all the other ways we add messages to the *lexical* content of our speech.[13]

It's not that writing is poverty stricken as a semiotic system. But writing has to achieve its subtleties with fewer resources. A harpsichord cannot make the gradations of volume of a piano, but harpsichordists use subtle cues of timing to communicate the *kind* of thing that pianos communicate with volume. Mozart had fewer harmonic resources to play with than Brahms, but he did quite a lot with his less. To write well is also to do a lot with less. If we are angry, we sometimes press harder with the pen or break the pencil lead or *hit* the keys harder or write the words all in a rush, and our speech would probably sound very angry; but none of these physical behaviors shows in our writing.

Consider the many ways we can say the sentence, "Listen to me"—from angry to fond—or in fact with a whole range of modes of anger. With writing, our options are comparatively small. We can underline or use all caps; we can end with a comma, a period, a question mark, an exclamation mark. We can create pauses by using the ellipsis sign. There are other textual resources of course—such as varying the spacing, sizing, or color of letters and words, playing with the shaping of letters and words, and so forth—but these are considered "informal" and inappropriate to "literate" writing. Perhaps the main resource in writing is word choice: choose different words, put them in different orders, set a context by what comes before or afterwards to affect how readers will experience any given sentence. These are the ways we convey significations in writing that we convey effortlessly in speech. In writing, we must do more with fewer channels.[14]

---

[13]See David Hoddeson, "The Reviser's Voices," *Journal of Basic Writing* 3.3 (Fall/Winter 1981): 91-108. For a masterful and scholarly treatment of all dimensions of intonation in speech, see Dwight Bolinger, *Intonation and its Parts: Melody in Spoken English* (Stanford: Stanford UP, 1986).

[14]For an exploration of how poets add to the resources of written language by the use of meter, line, and stanza, see Reuben Brower, "The Speaking Voice," in *The Fields of Light: An Experiment in Critical Reading* (New York: Oxford, 1962), 58-74.

Voice in Writing: A Family of Related Meanings

People have voices; radios, telephones, TV sets, and tape recorders have voices. Texts have no voices, they are silent. We can only talk about voice in writing by resorting to metaphor. It's my argument that this is a metaphor worth using, but we can't use it well unless we untangle five related meanings that have got caught up in it: audible voice, dramatic voice, recognizable or distinctive voice, voice with authority, and resonant voice or presence.

(1) *Audible voice or intonation in writing*

All texts are literally silent, but most readers experience some texts as giving more sense of sound—more of the illusion as we read that we are hearing the words sounded. Robert Frost insists that this is not just a virtue but a necessity: "A dramatic necessity goes deep into the nature of the sentence. . . . All that can save them is the speaking tone of voice somehow entangled in the words and fastened to the page for the ear of the imagination."[15]

How is it, then, that some texts have this audible voice? We have to sneak up on the answer by way of two facts I cited in the previous section: that most people have spoken longer and more comfortably than they have written, and that speaking has more channels of meaning than writing. As a result of these two things, when most people encounter a text—a set of words that just sit there silently on the page with no intonation, rhythm, accent, and so forth—they automatically *project aurally* some speech sounds onto the text. Given how conditioning and association work, most people cannot help it. Our most frequent and formative experiences with language have involved hearing speech.

In fact, people are virtually incapable of reading without nerve activity in the throat as though to speak—usually even *muscular* activity. We joke about people who move their lips as they read, but such movement is common even among the sophisticated and educated—and many poets insist that it is a travesty to read otherwise. (Have researchers checked out the *hearing* nerves while people read? I'll bet the circuits are busy.) Silent reading must be learned and is relatively recent. St. Augustine tells in his *Confessions* how amazed he was to see Ambrose reading without saying the words outloud.

In short hearing a text is the norm. We are conditioned to hear words, and the conditioning continues through life. Thus the fruitful question is not why we hear some texts but rather why we don't hear them all.

There are two main things that prevent us from hearing written words. The most obvious barriers come from the text itself: certain texts resist our conditioned habit to hear. The writer has chosen or arranged words so that it is hard or impossible to say them, and as a result we seem to experience them as hard to hear. This further illustrates the mediation of voice in hearing: for

---

[15]Robert Frost, Introduction, *A Way Out* (New York: Seven Arts, 1917).

of course, strictly speaking, we can *hear* any word at all. But when written words are easy to say, especially if we have frequently heard these phrases or cadences because they are characteristic of idiomatic speech, we tend to hear them more as we read; when written words are awkward or unidiomatic for speech, we tend to hear them less.

People produce unsayable writing in many ways. Some poets, for example, want to block sound and exploit vision (as in concrete poetry, some poems by e. e. cummings, and some L=A=N=G=U=A=G=E poetry). Much legal and bureaucratic writing is unidiomatic and unsayable and thus tends to be unheard because the writers so often create syntax by a process of "constructing" or roping together units (often jargon or even boiler plate units) in a way that has nothing to do with speech. Some scholarly writing is unsayable for various reasons. (A certain amount of technical and difficult terminology may be unavoidable; and consciously or not, scholars may want to sound learned or even keep out the uninitiated.) And of course many unskilled writers also lose all contact with the process of speech or utterance as they write: they stop so often in the middle of a phrase to wonder or worry about a word, to look up its spelling, or to change it to one that sounds more impressive, that they lose their syntactic thread and thereby produce many sentences that are wrong or completely unidiomatic.

But we can't blame inaudible writing only on awkward language or ungainly writers. There is a larger reason—culturally produced—why we often don't hear a voice in writing. Our culture of literacy has inculcated in most of us a habit of working actively to keep the human voice out of our texts when we write.

Notice, for example, the informal writing of adolescents or of people who are just learning the conventions of writing. Notice how often they use the language of speech. In addition they often use striking textual devices that are explicitly designed to convey some of the vividly audible features of speech—some of the music and drama of the voice: pervasive underlining— sometimes double or triple; three or four exclamation marks or question marks at once; pervasive all-caps; oversized letters, colors, parenthetical slang asides "(NOT!!)." (I'm sure I'm not alone in using too many underlinings in my rough drafts—as I'm trying to speak my emphases onto the page—and so I'm always having to get rid of them as I revise and try to find other means to give the emphasis I want.)

What interests me is how unthinkingly we all go along with the assumption that these textual practices are wrong for writing. That is, most of us are unconscious of how deeply our culture's version of literacy has involved a decision to keep voice out of writing, to maximize the difference between speech and writing—to prevent writers from using even those few crude markers that could capture more of the subtle and not so subtle semiotics of speech. Our version of literacy requires people to distance their writing behavior further from their speaking behavior than the actual modalities require. So when Derrida tries to remove connotations of voice from writing, (though he's not saying, "Stop all that informal language and that underlining and putting things in all caps!"), he is nevertheless giving an unnecessary fillip to a steamroller long at work in our version of literacy.

Thus it is *not* lack of skill or knowledge that keeps an audible voice out of the writing of so many poor writers. It's their worry about conforming to our particular conventions of writing and their fear of mistakes. Unskilled writers who are *not* worried—usually unschooled writers—tend to write prose that is very audible and speech-like. Here is a first grader writing a large story:

> One day, well if there was a day. There was sand and dust and rocks and stones and some other things. And it was a thunderclaps! And a planet began to rise. And they called it Earth. And do you know what? It rained and rained and rained for thirty days in the big holes. And see we began to grow. And the first animal was a little dinosaur. . . . Don't listen to the newspaperman, all that about the sun. Don't be afraid because the sun will last for ever. That's all there is.[16]

The very term "illiterate writing," as it is commonly used, tends in fact to imply that the writing suffers from being too much like speech. The culture of school and literacy seems to work *against* our tendency to write as we speak or to hear sounds in a text. (Two important exceptions: first, the still-evolving conventions for writing on E-mail—even scholarly writing—seem to be inviting more oral and voiced qualities into writing or literacy. Second, our culture sanctions more audible voice in poetry and fiction and literary nonfiction—perhaps because of the stronger or more recent the links to orality in these forms.)

So far I have been focusing on the question of how speech intonation gets into writing. But we mustn't forget the important prior question: how does intonation get into speech in the first place? For of course sometimes our speech *lacks* intonation. Sometimes we speak in a monotone; some people put more "expression" into their speech than others. Bakhtin, in the essay included here, focuses on intonation. He argues that intonation often carries the most important meaning in any discourse—meaning that may not be carried by the lexical, semantic meaning. As he puts it, intonation is the point where language intersects with life. And he points out that we often lose intonation in our speaking if we lack "choral support" from listeners—that is, if we have an audience that doesn't share our values. But it doesn't always work that way. In the face of an unsupportive or adversarial audience, we sometimes rise to the challenge or even lose our temper, and thus *raise* our voice and increase our intonation.

I sense even a gender issue here. Do not women in our culture tend to use more expression or intonation in their speech than men—more variation in pitch, accent, rhythm and so forth?—men tending on average to be a bit more

---

[16]Lucy McCormick Calkins, *The Art of Teaching Writing* (Portsmouth NH: Heinemann, 1986), 49. Of course this is a transcription of what the child wrote in "invented spelling," i.e., "1 day wel if thar was a day. . . ." And the text was only half the story: it went along with a series of vivid drawings.)

tight lipped and monotone? A recent extensive study shows that even in writing, women use more exclamation marks than men.[17] Perhaps the culture of literate writing is more inhospitable to women than to men.

Indeed, perhaps Derrida attacks voice so vehemently *because* he is living at a cultural moment when the old antipathy to voice in writing is beginning to fade and writing is more and more invaded by voice. What McLuhan and Ong call "secondary orality" is surely taking a toll in writing. Even academic writing is much more open to informal oral features.

Despite the two formidable barriers to audibility in writing, (frequently unsayable writing and a culture that wants to keep speech qualities out of writing), most humans come at writing with echoes of speech in their ears. We hear a text if it gives us half a chance. The onus is on people who object to the idea of voice in writing to show that hearing the words *isn't* a pervasive fact of reading.

Thus, "audible voice" is a necessary critical term because it points to one of the main textual features that affects how we respond to writing. Other things being equal, most readers prefer texts that they hear—that have audible voice. After all, when we *hear* the text, we can benefit from all those nuances and channels of communication that speech has and that writing lacks. Admittedly people sometimes find it useful to produce a voiceless, faceless text—to give a sense that these words were never uttered but rather just exist with ineluctable authority from everywhere and nowhere ("All students will. . . .")—and thus try to suppress any sense that there might be a voice or person behind them.

Naturally, not all readers agree about whether a text is audible. But there is at least as much agreement about the audibility of a text or passage as there is about the "structure" or "organization" of it—and we assume the usefulness of those critical concepts. A fruitful area for research lies here: What are the features of texts that many readers find audible? How much agreement do we get about audibility of texts—and among what kind of readers?[18]

---

[17]Donald L. Rubin and Kathryn Greene, "Gender-Typical Style in Written Language," *Research in the Teaching of English* 26.2 (Feb 1992): 22.

[18]Here are a couple of important points to keep in mind in such research. Idiomatic speech qualities are not the only source of audibility in a text. Certain rhythmic, rhetorical, or poetic features also increase audibility even though they are not characteristic of how people actually talk. Thus we are likely to hear audible voice in the following passage even though we don't hear people talk this way:

Because these men work with animals, not machines or numbers, because they live outside in landscapes of torrential beauty, because they are confined to a place and a routine embellished with awesome variables, because calves die in the arms that pulled others into life, because they go to the mountains as if on a pilgrimage to find out what makes a herd of elk tick, their strength is also a softness, their toughness, a rare delicacy. (Gretel Ehrlich, *The Solace of Open Spaces* [New York: Viking, 1985], 52-3).

Also, as Crismore points out in an interesting study, passages of "metadiscourse" in writing tend to be heard as more voiced (e.g., "Let me now turn to my second point"). But I think her insight is really part of a larger point: it's not just metadiscourse that creates audibility, but rather the signaling of any *speech-act*. "I disagree" is not metadiscourse, but as with any speech act, it highlights the presence and agency of a writer. See Palacas's essay in this volume for an analysis of other important syntactic features that heighten audibility.

(2) *Dramatic voice in writing*

Let me start again from a fact about literal voice. We identify people by their spoken voices—often even when we haven't talked to them in years. In fact we often identify someone's voice with what they are like. I don't mean to claim too much here. I'm not yet touching on voice and identity; I don't mean that we always believe that someone's voice fits their character. After all, we sometimes say of a friend: "He always sounds more confident than he really is." My point is simply that we do tend to read a human quality or characteristic into a voice. Even in that example, we are reading *confidence* into a voice in the very act of deciding that the person is *not* confident.

The same process occurs even with people we've never met before. When we hear them talk for more than a few minutes, we tend to hear character in their way of speaking. Again, the negative case clinches my point: we are struck when we *cannot* hear character: "She spoke so guardedly that you couldn't tell anything about what she was like" or even, "She sounded like a guarded kind of person."

Therefore it would be peculiar—habit and conditioning being what they are—if people *didn't* hear character or dramatic voice in written texts since they so habitually hear it in speech. And in fact I've simply been trying in the last two paragraphs to sneak up by a pathway of everyday empiricism on what has become a commonplace of literary criticism—at least since the New Critics and Wayne Booth, that there is always an implied author or dramatic voice in *any* written text. New Critics like to describe any piece of prose in terms of the "speaker." Where there is language, insist the New Critics, there is drama. Of course the speaker or implied author may not be the real author; in fact the New Critics brought in this terminology in order to heighten the *distinction* between the character implied by the text and the actual writer. (See Park's essay in this volume for an analysis of this change in critical attitude.)

My point is this: when we acknowledge that every text has an implied author, we are acknowledging that every text has a character or dramatic voice. Indeed, students usually do better at finding and describing the implied author in a text when we use the critical term *dramatic voice* and invite them to use their ears by asking them, "What kind of voice or voices do you hear in this essay or story or poem?" The New Critics, the people in the Amherst tradition (see Gibson and Coles in this volume), and those in the Stanford Voice Project tended to emphasize this kind of voice. In the Amherst tradition, students were always asked, "What kind of voice do you hear in your writing?" and "Is that the kind of person you want to sound like?" But people weren't identifying this textual voice with the writer's "real" voice.

Of course the dramatic voice in the text may be hard to hear. For example we may read certain wooden or tangled texts and say, "There's *no one* in there." But these good listeners among New Critics trained us to look again—listen again—and always find a speaker. It may just be "the bureaucratic speaker" hiding behind conventional forms, but it is a speaker. And Bakhtin continues this training—helping us hear *multiple voices* even when it looks at first like monologue.

Let me illustrate dramatic voice with a passage where D. H. Lawrence is talking about Melville in *Moby Dick*:

> The artist was so *much* greater than the man. The man is rather a tiresome New Englander of the ethical mystical-transcendentalist sort: Emerson, Longfellow, Hawthorne, etc. So unrelieved, the solemn ass even in humour. So hopelessly *au grand serieux* you feel like saying: Good God, what does it matter? If life is a tragedy, or a farce, or a disaster, or anything else, what do I care! Let life be what it likes. Give me a drink, that's what I want just now.
>
> For my part, life is so many things I don't care what it is. It's not my affair to sum it up. Just now it's a cup of tea. This morning it was wormwood and gall. Hand me the sugar.
>
> One wearies of the *grand serieux*. There's something false about it. And that's Melville. Oh, dear, when the solemn ass brays! brays! brays![19]

Lawrence's dramatic voice here is vivid: the sound of a brash, opinionated person who likes to show off and even shock. If we are critically naive we might say (echoing Lawrence himself), "And that's Lawrence." If we are more critically prudent we will say, "Notice the ways Lawrence constructs his dramatic voice and creates a role or persona. We sense him taking pleasure in striking this pose. It's a vivid role but let's not assume this is the 'real' Lawrence—or even that there is such a thing as a 'real' Lawrence." (Of course in saying this we would also be echoing Lawrence—in his dictum, "Never trust the teller, trust the tale.")

Compare the following passage by the Chicago critic, R. S. Crane:

> . . . a poet does not write poetry but individual poems. And these are inevitably, as finished wholes, instances of one or another poetic kind, differentiated not by any necessities of the linguistic instrument of poetry but primarily by the nature of the poet's conception, as finally embodied in his poem, of a particular form to be achieved through the representation, in speech used dramatically or otherwise, of some distinctive state of feeling, of moral choice, or action, complete in itself and productive of a certain emotion or complex of emotions in the reader.[20]

Crane has a less *vivid* dramatic voice here than Lawrence, but anyone who is following and entering into this admittedly more difficult prose (and such a short snippet makes it hard to do that) can sense a character here too. I hear a learned builder of distinctions, careful and deliberate and precise—and

---

[19]D. H. Lawrence, *Studies in Classic American Literature* (NY: Doubleday, 1951), 157-58.
[20]R. S. Crane. "The Critical Monism of Cleanth Brooks," in *Critics and Criticism: Ancient and Modern* (Chicago UP, 1951), 96.

someone who takes pleasure in building up syntactic architecture. But because his prose sounds less like a person talking—the syntax is more "constructed" than "uttered"—readers may disagree more about the character of the speaker than in the case of Lawrence. Such disagreements do not, however, undermine the well ensconced critical notion of an implied author in any text.

Let me try to sharpen *dramatic voice* and *audible voice* as critical terms by comparing them in these two samples. For most readers, Lawrence's words probably have more audible voice than Crane's. Notice in fact how Lawrence heightens the audible or spoken effect by embedding bits of tacit dialogue and mini-drama. He says, "You feel like saying: . . ." so that what follows ("Good God, what does it matter?" and so forth) is really a little speech in a different voice, and thus in implied quotation marks. Similarly, when he writes "Hand me the sugar," he's setting up a mini scene-on-stage that dramatizes the mood he's evoking.

But Crane's prose is not without audible voice. He starts out with a crisply balanced pronouncement (something pronounced): "a poet does not write poetry but individual poems." And the second sentence begins with a strikingly audible interrupted phrase or "parenthetical" ("And these are inevitably, as finished wholes, . . ."). But as he drifts from syntactic utterance to architectural construction, I find his words increasingly unidiomatic and difficult to say and hear.

So, whereas a text can have more or less audible voice, shall we say the same of dramatic voice? Yes and no. On the one hand, the critical world agrees that every text is 100% chock full of implied author. Even if the dramatic voice is subtle or hard to hear, even if there are multiple and inconsistent dramatic voices in a text, the word from Booth to Bakhtin is that the text is nothing but dramatic voices. But common sense argues the other way too, and this view shows itself most clearly in the everyday writerly or teacherly advice: "Why do you keep your voice or character so hidden here? Why not allow it into your writing?" (Palacas in his essay in this volume shows how parenthetical insertions heighten dramatic voice or the sense of an implied author. The fact that these parentheticals also increase audible voice shows that the different kinds of voice that I am working so hard to distinguish often blend into each other.)

So I would assert the same conclusion here as I did about audible voice. Just as it is natural and inevitable to hear *audible* voice in a text unless something stops us, so too with *dramatic* voice: we hear character in discourse unless something stops us.

(3) *Recognizable or distinctive voice in writing*

Like composers or painters, writers often develop styles that are recognizable and distinctive. And it is common for both popular and academic critics and writers themselves to go one step further and not just talk about a writer finding "a" distinctive voice but finding "her" voice.

There is nothing to quarrel with here. After all, writing is behavior, and it's hard for humans to engage in *any* behavior repeatedly without developing a habitual and thus recognizable way of doing it: a style. Perhaps the most striking example is the physical act of writing itself: handwriting (thus the force of one's literal signature). And we see the same thing in walking, tooth brushing, whatever. We can often recognize someone by how they walk—even how they stand—when we are too far away to recognize them by any other visual feature. If our walking and handwriting tend to be distinctive and recognizable and usually stable over time, why shouldn't that also be true of the kind of voice we use in our writing?

Of course if we seldom walk, and always with conscious effort, we probably don't develop a recognizable distinctive walking style. Early toddlers haven't yet "found their own walk." So it is natural that inexperienced writers often have no characteristic style or "signature" to their writing.

But it's worth questioning the positive *mystique* that sometimes surrounds the idea of "finding one's voice"—questioning the assumption that it is necessarily better to have a recognizable, distinctive voice in one's writing. Surely it doesn't make a writer *better* to have a distinctive style. It is just as admirable to achieve Keats' ideal of "negative capability": the ability to be a protean, chameleon-like writer. If we have become so practiced that our skills are automatic and habitual—and thus characteristic—we are probably pretty good, whether as walker or writer. But a *really* skilled or professional walker or writer will be able to bring in craft, art, and play so as to deploy different styles at will, and thus not necessarily have a recognizable, distinctive voice. Don't we tend to see Yeats as more impressive than Frost (not necessarily better)—Brahms than Elgar—for this ability to use a greater variety of voices?

Notice how I am still not broaching any of the sticky theoretical problems of self or identity that haunt arguments about voice in writing. If I have a "recognizable voice," that voice doesn't necessarily *resemble* me or imply that there is a "real me." Recognizable or distinctive voice is not about "real identity." We may *recognize* someone from their handwriting or their walk, but those behaviors are not necessarily pictures of what they are like. For example, we might find ourselves saying, "He has such a distinctively casual, laid-back walk, yet his personality or character is very up-tight."

So if we strip away any unwarranted mystique from the term "recognizable, distinctive voice in writing," it has a simple and practical use. We can ask about any author whether he or she tends to have a characteristic style or recognizable voice; and if so, whether a particular text displays that style or voice—whether it is characteristic or different from how that author usually writes. And we can ask our students to develop comfortable fluency and to notice if and where they seem to develop a distinctive style—and whether that style seems to be helpful for them. I tend to discourage students from lusting after a "distinctive voice," since that so often leads to pretension and over-writing.

So look again at our example from D. H. Lawrence: it may not be a picture of the "real" Lawrence (if there is such a thing) but it *is* vintage Lawrence criticism—not just a nonce style or voice he used in this essay.

(4) *Voice with authority—"having a voice"*

This is the sense of voice that is so current in much feminist work (see, for example, Belenky, Goldberger, Clinchy, and Tarule in *Women's Ways of Knowing*). But the sense is venerable too. Indeed the phrase "having a voice" has traditionally meant having the authority to speak or wield influence or to vote in a group. ("Does she have a voice in the faculty senate?")

As readers we often have no trouble agreeing about whether a text shows a writer having or taking the authority to speak out: whether the writer displays the conviction or the self-trust or gumption to make her voice heard. As teachers, we frequently notice and applaud the change when we see a timid writer finally speak out with some conviction and give her words some authority. We often notice the same issue in our own writing or that of our colleagues when we are asked for feedback. One of the traditional problems when we revise dissertations for publication is getting rid of the deferential, questioning, permission-asking, tone—getting more authority into the voice. It would be an interesting research project to try to figure out what textual features give readers a sense of authority. One source of authority is to bring in others who have written about one's topic and addressing their thoughts with some assurance—even "taking on" or "make one's own" their words and voices, in Bakhtin's sense.[21]

Notice that this sense of voice, like all the previous ones, does not entail any theory of identity or self, nor does it require making any inferences about the actual writer from the words on the page. When we see this kind of authority in writing, or the lack of it, we are not necessarily getting a good picture of the actual writer. It's not unusual, for example, for someone to develop a voice with strong authority that doesn't match their sense of who they are—or our sense of who they are. Indeed one of the best ways to find authority or achieve assertiveness of voice is to role-play and write in the voice of some "invented character" who is strikingly different from ourselves. We see this in simple role-playing exercises where the timid person "gets into" strong speech. And we see it in the complex case of Swift. He exerted enormous authority in the person of Gulliver and all his other ironic personae, and never published anything under his own name. (Ironically he wielded excoriating judgmental authority through personae that were nonjudgmental and self-effacing.)

Let's look at our examples again. Clearly D. H. Lawrence had no trouble using a voice with authority and making it heard in print. Some feel he overdid it. R. S. Crane uses a quieter voice but achieves a magisterial authority nevertheless. An authoritative voice in writing need not be loud; it often has a quality of quiet, centered calm. We see this in speech too: school

---

[21]See Don H. Bialostosky, "Liberal Education, Writing, and the Dialogic Self," *Contending with Words: Composition and Rhetoric in a PostModern Age*, ed. Patricia Harkin and John Schilb (NY: MLA, 1991), 11-22.

children often talk about "shouters"—teachers who shout a lot because they lack authority.

As teachers, most of us say we want our students to develop some authority of voice, yet many of our practices have the effect of making students more timid and hesitant in their writing. In the following passage Virginia Woolf writes about voice as authority—that is, about the struggle to take on authority in a situation where she was expected to be deferential:

> Directly . . . I took my pen in my hand to review that novel by a famous young man, she slipped behind me and whispered, "My dear, you are a young woman. You are writing about a book that has been written by a man. Be sympathetic; be tender; flatter; deceive; use all the arts and wiles of our sex. Never let anybody guess that you have a mind of your own . . . ." And she made as if to guide my pen. . . . [But in doing so] she would have plucked the heart out of my writing.[22]

We may write elegantly and successfully, she implies, but if we don't write with authority, with a mind of our own that is willing to offend, what we produce scarcely counts as real writing (the heart is plucked out of it).

(5) Resonant voice or presence

Here at last is trouble—the swamp. This the angle of meaning that has made voice such a disputed term—the arena of "authenticity," "presence," sincerity, identity, self, and what I called "real voice" in *Writing With Power*. Before wading in, let me pause to emphasize what I have gained by holding back so long—carefully separating what is solid from what is swampy. For my main argument in this essay is that there is little reason to dispute voice as a solid critical term that points to certain definite and important qualities in texts that cannot easily be gainsaid: audible voice, dramatic voice, recognizable or distinctive voice, and voice with authority. That is, even if we are completely at odds about the nature of selves or identities, about whether people even have such things, and about the relation of a text to the person who wrote it, we have a good chance of reaching agreement about whether any given text has audible voice, what kind of dramatic voice it has, whether it has a recognizable or distinctive voice, and whether the writer was able to achieve authority of voice. Similarly, even if teachers disagree completely about the nature of self and identity and about the value of sincerity in writing, they can probably agree that students would benefit from exploring and attending to these four dimensions of voice in their writing. With these meanings secure, *I* feel more authority to enter the arena of difficulty and conflict.

Indeed I can begin my account of resonant voice by showing that the

---

[22]Virginia Woolf, *Between Ourselves: Letters, Mothers, Daughters*, ed, Karen Payne (New York: Houghton Mifflen, 1983), 83.

ground is not as swampy as we might fear. That is, the concept of resonant voice or presence is certainly arguable, and it involves making inferences about the relation between the present text and the absent writer, but it does *not* assume any particular model of the self or theory of identity—and in particular it does not require a model of the self as simple, single, unique, or unchanging. I can make this point by describing resonant voice in contrast to *sincere voice* (something that enthusiasts of voice have sometimes mistakenly celebrated).

We hear sincere voices all around us. Lovers say, "I only have eyes for you"; parents say, "Trust me"; teachers say, "I am on your side." Even salesmen and politicians are sometimes perfectly sincere. Surely Reagan was sincere much of the time. But sometimes those sincere words, *even in their very sincerity*, ring hollow. Genuine sincerity can itself feel cloyingly false. Even the celebrations of sincerity by Tolstoy and Yeats (quoted in Part I) will grate on many teeth. Yet we mustn't flip all the way over to the cynical position of people who have been burned too often and say that sincerity *itself* is false ("never trust a guy who really thinks he loves you"), or to the sophisticated position of some literary folk ("sincere art is bad art"). *Sometimes* we can trust sincere words. Sincere discourse is not always tinny.

What is a sincere voice? When we say that someone speaks or writes sincerely, we mean that they "really really believe" what they are saying. This means that they experience no gap at all between utterance and intention, between words and available thoughts and feelings. But what about gaps between utterance and *unavailable* or *unconscious* thoughts and feelings?

Resonant voice is a useful concept because it points to the relationship between discourse and the unconscious. When we hear sincerity that is obviously tinny, we are hearing a *gap* between utterance and unconscious intention or feeling. Self-deception. Sensitive listeners can hear very small gaps. Thus they are also likely to be sensitive to the resonance that occurs when discourse *does* fit larger portions of the speaker—those precious moments in life and writing when a person actually does harness words to fit more than conscious intention—those words which seem to "have the heft of our living behind them" (Adrienne Rich's phrase—see note 28).

Such words are of course rare. For a discourse can never *fully* express or articulate a whole person. A person is usually too complex and has too many facets, parts, roles, voices, identities. But at certain lucky or achieved moments, writers or speakers *do* manage to find words which seem to capture the rich complexity of the unconscious; or words which, though they don't *express* or *articulate* everything that is in the unconscious, nevertheless somehow seem to *resonate with* or *have behind them* the unconscious as well as the conscious (or at least much larger portions than usual). It is words of this sort that we experience as resonant—and through them we have a sense of presence with the writer.

Notice now how the concept of resonant voice opens the door to irony, fiction, lying, and games; indeed it positively *calls for* these and other polyvocal or multivalent kinds of discourse. If we value the sound of resonance—the sound of more of a person behind the words—and if we get pleasure from a sense of the writer's presence in a text, we are often going to be drawn to what is ambivalent and complex and ironic, not just to earnest attempts to stay true to sincere, conscious feelings. Can two million New Critics be completely wrong in their preoccupation with irony? The most resonant language is often lying and gamey. Writing with resonant voice needn't be unified or coherent, it can be ironic, unaware, disjointed.

Any notion of resonant voice would have to include Swift's strongest works; even Pope's "Rape of the Lock" where he makes fun of the silliness and vanity he also loves. When Lawrence says of Melville, "The artist was so *much* greater than the man"—he is talking about the difference between Melville's sincere sentiments and those parts of his writing that express his larger darker vision—writing that resonates with more parts of himself or his vision or his feelings than he was sincerely, consciously able to affirm. In effect, Lawrence is saying that Melville "the man" has plenty of audible dramatic, distinctive and uthoritative voice ("And that's Melville. Oh dear when the solemn ass brays! brays! brays!"). But he lacks resonant voice ("But there's something false")—except where he functions "as artist" and renders more of his unconscious knowledge and awareness. It's no accident that the resonance shows up most in his discourse "as artist": that is, we tend to get more of our unconscious into our discourse when we use metaphors and tell stories and exploit the sounds and rhythms of language.

Once we see that resonance comes from getting more of ourselves behind the words, we realize that unity or singleness is not the goal. Of course we don't have simple, neatly coherent or unchanging selves. To remember the role of the unconscious is to remember what Bakhtin and social constructionists and others say in different terms: we are made of different roles, voices.

Indeed, Barbara Johnson sees a link between voice and *splitness* or *doubleness* itself—words which render multiplicity of self: ". . . the very notion of an 'authentic voice' must be redefined. Far from being an expression of Janie's new wholeness or identity as a character, Janie's increasing ability to speak grows out of her ability . . . to assume and articulate the incompatible forces involved in her own division. The sign of an authentic voice is thus not self-identity but self-difference."[23]

Keith Hjortshoj (exploring relations between writing and physical movement) makes the same point in a different context:

> Cohesion, then, isn't always a cardinal virtue, in [physical] movement or writing. . . . To appreciate fully the freedom, flexibility, and speed with which young children adapt to their surroundings, we have to remember that they continually come unglued and reassemble

---

[23]Barbara Johnson, "Metaphor, Metonymy, and Voice in Zora Neale Hurston's *Their Eyes Were Watching God*," ed. Mary Ann Caws, *Textual Analysis: Some Readers Reading* (NY: MLA, 1986), 238-39.

themselves—usually several times a day. They have wild, irrational expectations of themselves and others. They take uncalculated risks that lead them to frustration, anger, and fear. In the space of a few minutes they pass from utter despair to unmitigated joy, and sometimes back again, like your average manic-depressive.[24]

Selves tend to evolve, change, take on new voices and assimilate them. The concept of resonant voice explains the intriguing power of so much speech and writing by children: they wear their unconscious more on their sleeve, their defenses are often less elaborate. Thus they often get more of themselves into or behind their discourse.

One of the advantages that writing has over speech—and why writing provides a rich site for resonant voice or presence—is that writing has always served as a crucial place for trying out parts of the self or unconscious that have been hidden or neglected or undeveloped—to experiment and try out "new subject positions."[25]

When we see that the central question then for this kind of power in writing is not "How sincere are you?" but "How much of yourself did you manage to get *behind* the words?" we see why voice has been such a tempting metaphor. That is, the physical voice is more resonant when it can get more of the body resonating behind it or underneath it. "Resonant" seems a more helpful word than "authentic," and it is more to the point than "sincerity," because it connotes the "resounding" or "sounding-again" that is involved when distinct parts can echo each other (thus Coleridge's figure of the aeolian lyre). Just as a resonant physical voice is not in any way a *picture* of the body, but it has the body's resources behind or underneath it, so too resonant voice in writing is not a picture of the self, but it has the self's resources behind or underneath it. The metaphor of voice inevitably suggests a link with the body and with "weight," and this is a link that many writers call attention to. After all, the body often shows more of ourselves than the conscious mind does: our movements, our stance, our facial expressions often reveal our dividedness, complexity and splitness.

Here is a striking passage where William Carlos Williams sounds this theme of a link between writing, voice and the body:

> So poets . . . are in touch with "voices," but this is the very essence of their power, the voices are the past, the depths of our very beings. It is the deeper . . . portions of the personality speaking, the middle brain, the nerves, the glands, the very muscles and bones of the body itself speaking.[26]

---

[24]Keith Hjortshoj (Cornell U Writing Program), "Language and Movement," Unpublished MS.
[25]Sara Jonsberg (Montclair State U), "Rehearsing New Subject Positions: A Poststructuralist View of Expressive Writing," Presentation at Conference on College Composition and Communication, April 1993, San Diego.
[26]William Carlos Williams, in "How to Write," ed. J. Laughlin, *New Directions 50th Anniversary Issue* (New Directions Publishing Corp: New York, 1936).

Roland Barthes is particularly intriguing in this vein. Notice how he celebrates "the grain of the voice" by distinguishing it from the "dramatic expressivity" of opera—in effect, from sincerity:

> Listen to a Russian bass (a church bass—[since] opera is a genre in which the voice has gone over in its entirety to dramatic expressivity . . .): something is there, manifest and stubborn, (one hears only that), beyond (or before) the meaning of the words, their form . . . , the melisma, and even the style of execution: something which is directly in the cantor's body, brought to your ears in one and the same movement from deep down in the cavities, the muscles, the membranes, the cartilages, and from deep down in the Slavonic language, as though a single skin lined the inner flesh of the performer and the music he sings. The voice is not *personal*: it *expresses nothing of the cantor and his soul* [emphasis added]; it is not original . . . , and at the same time it is individual: it has us hear a body which has no civil identity, no 'personality', but which is nevertheless a separate body. . . . The 'grain" is that: the materiality of the body speaking its mother tongue.[27]

In a wonderful poem that serves, I feel, at once as a description and an example of resonant voice, Adrienne Rich uses the figure of weight to talk poetry that matters:

Even if every word we wrote by then
were honest   the sheer heft
of our living behind it
                              not these sometimes
lax indolent lines
                        these litanies[28]

Of course I'm not saying that writing with resonant voice *must* be ironic, gamey, split—cannot be sincere or personal. The Rich poem is surely sincere and personal. Nor that the self does not characteristically have a kind of coherence and even persistence of identity over time. I'm just insisting that the notion of resonant voice or presence in writing does not require these things.

Examples of resonant voice? I would venture the Adrienne Rich poem, but examples are hard to cite because we cannot point to identifiable features of language that are "resonant"—as we can point to features that are audible, dramatic, distinctive, or authoritative. Rather, we are in the dicey business of pointing to the *relation* of textual features to an inferred person behind the text. Of course this inferred presence can only come from other features of the

---

[27]Roland Barthes, "The Grain of the Voice" in *Image, Music, Text*, trans. Stephen Heath (New York: Hill and Wang, 1977), 181.
[28]Adrienne Rich, "Poetry: III," in *Your Native Land, Your Life* (NY: Norton, 1986), 68.

text. It's as though—putting it bluntly or schematically—any sentence, paragraph, or page can be resonant or not, depending on the context of a longer work or oeuvre.

Look, for example, at our passages from Lawrence and Crane. I hear so *much* voice in the Lawrence: audible, dramatic, distinctive, authoritative. With that much vividness and noise, I can't decide whether I hear resonance. The passage is gamey, tricky, show-offy—a pose. But of course that doesn't disqualify it either. I'm not sure; I'd have to read more.

Crane? Again we cannot decide from such a short passage. Certainly it is not rich in the kind of audible and dramatic voice that Robert Frost asked for (the "speaking tone of voice somehow entangled in the words and fastened to the page for the ear of the imagination"). But that's not the point with resonant voice. If we read more we might indeed hear in this somewhat forbidding prose the "sheer heft of his living," and experience a powerful resonance or presence in the passage.

For of course assertions about resonant voice will always be more arguable than about other kinds of voice. Not only because we are dealing with subtle inferences rather than pointing to particular linguistic features, but also because our main organ for listening to resonance is our own self. That is, we are most likely to hear resonance when the words resonate with us, fit us. This is an obvious problem, and it is enough to make some people insist that the only resonance we can talk about is between the text and the reader, not the text and the writer. I address this problem head on in the next section. (Bakhtin uses a metaphor of *literal* resonance between speaker and listener when he says, in the essay printed here, that we lose intonation in our speech unless we have "choral support" from sympathetic or like-minded listeners.)

I acknowledge that when we hear resonance, we are *most often* hearing a resonance of the words with our own predilections, tastes, obsessions. But something more than this is happening, surely, when readers of many different temperaments hear resonance in the same piece of writing—even a very idiosyncratic piece. And most of us have occasionally had a teacher or editor who is peculiarly good in possessing the ability to "hear around" her own temperament and predilections—to hear resonance even when it doesn't fit her. This is the ability to love and feel great power in a piece while still being able to say, "But this is not my kind of writing—it doesn't really fit me"— and still help the writer revise her piece in a direction different from one's own predilections or taste. To put it another way, this kind of reader is more expert at listening for resonance even when it involves what is "other" or "different" from herself.

The problem of the relationship between discourse and the actual author

The concept of resonant voice or presence may not require any ideology of self or identity, but it does assume something else controversial: that we can make inferences about the fit between the voice in a text and the actual unknown, unseen historical writer behind the text—on the basis of the written text alone. We can have audible, dramatic, distinctive, and authoritative voice without any sense of whether the voice fits or doesn't fit the real author. Not so here with resonant voice or presence.

Although it may seem peculiar to say that we can sense the fit between the voice in a text and the unknown writer behind it (especially in the light of much poststructural literary theory), in truth people have an ingrained habit of doing just that: listening not only *to* each others' words but also listening *for* the relationship between the words and the speaker behind the words. To put this in a nonstartling way, we habitually listen to see whether we can trust the speaker. If we know the speaker, these judgments are natural and un-problematic. ("Alice, your words make a lot of sense, but they just don't sound like you.")

But we sometimes make the same judgments with the discourse of people we *don't* know. When we hear an announcer or public speaker or we begin to converse with a stranger, we sometimes conclude that they sound unbelievable or fake, even when *what they say* is sensible and believable in itself. Something is fishy about the voice and we feel we don't trust this person. Sometimes the speaker sounds evasive, halting, awkward. But as often as not, on the contrary, we are bothered because the speaker seems too glib or fluent—as in the case of certain overzealous salesmen or politicians. Sometimes the speaker sounds insincere, but sometimes something sounds "off" even when the person sounds sincere.

Perhaps we are relying on visual cues from the speaker before our eyes. Yet we go on making these judgments without visual cues—when strangers speak over the phone or on the radio: nothing but literal voice to go on. Sometimes we still conclude that there is something untrustworthy about the voice of some politician or radio announcer or salesman. It's not that we necessarily distrust the message; sometimes we believe it. But we distrust the speaker—or at least we distrust the fit between the message and the speaker. How do we make these judgments about whether to trust someone when all we have is their language? Doubtless we go on auditory cues of intonation and rhythm: literal "tone of voice."

But tone of voice is nothing but a "way of talking," and when we only have *writing by a stranger*, we still have a "way of talking" to go on—that is, his or her way of writing. Even though we can't see or hear the writer, and even though writing provides fewer semiotic channels for nuance, we still draw inferences from the writer's syntax, diction, structure, strategies, stance, and so forth.

Obviously, these inferences are risky. But my point is that we've all had lots of training in making them. Repeatedly in our lives we face situations where our main criterion for deciding *whether* an utterance is true is whether to trust the speaker. When we take our car to a mechanic, most of us don't base our decision about whether the carburetor needs replacing on data about carburetors but rather on a decision about trustworthiness of voice. We often do the same thing when we take our body to a doctor—or decide to trust *anyone* about a matter we don't understand. We mustn't forget how practiced and skilled most of us have become at this delicate kind of judgment just because we remember so vividly the times we judged wrong. And we know that some people are strikingly good at figuring out whether someone can be trusted. They must be reading something. The practice of counseling and therapy depends on this kind of ear. Skilled listeners can sometimes even hear *through sincerity*: they can hear that even though the speaker is perfectly sincere, he cannot be trusted. There must be real cues in discourse—readable but subtle—about the relationship between discourse and speaker. Because we are listening for relationships between what is explicitly in the text and cues about the writer that are implicit in the text, we can seldom make these kinds of judgments unless we have extended texts—better yet two or three texts by the same writer.

Because our inferences about voice are so subtle, they are seldom based on conscious deliberation: we usually make these inferences with the *ear*—by means of how the discourse "sounds" or "feels" or whether it "rings true." We use the kind of tacit, nonfocal awareness that Polanyi addresses and analyzes so well, such as when we see a faint star better by not looking directly at it.[29]

Notice that this peculiar skill—evaluating the trustworthiness or validity of utterances by *how* things are said because we cannot evaluate *what* is said—often does not correlate with "school learning." Schools naturally emphasize texts, and when we are learning how to deal with texts (and especially when our culture becomes more text oriented or literate in the ways described by Olson and Ong and so many others) we are learning how to pay more attention to the relationship between words and their meanings and referents—and less attention to the relationship between words and their speakers or writers.

In a way, we've stumbled upon the very essence of schooling or literacy training: learning to attend better to the meaning and logic of words themselves and to stop relying on extra-textual cues such as how impressive or authoritative the author is or how you feel about her. School and the culture of literacy advise us to this effect: "Stop listening for the tone of voice and interpreting gestures. These are the tricks of illiterates and animals— evaluating speech on the basis of what they think of the speaker because they can't read or judge the message for itself." Sometimes the successful student or scholar is the *least* adept at this kind of meta-textual reading—at what we call "street smarts." Good teachers learn to integrate street smarts with literacy training, whether in first grade or college, for the sake of helping students be more sophisticated with purely silent textual language—instead of letting

---

[29]See the description by Oliver Sacks of certain aphasics watching Reagan give a talk on TV. Being unable to understand the propositional content of his speech, "they have an infallible ear for every vocal nuance, the tone, the rhythm, the cadences, the music, the subtlest modulations, inflections, intonations, which can give—or remove—verisimilitude to or from a man's voice. In this, then, lies their power of understanding—understanding without words what is authentic or inauthentic." "The President's Speech," in *The Man Who Mistook His Wife for a Hat: and Other Clinical Tales* (New York: Summit Books, 1987).

students feel that their skill at reading the person behind the text is a hindrance in school. (This is the message in Deborah Brandt's insightful *Literacy as Involvement*.)

I'm really making a simple claim here—and it's the same claim that I made earlier about audible and dramatic voice: that our primary and formative experiences with language were with words emerging audibly from physically present bodies—and most of us continue to encounter this kind of language as much as we encounter silent texts, if not more. For this reason, we can scarcely prevent ourselves from hearing the presence of human beings in language and attending to the relationship between the language and the person who speaks or writes it. Conditioning alone nudges us to do so, but more important, much of our functioning in the world depends on this skill. Many school practices blunt this skill—allegedly for the sake of literacy training, but Brandt argues intriguingly that these practices are based on a mistaken model of literacy.

If we explore Aristotle and the process of persuasion for a moment, we can find more corroboration for the nonstartling claim that humans naturally listen to discourse for cues about the actual person behind it. Aristotle defines *ethos* as a potent source of persuasion, but scholars argue about what he meant by the term.

Sometimes he emphasizes the author's real character, talking about "the personal character of the speaker," and saying "We believe good men more fully and more readily than others" (*Rhetoric* 1356a). But sometimes he emphasizes how speakers can fool listeners and persuade them with just dramatic voice or implied author. He talks about the ability to "make ourselves *thought to be* sensible and morally good. . . ." (1378a, my emphasis). And he notes that this is a matter of skill, not character:

> We can now see that a writer must disguise his art and give the impression of speaking naturally and not artificially. Naturalness is persuasive, artificiality is the contrary; for our hearers are prejudiced and think we have some design against them. . . . (1404b)

Scholars fight about this ambiguity in the *Rhetoric*, but the fight would disappear if they simply noticed and accepted the fact that he is affirming both positions in what is in fact the common sense view: "It's nice to *be* trustworthy; but if you're skilled you can fake it."

When Aristotle says that we can persuade people by creating a dramatic voice that is more trustworthy than we actually are—by saying, in effect, that a good rhetor can sometimes fool the audience—he is talking about the gap between implied author and real author, between dramatic voice and resonant voice or the writer's own voice. Because he's writing a handbook for authors, he's telling them how they can hide this gap if they are skilled. They can seem more trustworthy than they are, but to do so they must fool the audience into not seeing the gap. If he'd been writing a handbook for *audiences* rather than authors (writing "reception theory" instead of "transmission theory"), he would have looked at this gap from the other side. He would have emphasized how skilled *listeners* can *uncover* the gap that speakers are trying to hide. He would have talked about how skilled listeners can detect differences between the implied author and the real author—can detect, that is, dishonesty or untrustworthiness even through a sensible message or a fluent delivery. In short, by arguing in the *Rhetoric* that skilled speakers can seem better than they are, he is acknowledging that there is a gap to be detected, and implying that good listeners can make inferences about the character of the speaker from their words.

Since readers and listeners make these perceptions all the time about the trustworthiness of the speaker or writer on the basis of their words alone, any valid rhetorical theory must show that persuasiveness often comes from *resonant voice or communicated presence* as often as it comes from merely dramatic voice or implied author. Aristotle clearly implies what common sense tells us: we are not persuaded by implied author as such—that is, by the creation of a dramatic voice that sounds trustworthy; we are only persuaded if we believe that dramatic voice is the voice of the actual speaker or author. We don't buy a used car from someone just because we admire their dramatic skill in creating a fictional trustworthy voice. If ethos is nothing *but* implied author, it loses all power of persuasion.[30]

Identity politics, the nature of self, "Is there a real me?" We seem to hit the crunch when we have to write or teach writing.

So far, I have claimed that none of these senses of voice imply or require any particular theory of identity or self. We can have whatever ideological position we want and still agree with others in using the term *voice*. Even resonant voice accommodates the ideology of choice. Can I claim, then, that the identity issue *never* comes up? No. For so far I've emphasized the process of reading—the process of describing voice in texts produced by others. Once we set out to *write*, however, or to teach writing, it is hard to escape the identity issue.

For there is a momentous asymmetry between reading and writing. As readers we have access only to the text, not to the writer (assuming the text is not our own); but as writers we have access to *both* the text and the writer (ourselves). We can hear the sound of our text and we can also hear the sound of "us."

I won't define "us" because there's no need to: most of us don't define "us"—we simply have an intuitive sense of identity such that we can feel it

---

[30]This is a perplexing business. We are sometimes tempted to ascribe great power to the dramatic voice alone when we see people *seeming* to be persuaded by blatantly fake or inauthentic voice—for example, in the realm of politics and advertising. "Look at all those people voting for someone who is such an obvious crook. How can they be taken in?" But when people seem to be persuaded by glib dramatic voice, I think there are often dynamics of alienation, powerlessness, and cynicism at play. Those same people who vote for the speaker with glib dramatic voice often say things like, "Yeah, I can tell he is a crook. But what can you do?" It's not that they don't hear the gap between language and person. We need good research about what people actually hear and understand when they hear glib, untrustworthy dramatic voice.

when behavior, feelings, or discourse seem "not like me." Perhaps "me" is the sound of my most habitual or comfortable inner speech and outer speech. Who knows? We don't have to understand that issue here. Most of us have some breadth to our sense of "me" so that we have a range of voices or ways of speaking and writing and thinking that feels like us. We may feel just as natural and like ourselves in slangy talk with sporting pals and highly formal professional talk at conferences. Where some people's range is very narrow and they feel fake or inauthentic if they venture out of one or two kinds of voice or discourse, others have an enormous and surprising repertory of voices or modes that all feel perfectly like themselves.

But whatever the breadth and flexibility of our sense of identity (and whatever theory of identity we hold), most of us have occasions when we experience our writing or speaking or thinking somehow *not* like us— somehow artificial or pretended or distanced or stilted.[31]

I would point out that there are *certain* conditions where we *won't* notice whether our own textual voice feels like ours. a) We may be deaf to our text—that is, we may not pay any attention to the sound of our writing. After all, it is common for students and many others not to listen to the sound of their written words—never reading them over silently or outloud and never hearing anyone else read them outloud. (Many unskilled writers can't even imagine that their writing could be thought of as *having* a sound or a voice. This is why so many teachers emphasize having students read their work outloud. The Stanford Voice Project focused on this issue, for example by using lots of live and taped readings of speech and writing by students and professionals.) b) Or we may not have any sense of an "ours" against which to compare the sound of a text. Either we don't pay any attention to any sense of "ours" in our discourse—or we have a sense of "ours" that is completely fluid or boundless: what *ever* words we put out in speech or writing always feel like "ours."

Thus it is *possible* to hold off all identity issues and try to write with audible voice, distinctive voice, authoritative voice; we can try to use the dramatic voice or persona that seems most appropriate for the audience; we can try to use a voice that "situates itself within the conversation" we are trying to enter into—and thus do our best to "take on" the voices that make up that conversation; this is what Don Bialostosky, drawing on Bakhtin, calls "well-situated voice," and it is surely one of the main ways in which we give

---

[31]Of course we can decide that people are *wrong* to have the sense of identity they do. It is common to criticize adolescents for having a restricted sense of identity (though it's also a time of life when you sometimes feel as though you are bouncing around with no boundary to your identity at all). One of the postmodern critiques in identity theory is that the conventional Western sense of self is an illusion: that Christianity and Romanticism have given us too much sense of uniqueness in self/soul; and that capitalism has given us too much sense of "ownership." The Buddhist doctrine of "no-soul" also proclaims that the sense of self is an illusion.

[32]Don H. Bialostosky, "Liberal Education, Writing, and the Dialogic Self," in *Contending with Words: Composition and Rhetoric in a Postmodern Age*, ed. Patricia Harkin and John Schilb (NY: MLA, 1991), 11-22.

authority to our writing.[32] We can do all those things and still never ask or notice whether the words feel like ours.

But surely this not noticing is fairly rare. Thus for many people (not just those women interviewed by Gilligan or by Belenky and her colleagues) the question is not just whether one *has* a strong or distinctive voice but whether that voice feels like "one's own." For of course it's not uncommon for people to develop a voice that is strong or lively or distinctive or authoritative, but which feels somehow alien—and to feel like using it means remaining without power or authority. Here is a passage from an interview with a woman talking about a striking case of this experience:

> Writing has always been so hard and I've always felt trapped inside myself in terms of having to put stuff on paper, um. So that ultimately when I did have to write stuff like reports, I managed to get somebody inside me to do them, but it wasn't like it was me doing it. And that's continued as an adult. . . .
>
> And I think I have sort of grown up and been an adult for a long time, thinking of myself as not having any voice. . . . [But I] started thinking of all my work with children and how my voice is in that work [she is a teacher] and that it's, you know, it's not a loud voice that says, but it's, you know, it's more like a voice like the wind or something [pause] that's there. . . .
>
> [About an important report:] it was still as though, you know, I had finally set a deadline and I got the person inside me who does that piece of writing when the deadline happens [to do it]. . . . [And about another paper for a course:] I wanted to write it in my own voice and not make the ghost writer in me, or whoever that is, basically [do] it.[33]

When we write, then, most of us cannot help brushing against the identity issue and noticing whether our words feel like us or ours. Ideally we have a *choice* about whether to use prose that feels as though it fits us. (Of course plenty of people—among inexperienced and even professional writers—don't feel as though it's possible to let writing actually sound like themselves. They don't feel capable of just uttering themselves on paper—as extensive freewriting shows one how to do.) In making this choice we notice that there are two extreme ideological or theoretical positions here about language and self. At one extreme, the "sentimental" position says, "Hold fast to your 'you' at all costs. Don't give in and write in the voice 'they' want. Your voice is the only powerful voice to use. Your true voice will conquer all difficulties." At the other extreme, the "sophisticated" position says, "Your sense of 'you' is just an illusion of late Romantic, bourgeois, capitalism. Forget it. You have no self. There is no such thing. You are nothing but roles. Write in the role

---

[33]Fern Tavalin, *Voice, A Call and Response: Understanding Voice in Writing Through Storytelling*, Dissertation, U of Mass, 1994.

that is appropriate for this situation."

But in practice we don't have to choose *between* such extreme positions. It is far more helpful to move somewhat back and forth between some version of them—especially with regard to *practices*. (The purely theoretical fight loses interest after a while.) We can come at our writing from both sides of the identity fence.

First the "sentimental" side. Suppose I've been told that my characteristic voice—the voice that feels like me or mine—tends to be too insecure or emotional or tied in knots or angry; and I've become convinced that this voice of mine has repeatedly undermined my writing—at least for most audiences. I don't have to slap my wrists and say, "I guess I've just got a bad, ineffective voice, and so I'll have to get a better one." I *can* use whatever voice feels comfortably mine—particularly for exploratory writing, private writing, and early draft writing.

For it turns out not so hard to revise late drafts from a pragmatic and audience-oriented frame of reference and make a limited number of changes and get rid of most of the voice problems for readers—to get rid of the worst pieces of insecurity or emotionality or knottedness or anger. When I do this, the underlying plasma of my prose still feels as though it is me, is my own voice. I think good readers feel something lacking or some lack of resonance when people *don't* use their own plasma.

And, perhaps more important, in the *long run*, when I use the voice or voices that I experience as mine—such as they are and with all their limitations—use them a lot for exploratory and private and early draft writing and try them out on myself and others—listening to them and even appreciating them—these voices tend to get richer and develop. As I use my insecure voice more, I write myself into more passages of confidence; as I use my emotional voice more, I write myself into more passages of calmness and control; giving more permission to my angry voice leads to more passages in other moods. It's not that I give up the original voices, but I develop more options. Gradually I find I have more flexibility of voice—more voices that feel like me.

But I can also work from the "sophisticated" side of this identity issue. I can think of all discourse as the taking on of roles or as the use of the voices of others. I can take on the mentality that Auden celebrated in his wonderful poem, "The Truest Poetry is the Most Feigning," and consciously practice role-playing and ventriloquism and heteroglossia. Role playing and irony and make-believe often get at possible or temporary selves or dimensions of the protean self that are important and useful but unavailable to consciousness. To take a concrete example, people who are characteristically timid, quiet, self-effacing—who have a hard time getting heard or getting any force into language—often come up with a powerfully angry voice when they let themselves play that role. It's as though they have an angry voice in their unconscious. (Does the sophisticated position posit an unconscious?) When this angry voice gets a hold of the pen, the resulting language is often very powerful indeed—though hard to control. At first this voice feels alien, but gradually one often comes to own or claim it.

Notice that in both approaches, sentimental and sophisticated, we see the same crucial process: a gradual development and enrichment of voice. In one case it is a matter of using, trusting, and "playing in" (as with an unplayed violin) a voice that feels like one's own—and seeing it become more flexible. In the other case it is a matter of trusting oneself to use unaccustomed or even alien voices in a spirit of play and non-investment—and seeing those voices become more comfortable and owned.

Bakhtin provides us with a good example of someone trying to do justice to both positions. All the while he is arguing that every word we speak or write comes from the mouths and voices of others, he never stops being interested in the process by which we take these alien words and "make them our own."

> The importance of struggling with another's discourse, its influence in the history of an individual's coming to dialogical consciousness, is enormous. One's own discourse and one's own voice, although born of another or dynamically stimulated by another, will sooner or later begin to liberate themselves from the authority of the other's discourse.[34]

William Coles and Walker Gibson provide two more examples of midway positions on the issue of voice and identity. They may not have intended to take a middle position, for in fact both of them repeatedly insist that they are not interested in the real writer at all, only in the textual voice; they insist that we create ourselves anew every time we speak or write. Yet the test they often use for language is not whether it is strong in itself or well suited to the audience but rather a certain sense of authenticity. Here is Coles writing about the textual voice in a letter by Nicola Sacco (of Sacco and Vanzetti): ". . . for me there's no 'facade' here, not any more than Sacco is 'behind' anything. That language of his so far as I'm concerned, he's in. He's it. And it's him."[35] When they criticize a textual voice, they often call it "fake"; Coles sometimes even calls it "bullshit." (If we create ourselves anew every time we speak or write, how can our creation ever be anything but real?) Here in the same book is Coles doing a kind of justice to both sides of the voice/identity issue in two adjacent sentences. He is talking about revising his book and the unavoidable process of "rewriting" himself. In one sentence he says he is doing "no more than trying to solve a writing problem." But in the next sentence he says his revising is "a way of seeing what it could mean to belong to one's self . . ."(276). I sense an ambivalence in Coles and Gibson—an ambivalence that seemed shared in the culture of the Amherst College course they both

---

[34]Mikhail Bakhtin, "Discourse in the Novel," in *The Dialogic Imagination: Four Essays*, ed. Michael Holquist, trans. Caryl Emerson and Michael Holquist (Austin: U of Texas P Slavic Series, no. 1, 1981), 348. See 343 ff on this issue.

[35]William E. Coles, Jr., *The Plural I—And After* (Portsmouth NH: Boynton/Cook Heinemann, 1988), 179.

taught in: on the one hand, an insistence that voice is nothing but a phenomenon of text; yet on the other hand a continual, intuitive listening for how textual voice reverberates in relation to a person behind the page. Gibson's *Tough, Sweet and Stuffy* seems to me one of the best books around about voice and writing.

Concluding

When it comes to our own writing, then, we often notice whether the words we put down on the page feel like our words—whether they sound like our voice or one of our owned voices. Yet even here, I hope I've persuaded you that we write best if we learn to move flexibly back and forth between on the one hand using and celebrating something we feel as our *own* voice, and on the other hand operating as though we are nothing but ventriloquists playfully using and adapting and working against an array of voices we find around us.

And for my larger argument, I hope I've made it clear why voice should be such a tempting metaphor for this family of related dimensions of texts—dimensions that are so important and often neglected. Of course voice is a lightning rod that attracts ideological dispute, but I hope I've provided the kind of analysis needed to make voice a practical critical tool that we can *use* rather than just fight about. We may not agree about the presence or absence in a particular text of audible, dramatic, distinctive, or authoritative voice, but we can agree about what these terms mean. Even for resonant voice, we don't have to agree on the nature of self.

In order to stabilize and solidify the concept of voice in writing, I think we need to distinguish the five different kinds of voice I have spelled out here. But once we have had our critical conversation about voice in writing so as to make the concept more solidly understood and widely accepted, I don't think we'll always have to be so fussy about distinctions. We'll be able to say to a friend or student, "I hear more voice in these passages; something rich and useful and interesting is going on there; can you get more of that?" and not necessarily have to make careful distinctions between audible, dramatic, distinctive, authoritative, and resonant voice. There are substantive differences between the various kinds of voice in writing—but more often than not they go together. And surely the richly bundled dimensions and connotations of the human voice are what hold them all together.

Section 1:
Essays

Discourse in Life and Discourse in Art
by Michael Bakhtin

III

In life, verbal discourse is clearly not self-sufficient. It arises out of an extraverbal pragmatic situation and maintains the closest possible connection with that situation. Moreover, such discourse is directly informed by life itself and cannot be divorced from life without losing its import.

The kind of characterizations and evaluations of pragmatic, behavioral utterances we are likely to make are such things as: "that's a lie," "that's the truth," "that's a daring thing to say," "you can't say that," and so on and so forth.

All these and similar evaluations, whatever the criteria that govern them (ethical, cognitive, political, or other), take in a good deal more than what is enclosed within the strictly verbal (linguistic) factors of the utterance. *Together with the verbal factors, they also take in the extraverbal situation of the utterance.* These judgments and evaluations refer to a certain whole wherein the verbal discourse directly engages an event in life and merges with that event, forming an indissoluble unity. The verbal discourse itself, taken in isolation as a purely linguistic phenomenon, cannot, of course, be true or false, daring or diffident.

How does verbal discourse in life relate to the extraverbal situation that has engendered it? Let us analyze this matter, using an intentionally simplified example for the purpose.

Two people are sitting in a room. They are both silent. Then one of them says, "Well!" The other does not respond.

For us, as outsiders, this entire "conversation" is utterly incomprehensible. Taken in isolation, the utterance "Well!" is empty and unintelligible. Nevertheless, this peculiar colloquy of two persons, consisting of only one—although, to be sure, one expressively intoned—word, does make perfect sense, is fully meaningful and complete.

In order to disclose the sense and meaning of this colloquy, we must analyze it. But what is it exactly that we can subject to analysis? Whatever pains we take with the purely verbal part of the utterance, however subtly we define the phonetic, morphological, and semantic factors of the word *well*, we shall still not come a single step closer to an understanding of the whole sense of the colloquy.

Let us suppose that the intonation with which this word was pronounced is known to us: indignation and reproach moderated by a certain amount of humor. This intonation somewhat fills in the semantic void of the adverb *well* but still does not reveal the meaning of the whole.

What is it we lack, then? We lack the "extraverbal context" that made the word *well* a meaningful locution for the listener. This *extraverbal context* of the utterance is comprised of three factors: (1) the *common spatial purview* of the interlocutors (the unity of the visible—in this case, the room, the window, and so on), (2) the interlocutor's *common knowledge and understanding of the situation*, and (3) their *common evaluation* of that situation.

At the time the colloquy took place, both interlocutors *looked up* at the window and *saw* that it had begun to snow; *both knew* that it was already May and that it was high time for spring to come; finally, *both* were *sick and tired* of the protracted winter—*they both were looking forward* to spring and *both were bitterly disappointed* by the late snowfall. On this "jointly seen" (snowflakes outside the window); "jointly known" (the time of year—May) and "unanimously evaluated" (winter wearied of, spring looked forward to)— on all this the utterance *directly depends*, all this is seized in its actual, living import—is its very sustenance. And yet all this remains without verbal specification or articulation. The snowflakes remain outside the window; the date, on the page of a calendar; the evaluation, in the psyche of the speaker; and nevertheless, all this is *assumed* in the word *well*.

Now that we have been let in on the "assumed," that is, now that we know the *shared spatial and ideational purview*, the whole sense of the utterance "Well!" is perfectly clear to us and we also understand its intonation.

How does the extraverbal purview relate to the verbal discourse, how does the said relate to the unsaid?

First of all, it is perfectly obvious that, in the given case, the discourse does not at all reflect the extraverbal situation in the way a mirror reflects an object. Rather, the discourse here *resolves the situation*, bringing it to an *evaluative conclusion*, as it were. Far more often, behavioral utterances actively continue and develop a situation, adumbrate a plan for future action, and organize that action. But for us it is another aspect of the behavioral utterance that is of special importance: Whatever kind it be, the behavioral utterance always joins the participants in the situation together as *co-participants* who know, understand, and evaluate the situation in like manner. *The utterance*, consequently, *depends on their real, material appurtenance to one and the same segment of being and gives this material commonness ideological expression and further ideological development.*

Thus, the extraverbal situation is far from being merely the external cause of the utterance—it does not operate on the utterance from outside, as if it were a mechanical force. Rather, *the situation enters into the utterance as an essential constitutive part of the structure of its import.* Consequently, a behavioral utterance as a meaningful whole is comprised of two parts: (1) the part realized or actualized in words and (2) the assumed part. On this basis, the behavioral utterance can be liked to the enthymeme.[1]

However, it is an enthymeme of a special order. The very term enthymeme (literally translated from the Greek, something located in the heart or mind) sounds a bit too psychological. One might be led to think of the situation as something in the mind of the speaker on the order of a subjective-psychical act (a thought, idea, feeling). But that is not the case. The individual and subjective are backgrounded here by *the social and objective*. What *I* know, see, want, love, and so on cannot be assumed. Only what all of us speakers know, see, love, recognize—only those points on which we are all united can become the assumed part of an utterance. Furthermore, this fundamentally social phenomenon is completely objective; it consists, above all, of *the material unity of world that enters the speakers' purview* (in our example, the room, the snow outside the window, and so on) and of *the unity of the real conditions of life* that generate a *community of value judgments*—the speakers' belonging to the same family, profession, class, or other social group, and their belonging to the same time period (the speakers are, after all, contemporaries). Assumed value judgments are, therefore, not individual emotions but regular and essential social acts. *Individual* emotions can come into play only as *overtones* accompanying the *basic tone of social evaluation*. "I" can realize itself verbally only on the basis of "we."

Thus, every utterance in the business of life is an objective social enthymeme. It is something like a "password" known only to those who belong to the same social purview. The distinguishing characteristic of behavioral utterances consists precisely in the fact that they make myriad connections with the extraverbal context of life and, once severed from that context, lose almost all their import—a person ignorant of the immediate pragmatic context will not understand these utterances.

This immediate context may be of varying scope. In our example, the context is extremely narrow: It is *circumscribed by the room and the moment of occurrence*, and the utterance makes an intelligible statement only for the two persons involved. However, the unified purview on which an utterance depends can expand in both space and time: *The "assumed" may be that of the family, clan, nation, class and may encompass days or years or whole epochs.* The wider the overall purview and its corresponding social group, the more *constant* the assumed factors in an utterance become.

When the assumed real purview of an utterance is narrow, when, as in our example, it coincides with the actual purview of two people sitting in the same room and seeing the same thing, then even the most momentary change within that purview can become the assumed. Where the purview is wider, the utterance can operate only on the basis of constant, stable factors in life and substantive, fundamental social evaluations.

---

[1] The enthymeme is a form of syllogism one of whose premises is not expressed but assumed. For example: "Socrates is a man, therefore he is mortal." The assumed premise: "All men are mortal."

Especially great importance, in this case, belongs to assumed evaluations. The fact is that all the basic social evaluations that stem directly from the distinctive characteristics of the given social group's economic being are usually not articulated: They have entered the flesh and blood of all representatives of the group; they organize behavior and actions; they have merged, as it were, with the objects and phenomena to which they correspond, and for that reason they are in no need of special verbal formulation. We seem to perceive the value of a thing together with its being as one of its qualities, we seem, for instance, to sense, along with its warmth and light, the sun's value for use, as well. All the phenomena that surround us are similarly merged with value judgments. If a value judgment is in actual fact conditioned by the being of a given community, it becomes a matter of dogmatic belief, something taken for granted and not subject to discussion. On the contrary, whenever some basic value judgment is verbalized and justified, we may be certain that it has already become dubious, has separated from its referent, has ceased to organize life, and, consequently, has lost its connection with the existential conditions of the given group.

A healthy social value judgment remains within life and from that position organizes the very form of an utterance and its intonation, but it does not at all aim to find suitable expression in the content side of discourse. Once a value judgment shifts from formal factors to content, we may be sure that a reevaluation is in the offing. Thus, a viable value judgment exists wholly without incorporation into the content of discourse and is not derivable therefrom; instead, it determines the *very selection of the verbal material and the form of the verbal whole*. It finds its purest expression in *intonation*. Intonation establishes a firm link between verbal discourse and the extraverbal context—genuine, living intonation moves verbal discourse beyond the border of the verbal, so to speak.

Let us stop to consider in somewhat greater detail the connection between intonation and the pragmatic context of life in the example utterance we have been using. This will allow us to make a number of important observations about the social nature of intonation.

IV

First of all, we must emphasize that the word *well*—a word virtually empty semantically—cannot to any extent predetermine intonation through its own content. Any intonation—joyful, sorrowful, contemptuous, and so on— can freely and easily operate in this word; it all depends on the context in which the word appears. In our example, the context determining the intonation used (indignant-reproachful but moderated by humor) is provided entirely by the extraverbal situation that we have already analyzed, since, in this instance, there is no immediate verbal context. We might say in advance that even were such an immediate verbal context present and even, moreover, if that context were entirely sufficient from all other points of view, the intonation would still take us beyond its confines. Intonation can be thoroughly understood only when one is in touch with the assumed value judgments of the given social group, whatever the scope of that group might be. *Intonation always lies on the border of the verbal and the nonverbal, the said and the unsaid.* In intonation, discourse comes directly into contact with life. And it is in intonation above all that the speaker comes into contact with the listener or listeners—intonation is social par excellence. It is especially sensitive to all the vibrations in the social atmosphere surrounding the speaker.

The intonation in our example stemmed from the interlocutors' shared yearning for spring and shared disgruntlement over the protracted winter. This commonness of evaluations assumed between them supplied the basis for the intonation, the basis for the distinctness and certitude of its major tonality. Given an atmosphere of sympathy, the intonation could freely undergo deployment and differentiation within the range of the major tone. But if there were no such firmly dependable "choral support," the intonation would have gone in a different direction and taken on different tones—perhaps those of provocation or annoyance with the listener, or perhaps the intonation would simply have contracted and been reduced to the minimum. When a person anticipates the disagreement of his interlocutor or, at any rate, is uncertain or doubtful of his agreement, he intones his words differently. We shall see later that not only intonation but the whole formal structure of speech depends to a significant degree on what the relation of the utterance is to the assumed community of values belonging to the social milieu wherein the discourse figures. A creatively productive, assured, and rich intonation is possible only on the basis of presupposed "choral support." Where such support is lacking, the voice falters and its intonational richness is reduced, as happens, for instance, when a person laughing suddenly realizes that he is laughing alone—his laughter either ceases or degenerates, becomes forced, loses its assurance and clarity and its ability to generate joking and amusing talk. *The commonness of assumed basic value judgments constitutes the canvas upon which living human speech embroiders the designs of intonation.*

Intonation's set toward possible sympathy, toward "choral support," does not exhaust its social nature. It is only one side of intonation—the side turned toward the listener. But intonation contains yet another extremely important factor for the sociology of discourse.

If we scrutinize the intonation of our example, we will notice that it has one "mysterious" feature requiring special explanation.

In point of fact, the intonation of the word *well* voiced not only passive dissatisfaction with an occurring event (the snowfall) but also active indignation and reproach. To whom is this reproach addressed? Clearly not to the listener but to somebody else. This tack of the intonational movement patently makes an opening in the situation for a *third participant*. Who is this third participant? Who is the recipient of the reproach? The snow? Nature? Fate, perhaps?

Of course, in our simplified example of a behavioral utterance the third participant—the "hero" of this verbal production—has not yet assumed full and definitive shape; the intonation has demarcated a definite place for the hero but his semantic equivalent has not been supplied and he remains nameless. Intonation has established an active attitude toward the referent, toward the object of the utterance, an attitude of a kind verging on *apostrophe* to that object as the incarnate, living culprit, while the listener—the second participant—is, as it were, called in *as witness and ally*.

Almost any example of live intonation in emotionally charged behavioral speech proceeds as if it addressed, behind inanimate objects and phenomena, animate participants and agents in life; in other words, it has an inherent *tendency toward personification*. If the intonation is not held in check, as in our example, by a certain amount of irony, then it becomes the source of the mythological image, the incantation, the prayer, as was the case in the earliest stages of culture. In our case, however, we have to do with an extremely important phenomenon of language creativity—*the intonational metaphor*: The intonation of the utterance "Well!" makes the word sound as if it were reproaching the living culprit of the late snowfall—winter. We have in our example an instance of *pure* intonational metaphor wholly confined within the intonation; but latent within it, in cradle, so to speak, there exists the possibility of the usual *semantic metaphor*. Were this possibility to be realized, the word *well* would expand into some such metaphorical expression as: "What a *stubborn winter! It just won't give up*, though goodness knows it's time!" But this possibility, inherent in the intonation, remained unrealized and the utterance made do with the almost semantically inert adverb *well*.

It should be noted that the intonation in behavioral speech, on the whole, is a great deal more metaphorical than the words used: The aboriginal myth-making spirit seems to have remained alive in it. Intonation makes it sound as if the world surrounding the speaker were still full of animate forces—it threatens and rails against or adores and cherishes inanimate objects and phenomena, whereas the usual metaphors of colloquial speech for the most part have been effaced and the words become semantically spare and prosaic.

Close kinship unites the intonational metaphor with the *gesticulatory metaphor* (indeed, words were themselves originally lingual gestures constituting one component of a complex, omnicorporeal gesture)—the term "gesture" being understood here in a broad sense including miming as facial gesticulation. Gesture, just as intonation, requires the choral support of surrounding persons: only in an atmosphere of sympathy is free and assured gesture possible. Furthermore, and again just as intonation, gesture makes an opening in the situation and introduces a third participant—the hero. Gesture always has latent within itself the germ of attack or defense, of threat or caress, with the contemplator and listener relegated to the role of ally or witness. Often, the "hero" is merely some inanimate thing, some occurrence or circumstance in life. How often we shake our fist at "someone" in a fit of temper or simply scowl at empty space, and there is literally nothing we cannot smile at—the sun, trees, thoughts.

A point that must constantly be kept in mind (something that psychological aesthetics often forgets to do) is this: *Intonation and gesture are active and objective by tendency*. They not only express the passive mental state of the speaker but also always have embedded in them a living, forceful relation with the external world and with the social milieu—enemies, friends, allies. When a person intones and gesticulates, he assumes an active social position with respect to certain specific values, and this position is conditioned by the very bases of his social being. It is precisely this objective and sociological, and not subjective and psychological, aspect of intonation and gesture that should interest theorists of the various relevant arts, inasmuch as it is here that reside forces in the arts that are responsible for aesthetic creativity and that devise and organize artistic form.

As we see then, every instance of intonation is oriented *in two directions*: with respect to the listener as ally or witness and with respect to the object of the utterance as the third, living participant whom the intonation scolds or caresses, denigrates or magnifies. *This double social orientation is what determines all aspects of intonation and makes it intelligible.* And this very same thing is true for all the other factors of verbal utterances: They are all organized and in every way given shape in the same process of the speaker's *double orientation*; this social origin is only most easily detectable in intonation since it is the verbal factor of greatest sensitivity, elasticity, and freedom.

Thus, as we now have a right to claim, *any locution actually said aloud or written down for intelligible communication* (i.e., anything but words merely reposing in a dictionary) *is the expression and product of the social interaction of three participants: the speaker* (author), *the listener* (reader), and *the topic* (the who or what) *of speech* (the hero). Verbal discourse is a social event; it is not self-contained in the sense of some abstract linguistic quantity, nor can it be derived psychologically from the speaker's subjective consciousness taken in isolation. Therefore, both the formal linguistic approach and the psychological approach equally miss the mark: The concrete, sociological essence of verbal discourse, that which alone can make it true or false, banal or distinguished, necessary or unnecessary, remains beyond the ken and reach of both these points of view. Needless to say, it is also this very same "social soul" of verbal discourse that makes it beautiful or ugly, that is, that makes it artistically meaningful, as well. To be sure, once subordinated to the basic and more concrete sociological approach, both abstract points of view—the formal linguistic and the psychological—retain their value. Their collaboration is even absolutely indispensable; but separately, each by itself in isolation, they are inert.

The concrete utterance (and not the linguistic abstraction) is born, lives, and dies in the process of social interaction between the participants of the utterance. Its form and meaning are determined basically by the form and character of this interaction. When we cut the utterance off from the real grounds that nurture it, we lose the key to its form as well as to its import— all we have left is an abstract linguistic shell or an equally abstract semantic scheme (the banal "idea of the work" with which earlier theorists and historians of literature dealt)—two abstractions that are not mutually joinable because there are no concrete grounds for their organic synthesis.

It remains for us now only to sum up our short analysis of utterance in life and of those *artistic potentials, those rudiments of future form and content,* that we have detected in it.

The meaning and import of an utterance in life (of whatever particular kind that utterance may be) do not coincide with the purely verbal composition of the utterance. Articulated words are impregnated with assumed and unarticulated qualities. What are called the "understanding" and "evaluation" of an utterance (agreement or disagreement) always encompass the extraverbal pragmatic situation together with the verbal discourse proper. Life, therefore, does not affect an utterance from without; it penetrates and exerts an influence on an utterance from within, as that unity and commonness of being surrounding the speakers and that unity and commonness of essential social value judgments issuing from that being without all of which no intelligible utterance is possible. Intonation lies on the border between life and the verbal aspect of the utterance; it, as it were, pumps energy from a life situation into the verbal discourse, it endows everything linguistically stable with living historical momentum and uniqueness. Finally, the utterance reflects the social interaction of the speaker, listener, and hero as the product and fixation in verbal material of the act of living communication among them.

Verbal discourse is like a *"scenario"* of a certain event. A viable understanding of the whole import of discourse must *reproduce* this event of the mutual relationship between speakers, must, as it were, "reenact" it, with the person wishing to understand taking upon himself the role of the listener. But in order to carry out that role, he must distinctly understand the positions of the other two participants, as well.

For the linguistic point of view, neither this event nor its living participants exist, of course; the linguistic point of view deals with abstract, bare words and their equally abstract components (phonetic, morphological, and so on). Therefore, the *total import of discourse* and *its ideological value*—the cognitive, political, aesthetic, or other—are inaccessible to it. Just as there cannot be a linguistic logic or linguistic politics, so there cannot be a linguistic poetics.

The "Speaking Voice" and the Teaching of Composition

by Walker Gibson

This is an effort to say something useful to English teachers about the teaching of composition. Not composition in general, but composition in relation to one particular problem of writing—the problem of "focus" or "point of view." In making this effort I'm going to borrow from literary criticism a term that I think we composition teachers can put to work for us. This is the term "speaking voice."

Now what is a speaking voice? First let's talk about it as it relates to the teaching of literature, the appreciation of reading. We all know about it there—or anyway we should. It's one of those concepts that we've learned, in part at least, from what used to be called New Criticism, and it's familiar now in much critical writing and much classroom practice. It provides a way, for one thing, of concentrating on language by drawing attention to the fictitious speaker who is addressing us in a text. It is a way of looking hard at what is before us, the words on the page.

To remind ourselves how the term "speaking voice" is used, let's begin with a familiar example:

> "You don't know about me, without you have read a book by the name of *The Adventures of Tom Sawyer,* but that ain't no matter. That book was made by Mr. Mark Twain, and he told the truth, mainly."

The question is simple, or at least it's easy to put: who's talking? What sort of person is it that we infer from this language? What voice do we hear? As every schoolboy knows, the voice of Huck Finn is an easy backwoodsy sort of voice whose colloquial character is defined in the very first sentence. The use of "without" for "unless" and the unblushing "ain't" are two pieces of evidence that the most elementary reader recognizes immediately. "That book was made by Mr. Mark Twain"—the author has adopted a role from which he can refer to himself, his author-self by name (or pseudo-name!). No one could possibly confuse the "I" of the book with its author and the language of Huck's reference to his creator has even something of respectful formality and distance about it: *Mr.* Mark Twain. This is a useful passage to talk over with

---

Reprinted from New York: The College Entrance Examination Board, filmed 1963, published 1965: 3-13. Reprinted with permission.

young readers since, among its other interests, it so clearly and obviously defines a situation where author and narrator are distinct.

But there is another voice at the beginning of *Huckleberry Finn* that is worth pausing over too, and that is the voice of the famous NOTICE:

"Persons attempting to find a motive in this narrative will be prosecuted; persons attempting to find a moral in it will be banished; persons attempting to find a plot in it will be shot."

Who's talking now? A government official of some sort? A military commander, as the signature "Chief of Ordinance" suggests? How do we know that this is a "pretend-voice"—a joker? A class can be challenged with this question in order to make a discovery about the composition of humor. Such a discovery will rest on two perceptions. First, the language of the NOTICE is indeed the language of legalistic officialese: "persons attempting . . . will be prosecuted." Second, however, the "crimes" we are warned against are trivial—the mere finding of a plot in a book. The reader is faced with a dilemma: on the one hand an official-sounding voice warns of terrible punishments for crimes; on the other hand we know that these are not crimes at all. A world in which such acts could be followed by such punishments is a world inconceivable to us, insupportable. And so, of course, we laugh, and our laughter is our recognition that we have not identified this wild terrible world with any real world that we know and live in.

At the same time (a class should be able to add), through the joking voice, we *are* being warned not to take the novel that follows too solemnly— though our hearing that voice does not prevent us from taking it just as solemnly as we choose.

Now this rather cumbersome analysis, which is nevertheless much worth dragging out of students, serves to help them see a humorous speaker in action. It is not an official voice speaking; it is mock-official. The voice of a joker. One could ask students how to read this aloud, exaggerating the tone of formal stuffiness, the tone of an adjutant reading an order to the troops. Compare this reading with an appropriate voice for reading aloud the first sentence of the novel itself.

As you recall, there is still a third voice available to us at the beginning of *Huckleberry Finn,* the voice of the little passage on dialects headed EXPLANATORY:

"In this book a number of dialects are used, to wit: the Missouri Negro dialect; the extremest form of the backwoods Southwestern dialect; the ordinary "Pike County" dialect; and four modified varieties of this last. The shadings have not been done in a haphazard fashion, or by guess-work; but painstakingly, and with the trustworthy guidance and support of personal familiarity with these several forms of speech.

I make this explanation for the reason that without it many readers would suppose that all these characters were trying to talk alike and not succeeding."–THE AUTHOR

Now who's talking? The passage is signed THE AUTHOR, and students will be tempted perhaps to say that this is "really" Mark Twain at last. Let them say it if they like, as long as they see that here too the author is taking on a role, playing a part. It is a fairly formal role, in that first paragraph, and perhaps a student might observe that it seems rather on the defensive. The language is strikingly different, in its self-consciousness, from either Huck's monosyllables or the officialese of the Notice: "the trustworthy guidance and support of personal familiarity." But there is a semi-jocular ease in the last sentence that students should also be sensitive to; it rests on the absurd assumption that characters in a book could possibly be engaged in "trying to talk alike and not succeeding." The shift in tone is supported by a grammatical shift, from passive to active verbs, and such interactions of grammar and tone are crucial in our teaching of composition.

All this, then, is meant to remind ourselves how, in our teaching of reading, we can make use of the term "speaking voice" to help students become more sensitive to language. Now let's enlarge this concept a little, and consider its relevance to our daily lives.

We all play roles all the time. I don't mean that this is dishonesty—it is simply a way we have of making ourselves understood. And when I say "ourselves," I stress the plural, for each of us has many selves as we confront the various situations of our ordinary lives. Someone walks in the door and we throw a greeting at him—or her. We can say HELLo, meaning I'm a bored and irascible fellow, or I'm kiddingly pretending to be, and O golly, you again! We can say hellO, cheerfully, meaning you and I are friendly enough but not really intimate. Or we can say hellooo, which defines, of course, quite a different speaker and quite a different relation. Notice how, in making these self-definitions, one uses the complex muscles of the throat to produce, literally, a Tone, a certain significant noise out of the voicebox. Not only that: we use other facilities at our disposal for communication—gestures, facial grimaces, eyebrows. These last resources make up what some modern linguists call kinesics—those techniques of expression in addition to language. The problem that all writers face is the loss of both voicebox and kinesics. The writer's task is to so surround his words with other words on the page that readers may infer the quality of the desired speaking voice. This is an art, at all levels of writing.

And so we come, more directly, to the teaching of composition, and high time.

There is good reason to believe that this concept of the speaking voice, the *role* chosen by the author in a piece of writing, may provide a tool for the teacher of composition just as useful as for the teacher of literature. Furthermore, the use of the identical term—voice—in both the reading and writing process should assist the teacher in reminding his students that reading and writing do, after all, have something in common. Most of us teach reading *and* writing, and perhaps we're operating at our best when we're actually teaching them simultaneously.

Now, just how, in the teaching of composition, can this matter of "voice" be made to pay off? Consider simply a crude problem of voice inconsistency. A student writes a paper in which his first paragraph moves along in what we call acceptable English, but in his second paragraph he has a run-on sentence and a comma splice. Or take the student I was reading recently who interrupted a fairly solemn piece of literary discussion with the statement, "This kills me." What to do about this? Well, of course, one thing we all do is make some big red circles, and in the margin we refer nastily to the relevant sections of a handbook—31b or whatever. Or we write COLLOQ! That's all very well and no doubt has to be done, but it relies on that old weapon of the pedagogue, the Absolutely Right and Wrong. It isn't so much that the comma splice is wrong, immoral, wicked—it's that it expresses a voice inconsistent with the voice of the first paragraph. And one might, at least occasionally, say to one's class, Look, the problem here is that a more-or-less formal tone and voice in the first paragraph have collapsed in the second paragraph into the unbuttoned voice of oral speech. (Of course we always have to leave open the possibility that an abrupt shift of tone may be just the right touch for the situation. "This kills me" *could* be the perfect remark.) It is a degree of self-consciousness that we are trying to impress on the student. You orated to me, we say to him, in your first paragraph, from a podium and dressed in a black gown; in your second you spoke to me in a locker-room. I can appreciate both situations, mind, but I don't like getting shoved around so—unless I can see some point in being shoved around.

All language, certainly including the language I am now uttering, expresses a personality, defines a self. I don't at all mean that our language necessarily reveals our True Self, whatever that is. The self I am trying to dramatize to you at this moment is not at all the one I'd want to be stuck with forever—it is a particular voice, chosen, skillfully or not, to meet the apparent requirements of a particular and temporary situation—the making of a kinescope for English teachers.

Let me indicate now some other ways in which the "voice" approach might be applied to our work with student writing. Just about at random, I give you these two opening sentences from a freshman's response to his first assignment: to take a walk through a park and say what he sees.

> "Washington Square—A small plot of land, where nature attempts to display a small portion of the infinite beauty that she possesses to the hurrying inhabitants of metropolitan New York. People who desire to escape the worries and the bustle of their city life for a few short moments may consider Washington Square Park a haven, a God-sent cove where they might anchor their ship of burden for a while and escape the sometimes troubled sea of life."

Suppose you put a class to work discussing answers to this question: What sort of personality, what voice, do you hear in these lines, and just where do you hear it? The corny romanticism and sentimentality of the language will emerge from such a discussion in a way likely to be revealing and memorable to the writer. Instead, that is, of inviting from the class such comments as

"The phrase 'troubled sea of life' is a cliché and should not be used," I suggest inviting such comments as this: "I hear in this passage the voice of a silly and stuffy old fool. When I hear somebody talk about the troubled sea of life, I stop listening because I associate that kind of talk with people, especially older people, who haven't anything much to say to me." Now the student who wrote the piece, of course, is not a silly old fool at all—or anyway he's not old. Why, he must ask himself, did I choose to dramatize myself in that role? Partly, of course, the answer is that his whole TV-and-journalism world has encouraged him to take on such masks. It is true also, too often, that his English teachers have rewarded him in the past for just such performances.

Obviously I'm not arguing that this procedure of seeing all language as a drama—as an act of defining a particular voice—is going to solve all our difficulties in reading and writing. It is simply another way of saying what good teachers have been always saying. It provides, for instance, a slightly different way of getting at familiar traditional problems of "point of view." When the writer adopts a particular role or personality, he *places* himself, not only as a character with a voice and a relation with his reader, but also in time and space. In the writing of short exercises in fiction, especially, some traditional matters involving control of the narrator can be related to the student's experience with "voice." Just how knowledgeable is the narrator to be—how "omniscient"? If the person telling the story is launching himself into the consciousness of one character, one "point of view," does he not change his voice when he capriciously moves into the consciousness of some other character? Both crude and sophisticated literary problems of style, in other words, are approachable (I don't say solvable) through the concept of the author's speaking voice.

In a more elementary way, a good practice for flexing student muscles is simply to offer constant exercise in recognizing "voices" in the language of daily life. Any day's newspaper, for instance, will provide dozens of examples, and don't neglect the advertisers.

> "Remember that heat in October? Sure burned us! You should see the huge stock of suits and overcoats we didn't sell!"

The cute clubbiness of this speaking voice is supported—no, created—by its own rhetoric. The brevity of the sentences, their simple structure, the punctuation (exclamations and interrogatives) are all relevant. Everything fits—not of course that you have to *like* it. Diction largely Anglo-Saxon. Direct involvement of the reader ("You should see . . ."). Use of italics to echo the stresses of informal oral speech. Omission of subjects in the first two sentences, again to echo oral patterns. Students can quickly recognize how precisely different rhetorical devices define a radically different speaking voice:

> "A strong possibility has arisen that the artistic administration of the new center will be taken over by the Metropolitan Opera Company."

The longer and more complex sentence is obvious, and the formal diction, expressing the voice of a solemn news account, or editorial. The tone is unexcited, distant from the reader. The passive verb is characteristic, and so is the placing of the principal information in the dependent clause. The subject of the sentence, grammatically, is a mere abstraction ("possibility"). Much good experience with language can be gained by asking students to rewrite such passages in a different voice:

> "The Metropolitan Opera Company will very possibly take over the artistic administration of the new center.

Here, without even varying the vocabulary, and by changing only the word order, we create a speaker who is closer both to his subject and to his reader. Instead of asserting that only a "possibility has arisen," he now asserts somebody will possibly do something: a more forthright stand. Neither is "better," really: it depends on the degree of assurance and intimacy one wishes one's speaker to have. It is often desirable to produce a speaking voice that is almost faceless, dry, distant, impersonal. You can find this in the newspaper too:

> "Pursuant to the provisions of the amended Certificate of Incorporation, notice is hereby given that the Board of Directors will dispose of said property on Wednesday, 16 May, at ten o'clock in the forenoon."

Somebody may be about to be sold down the river, but the speaker's voice couldn't care less. This is a voice you just can't argue with, and that of course is the writer's intention. The speaker doesn't even "give notice"—he merely announces that "notice is hereby given."

Now let's return to composition and try out some generalizations.

To write a composition, of any sort, is to decide at least these three things and these are traditional things that I'm going to list. Who you are. What your situation is (your "subject"). Who your audience is. The teacher who thinks of composition in terms of "voice" would be likely to place special importance on the first of these decisions—who you are. But notice that the teacher does not ask "Who are you?" in any cosmic sense, and certainly not in any psychoanalytical sense. The definition of the speaker is made in relation to other immediate considerations: the situation certainly, and the audience. "Who are you," the teacher asks, "for the purposes of this particular composition? Are you this person consistently through the composition? Is this person the best one for the job?"

Not long ago I visited a class of bright tenth graders where a well-trained and resourceful teacher was using this approach that I've been describing. She was differentiating between *authors* of pieces of writing and *speakers* or voices dramatized within those pieces of writing. Midway through the class, she had a boy named Jimmy read a paper he'd written. When that was over she turned to the class and said, "Now what's the trouble here? What voice did you hear in that paper? Is it Jimmy's voice? Is that Jimmy speaking or is it some artificial, insincere voice?"

I'm sure you see what happened here. The teacher was fine in making our author-speaker distinction in reading literature, but she forgot it momentarily when she turned to composition. Instantly she was in trouble, because Jimmy, who was a very alert young man, cried out in his defense, and sensibly too. "Look," he said, "we just finished saying that real authors and 'voices' don't sound the same. I don't *have* to sound like *me*, whoever that is." I'm afraid I was on Jimmy's side in that argument. Though of course as a polite visitor in the back row I couldn't quite say so.

Naturally there are times, lots of times, when we might properly challenge a student about his choice of a voice. Are you really prepared to commit yourself to this personality, this set of attitudes, we may ask, even though we recognize it's only temporary and dramatic? Is *this* the sort of person you want to be taken to be by your reader? The responsibility implicit in such choices is surely something that we teachers mustn't ever forget. But it's also true that we cannot, usually, ask a student what his "real" voice is, any more than we can ask, after reading those three passages from *Huck Finn,* who the "real" Mark Twain is.

We are all made up of all the selves we act out, all day long and every day.

It's arguable that the young are proficient and uninhibited actors, at least compared with us straightfaced elders. Their facility in changing roles ought to be useful to them in learning to write. The teenager's day presents him with a series of social situations which call for different linguistic performances: to his parents and his siblings, in his various classrooms, the lunchroom and athletic field, drugstore and drive-in movie. He is accustomed to sizing up situations and adapting himself to the expectations of varying audiences, from guidance counselor to girlfriend. Indeed, some young people seem to know already, in a practical way, what it takes the rest of us half our lives to understand consciously: that the question of the "appropriate" voice is not so much a function of the situation as it is a function of ourselves. Or to put it more drastically: the world is the world we make by our own creative acts, as the poets have been saying for some time. We are the woods we wander in. Perhaps one way of becoming "mature" is to recognize that one does not slavishly adopt new voices simply in response to situations, but that on the contrary one creates and shapes one's situations by the very language one chooses on the spot. We do not select our words simply in recognition of outer circumstances, but also to satisfy inner desires. It's in this sense that the name of our subject, composition, bears extra meaning, with huge implications of freedom and responsibility. By composing our language we compose ourselves, and while there are other ways of presenting ourselves to the world, our language remains the most persuasive, the most delicate, the best way we have for defining ourselves.

Word as Sound

by Walter Ong

Auditory Synthesis: Word as Event

In discussing the phonetic alphabet we have treated the alliance of sound with the passage of time and the consequent irreducibility of sound to purely spatial categories. There are also other features of sound which give it special importance within man's life-world and which have strong religious significance but which are likely to elude us in today's still highly visualist culture. It is a commonplace that early man, strongly if by no means exclusively oral-aural, experiences words—which for him typically are spoken words—as powerful, effective, of a piece with other actuality far more than later visualist man is likely to do. A word is a real happening, indeed a happening par excellence.

Some are tempted to regard the primitive attitude toward the word as superstition, but there is an abiding truth about it which we can see if we reflect further on the implications of sound in terms of man's life-world and in terms of actuality in general.

Sound is more real or existential than other sense objects, despite the fact that it is also more evanescent. Sound itself is related to present actuality rather than to past or future. It must emanate from a source here and now discernibly active, with the result that involvement with sound is involvement with the present, with here-and-now existence and activity.

Sound signals the present use of power, since sound must be in active production in order to exist at all. Other things one senses may reveal actual present use of power, as when one watches the drive of a piston in an engine. But vision can reveal also mere quiescence, as in a still-life display. Sound can induce repose, but it never reveals quiescence. It tells us that something is going on. In his *Sound and Symbol,* writing on the effect of music, Victor Zuckerkandl notes that, by contrast with vision and touch, hearing registers force, the dynamic. This can be perceived on other grounds, too. A primitive hunter can see, feel, smell, and taste an elephant when the animal is quite dead. If he hears an elephant trumpeting or merely shuffling his feet, he had better watch out. Something is going on. Force is operating.

Hence cultures which do not reduce words to space but know them only

Reprinted from Chapter 3, *The Presence of the Word: Some Prolegomena for Cultural and Religious History.* (New Haven: Yale UP, 1967): 111-138. Reprinted with permission.

as oral-aural phenomena, in actuality or in the imagination, naturally regard words as more powerful than do literate cultures. Words *are* powerful. We take them in tiny doses, a syllable at a time. What would the shattering psychological experience of the hearer be if all the knowledge written in books were somehow suddenly *uttered* all at once? What would it do to the nervous system and the psyche to assimilate all these words simultaneously? Being powered projections, spoken words themselves have an aura of power. In personal relations—and spoken words of their very nature entail real, not imagined, personal relations, since the audience is on hand and reacting— words do have real power: the king's statement that so-and-so is his representative makes him his representative as nothing else does. Words in an oral-aural culture are inseparable from action for they are always sounds. Thus they appear of a piece with other actions, including even grossly physical actions. The Hebrew use of the word *dabar* to mean both word and event is, as Barr would have it, probably not so distinctive a phenomenon as it has been made out to be. But, however common the usage may or may not be, this sense is perfectly consistent not only with the oral-aural state of mind but with the very nature of words themselves. For every word even today in its primary state of existence, which is its spoken state, is indeed an event.

In oral-aural cultures it is thus eminently credible that words can be used to achieve an effect such as weapons or tools can achieve. Saying evil things of another is thought to bring him direct physical harm. Charms and magic formulas abound. This attitude toward words in more or less illiterate societies is an anthropological commonplace, but the connection of the attitude with the nature of sound and the absence of writing has not until recently begun to grow clear.

Moreover, since sound is indicative of here-and-now activity, the word as sound establishes here-and-now personal presence. Abraham knew God's presence when he heard his "voice." (We should not assume that the Hebrews necessarily thought of a physical sound here, only that what happened to Abraham was more like hearing a voice than anything else.) "After these events God put Abraham to a test. He said to him, 'Abraham.' He answered, 'Here I am'" (Gen. 22:1). As establishing personal presence, the word has immediate religious significance, particularly in the Hebrew and Christian tradition, where so much is made of a personal, concerned God. Mircea Eliade has brilliantly discussed the relationship of religion to sacred time and sacred space. Religious awareness grows out of regard for sacred times and sacred places. But sacred time and sacred space are space plus and time plus. The divine presence irrupts into time and space and "inhabits" them. Presence does not irrupt *into* voice. One cannot have voice without presence, at least suggested presence. And voice, as will be seen, being the paradigm of all sound for man, sound itself thus of itself suggests presence. Voice is not inhabited by presence as by something added: it simply conveys presence as nothing else does.

My nerves are bad to-night. Yes, bad. Stay with me.

Speak to me. Why do you never speak. Speak.
What are you thinking of? What thinking? What?
I never know what you are thinking. Think.

The distressed person in *The Waste Land* of T. S. Eliot expresses the agony of one to whom presence is denied because vocal communication is denied.

Only with writing, and particularly with the phonetic alphabet, do words readily appear to be disengaged from nonverbal actuality to the extent to which technological man today commonly takes them to be. This is to say, only when words are made out to be something different from what they really are do they readily take any radically distinctive characteristics. We are faced with a paradox here. Reduced by writing to objects in space, words can be compared with other objects and seen to be quite different. But reduced by writing to objects in space, they are one remove from actuality, less real (although more permanent) than when they are spoken. In this sense the spoken word, evanescent though it is and elusive though it is and lumped with other nonverbal actuality though it is, is nevertheless in the deepest sense more real and more really a word than the word sensed, through writing (and even more through print), as something different from "things."

The greater reality of words and sound is seen also in the further paradox that sound conveys meaning more powerfully and accurately than sight. If words are written, they are on the whole far more likely to be misunderstood than spoken words are. The psychiatrist J. C. Carothers, in a brilliant study, "Culture, Psychiatry, and the Written Word," on which I have drawn here, puts it this way (p. 311):

> Few people fail to communicate their messages and much of themselves in speech, whereas writings, unless produced by one with literary gifts, carry little of the writer and are interpreted far more according to the reader's understanding or prejudice.

That is to say, the spoken word does have more power than the written to do what the word is meant to do, to communicate. We are inclined to think of writing in terms of the very specially gifted and specially trained individuals, professional writers or literary artists who can use writing often in specially controlled or limited circumstances, in truly exceptional ways. We are also likely to forget how very small a part of spoken speech can be put into writing that makes sense. The ordinary individual who can manage dismayingly complicated situations—his relations to scores of other persons and things in the intricacies of day-by-day activities—quite well through oral communication, is utterly incapable of managing comparably complex situations in writing at all. He can fill out forms or, after a long telephone conversation in which the real understanding was worked out (as it could never have been worked out by correspondence alone), he can "confirm the conversation in this letter." The letter only seems to be the definitive action. In reality it is a mere footnote to a complex of interrelationships which he could never write down. Our literate and now electronically computerized culture relies on the recorded word as never before, and yet at the planning level turns to conferences and idea-exchange meetings as no earlier culture ever did. The technological age is the age of the convention and conference and discussion group, and of the oral brainstorming session.

Such are the special demands of the written and printed media that it is rare ever to get into writing an exact, unedited version of oral verbalization, and virtually impossible to get it into print. Stenotype operators and stenographers transcribing from tape inevitably edit. Editors of printed works do what their title of editor has come to suggest: they "edit," that is alter, the expression that passes through their hands. (Yale's editor altered the foregoing sentence!) The written medium simply will not tolerate all of what actually goes on in oral speech. It has rules. If you cannot fit what you want to verbalize into the rules of writing, you are obligated not to write it.

The spoken word thus lends itself in quite full pliability to virtually everyone, the written word only to the select few, and even these cannot transact in writing all the complexities they can handle with little trouble in speech. One reason for this situation is of course that the spoken word is part of present actuality and merges with a total situation to convey meaning. Context for the spoken word is furnished ready-made. In written performance the writer must establish both meaning and context. This is one of the most difficult tasks in communication simply because the person or persons being communicated with are not *there* at all: the writer has to project them totally out of his own imagination. And they themselves, the readers, have to learn the game of literacy: how to conform to the other's projection, or at least operate in terms of it.

Sound is a special sensory key to interiority. Sound has to do with interiors as such, which means with interiors as manifesting themselves, not as withdrawn into themselves, for true interiority is communicative.

Sound is a clue to interiors in the physical as well as in the psychological sense. More than other sensory phenomena, sound makes interiors known as interiors (although it is of course true that the *concept* of an interior is derived also from other senses, notably the tactile and kinesthetic senses).

Sight presents surfaces (it is keyed to *reflected* light; light coming directly from its source, such as fire, an electric lamp, the sun, rather dazzles and blinds us); smell suggests presences or absences (its association with memory is a commonplace) and is connected with the attractiveness (especially sexual) or repulsiveness of bodies which one is near or which one is seeking ("I smelled him out"): smell is a come-or-go signal. Hence "It stinks" expresses maximum rejection or repulsion: do not even go near—the farther away the better—do not even think about it.   Taste above all discriminates, distinguishing what is agreeable or disagreeable for intussusception by one's own organism (food) or psyche (aesthetic taste). Touch, including kinesthesia, helps form the concepts of exteriority and interiority. We feel ourselves inside our own bodies, and the world as outside. We can feel free, not "boxed in." We explore tactually the inside of a box, and there are jokes about the drunk feeling his way confusedly around a lamp post and exclaiming in his confusion, "I'm walled in." But to explore an interior, touch must violate the interior, invade it, even break it open. Kinesthesia, it is true, gives me access to my own interior without violation—I feel myself somehow inside my own body and feel my body inside my own skin—but kinesthesia gives me direct access to nothing but myself. Other interiors are inaccessible to it (except through empathy, indirectly).

Sound, on the other hand, reveals the interior without the necessity of physical invasion. Thus we tap a wall to discover where it is hollow inside, or we ring a silver-colored coin to discover whether it is perhaps lead inside. To discover such things by sight, we should have to open what we examine, making the inside an outside, destroying its interiority as such. Sound reveals interiors because its nature is determined by interior relationships. The sound of a violin is determined by the interior structure of its strings, of its bridge, and of the wood in its sound-board, by the shape of the interior cavity in the body of the violin, and other interior conditions. Filled with concrete or water, the violin would sound different.

We should recall here that in dealing with interior and exterior we are not, strictly speaking, dealing with mathematical concepts. Like left and right, or up and down, or the directions north, south, east, and west, the concepts interior and exterior cannot be defined mathematically or distinguished from each other mathematically, although they may be accepted as given and then assigned different mathematical values. These are strictly "existential" terms. Many attempts to define such terms are circular. *Webster's New World Dictionary of the American Language*, College Edition (World Publishing Co., 1954) defines left as "of or designating that side of man's body which is toward the west when one faces north" and then defines "west" as "the direction to the left of a person facing north." This is hopeless, and thus the same dictionary adds to this definition of left, the phrase "usually the side of the less-used hand." This is the better definition. The Merriam *Webster's Seventh New Collegiate Dictionary* (1963), based on *Webster's New International Dictionary,* Third Edition, proposes such a definition first: "left" means "related to or being nearer the weaker hand in most persons" and "west" is "the general direction of sunset." These latter definitions are existential in the sense that they point not to an abstract set of relations but to an existent historical situation or event or series of events: matters have so worked out that most persons do have their weaker hand on the same side; the sun sets regularly in a certain position. The definition can point only to the historical, existential fact and structure itself on this fact.

"Interior" and "exterior" are similarly existential or historically grounded, and dictionary definitions of them tend to be even more relentlessly circular. Interior is referred to "in," which in turn is referred to "within," "inside," and so on—always the "in" or some variant of it, such as "between" or "bounded," eludes definition. The same is true of out and exterior. Ultimately the meaning of in and out or interior and exterior depends on pointing to a historical or existential fact, a fact which appears ultimately to be that of self and other, our experience of ourselves as existing somehow inside our bodies with an exterior world outside. What we mean by in and out comes from our experience of ourselves. We find ourselves situated in insideness and outsideness. Our bodies are a frontier, and the side which is most ourselves is "in."

As material being develops higher forms, interiority increases. This has been spelled out in great detail by Pierre Teilhard de Chardin. It appears also that, in some general way, this interiority is involved with the interiorizing economy of sound itself. The lowest forms of life, such as protozoans, would appear to have no real voice, although something like it may exist for them in the form of vibrations. Mollusks, too, appear voiceless. Crustaceans and arthropods have voice of a sort, but curiously externalized for the most part, produced from the exoskeleton; however, it thereupon resonates within the body. Exceptions to this rule among arthropods would be the death's-head hawk-moth and a few other insects noted by V. C. Wynne-Edwards in *Animal Dispersion in Relation to Social Behaviour* (p. 43). These have more interior sources of sound, as do also a few fishes which produce swim-bladder vibrations. Nevertheless, true voice in the sense of sound emergent from within is for the most part a characteristic of the higher animals—amphibians, reptiles, birds, and mammals—and rather more common among these as one moves up the scale to more advanced orders. Only some amphibians (frogs and toads but not salamanders) are highly vocal, reptiles only occasionally so (as the alligator). Birds as a group are more persistently vocal than lower forms. Mammals vary in their use of vocalization but, like birds, they regularly have highly developed interior sound organs (vocal chords). The large hammerheaded fruit bat has pharyngeal air sacs almost a third of the size of its entire body to aid in the production of sound, and some apes (howler monkeys, gibbons, gorillas) also have fantastically developed interior resonating structures (Wynne-Edwards, pp. 55-57). One can thus say that, speaking generally, voice becomes more operative as we move up the evolutionary scale and that bodily structure becomes somehow more resonant.

The increasing exploitation of voice as one moves up the evolutionary scale toward greater "interiority" of being parallels the movement toward intelligence, suggesting what will be treated in the next section of this chapter, "The Affinity of Sound and Thought." Intelligence, in its subhuman analogue as in its human form, is closely associated with sound.

Recent studies by Winthrop Kellogg and others, and not a little semipopular and popular literature, have called attention to the case of porpoises. It has been suggested that much of the "intelligence" of these mammals may be due to their extremely high discriminatory ability regarding sound, made possible by the extraordinarily fine construction of their ear. This much involvement in a world of sound creates the impression of humanness.

Many differences as well as similarities between porpoises' use of sound and man's can be noted. One of some significance here is that, while porpoises use sound signals as do other animals for communication between individuals, their principal use of sound appears to be a type of sonar. Sound is less porpoise-to-porpoise than it is porpoise-to-inert-object-and-back;

"voice" here is less communication than probe. Porpoises produce sound (by what means is not yet sure; perhaps through structures in the blowhole, for they have no vocal cords) largely to bounce it off objects, as bats do, so as to locate objects and define them with remarkable accuracy. Insofar as this sound-probe technique reports surface extent and shape, it makes hearing into a kind of vision. Because the objects involved not only reflect sound but also resonate in various ways, sending back variously sounding echoes according to their constitution, porpoises can also through sonar distinguish the quality of objects (soft, hard—fish from wooden models of fish, for example). Even though it resonates, however, sound thus used is less interiorized than voice as typically used by man for communication between the deep interior and essentially private consciousnesses of unique human beings. The hyperdevelopment of the porpoises's "voice" and hearing is largely for dealing with objects; man's corresponding development is interpersonal.

In *The Miraculous Birth of Language,* Richard Albert Wilson explores the origin of language in terms of the development of life. He suggests that the animal's resort to sound in its calls, a kind of "rudi-language," effects a change in the cosmic totality because "it explicitly anticipates time," since, although sound thus used "is also no doubt a report of the animal's present or immediate past state, . . . its chief significance is its reference to the future and thus its involvement in purposiveness" (p. 160). This suggestion of Wilson's and those which I have just presented above were developed independently, but they seem to jibe with one another. One might combine them in the further suggestion that sound is in certain ways a preferred field for the movement from inertness to intelligence, from object-like exteriority to the interiority of living beings and finally of persons. Wilson's "purposiveness" is a function of intelligence. It is also by the same token a function of interiority. To act with purpose is to determine even exterior process and structures from within consciousness itself.

Sound unites groups of living beings as nothing else does. There is some relationship between resort to sound and socialization of life. The relationship is not absolute; many animals, such as ants or some fish, have a kind of group organization which appears quite independent of the use of sound. Many others use all their senses, or most of them, for social purposes. Niko Tinbergen has shown this beautifully and circumstantially in *The Herring Gull's World.* Nevertheless, once production of sound is arrived at in evolutionary development, the fact that sound signals present, ongoing activity gives it immediate value in establishing social relations, particularly flexible ones in variable situations. Sound reciprocates. Sounds which I produce tend to evoke responses from outside me in a way that very few of my visible or tangible activities do. Sound even reciprocates between living and nonliving things, as was shown for porpoises and bats. The response here is from an object, a thing—although, since sound makes the thing to a degree resonate from its interior, the object or thing is less a pure surface than it is to sight. A fortiori, sound is useful for eliciting true responses from other living organisms, and that even at a distance. In *Animal Dispersion in Relation to*

Social Behaviour Wynne-Edwards (p. 63) calls attention to the fact that animal sound almost always is a signal to others *within* the species (it operates in a *communal* framework) and that interspecific use of sound is rare to the point of virtual nonexistence. Normally lions roar not to frighten their prey or even other competing carnivores but to signal other lions (this may include occasionally frightening *them).* On the other hand, visual and olfactory as well as tactual signals are regularly used to affect other species; for example, to frighten or discourage predators.

Touch is also a reciprocating sense, but the distance tolerated in sound as against touch is important, for socialization commonly demands a certain distance. Although sometimes it may have tactile aspects, of itself socialization is not physical compactness. This is true even of organisms lower than man. "Individual distance" is enforced in the social life of animals, as Wynne-Edwards details (pp. 133-34). The colonies of sea birds reported by Tinbergen, by Peter Marler and William Hamilton, and by many others are true social groups, but in their nesting colonies they enforce rigid territorial rules which preclude not only contact but even proximity except between mates and between parents and their young. The social structures of the colony are maintained by visual signals and in a special way by cries, which can simultaneously relate individuals to one another and warn each to keep his distance. Physical contact would destroy this complex social organization. A fortiori, human privacy or dignity imposes severe limits on reciprocity achieved by touch. Sound provides reciprocity and communication without collision or friction.

Thus because of the very nature of sound as such, voice has a kind of primacy in the formation of true communities of men, groups of individuals constituted by shared awarenesses. A common language is essential for a real community to form. It binds man not only in pairs or families but, as nothing else does, in large groups, and as a consequence it has a kind of primacy in communication even between individuals. It would appear that precisely because sound is so interiorizing and thus exploitable by man at depths unknown to less interiorized creatures, it implements socialization or even forces it as nothing else can. True interiority makes it possible to address others: only insofar as a person has interior resources, insofar as he experiences his full self, can he also relate to others, for addressing or relating to them involves him precisely in interiority, too, since they are interiors. Thus addressing others is not quite "facing" them insofar as facing is a visually based concept that calls for a turning outward. Communication is more inwardness than outwardness. It is not entirely satisfactory even to say that man is an interior exteriorizing himself. To exteriorize oneself without interiorization is to devote oneself to things, which alone are not satisfying. To address or communicate with other persons is to participate in their inwardness as well as in our own.

The word, and particularly the spoken word, is curiously reciprocating not only intentionally, in what it is meant to do (establish relationships with another), but also in the very medium in which it exists. Sound binds interiors to one another as interiors. Even in the physical world this is so; sounds echo and resonate, provided that reciprocating physical interiors are at hand. Sights may reflect, from surfaces. Strumming on a bass viol will make a nearby one sound, by virtue of outside impact of energy but in such a way as to reveal its interior structures.

Because the spoken word moves from interior to interior, encounter between man and man is achieved largely through voice. The modes of encounter are innumerable—a glance, a gesture, a touch, even an odor—but among these the spoken word is paramount. Encounters with others in which no words are ever exchanged are hardly encounters at all. The written word alone will not do, for it is not sufficiently living and refreshing. The scholar, isolated in his den with his books and sheets of writing paper, is plunged into words, but he is still liable to the charge of being "dead"; one thinks again of Browning's poem, *The Grammarian's Funeral.* Despite the nourishment they furnish, books taken alone are killing. Renaissance humanists such as Machiavelli could think of the authors in their libraries as living men: "They receive me with friendship; in their company I feed upon the only nourishment which is truly mine, the nourishment I was born to receive. Without false shame I venture to converse with them." But afterward, Machiavelli also ventured to tell others who were truly living all about it. He gives us this account in a letter of December 10, 1513, to Francesco Vettori, and we can be sure that he conversed with friends such as Vettori about his conversations with his books, so that this letter itself, though a written instrument, was close to the world of real conversation, oral exchange, as humanists' letters commonly were. Man must give meaning and life to his actions, including his study of books, by his encounters with others, which means that in one way or another, explicitly or implicitly, he must relate his other actions to spoken words.

Since pure interiors (persons) do communicate with one another so largely by voice, the silencing of words portends in some way withdrawal into oneself. Such withdrawal need not be antisocial, for the interior into which one withdraws is the ground of all communication. Religious silence, for example, undertaken in union with others and out of regard for God and all mankind, can be fruitful and is, but such silence relates at many points to the spoken word and constitutes itself a kind of communication and encounter. So does writing, of course. And yet, because it consists of silent words, writing introduces a whole new set of structures within the psyche: communication which lacks the normal social aspect of communication, encounter with one who is not present, participation in the thought of others without commitment or involvement. Oral or illiterate peoples are understandably suspicious of literates as "slickers," the noncommitted and disinterested whom one cannot trust.

Although oral-aural cultures certainly differ vastly from one another both in explored and unexplored ways, it appears that at least a great many of them commonly conceive of actuality as united in some kind of harmony rather than in the visualist terms whereby cosmological unity is commonly pictured in modern technological society. Spitzer's *Classical and Christian Ideas of World Harmony* provides massive detail illustrating the more aural bent of the Western mind in its earlier phases by contrast with the present visualist bent in the West and to a growing extent elsewhere. Reviewing psychological and anthropological studies of present-day cultures still relatively illiterate, Carothers describes such culture as encouraging habits of "auditory synthesis" as against the habits of "visual synthesis" enforced by modern science and grounded in literacy.

We should remember, however, that auditory synthesis does not quite entirely describe the earlier or more primitive, residually oral state of mind, for the term synthesis is itself a visualist construct, meaning at root a putting together—that is, an operation conceived of as local motion in a spatial field, a visually (or visually-tactually) conceived operation. It would be more accurate to oppose "visual synthesis" with "(auditory) harmony," conceiving the auditory in auditory terms. However, auditory synthesis has something to recommend it, for all explanation entails some conversion to visual-tactile concepts. To call for explanation (root meaning: unfolding, laying out flat) is to call for analysis, the fragmentation that belongs more properly to vision than to the other senses. While explanation thus helps understanding, it provides of its very nature an extremely limited participation in actuality—knowing more and more about less and less—unless it is accompanied by other modes of understanding.

Habits of dominantly auditory synthesis long survive the introduction of writing, as can be seen for the seventeenth and eighteenth centuries in John Hollander's *The Untuning of the Sky* and for the earlier periods of Western culture in Spitzer's book just mentioned. Spitzer sees the old auditory sense of unity (although he does not use this precise term) encapsulated permanently in the German word *Stimmung* and its cognates *(dass stimmt, Stimme,* etc.), on which his entire book is simply a comment. *Stimmung* is of course untranslatable, but a close English equivalent would be "tunedness"—a sense of unity working out from the world of sound to all actuality. There are of course many other points in other languages and cultures at which the old oral-aural awareness of fullness, completeness, and unity works itself out. And there are movements to strengthen this awareness in new ways today. Milič Čapek's *Philosophical Impact of Contemporary Physics* (pp. 170-71) proposes that modern physics resort to sound-based concepts to supplement (but of course without abandoning) the visually based apparatus in which physics has specialized.

Sound situates man in the middle of actuality and in simultaneity, whereas vision situates man in front of things and in sequentiality. Since technological man is more addicted to sight than to sound, we can start here with sight. Sight presents surfaces, as we have seen; but it does not present all surfaces, only those that are in front of us. We speak of sight as man knows it; what the world looks like to an insect with compound eyes presenting dozens of slightly different views of the same object simultaneously, or to a crustacean with eyes on stalks capable of viewing opposed sides of an object simultaneously is another thing. And yet not entirely another thing for even here we encounter surface as surface: sight is feedback, because all sight registers reflected light.

As a human being, I see only what is ahead, not what I know is behind. To view the world around me, I must turn my eyes, taking in one section after another, establishing a sequence. To view a friend from all sides, I must walk around him or have him turn around. There is no way to view all that is visible around me at once. As Merleau-Ponty has nicely put it in his "L'Oeil et l'esprit," vision is a dissecting sense. Or, to put it another way, one can say that it is sequential. It presents one thing after another. Even though each part of the landscape surrounding me on all sides is contemporaneous with every other part, sight splits it up temporally, gives it a one-piece-after-another quality. Sight, despite the fact that it is seemingly more independent of time than sound (which exists only when it is perishing in time) nevertheless is nonsimultaneous. The actuality around me accessible to sight, although it is all simultaneously on hand, can be caught by vision only in a succession of "fixes."

Sound is quite different. At a given instant I hear not merely what is in front of me or behind me or at either side, but all these things simultaneously, and what is above and below as well. We have just noted that there is no way to view all that is around me at once. By contrast, I not only can but must hear all the sounds around me at once. Sound thus situates me in the midst of a world.

Because it situates me in the midst of a world, sound conveys simultaneity. Although sound itself is fleeting, as we have seen, what it conveys at any instant of its duration is not dissected but caught in the actuality of the present, which is rich, manifold, full of diverse action, the only moment when everything is really going on at once. The ticking of my watch, the ringing of a church bell, a quick step on the floor, and the lowing of a diesel horn merge. One of the special terrors of those addicted chiefly to auditory syntheses is due to the disparity between this world of sound and that of sight: hearing makes me intimately aware of a great many goings-on which it lets me know are simultaneous but which I cannot possibly view simultaneously and thus have difficulty in dissecting or analyzing, and consequently of managing. Auditory syntheses overwhelm me with phenomena beyond all control.

Hearing does not of itself dissect as sight does. It will register all the sounds within its range, which are selected out only by specific acts of attention, and then only if competing sounds are not too loud. Of itself, hearing unites the sounds. It moves toward harmony. When the sounds will not unite, when they are cacophonous, hearing is in agony, for it cannot eliminate selectively—there is no auditory equivalent of averting one's face or eyes—even though with proper stimulus or effort the individual organism can attend to a select band of sound.

Although, as we have seen, sound perishes each instant that it lives, the instant when it does live is rich. Through sound we can become present to a totality which is a fullness, a plenitude. A symphony, produced by an orchestra which is seen as merely in front of us, fills the entire hall and assaults us from all sides. Stereophonic sound is sound in its full normalcy. Of its very nature, the sound world has depth, dimension, fullness such as the visual, despite its own distinctive beauties, can never achieve.

This is to say, too, that sound and hearing have a special relationship to our sense of presence. When we speak of a presence in its fullest sense—the presence which we experience in the case of another human being, which another person exercises on us and which no object or living being less than human can exercise—we speak of something that surrounds us, in which we are situated. "I am *in* his presence," we say, not "in front of his presence." Being in is what we experience in a world of sound.

Specializing in auditory syntheses and specializing in visual syntheses foster different personality structures and different characteristic anxieties. Personality structure varies in accordance with variations in communications media and consequent variations in the organization of the sensorium. Obviously, these variations will not be the same or equally discernible in all cultures, but they are recognizable at times and analyzable to a degree.

In a world dominated by sound impressions, the individual is enveloped in a certain unpredictability. As has been seen, sound itself signals that action is going on. Something is happening, so you had better be alert. Sounds, moreover, tend to assimilate themselves to voices, whether in primitive cultures where thunder is heard as the voice of God or in our present-day imagination where in the depths of a dark wood the noises which even the most "advanced" technologically educated person hears about him strongly suggest voices, living beings, very likely persons, for intersubjectivity is one of the primary modes by which man's life-world is constituted. A world of sounds thus tends to grow into a world of voices and of persons, those most unpredictable of all creatures. Cultures given to auditory syntheses have this background for anxieties, and for their tendencies to animism.

Whatever the influence of this background, it appears from other evidence that at least a good many oral-aural cultures manifest characteristic anxiety syndromes which are far from typical in societies where the effects of literacy have been assimilated. Research in diverse non-literate cultures of Asia, Oceania, Africa, and the Americas, reported by Marvin K. Opler in *Culture, Psychiatry, and Human Values* (p. 135) has shown in these cultures, by contrast with literate cultures, a "uniformly ... high incidence of states of confused excitement, with disorganizing amounts of anxiety, fear, and hostility present, ... frequently associated with either indiscriminate homicidal behaviour or self-mutilation, or both, in a setting of catathymic outbursts of activity." In other words, when they are under emotional pressure, individuals in these cultures tend far more than do literates to break out in frenzied rages which often lead to indiscriminate slaughter.

Linguistic history appears to confirm these results of anthropological and psychological studies by attesting to standard anxiety-hostility syndromes in primitive populations. The terms "to go berserk" or "to run amok" attest that among the basically illiterate primitive Scandinavians and Southeast Asians respectively this sort of frenzied behavior was regular enough to generate the special terms which we have imported into English. Opler (p. 133) notes additional terms for similar behavior among other nonliterate peoples. Scandinavian berserkers (bear-shirts), as in the *Ynglingasaga,* could apparently work themselves into a frenzy more or less at will. In *Birth and Rebirth* (p. 81) Mircea Eliade has related the berserkers to members of the other *Männerbünde* of the ancient Germanic civilization: one entered these men's societies by undergoing terrifying ordeals (such as fighting unarmed) during which one had to behave as a beast of prey. In the perspectives suggested by Carothers one might say that the candidates for these societies learned to respond to psychological stress by outbursts of wild anxiety and hostility.

The riots in the Republic of the Congo at the achievement of independence a few years ago perhaps provide more recent evidence of oral-aural anxiety syndromes. I recall in particular the press reports of a Congolese officer whose comment, when he was asked about the riots, was quite simply, "What did you expect?" That is to say, "Don't armies everywhere riot this way from time to time when the pressure builds up?"

One thinks further in this connection of the wrath of epic warriors, recalling that the epic is a form with its roots and its persistent conventions deriving from oral cultures. Achilles' wrath does not occur directly in battle, it is true, but the weight given it, which to speak frankly is quite unconvincing today, may well derive from association between warriors and states of blind frenzy. It is not impossible that the highly conventional (if also erratic) wrath of epic warriors all the way down to Orlando is referable to confused cultural memories of earlier favored frenzied states retained as epic conventions even when they had grown less understandable and more palpably histrionic as social conditions and personality structures changed with the growing effects of literacy. The "fury" of Orlando in Ariosto's *Orlando furioso* would appear to be such a confused and adjusted wrath, partly a takeoff on courtly love madness but given an epic military turn which evokes Ariosto's indulgent irony shot through at times with high comedy showing a basic uneasiness about epic conventions in general.

Whatever the traces which may have appeared in the epic, and survived more or less equivocally as this oral genre adjusted itself to writing and finally was driven to suicide by print, the outburst of confused, violently hostile anxiety is real enough in many oral cultures. (One cannot of course say with surety in all of them.) The psychological studies by Carothers, Seligman, and others, summarized by Opler in the work cited above, suggest that these outbursts, "often self-terminating in natural course" (you actually cure yourself by massacring others) result from a lack of systematized fancy or delusions acting as ego defenses. A great variety of studies shows that illiterates seldom if ever indulge in the schizophrenic delusional systematization which is a regular syndrome of individuals under great stress in literate cultures. That is to say, under psychological pressure, illiterates do not commonly withdraw into themselves to create a little dream-world where everything can be ideally ordered. In the study earlier cited, Carothers notes (p. 307) that among African illiterates "categories described as 'paranoic,' 'paraphrenic,' and 'paranoid' are seldom seen" and that among these illiterates "in general, the clinical picture in schizophrenic patients is marked by confusion." The individual is psychologically faced outward, he is a "tribal" man, and, under duress, he directs his anxieties and hostilities outward toward the material world around him and chiefly to what he is most intimately aware of in that aurally or vocally conceived world, that is, to his fellow man.

The extremely confused anxiety and hostility syndromes reported by Carothers and those he draws on are of course not necessarily the only behavioral manifestations in oral cultures related to schizoid phenomena of the sort found among literates. In *Magic and Schizophrenia* Géza Róheim has shown relationships between magical practices and schizophrenic behavior. There is some sort of connection, it would appear, between magic and anxiety, and it would seem not impossible to correlate Carothers' work and that of Róheim, who traces schizophrenia in general to an oral trauma (p. 221).

With writing, and more intensely with print, the individual first becomes aware of himself as capable of thinking for himself to a degree impossible for relatively overcommunalized tribal man. Without literacy man tends to solve problems in terms of what people do or say—in the tradition of the tribe, without much personal analysis. He lives in what anthropologists call a "shame" culture, which institutionalizes public pressures on individuals to ensure conformity to tribal modes of behavior. With literacy, the individual finds it possible to think through a situation more from within his own mind out of his own personal resources and in terms of an objectively analyzed situation which confronts him. He becomes more original and individual, detribalized.

This withdrawal into the self, however, involves special strains of its own. Carothers has associated literacy with growth in guilt feelings, pointing out that among African illiterates, "depressive syndromes with retardation and ideas of guilt, unworthiness, or remorse are hardly to be found." The guilt is associated, of course, with the sense of responsibility, the responsibility connected with a sense of one's interior as one's own, keener among literates than among illiterates. Where the schizophrenic illiterate is marked by confusion with resulting outbursts of anxiety and hostility, the schizophrenic literate can withdraw within himself to construct his own world, self-consistent but maintained by his own effort.

The literacy with which illiteracy is contrasted in the studies reported by Carothers and Opler is uniformly alphabetic literacy. We do not know what effect learning Chinese character writing or other nonalphabetic scripts would have on personality structures. But one can conjecture how the phonetic alphabet encourages schizophrenic delusional systematization.

First, reading of any sort forces the individual into himself by confronting him with thought in isolation, alone. The book takes the reader out of the tribe. His thought still has a minimal social guise: it is in a book, which comes from another. But the other is not there. The reader follows thought all alone.

Beyond this, script, and particularly the alphabet, provides a heightened experience of order. The world of thought is itself a beautifully intricate world, and the world of words is likewise impressively, if mysteriously, organized. But visual space appears to be, as we have seen, a special symbol of order and control. When the exquisitely organized worlds of thought and speech (with their natural affinity for each other) are further ordered by reduction to segmentation, to spatial surface, the possibility of control and organization of the world represented through thought and word becomes overpowering. Print, because it is still more spatially tidy, is more convincing than even writing: "I saw it in the book." The expression registers the automatic, subconsciously driven reaction. To attack the printed word would be to attack *the* symbol of order.

In his sensitive novel *No Longer at Ease,* concerned with the acculturation of his native Nigeria, Chinua Achebe cogently portrays (pp. 126-27) the awesome impression which knowledge of writing has made on a thoughtful elderly man, who is fascinated by its order and stability and rather given to explaining this order and stability to illiterate kinsmen. He urges them to meditate on Pilate's words (which he quotes in oral fashion, that is thematically, not verbatim, suppressing Pilate's "I"): "What is written is written." The same man is even more impressed by print. He never destroys a piece of printed paper, but in boxes and the corners of his room saves every bit of it he can find. Order so assured as that of printed words deserves to be preserved, whatever the words say. It appears reasonable that such experience of this spectacularly ordered environment for thought, free from interference, simply there, unattended and unsupervised by any discernible person, would open to the overstrained psyche the new possibility of withdrawal into a world away from the tribe, a private world of delusional systematization—an escape not into violence or tribal magic, but into the interior of one's own consciousness, rendered schizoid but once and for all consistent with itself.

We can go even further than this. The alphabet, useful and indispensable as it has certainly proved to be, itself entails to some extent delusional systematization if not necessarily schizophrenia properly so called. The alphabet, after all, is a careful pretense. Letters are simply not sounds, do not have the properties of sounds. As we have seen, their whole existence and economy of operation is in a temporally neuter space rather than within the living stream of time. With alphabetic writing, a kind of pretense, a remoteness from actuality, becomes institutionalized.

Of course it can be maintained that even spoken words are pretenses too, in the sense that they are out of contact with the actuality they represent. Words are symbols, and all symbolization proceeds by indirection and to this extent demands a lack of contact with reality. It is of the nature of symbolization that the symbol stands for something other than itself. Man's knowledge is roundabout, and he conceives of reality not by dealing with it in the raw but by removing himself from it through symbolization, thus to achieve a more fruitful union. He re-presents in symbols, conceptual and verbal, what is present on other grounds. We shall not enter into the question of conceptual symbolization here, but consider only the sensible word. To the extent that he uses symbols to re-present actuality to himself, and especially in his use of perishing vocal symbols, words, to achieve contact with truth which he knows as extratemporal and permanent, man, too, resorts to pretense. But the pretense in oral verbalization is less contrived than in alphabetic writing. For reasons which we can suggest later, resort to sound for intelligibility comes about naturally. Reduction of this sound to space is by contrast artificial, contrived.

Even though chirographic and typographic man is less inclined to manifest the frenzied anxiety-hostility syndrome of oral-aural man, he does have special anxieties of his own, for, as was noted earlier in connection with the Freudian psychosexual sequences, chirographic and typographic man must keep order in an artificial spatial world of speech, not only far removed from the real habitat of speech but at root not entirely compatible with it. Though serviceable and enriching beyond all measure, nevertheless, by comparison with the oral medium, writing and print are permanently decadent. However vaguely, they entail some special threat of death. "The letter kills, but the spirit gives life" (II Cor. 3:6). The spirit (Latin, *spiritus),* we remember, meant the breath, the vehicle of the living word in time.

Assignment 19: J. D. Salinger

by William E. Coles, Jr.

[For this assignment I gave the students a passage from *The Catcher in the Rye* by J. D. Salinger. The passage, a paragraph that begins with "The book" and ends with "Eustacia Vye," may be found on pages 24-25 of the original edition published by Little, Brown and Company and on pages 18–19 of the Bantam paperback edition. Permission to reprint this paragraph has been denied by Mr. Salinger.]

Describe the voice you hear speaking in this passage [from *The Catcher in the Rye*, identified above] *and its ideal audience. What is it you call professional here? What do you call amateur?*

Holden Caulfield is no more dated in his appeal for college freshmen than the Cinderella story is for children. In fact, by his admirers he is thought of less as a character than as a person, less as a person than as a myth—an effect that is as carefully calculated as it is insidious. For the appeal of Salinger's ingeniously extended sentimentalization of the already sentimental tradition of the Noble Savage is based on an attempt to seduce the young into believing that Holden Caulfield is who they are. Holden Caulfield is *not* who young people are, of course, any more than they sound the way he does, but in being made to sound the way young people would like to *believe* they sound, and to behave as they would like to believe they behave—with a touching fumble-tongued awkwardness that is but the rough side of an absolutely unerring instinct for the true, the good, and the beautiful—Salinger's character, or rather the effect of Salinger's character, is to confirm the young in the lie they wish most to believe about themselves as young people: that they already know what in fact no one can know without learning; that they already are what in fact no one can be without trying to become. More than a fiction, Holden Caulfield is an impossibility. *The Catcher in the Rye*, for this reason, is a lie about life. Its ideal audience is adolescents of whatever age who wish to remain adolescents at the same time they have the need to pretend they are all grown up. The novel may traffic in the myth of the Noble Savage, but in its workings it enacts the myth of Frankenstein.

The passage I picked from the novel for the students to work with is a good example of both Salinger's ability as a writer, the source of his

Reprinted from *The Plural I—And After*, Portsmouth NH: Boynton/Cook Heinemann, 1988: 163-72. Reprinted with permission.

popularity; and what I would call the betrayal of that ability, the fraudulence of his appeal. The amateurish sounding voice of the passage, for example, is actually a very slick professional achievement; there is no question of Salinger's skill to manipulate dead language in order to produce the illusion of a sensitive and knowing creature. This effect he creates mainly through the yoking of certain kinds of contrasts.

"I'm quite illiterate, but I read a lot," immediately following the explanation of how Holden has come to read Isak Dinesen, connects a sterile, teacherish conception of education ("illiterate") with a phrase that not only explodes it, but in so doing suggests that the speaker (even though he does not realize it) actually reads with more insight and appreciation than does the reader who is conventionally "literate." The word "killed" is played with in an analogous way. When "this girl gets killed," the word signifies death—a meaning that carries into and deepens the more slangy connotations of the same word in the following sentence. The montage-like juxtaposition of these two meanings is what creates the image of Holden's hypersensitivity, particularly in that he is responding to an artistic rendering of an optionless situation (developed by the repetition of "married"). "Funny" is first used in its ordinary sense, but is jiggled in meaning almost immediately by "crazy" and so takes on the overtones of "queer" or "odd." The two meanings coalesce in the second use of "funny" to suggest that the speaker "likes" literature that makes use of the sort of pattern he describes in the Lardner story, and possibly that he needs the humorous to alleviate the pain of his hypersensitive response to what "just about" kills him.

The fraud of the passage, however, is a matter of its being based on a lie that is made to seem like something other than a lie. Holden Caulfield cannot be what he is said to be and know what he is said to know without also knowing that he knows what he does. But since such an admission would expose the myth of the Natural Sophisticate as a fiction, Salinger must arrange things in the passage to suggest that it *is* possible for someone to possess an awareness he can neither display nor act on, that the capacity for appreciation and the ability to discriminate *can* exist in total independence of the understanding, that in fact one *may* live on a level other than the languages he knows. He must, that is, arrange Holden's values and preferences *for* him—without getting caught at it.

I wanted to catch him at it, particularly after reading a set of papers that showed the students, almost to a man, solidly hooked by Salinger. But even in their praise, a number of writers had had trouble finding language to describe the speaker of the passage, so I began class with an excerpt from a paper the last sentence of which seemed a good way into this as a problem:

> To use proper English would have restricted him even further, to the point where understanding would become virtually impossible. As it is, he is trying to express concepts he doesn't understand in a medium he hasn't mastered. These are not the neat, logical sentences of a professional writer; instead it is the painfully wrought prose of a

boy who is unable to express himself, but does so with a beautiful, illuminating clarity.

"How is it that someone can express 'concepts he doesn't understand in a medium he hasn't mastered' and yet do this with what this writer calls 'a beautiful, illuminating clarity'? Who *is* speaking in Salinger's passage, anyway?"

"Well, it's a young boy, I think—I mean to judge from the language he's using."

"You mean Salinger wrote this when he was about fifteen?"

"No. I mean he's imitating a young boy. He's talking the way he thinks a young boy would talk."

"So it isn't just a young boy's talking?"

"No. It's Salinger too. He's pretending to be a young boy."

When we stalled on the question of how one knew it was Salinger's pretending to be a young boy, I turned to an excerpt from another paper:

> So the voice of the speaker is what is amateur in this picture. It does not know the correct English to use, but that doesn't mean that the voice is not interesting. It merely means that I wouldn't identify the speaker with any person who is a professional.
>
> What is professional in this passage is J. D. Salinger's ability to make me actually visualize the speaker talking to me. He makes simple talk seem appealing in this passage. Such things as "My favorite author is my brother D.B." make me take an interest in the speaker and in what he feels. It takes talent to create a subject like the one talking in this passage. This talent is what I would link with professionalism.

"Is this the sort of thing you meant, Rick, that Salinger has the ability to make you 'visualize' the speaker?"

"Yes, I think he does."

"How does 'my favorite author is my brother D.B.' make you 'visualize' the speaker? Do you know anything about him from a remark like that?"

"I know his brother means a lot to him. He doesn't seem jealous of him or anything."

"OK. You know that he has strong affections and that there's nothing mean about them. There's a kind of openness to him, a kind of honesty and decency. In other words, your response is a lot more specific than just 'taking an interest in the speaker'—talk that won't get you much farther than the dust-jacket rhetoric of 'beautiful, illuminating clarity.' It's a certain *kind* of interest you have, and it's a lot more than visual. In some mysterious way you move from an order of words to a sense of character, from language to what that language is symbolic of. Anybody, for example, could have said 'I'm quite illiterate.' Anybody could have said 'I read a lot.' But when you put them together the way Salinger does you don't get just anybody."

"You get a guy who's smarter than he thinks he is."

"You get that as an image I think, yes, along with the pathos of the fact that he doesn't know it and maybe never will. Where do you think Holden Caulfield got the term 'illiterate'?"

"From a teacher, I suppose."

"From a teacher, a parent, some so-called authority figure anyway. And the term embodies a concept which the boy seems to accept at the same time the context of his talk suggests how ridiculous it is for such a concept to be connected with him. He not only reads a lot; he reads good stuff."

"So the passage has to be translated, then?"

"Does translate, I think, as all language does. Let's look at an example of this translating process at work in another paper:"

> This character is trying awfully hard to act big and be noticed, but at the same time he wants to learn. His use of slang points toward his desire to be a member of the in group; as does the way he talked about the girl being killed. He didn't really think it was funny. He was just expecting a storybook ending, and he was shocked by the way she was treated by Lardner. It was different; and he didn't quite know what words to use to describe it; but instead of seeming to be at a loss for words, he uses "funny." As soon as he says it he is kind of scared by the way it sounds and to avoid going into it further, he changes the subject to "classical books." He is hungry for knowledge, not the kind you get from a classroom, but rather learning about life. He reads books and especially likes those that seem real to him. Wars and mysteries are something he can't quite comprehend (or doesn't want to), so he doesn't like them too well. He likes Lardner because Lardner seems to paint a picture of life that he could accept; and he likes his brother's writing, I suppose, because he can easily recognize life as depicted by him, having lived with him. Also, that sentence about calling up an author of a book that he liked particularly well shows his hunger for knowledge. He isn't satisfied with a good book; it only whets his appetite. Although he tries very hard, as I have said, to be big and noticeable, I don't think he is really that way. When he says that he is "quite illiterate," it is his way of shamefacedly, maybe humbly, admitting that he doesn't read as well as he should.
>
> He also does a lot of daydreaming. When he gets the wrong book from the library, he doesn't even notice it until he gets home. Most people, if they didn't pick it out themselves, would at least make sure that they were getting the right book. When he does get home and finds the mistake, instead of taking the book back he reads it (even though at first he thought it was going to stink).
>
> So what is this a voice of? The voice of someone growing up— fast; in a way wanting to slow down and yet wanting, to go faster.

"I see. I can follow what he means when he says that the character uses slang to be a member of the 'in group.'"

"And the way he translates 'that story just about killed me' into someone capable of being 'shocked,' or the remark about 'war books and mysteries' into someone who 'doesn't want to' comprehend war and mystery. The translation going on here is a matter of the writer's moving the way words fall on a page into the human terms for which they're the symbolic equivalents. There was another paper I admired for the same thing:"

> The strange part about the voice in this piece of writing is what lies beneath the voice, namely the person. The "flowered shirt" critic, the guy picking his teeth in front of the "hills like white elephants," is the type of man who might pick up *Out of Africa* by mistake, instead of *Day of the Guns* by Mickey Spillane, but he is not the type of man who would read it instead of taking it back. I don't know whether or not it might be a touch of professionalism, but here is a person who doesn't read what someone else has suggested, or what he started out to, but who rather takes advantage of discovering a book he didn't plan on. While the average slob might have picked up *Origin of Species* or *Mein Kampf* by mistake and immediately have taken it back, this person sounds like the type of person who would keep it, read it, and possibly profit by it.
>
> Here is a person who prefers the classics to the usual drugstore selection of war stories and mysteries, and yet who cannot explain why he prefers the classics. He reads a lot, yet he is illiterate; he rationalizes his feelings at the end of a book by his desire to meet the author, yet he reads Lardner unaware that Lardner is dead. *The Catcher in the Rye* is indeed a strange mixture of outward ignorance with an inner knowledge.

As with the last paper, what I praised here was a critical reading become a creative act. I mentioned particularly liking the way that the paradoxes of the writer's final paragraph seem to correspond to the paradox of Salinger's achievement in the passage as a whole, in his having been able to evolve a living voice from dead terminology.

"Does either of these two papers, by the way, give anyone an idea of how to address the question we bogged down with earlier, the question of whether this is a young boy's speaking or whether it's someone's making a young boy speak? 'Pretending to be a young boy' was Bob's phrase."

"I think it's definitely Salinger talking."

"Why?"

"Because I don't think a fifteen-year-old could show all this. I don't think he could mean what we've said the passage means.

"You mean he wouldn't talk bad English this well, this artfully?"

"That's part of it. No, I don't think he would."

"OK. Now, is Salinger believably rendering the consciousness of a fifteen-year-old, do you think, or is he simply making his mouth move, using him for his own purposes?"

"I don't understand what you mean."

I then turned to the last paper:

Just as it is difficult to separate what is said in a paper from the way it is said, it is difficult here to separate the voice of the writer and what his character is saying from the voice of the character and what the author is saying. Just what *is* being said here? On a superficial level, the voice of the character, someone with poor grammar, explains that while he doesn't read too well, he reads a lot of books that are funny at least once in a while and that he wishes he knew the authors of the ones he likes. Does the character actually mean this, or may Salinger be saying that the best literature gives the reader (even one who calls himself an illiterate) a picture of the author that carries his personality vividly enough to make the reader wish he were his friend? What makes *The Return of the Native* or *Out of Africa* seem better than *Of Human Bondage* in this respect and in this or any instance? Could this be one of the reasons that writing is an art instead of a science—the fact that what makes outstanding literature better than good literature for a given reader is something called style or tone, something a writer must develop for himself, something that cannot be taught, an intangible characteristic of the writing that strikes each reader differently?

Another characteristic of the voice of this paragraph is contradiction, such as "I'm quite illiterate, but I read a lot." Contradictions are here too in another less obvious sense coupled with the question of who is really speaking. The character's grammar and vocabulary aren't the best, but he has the discernment to give *Return* the title of classic in the sense of worth rather than of age (does he really know what he's saying?). In what appears to be a deliberate refutation of his apparent ignorance of good English, Salinger's character proceeds to sit in judgment on Maugham. "He just isn't the kind of guy I'd want to call up, that's all." What kind of illiterate reads Dinesen, Lardner, Maugham, and Hardy—and has the audacity to evaluate them, even on his own terms? Isn't the term "illiterate" a contradiction, whether by the character or by Salinger?

The first level of writing in this paragraph presents an amateur in the field of English and literature, but read on and listen to what the character has to say; isn't there a professional hidden in the bushes? Perhaps a professional amateur? The question of where one begins and the other leaves off must, within the context of this paragraph, remain unanswered, as does the question of whether such a point exists. The voice is that of a professional presenting an amateur who is a professional.

The voice of this paragraph has as its ideal audience anyone interested in paradoxes—which here include the writer, the character, the voices of both, and the style of writing. It also includes me. I've been persuaded that I should read the book.

"Now, one of the things that interests me most about that paper is the writer's talk of the passage as 'a strange mixture.' He talks first of the 'contradiction' of the paragraph, but then concludes by saying that the ideal audience for it would be those who are interested in 'paradoxes.' I'd like to raise the question of which is the better term by looking at the passage from Salinger in a slightly different way. Let me read it through with no more than some changes of proper nouns."

I picked up with Salinger's reference to *The Return of the Native*, but for that title substituted *Gone with the Wind*. For "Isak Dinesen" I read "Margaret Mitchell"; for "Ring Lardner," "the writer of Dick Tracy." And instead of Maugham I had Holden not wanting to call up the author of *Crime and Punishment*. He'd rather have called up old Margaret Mitchell. He liked that Scarlett O'Hara.

"OK," I said. "Now what's happened to the voice we've been talking about?"

"The kid's turned into a jerk."

"Do you think it's possible then that the writer of this last paper had a real question in asking 'What kind of illiterate reads Dinesen, Lardner, Maugham, and Hardy—and has the audacity to evaluate them'?"

"You mean he wouldn't be smart enough to evaluate them?"

"I mean would he have the knowledge to evaluate them when the whole structure of his talk, the syntax of it, suggests that what we have here is a mind at best naive, at worst slobby. How many of you in here have read *Of Human Bondage*?"

A couple of students had.

"Do you know why it's a cheap book?"

"No. I kind of liked it."

"So did I when I read it. I was seventeen. All that stuff about the meaning of life, or rather why life has no meaning. I thought it was real art, and it took me a while, and the help of a teacher, to be able to see how it wasn't. But Holden knows that it's a cheap book right away. That is, he's said to, in the same way that he's said to like Hardy and not be too knocked out by mysteries and war books and all. He doesn't know why, of course, but he knows. You just take Salinger's word for it. Do you see now, Bob, what I meant by asking whether Salinger is making Holden's mouth move?"

"You mean he makes him a great guy by having him like the right things?"

"Exactly. And not the other way around. Using the same technique, and maintaining Holden as the same sort of character, how would you take him to an art museum? What would you have him knocked out by and not knocked out by?"

"Well, I'd have him hate the billboards on the way there, but go nuts over Rembrandt."

"Or you'd have him really flattened by the Impressionists but not so turned on by Claude or some of the more conventional landscape artists. He'd like passion and sincerity and force but nothing stylized. And so on. And what would you have him give as his reasons for his preferences? What's all you'd *have* to have him say about them?"

"I know what I like."

"Right on. You'd never have to give a reason. All you'd have to have your character say is, 'I just like it, that's all. I don't know. Those Impressionists just turn me on. That Monet is the kinda guy I'd like to have pizza with, except I hear he's like dead.' And you could work the same trick with Holden on music or politics or life-styles or on any damned thing you wanted."

"Just so he liked the right things and didn't like the wrong ones."

"And just so you were careful to set it all to these rhythms—and all."

"I know what you mean there. When I finished the book I even talked that way."

"Sure. It's the key to Salinger's style—a set of attitudes marching like a parade of circus elephants, tail in trunk, trunk around tail. Only it's hypnotic, that style. I don't know. You just can't get it out of your head, that's all. What I like is a style you can at least get out of your head once in a while. Let me try one more change with the passage:

> The potato chips I was eating were these potato chips I took out of the supermarket by mistake. They gave me the wrong potato chips, and I didn't notice it till I got back to my room. They gave me Stateline Potato Chips. I thought they were going to stink, but they didn't. They were very good potato chips, etc., etc.

"What do you say about Holden on the basis of that change?"

"He's crazy."

"Meaning what, exactly?"

"That I don't understand him. He's either awfully dumb or a mental case."

"Why didn't you say that about him when the subject had to do with getting a book out of the library? That's just as much of an everyday thing as buying potato chips, isn't it?"

"Not for me. I don't take books out of the library that much."

Which, of course, is just the sort of thing that Salinger's stuff depends on. We concluded with my saying that so far as I was concerned, there is indeed, as the writer of the last paper suggests, "a professional hidden in the bushes" here. The metaphor, however, I think is appropriate in more than one sense.

Translator's Introduction

to Dissemination

by Barbara Johnson

I. *A Critique of Western Metaphysics*

Best known in this country for having forged the term "deconstruction," Jacques Derrida follows Nietzsche and Heidegger in elaborating a critique of "Western metaphysics," by which he means not only the Western philosophical tradition but "everyday" thought and language as well. Western thought, says Derrida, has always been structured in terms of dichotomies or polarities: good vs. evil, being vs. nothingness, presence vs. absence, truth vs. error, identity vs. difference, mind vs. matter, man vs. woman, soul vs. body, life vs. death, nature vs. culture, speech vs. writing. These polar opposites do not, however, stand as independent and equal entities. The second term in each pair is considered the negative, corrupt, undesirable version of the first, a fall away from it. Hence, absence is the lack of presence, evil is the fall from good, error is a distortion of truth, etc. In other words, the two terms are not simply opposed in their meanings, but are arranged in a hierarchical order which gives the first term *priority*, in both the temporal and the qualitative sense of the word. In general, what these hierarchical oppositions do is to privilege unity, identity, immediacy, and temporal and spatial *presentness* over distance, difference, dissimulation, and deferment. In its search for the answer to the question of Being, Western philosophy has indeed always determined Being as *presence*.

Derrida's critique of Western metaphysics focuses on its privileging of the spoken word over the written word. The spoken word is given a higher value because the speaker and listener are both present to the utterance simultaneously. There is no temporal or spatial distance between speaker, speech, and listener, since the speaker hears himself speak at the same moment the listener does. This immediacy seems to guarantee the notion that in the spoken word we know what we mean, mean what we say, say what we mean, and know what we have said. Whether or not perfect understanding always occurs *in fact*, this image of perfectly self-present meaning is, according to Derrida, the underlying ideal of Western culture. Derrida has

Reprinted from Jacques Derrida, *Dissemination* (Chicago: Univ. of Chicago Press, 1981): viii-xvi. Reprinted with permission.

termed this belief in the self-presentation of meaning "Logocentrism," from the Greek word *Logos* (meaning speech, logic, reason, the Word of God). Writing, on the other hand, is considered by the logocentric system to be only a *representation* of speech, a secondary substitute designed for use only when speaking is impossible. Writing is thus a second-rate activity that tries to overcome distance by making use of it: the writer puts his thought on paper, distancing it from himself, transforming it into something that can be read by someone far away, even after the writer's death. This inclusion of death, distance, and difference is thought to be a corruption of the self-presence of meaning, to open meaning up to all forms of adulteration which immediacy would have prevented.

In the course of his critique, Derrida does not simply reverse this value system and say that writing is better than speech. Rather, he attempts to show that the very possibility of opposing the two terms on the basis of presence vs. absence or immediacy vs. representation is an illusion, since speech is *already* structured by difference and distance as much as writing is. The very fact that a word is divided into a phonic *signifier* and a mental *signified,* and that, as Saussure pointed out, language is a system of differences rather than a collection of independently meaningful units, indicates that language as such is already constituted by the very distances and differences it seeks to overcome. To mean, in other words, is automatically *not* to be. As soon as there is meaning, there is difference. Derrida's word for this lag inherent in any signifying act is *différance*, from the French verb *différer*, which means both "to differ" and "to defer." What Derrida attempts to demonstrate is that this *différance* inhabits the very core of what appears to be immediate and present. Even in the seemingly nonlinguistic areas of the structures of consciousness and the unconscious, Derrida analyzes the underlying necessity that induces Freud to compare the psychic apparatus to a structure of scriptural *différance*, a "mystic writing-pad."[1] The illusion of the self-presence of meaning or of consciousness is thus produced by the repression of the differential structures from which they spring.

Derrida's project in his early writings is to elaborate a science of writing called *grammatology*: a science that would study the effects of this *différance* which Western metaphysics has systematically repressed in its search for self-present Truth. But, as Derrida himself admits, the very notion of a perfectly adequate *science* or *–logy* belongs to the logocentric discourse which the science of writing would try, precisely, to put in question. Derrida thus finds himself in the uncomfortable position of attempting to account for an error by means of tools derived from that very error. For it is not possible to show that the belief in truth is an error without implicitly believing in the notion of Truth. By the same token, to show that the binary oppositions of metaphysics

---

[1] See "Freud and the Scene of Writing," in *Writing and Difference*, trans. Alan Bass (Chicago: University of Chicago Press, 1978), pp. 196-231.

are illusions is *also*, and perhaps most importantly, to show that such illusions cannot simply in turn *be opposed* without repeating the very same illusion. The task of undoing the history of logocentrism in order to disinter *différance* would thus appear to be a doubly impossible one: on the one hand, it can only be conducted by means of notions of revelation, representation, and rectification, which are *the* logocentric notions par excellence, and, on the other hand, it can only dig up something that is really nothing—a difference, a gap, an interval, a trace. How, then, can such a task be undertaken?

II. Supplementary Reading

Any attempt to disentangle the weave of *différance* from the logocentric blanket can obviously not long remain on the level of abstraction and generality of the preceding remarks. Derrida's writing, indeed, is always explicitly inscribed in the margins of some preexisting text. Derrida is, first and foremost, a *reader*, a reader who constantly reflects on and transforms the very nature of the act of reading. It would therefore perhaps be helpful to examine some of the specific reading strategies he has worked out. I begin with a chapter from *Of Grammatology* entitled "That Dangerous Supplement," in which Derrida elaborates not only a particularly striking reading of Rousseau's *Confessions* but also a concise reflection on his own methodology.

Derrida's starting point is the rhetoric of Rousseau's discussions of writing, on the one hand, and masturbation, on the other. Both activities are called *supplements* to natural intercourse, in the sense both of conversation and of copulation. What Derrida finds in Rousseau's account is a curious bifurcation within the values of writing and masturbation with respect to the desire for presence.

Let us take writing first. On the one hand, Rousseau condemns writing for being only a representation of direct speech and therefore less desirable because less immediate. Rousseau, in this context, privileges speech as the more direct expression of the self. But on the other hand, in the actual experience of living speech, Rousseau finds that he expresses himself much less successfully in person than he does in his writing. Because of his shyness, he tends to blurt out things that represent him as the opposite of what he thinks he is:

> I would love society like others, if I were not sure of showing myself not only at a disadvantage, but as completely different from what I am. The part that I have taken of *writing and hiding myself* is precisely the one that suits me. If I were present, one would never know what I was worth.[2]

---

[2] Quoted in *Of Grammatology* (trans. Gayatri Chakravorty Spivak [Baltimore: Johns Hopkins University Press, 1974]), p. 142. Page numbers in brackets following references to *Of Grammatology* refer to J. M. Cohen's translation of Rousseau's *Confessions* (Penguin, 1954), which I have sometimes substituted for the translation used by Spivak.

It is thus absence that assures the presentation of truth, and presence that entails its distortion. Derrida's summation of this contradictory stance is as follows:

> Straining toward the reconstruction of presence, [Rousseau] valorizes and disqualifies writing at the same time. . . . Rousseau condemns writing as destruction of presence and as disease of speech. He rehabilitates it to the extent that it promises the reappropriation of that of which speech allowed itself to be dispossessed. But by what, if not already a writing older than speech and already installed in that place? (Pp. 141-42)

In other words, the loss of presence has always already begun. Speech itself springs out of an alienation or differance that has the very structure of writing.

It would seem, though, that it is precisely through this assumption of the necessity of absence that Rousseau ultimately succeeds in reappropriating the lost presence. In sacrificing himself, he recuperates himself. This notion that self-sacrifice is the road to self-redemption is a classical structure in Western metaphysics. Yet it can be shown that this project of reappropriation is inherently self-subverting because its very starting point is not presence itself but the *desire* for presence, that is, the *lack* of presence. It is not possible to desire that with which one coincides. The starting point is thus not a *point* but a differance:

> Without the possibility of differance, the desire of presence as such would not find its breathing-space. That means by the same token that this desire carries in itself the destiny of its nonsatisfaction. Differance produces what it forbids, making possible the very thing that it makes impossible. (P. 143)

The same paradoxical account of the desire for presence occurs in Rousseau's discussions of sexuality. On the one hand, masturbation is condemned as a means of "cheating Nature" and substituting a mere image (absence) for the presence of a sexual partner. On the other hand:

> This vice, which shame and timidity find so convenient, has a particular attraction for lively imaginations. It allows them to dispose, so to speak, of the whole female sex at their will, and to make any beauty who tempts them serve their pleasure without the need of first obtaining her consent. (P. 151 [109])

It is thus the woman's absence that gives immediacy to her imaginary possession, while to deal with the woman's presence would inevitably be to confront differance. Masturbation is both a symbolic form of ideal union, since in it the subject and object are truly one, and a radical alienation of the self from any contact with an other. The union that would perfectly fulfill desire would also perfectly exclude the space of its very possibility.

Just as speech was shown to be structured by the same differance as writing, so, too, the desire to possess a "real" woman is grounded in distance, both because the prohibition of incest requires that one's love-object always be a substitute for the original object, and because of the fundamental structure of desire itself. Rousseau's autobiography offers us a particularly striking example of the essential role of differance in desire. Faced with the possibility of a quasi-incestuous relation with the woman he called "Mama"—incest being the very model of the elimination of differance—Rousseau finds that his desire manifests itself in inverse proportion to Mama's physical proximity: "I only felt the full strength of my attachment to her when she was out of my sight." (p. 152 [107]) Not only does the enjoyment of presence appear to Rousseau to be impossible; it also could be fatal: "If I had ever in my life tasted the delights of love even once in their plenitude," he writes, "I do not imagine that my frail existence would have been sufficient for them. I would have been dead in the act." (p. 155)

Presence, then, is an ambiguous, even dangerous, ideal. Direct speech is self-violation; perfect heteroeroticism is death. Recourse to writing and autoeroticism is necessary to recapture a presence whose lack has not been preceded by any fullness. Yet these two compensatory activities are themselves condemned as unnecessary, even dangerous, supplements.

In French, the word *supplément* has two meanings: it means both "an addition" and "a substitute." Rousseau uses this word to describe both writing and masturbation. Thus, writing and masturbation may *add to* something that is already present, in which case they are *superfluous,* AND/OR they may *replace* something that is *not* present, in which case they are *necessary.* Superfluous and necessary, dangerous and redemptive, the supplement moves through Rousseau's text according to a very strange logic.

What Derrida's reading of Rousseau sketches out is indeed nothing less than a revolution in the very logic of meaning. The logic of the supplement wrenches apart the neatness of the metaphysical binary oppositions. Instead of "A is opposed to B" we have "B is both added to A and replaces A." A and B are no longer opposed, nor are they equivalent. Indeed, they are no longer even equivalent to themselves. They are their own differance from themselves. "Writing," for example, no longer means simply "words on a page," but rather any differential trace structure, a structure that *also* inhabits speech. "Writing" and "speech" can therefore no longer be simply opposed, but neither have they become identical. Rather, the very notion of their "identities" is put in question.

In addition to this supplementary logic in the text's *signified*, the inseparability of the two senses of the *word* "supplément" renders any affirmation that contains it problematic. While Rousseau's explicit intentions are to keep the two senses rigorously distinct—to know when he means "substitute" and when he means "addition"—the shadow presence of the other meaning is always there to undermine the distinction. On the level both of the signified and of the signifier, therefore, it is not possible to pin down the dividing lines between excess and lack, compensation and corruption. The doubleness of the word *supplément* carries the text's signifying possibilities beyond what could reasonably be attributed to Rousseau's conscious intentions. Derrida's reading shows how Rousseau's text functions *against* its own explicit (metaphysical) assertions, not just by creating ambiguity, but by inscribing a *systematic* "other message" behind or through what is being said.

III. Deconstruction

Let us now examine more closely the strategies and assumptions involved in this type of critical reading. It is clear that Derrida is not seeking the "meaning" of Rousseau's text in any traditional sense. He neither adds the text up into a final set of themes or affirmations nor looks for the reality of Rousseau's life outside the text. Indeed, says Derrida, there *is* no outside of the text:

> There is nothing outside of the text [*il n'y a pas de hors-texte*]. And that is neither because Jean-Jacques' life, or the existence of Mama or Thérèse *themselves*, is not of prime interest to us, nor because we have access to their so-called "real" existence only in the text and we have neither any means of altering this, nor any right to neglect this limitation. All reasons of this type would already be sufficient, to be sure, but there are more radical reasons. What we have tried to show by following the guiding line of the "dangerous supplement," is that in what one calls the real life of these existences "of flesh and bone," beyond and behind what one believes can be circumscribed as Rousseau's text, there has never been anything but writing; there have never been anything but supplements, substitutive significations which could only come forth in a chain of differential references, the "real" supervening, and being added only while taking on meaning from a trace and from an invocation of the supplement, etc. And thus to infinity, for we have read, *in the text*, that the absolute present, Nature, that which words like "real mother" name, have always already escaped, have never existed; that what opens meaning and language is writing as the disappearance of natural presence. (Pp. 158-59; emphasis in original)

Far from being a simple warning against the biographical or referential fallacy, *il n'y a pas de hors-texte* is a statement derived from Rousseau's autobiography itself. For what Rousseau's text tells us is that our very relation to "reality" already functions like a text. Rousseau's account of his life is not only itself a text, but it is a text that speaks only about the textuality of life. Rousseau's life does not *become* a text through his writing: it always already *was* one. Nothing, indeed, can be said to be *not* a text.

Derrida's reading of Rousseau's autobiography thus proposes a "deconstruction" of its logocentric claims and metaphysical assumptions. Deconstruction is not a form of textual vandalism designed to prove that meaning is impossible. In fact, the word "de-construction" is closely related not to the word "destruction" but to the word "analysis," which etymologically means "to undo"—a virtual synonym for "to de-construct." The deconstruction of a text does not proceed by random doubt or generalized skepticism, but by the careful teasing out of warring forces of signification *within the text itself*. If anything is destroyed in a deconstructive reading, it is not meaning but the claim to unequivocal domination of one mode of signifying over another. This, of course, implies that a text signifies in more than one way, and to varying degrees of explicitness. Sometimes the discrepancy is produced, as here, by a double-edged word, which serves as a hinge that both articulates and breaks open the explicit statement being made. Sometimes it is engendered when the figurative level of a statement is at odds with the literal level. And sometimes it occurs when the so-called starting point of an argument is based on presuppositions that render its conclusions problematic or circular.

Derrida defines his reading strategy as follows:

> The reading must always aim at a certain relationship, unper-
> ceived by the writer, between what he commands and what he does
> not command of the patterns of the language that he uses. This
> relationship is not a certain quantitative distribution of shadow and
> light, of weakness or of force, but a signifying structure that the
> critical reading should *produce*. (p. 158; emphasis in original)

In other words, the deconstructive reading does not point out the flaws or weaknesses or stupidities of an author, but the *necessity* with which what he *does* see is systematically related to what he does *not* see.

It can thus be seen that deconstruction is a form of what has long been called a *critique*. A critique of any theoretical system is not an examination of its flaws or imperfections. It is not a set of criticisms designed to make the system better. It is an analysis that focuses on the grounds of that system's possibility. The critique reads backwards from what seems natural, obvious, self-evident, or universal, in order to show that these things have their history, their reasons for being the way they are, their effects on what follows from them, and that the starting point is not a (natural) given but a (cultural) construct, usually blind to itself. For example, Copernicus can be said to have written a critique of the Ptolemeic conception of the universe. But the idea that the earth goes around the sun is not an *improvement* of the idea that the sun goes around the earth. It is a shift in perspective which literally makes the ground move. It is a deconstruction of the validity of the commonsense perception of the obvious. In the same way, Marx's critique of political economy is not an improvement in it but a demonstration that the theory which starts with the commodity as the basic unit of economy is blind to what *produces* the commodity—namely, labor. Every theory starts somewhere; every critique exposes what that starting point conceals, and thereby displaces all the ideas that follow from it. The critique does not ask "what does this statement *mean*?" but "where is it being made from? What does it presuppose? Are its presuppositions compatible with, independent of, and anterior to the statement that seems to follow from them, or do they already follow from it, contradict it, or stand in a relation of mutual dependence such that neither can exist without positing that the other is prior to it?"

In its elaboration of a critique of the metaphysical forces that structure and smother differance in every text, a deconstructive reading thus assumes:

1. That the rhetoric of an assertion is not necessarily compatible with its explicit meaning.

2. That this incompatibility can be read as systematic and significant *as such*.

3. That an inquiry that attempts to study an object by means of that very object is open to certain analyzable aberrations (this pertains to virtually all important investigations: the self analyzing itself, man studying man, thought thinking about thought, language speaking about language, etc.).

4. That certain levels of any rigorous text will engender a systematic double mark of the insistent but invisible contradiction or differance (the repression of) which is necessary for and in the text's very elaboration.

But if the traditional logic of meaning as an unequivocal structure of mastery *is* Western metaphysics, the deconstruction of metaphysics cannot simply combat logocentric meaning by opposing some other meaning to it. Differance is not a "concept" or "idea" that is "truer" than presence. It can only be a process of textual *work*, a strategy of *writing*.

"When I Was a Young Soldier for the Revolution": Coming to Voice

by bell hooks

Angela Davis spoke these words. They moved me. I say them here and hope to say them in many places. This is how deeply they touched me— evoking memories of innocence, of initial passionate commitment to political struggle. They were spoken in a talk she gave at a conference focusing on "Poetry and Politics: Afro-American Poetry Today." I began writing poetry when I was young, ten years old. Poetry came into my life, the sense of poetry, with reading scripture with those awkward and funny little rhymes we would memorize and recite on Easter Sunday. Then it came into my life at Booker T. Washington grade school where I learned that poetry was no silent subject. That moment of learning was pure enchantment, for we learned by listening and reciting, that words put together just so, said just so, could have the same impact on our psyches as song, could lift and exalt our spirits, enabling us to feel tremendous joy, or carrying us down into that most immediate and violent sense of loss and grief.

Like many African-Americans, I became a writer through making poems. Poetry was one literary expression that was absolutely respected in our working-class household. Nights when the lights would go out, when storms were raging, we would sit in the dim candlelight of our living room and have a talent show. I would recite poems: Wordsworth, James Weldon Johnson, Langston Hughes, Elizabeth Barrett Browning, Emily Dickinson, Gwendolyn Brooks. Poetry by white writers was always there in schools and on family bookshelves in anthologies of "great" works sold to us by door-to-door salesmen, book peddlers, who came spreading their wares as though we were a dark desert people and they weary travelers bringing us light from a faraway place. Poetry by black writers had to be searched for, a poem copied from books no one would let you borrow for fear of loss, or taken from books found by puzzled white Southern librarians eager to see that you "read right." I was in high school before I discovered James Weldon Johnson's collection of *American Negro Poetry*. It had never been checked out of the library even though it had been on the shelves for some time. I would keep this book as

Reprinted from *Talking Back: thinking feminist, thinking black* (Boston: South End, 1984). Reprinted with permission.

long as I could, working to memorize every poem so I would know them all
by heart.

For me, poetry was the place for the secret voice, for all that could not be
directly stated or named, for all that would not be denied expression. Poetry
was privileged speech—simple at times, but never ordinary. The magic of
poetry was transformation; it was words changing shape, meaning, and form.
Poetry was not mere recording of the way we Southern black folks talked to
one another, even though our language was poetic. It was transcendent
speech. It was meant to transform consciousness, to carry the mind and heart
to a new dimension. These were my primitive thoughts on poetry as I
experienced and knew it growing up.

When I became a student in college creative writing classes, I learned a
notion of "voice" as embodying the distinctive expression of an individual
writer. Our efforts to become poets were to be realized in this coming into
awareness and expression of one's voice. In all my writing classes, I was the
only black student. Whenever I read a poem written in the particular dialect
of Southern black speech, the teacher and fellow students would praise me for
using my "true," authentic voice, and encouraged me to develop this "voice,"
to write more of these poems. From the onset this troubled me. Such
comments seemed to mask racial biases about what my authentic voice would
or should be.

In part, attending all-black segregated schools with black teachers meant
that I had come to understand black poets as being capable of speaking in
many voices, that the Dunbar of a poem written in dialect was no more or
less authentic than the Dunbar writing a sonnet. Yet it was listening to black
musicians like Duke Ellington, Louis Armstrong, and later John Coltrane that
impressed upon our consciousness a sense of versatility—they played all
kinds of music, had multiple voices. So it was with poetry. The black poet, as
exemplified by Gwendolyn Brooks and later Amiri Baraka, had many
voices—with no single voice being identified as more or less authentic. The
insistence on finding one voice, one definitive style of writing and reading
one's poetry, fit all too neatly with a static notion of self and identity that was
pervasive in university settings. It seemed that many black students found our
situations problematic precisely because our sense of self, and by definition
our voice, was not unilateral, monologist, or static but rather multidimensional. We were as at home in dialect as we were in standard English.
Individuals who speak languages other than English, who speak patois as well
as standard English, find it a necessary aspect of self-affirmation not to feel
compelled to choose one voice over another, not to claim one as more
authentic, but rather to construct social realities that celebrate, acknowledge,
and affirm differences, variety. In *Borderlands: La Frontera,* Gloria Anzaldúa
writes of the need to claim all the tongues in which we speak, to make speech
of the many languages that give expression to the unique cultural reality of a
people:

For a people who are neither Spanish nor live in a country in which

Spanish is the first language; for a people who live in a country in which English is the reigning tongue but who are not Anglo; for a people who cannot entirely identify with either standard (formal, Castilian) Spanish nor standard English, what recourse is left to them but to create their own language? A language which they can connect their identity to, one capable of communicating the realities and values true to themselves. . . .

In recent years, any writing about feminism has overshadowed writing as a poet. Yet there are spaces where thoughts and concerns converge. One such space has been the feminist focus on coming to voice—on moving from silence into speech as revolutionary gesture. Once again, the idea of finding one's voice or having a voice assumes a primacy in talk, discourse, writing, and action. As metaphor for self-transformation, it has been especially relevant for groups of women who have previously never had a public voice, women who are speaking and writing for the first time, including many women of color. Feminist focus on finding a voice may seem clichéd at times, especially when the insistence is that women share a common speech or that all women have something meaningful to say at all times. However, for women within oppressed groups who have contained so many feelings— despair, rage, anguish—who do not speak, as poet Audre Lorde writes, "for fear our words will not be heard nor welcomed," coming to voice is an act of resistance. Speaking becomes both a way to engage in active self-transformation and a rite of passage where one moves from being object to being subject. Only as subjects can we speak. As objects we remain voiceless—our beings defined and interpreted by others. It is this liberating speech that Mariana Romo-Carmona writes about in her introduction to *Compañeras: Latina Lesbians:*

Each time a woman begins to speak, a liberating process begins, one that is unavoidable and has powerful implications. In these pages we see repeated the process of self-discovery, of affirmation in coming out of the closet, the search for a definition of our identity within the family and our community, the search for answers, for meaning in our personal struggles, and the commitment to a political struggle to end all forms of oppression. The stages of increasing awareness become clear when we begin to recount the story of our lives to someone else, someone who has experienced the same changes. When we write or speak about these changes we establish our experiences as valid and real, we begin to analyze, and that analysis gives us the necessary perspective to place our lives in a context where we know what to do next.

Awareness of the need to speak, to give voice to the varied dimensions of our lives, is one way women of color begin the process of education for critical consciousness.

Need for such speech is often validated in writings by people engaged in liberation struggles in the Third World, in the literatures of people struggling globally from oppression and domination. El Salvadoran writer Manlio Argueta structures his powerful novel, *One Day of Life,* around the insistence on the development of political awareness, the sharing of knowledge that makes the revolutionary thinker and activist. It is the character José who is most committed to sharing his awareness with family and community, and most importantly with Lupé, his friend and wife, to whom he says:

> ... that's why the problems can't be solved by a single person, but only by all of us working together, the humble, the clearheaded ones. And this is very important; you can be humble and live in darkness. Well, the thing is not a matter of being or not being humble. The problem lies in our awareness. The awareness we will have. Then life will become as clear as spring water.

I first read this novel in a course I taught on Third World literature and it was clear then that speaking freely, openly has different meaning for people from exploited and oppressed groups.

Nonliterary works by writers opposing domination also speak to the primacy of coming to voice, of speaking for the oppressed. In keeping with this emphasis on speech, Alicia Partnoy proclaims, in her brave work, *The Little School: Tales of Disappearance and Survival in Argentina,* "They cut off my voice so I grew two voices, into different tongues my songs I pour." Here speech has a dual implication. There is the silence of the oppressed who have never learned to speak and there is the voice of those who have been forcefully silenced because they have dared to speak and by doing so resist. Egyptian writer Nawal El Sa'adawi protests against such silences in her *Memoirs from the Women's Prison.* She dedicated her book "To all who have hated oppression to the point of death, who have loved freedom to the point of imprisonment, and have rejected falsehood to the point of revolution." Or the resistance to being silenced Theresa Hak Kyung Cha describes in *Dictee:*

> Mother, you are a child still. At eighteen. More of a child since you are always ill. They have sheltered you from the others. It is not your own. Even if it is not you know you must. You are bi-lingual. You are tri-lingual. The tongue that is forbidden is your own mother tongue. You speak in the dark, in the secret. The one that is yours. Your own ... Mother tongue is your refuge. It is being home. Being who you are. Truly. To speak makes you sad. To utter each word is a privilege you risk by death.

In fiction as well as in confessional writing, those who understand the power of voice as gesture of rebellion and resistance urge the exploited, the oppressed to speak.

To speak as an act of resistance is quite different than ordinary talk, or the personal confession that has no relation to coming into political awareness, to developing critical consciousness. This is a difference we must talk about in the United States, for here the idea of finding a voice risks being trivialized or romanticized in the rhetoric of those who advocate a shallow feminist politic that privileges acts of speaking over the content of speech. Such rhetoric often turns the voices and beings of nonwhite women into commodity, spectacle. In a white-supremacist, capitalist, patriarchal state where the mechanisms of co-optation are so advanced, much that is potentially radical is undermined, turned into commodity, fashionable speech as in "black women writers are in right now." Often the questions of who is listening and what is being heard are not answered. When reggae music became popular in the United States, I often pondered whether the privileged white people who listened were learning from this music to resist, to rebel against white supremacy and white imperialism. What did they hear when Bob Marley said, "We refuse to be what you wanted us to be"—did they think about colonization, about internalized racism? One night at a Jimmy Cliff concert attended predominantly by young white people, Cliff began a call-and-response refrain where we the listeners were to say "Africa for Africans." There was suddenly a hush in the room, as though the listeners finally heard the rebellion against white supremacy, against imperialism in the lyrics. They were silent, unable apparently to share in this gesture affirming black solidarity. Who is listening and what do they hear?

Appropriation of the marginal voice threatens the very core of self-determination and free self-expression for exploited and oppressed peoples. If the identified audience, those spoken to, is determined solely by ruling groups who control production and distribution, then it is easy for the marginal voice striving for a hearing to allow what is said to be overdetermined by the needs of that majority group who appear to be listening, to be tuned in. It becomes easy to speak about what that group wants to hear, to describe and define experience in a language compatible with existing images and ways of knowing, constructed within social frameworks that reinforce domination. Within any situation of colonization, of domination, the oppressed, the exploited develop various styles of relating, talking one way to one other, talking another way to those who have power to oppress and dominate, talking in a way that allows one to be understood by someone who does not know your way of speaking, your language. The struggle to end domination, the individual struggle to resist colonization, to move from object to subject, is expressed in the effort to establish the liberatory voice—that way of speaking that is no longer determined by one's status as object—as oppressed being. That way of speaking is characterized by opposition, by resistance. It demands that paradigms shift—that we learn to talk—to listen—to hear in a new way.

To make the liberated voice, one must confront the issue of audience—we must know to whom we speak. When I began writing my first book, *Ain't I A Woman: black women and feminism,* the initial completed manuscript was excessively long and very repetitious. Reading it critically, I saw that I was trying not only to address each different potential audience—black men, white women, white men, etc.—but that my words were written to explain, to placate, to appease. They contained the fear of speaking that often characterizes the way those in a lower position within a hierarchy address those in a higher position of authority. Those passages where I was speaking most directly to black women contained the voice I felt to be most truly mine—it was then that my voice was daring, courageous. When I thought about audience—the way in which the language we choose to use declares who it is we place at the center of our discourse—I confronted my fear of placing myself and other black women at the speaking center. Writing this book was for me a radical gesture. It not only brought me face-to-face with this question of power; it forced me to resolve this question, to act, to find my voice, to become that subject who could place herself and those like her at the center of feminist discourse. I was transformed in consciousness and being.

When the book was first published, white women readers would often say to me, "I don't feel this book is really talking to me." Often these readers would interpret the direct, blunt speech as signifying anger and I would have to speak against this interpretation and insist upon the difference between direct speech and hostility. At a discussion once where a question about audience was raised, I responded by saying that while I would like readers to be diverse, the audience I most wanted to address was black women, that I wanted to place us at the center. I was asked by a white woman, "How can you do that in a cultural context where black women are not primary book buyers and white women are the principal buyers of feminist books?" It seemed that she was suggesting that audience should be determined by who buys certain books. It had never occurred to me that white women would not buy a book if they did not see themselves at the center because, more than any group of people I could identify, white people have traveled the globe consuming cultural artifacts that did not place them at the center. My placement of black women at the center was not an action to exclude others but rather an invitation, a challenge to those who would hear us speak, to shift paradigms rather than appropriate, to have all readers listen to the voice of a black woman speaking as subject and not as underprivileged other. I wrote *Ain't I A Woman* not to inform white women about black women but rather as an expression of my longing to know more and think deeply about our experience.

In celebrating our coming to voice, Third World women, African-American women must work against speaking as "other," speaking to difference as it is constructed in the white-supremacist imagination. It is therefore crucial that we search our hearts and our words to see if our true aim is liberation, to make sure they do not suppress, trap, or confine. Significantly, knowing who is listening provides an indication of how our voices are heard. My words are heard differently by the oppressive powerful. They are heard in a different way by black women who, like me, are struggling to recover ourselves from the ravages of colonization. To know our audience, to know who listens, we must be in dialogue. We must be speaking with and not just speaking to. In hearing responses, we come to understand whether our words act to resist, to transform, to move. In a consumer culture where we are all led to believe that the value of our voice is not determined by the extent to which it challenges, or makes critical reflection possible, but rather by whether or not it (and sometimes even we) is liked, it is difficult to keep a liberatory message. It is difficult to maintain a sense of direction, a strategy for liberated speaking, if we do not constantly challenge these standards of valuation. When I first began to talk publicly about my work, I would be disappointed when audiences were provoked and challenged but seemed to disapprove. Not only was my desire for approval naive (I have since come to understand that it is silly to think that one can challenge and also have approval), it was dangerous precisely because such a longing can undermine radical commitment, compelling a change in voice so as to gain regard.

Speaking out is not a simple gesture of freedom in a culture of domination. We are often deceived (yes, even those of us who have experienced domination) by the illusion of free speech, falsely believing that we can say whatever we wish in an atmosphere of openness. There would be no need to even speak of the oppressed and exploited coming to voice, articulating and redefining reality, if there were not oppressive mechanisms of silencing, suppressing, and censoring. Thinking we speak in a climate where freedom is valued, we are often shocked to find ourselves assaulted, our words devalued. It should be understood that the liberatory voice will necessarily confront, disturb, demand that listeners even alter ways of hearing and being. I remember talking with Angela Davis a few years ago about the death threats that she often received before speaking. Our conversations had a profound effect on my consciousness, on me as a listener; it changed my understanding of what it means to speak from a radical position in this society. When one threatens—one is at risk.

Often I am amazed as a teacher in the classroom at the extent to which students are afraid to speak. A young black woman student wrote these words to me:

> *My voice is not fit to be heard by 120 people. To produce such a voice, my temperature increases and my hands shake. My voice is calm and quiet and soothing; it is not a means of announcing the many secrets my friends have told me—it quiets the rush of the running stream that is their life, slowing to make a mirror to reflect their worries, so that they can be examined and problems be rectified. I am not relieved by voicing my opinions. Placing my opinion up to be judged by the public is a form of opening myself to criticism and pain. Those who do not share my eyes cannot see where to tread lightly on me.*
>
> *I am afraid. I am, and will always be afraid. My fear is that I will not be understood. I try to learn the vocabulary of my friends to ensure my communication on their terms. There is no singular vocabulary of 120 people. I will be misunderstood; I will not be respected as a speaker; they will name me Stupid in their minds; they will disregard me. I am afraid.*

Encouraging students to speak, I tell them to imagine what it must mean to live in a culture where to speak one risks brutal punishment—imprisonment, torture, death. I ask them to think about what it means that they lack the courage to speak in a culture where there are few if any consequences. Can their fear be understood solely as shyness or is it an expression of deeply embedded, socially constructed restrictions against speech in a culture of domination, a fear of owning one's words, of taking a stand? Audre Lorde's poem, "Litany for Survival," addresses our fear of speech and urges us to overcome it:

> *and when we speak we are afraid*
> *our words will not be heard*
> *nor welcomed*
> *but when we are silent*
> *we are still afraid*
> *So it is better to speak*
> *remembering*
> *we were never meant to survive.*

To understand that finding a voice is an essential part of liberation struggle— for the oppressed, the exploited a necessary starting place—a move in the direction of freedom, is important for those who stand in solidarity with us. That talk which identifies us as uncommitted, as lacking in critical consciousness, which signifies a condition of oppression and exploitation, is utterly transformed as we engage in critical reflection and as we act to resist domination. We are prepared to struggle for freedom only when this groundwork has been laid.

When we dare to speak in a liberatory voice, we threaten even those who may initially claim to want our words. In the act of overcoming our fear of speech, of being seen as threatening, in the process of learning to speak as subjects, we participate in the global struggle to end domination. When we end our silence, when we speak in a liberated voice, our words connect with anyone, anywhere who lives in silence. Feminist focus on women finding a voice, on the silence of black women, of women of color, has led to increased interest in our words. This is an important historical moment. We are both speaking of our own volition out of our commitment to justice, to revolutionary struggle to end domination, and simultaneously called to speak, "invited" to share our words. It is important that we speak. What we speak about is more important. It is our responsibility collectively and individually to distinguish between mere speaking that is about self-aggrandizement, exploitation of the exotic "other," and that coming to voice which is a gesture of resistance, an affirmation of struggle.

Nobody Mean More to Me Than You[1]
And the Future Life of Willie Jordan

July, 1985

by June Jordan

Black English is not exactly a linguistic buffalo; as children, most of the thirty-five million Afro-Americans living here depend on this language for our discovery of the world. But then we approach our maturity inside a larger social body that will not support our efforts to become anything other than the clones of those who are neither our mothers nor our fathers. We begin to grow up in a house where every true mirror shows us the face of somebody who does not belong there, whose walk and whose talk will never look or sound "right," because that house was meant to shelter a family that is alien and hostile to us. As we learn our way around this environment, either we hide our original word habits, or we completely surrender our own voice, hoping to please those who will never respect anyone different from themselves: Black English is not exactly a linguistic buffalo, but we should understand its status as an endangered species, as a perishing, irreplaceable system of community intelligence, or we should expect its extinction, and, along with that, the extinguishing of much that constitutes our own proud, and singular identity.

What we casually call "English," less and less defers to England and its "gentlemen." "English" is no longer a specific matter of geography or an element of class privilege; more than thirty-three countries use this tool as a means of "intranational communication."[2] Countries as disparate as Zimbabwe and Malaysia, or Israel and Uganda, use it as their non-native currency of convenience. Obviously, this tool, this "English," cannot function inside thirty-three discrete societies on the basis of rules and values absolutely determined somewhere else, in a thirty-fourth other country, for example.

In addition to that staggering congeries of non-native users of English, there are five countries, or 333,746,000 people, for whom this thing called

---

Reprinted from *On Call: Political Essays* (Boston: South End, 1985): 123-39. Reprinted with permission.

[1] Black English aphorism crafted by Monica Morris, a Junior at S.U.N.Y. at Stony Brook, October, 1984.

[2] *English is Spreading, But What Is English.* A presentation by Professor S.N. Sridahr, Dept. of Linguistics, S.U.N.Y. at Stonybrook, April 9, 1985: Dean's Conversation Among the Disciplines.

"English" serves as a native tongue.[3] Approximately 10% of these native speakers of "English" are Afro-American citizens of the U.S.A. I cite these numbers and varieties of human beings dependent on "English" in order, quickly, to suggest how strange and how tenuous is any concept of "Standard English." Obviously, numerous forms of English now operate inside a natural, an uncontrollable, continuum of development. I would suppose "the standard" for English in Malaysia is not the same as "the standard" in Zimbabwe. I know that standard forms of English for Black people in this country do not copy that of whites. And, in fact, the structural differences between these two kinds of English have intensified, becoming more Black, or less white, despite the expected homogenizing effects of television[4] and other mass media.

Nonetheless, white standards of English persist, supreme and unquestioned, in these United States. Despite our multi-lingual population, and despite the deepening Black and white cleavage within that conglomerate, white standards control our official and popular judgements of verbal proficiency and correct, or incorrect, language skills, including speech. In contrast to India, where at least fourteen languages co-exist as legitimate Indian languages, in contrast to Nicaragua, where all citizens are legally entitled to formal school instruction in their regional or tribal languages, compulsory education in America compels accommodation to exclusively white forms of "English." White English, in America, is "Standard English."

This story begins two years ago. I was teaching a new course, "In Search of the Invisible Black Woman," and my rather large class seemed evenly divided between young Black women and men. Five or six white students also sat in attendance. With unexpected speed and enthusiasm we had moved through historical narratives of the 19th century to literature by and about Black women, in the 20th. I had assigned the first forty pages of Alice Walker's *The Color Purple*, and I came, eagerly, to class that morning:

"So!" I exclaimed, aloud. "What did you think? How did you like it?"

The students studied their hands, or the floor. There was no response. The tense, resistant feeling in the room fairly astounded me.

At last, one student, a young woman still not meeting my eyes, muttered something in my direction:

"What did you say?" I prompted her.

"Why she have them talk so funny. It don't sound right."

"You mean the language?"

Another student lifted his head: "It don't look right, neither. I couldn't hardly read it."

At this, several students dumped on the book. Just about unanimously, their criticisms targeted the language. I listened to what they wanted to say

---

[3] Ibid.
[4] *New York Times*, March 15, 1985, Section One, p. 14: Report on study by Linguistics at the University of Pennsylvania.

and silently marvelled at the similarities between their casual speech patterns and Alice Walker's written version of Black English.

But I decided against pointing to these identical traits of syntax; I wanted not to make them self-conscious about their own spoken language—not while they clearly felt it was "wrong." Instead I decided to swallow my astonishment. Here was a negative Black reaction to a prize winning accomplishment of Black literature that white readers across the country had selected as a best seller. Black rejection was aimed at the one irreducibly Black element of Walker's work: the language—Celie's Black English. I wrote the opening lines of *The Color Purple* on the blackboard and asked the students to help me translate these sentences into Standard English:

> *You better not never tell nobody but God. It'd kill your mammy.*
> Dear God,
>   I am fourteen years old. I have always been a good girl. Maybe you can give me a sign letting me know what is happening to me.
>   Last spring after Little Lucious come I heard them fussing. He was pulling on her arm. She say it too soon, Fonso. I ain't well. Finally he leave her alone. A week go by, he pulling on her arm again. She say, Naw, I ain't gonna. Can't you see I'm already half dead, an all of the children.[5]

Our process of translation exploded with hilarity and even hysterical, shocked laughter: The Black writer, Alice Walker, knew what she was doing! If rudimentary criteria for good fiction includes the manipulation of language so that the syntax and diction of sentences will tell you the identity of speakers, the probable age and sex and class of speakers, and even the locale—urban/rural/southern/western—then Walker had written, perfectly. This is the translation into Standard English that our class produced:

> *Absolutely, one should never confide in anybody besides God. Your secrets could prove devastating to your mother.*
> Dear God,
>   I am fourteen years old. I have always been good. But now, could you help me to understand what is happening to me?
>   Last spring, after my little brother, Lucious, was born, I heard my parents fighting. My father kept pulling at my mother's arm. But she told him, "It's too soon for sex, Alfonso. I am still not feeling well." Finally, my father left her alone. A week went by, and then he began bothering my mother, again: Pulling her arm. She told him, "No, I won't! Can't you see I'm already exhausted from all of these children?"

(Our favorite line was "It's too soon for sex, Alphonso.")
Once we could stop laughing, once we could stop our exponentially wild

---

[5] Alice Walker, *The Color Purple*, p. 11, Harcourt Brace, N.Y.

improvisations on the theme of Translated Black English, the students pushed me to explain their own negative first reactions to their spoken language on the printed page. I thought it was probably akin to the shock of seeing yourself in a photograph for the first time. Most of the students had never before seen a written facsimile of the way they talk. None of the students had ever learned how to read and write their own verbal system of communication: Black English. Alternatively, this fact began to baffle or else bemuse and then infuriate my students. Why not? Was it too late? Could they learn how to do it, now? And, ultimately, the final test question, the one testing my sincerity: Could I teach them? Because I had never taught anyone Black English and, as far as I knew, no one, anywhere in the United States, had ever offered such a course, the best I could say was "I'll try."

He looked like a wrestler.

He sat dead center in the packed room and, every time our eyes met, he quickly nodded his head as though anxious to reassure, and encourage, me.

Short, with strikingly broad shoulders and long arms, he spoke with a surprisingly high, soft voice that matched the soft bright movement of his eyes. His name was Willie Jordan. He would have seemed even more unlikely in the context of Contemporary Women's Poetry, except that ten or twelve other Black men were taking the course, as well. Still, Willie was conspicuous. His extreme fitness, the muscular density of his presence underscored the riveted, gentle attention that he gave to anything anyone said. Generally, he did not join the loud and rowdy dialogue flying back and forth, but there could be no doubt about his interest in our discussions. And, when he stood to present an argument he'd prepared, overnight, that nervous smile of his vanished and an irregular stammering replaced it, as he spoke with visceral sincerity, word by word.

That was how I met Willie Jordan. It was in between "In Search of the Invisible Black Women" and "The Art of Black English." I was waiting for Departmental approval and I supposed that Willie might be, so to speak, killing time until he, too, could study Black English. But Willie really did want to explore Contemporary Women's poetry and, to that end, volunteered for extra research and never missed a class.

Towards the end of that semester, Willie approached me for an independent study project on South Africa. It would commence the next semester. I thought Willie's writing needed the kind of improvement only intense practice will yield. I knew his intelligence was outstanding. But he'd wholeheartedly opted for "Standard English" at a rather late age, and the results were stilted and frequently polysyllabic, simply for the sake of having more syllables. Willie's unnatural formality of language seemed to me consistent with the formality of his research into South African apartheid. As he projected his studies, he would have little time, indeed, for newspapers. Instead, more than 90% of his research would mean saturation in strictly historical, if not archival, material. I was certainly interested. It would be tricky to guide him into a more confident and spontaneous relationship both with language and apartheid. It was going to be wonderful to see what happened when he could catch up with himself, entirely, and talk back to the world.

September, 1984: Breezy fall weather and much excitement! My class, "The Art of Black English," was full to the limit of the fire laws. And, in Independent Study, Willie Jordan showed up, weekly, fifteen minutes early for each of our sessions. I was pretty happy to be teaching, altogether!

I remember an early class when a young brother, replete with his ever present pork-pie hat, raised his hand and then told us that most of what he'd heard was "all right" except it was "too clean." "The brothers on the street," he continued, "they mix it up more. Like 'fuck' and 'motherfuck.' Or like 'shit.' " He waited. I waited. Then all of us laughed a good while, and we got into a brawl about "correct" and "realistic" Black English that led to Rule 1.

Rule 1: *Black English is about a whole lot more than motha-fuckin.*

As a criterion, we decided, "realistic" could take you anywhere you want to go. Artful places. Angry places. Eloquent and sweetalkin places. Polemical places. Church. And the local Bar & Grill. We were checking out a language, not a mood or a scene or one guy's forgettable mouthing off.

It was hard. For most of the students, learning Black English required a fallback to patterns and rhythms of speech that many of their parents had beaten out of them. I mean *beaten*. And, in a majority of cases, correct Black English could be achieved only by striving for *incorrect* Standard English, something they were still pushing at, quite uncertainly. This state of affairs led to Rule 2.

Rule 2: *If it's wrong in Standard English it's probably right in Black English, or, at least, you're hot.*

It was hard. Roommates and family members ridiculed their studies, or remained incredulous, "You *studying* that shit? At school?" But we were beginning to feel the companionship of pioneers. And we decided that we needed another rule that would establish each one of us as equally important to our success. This was Rule 3.

Rule 3: *If it don't sound like something that come out somebody mouth then it don't sound right. If it don't sound right then it ain't hardly right. Period.*

This rule produced two weeks of compositions in which the students agonizingly tried to spell the sound of the Black English sentence they wanted to convey. But Black English is, pre-eminently, an oral/spoken means of communication. *And spelling don't talk.* So we needed Rule 4.

Rule 4: *Forget about the spelling. Let the syntax carry you.*

Once we arrived at Rule 4 we started to fly because syntax, the structure of an idea, leads you to the world view of the speaker and reveals her values. The syntax of a sentence equals the structure of your consciousness. If we insisted that the language of Black English adheres to a distinctive Black syntax, then we were postulating a profound difference between white and Black people, *per se*. Was it a difference to prize or to obliterate?

There are three qualities of Black English—the presence of life, voice, and clarity—that testify to a distinctive Black value system that we became excited about and self-consciously tried to maintain.

1. Black English has been produced by a pre-technocratic, if not anti-technological, culture. More, our culture has been constantly threatened by annihilation or, at least, the swallowed blurring of assimilation. Therefore, our language is a system constructed by people constantly needing to insist that we exist, that we are present. Our language devolves from a culture that abhors all abstraction, or anything tending to obscure or delete the fact of the human being who is here and now/the truth of the person who is speaking or listening. Consequently, *there is no passive voice construction possible in Black English*. For example, you cannot say, "Black English is being eliminated." You must say, instead, "White people eliminating Black English." The assumption of the presence of life governs all of Black English. Therefore, overwhelmingly, *all action takes place in the language of the present indicative*. And every sentence assumes the living and active participation of at least two human beings, the speaker and the listener.

2. A primary consequence of the person-centered values of Black English is the delivery of voice. If you speak or write Black English, your ideas will necessarily possess that otherwise elusive attribute, *voice*.

3. One main benefit following from the person-centered values of Black English is that of *clarity*. If your idea, your sentence, assumes the presence of at least two living and active people, you will make it understandable because the motivation behind every sentence is the wish to say something real to somebody real.

As the weeks piled up, translation from Standard English into Black English or vice versa occupied a hefty part of our course work.

> Standard English (hereafter S.E.): "In considering the idea of studying Black English those questioned suggested—"

> (What's the subject? Where's the person? Is anybody alive in there, in that idea?)

> Black English (hereafter B.E.): "I been asking people what you think about somebody studying Black English and they answer me like this:"

But there were interesting limits. You cannot "translate" instances of Standard English preoccupied with abstraction or with nothing/nobody evidently alive, into Black English. That would warp the language into uses antithetical to the guiding perspective of its community of users. Rather you must first change those Standard English sentences, themselves, into ideas consistent with the person-centered assumptions of Black English.

Guidelines For Black English

1. Minimal number of words for every idea: This is the source for the aphoristic and/or poetic force of the language; eliminate every possible word.
2. Clarity: If the sentence is not clear it's not Black English.
3. Eliminate use of the verb *to be* whenever possible. This leads to the deployment of more descriptive and therefore, more precise verbs.
4. Use *be* or *been* only when you want to describe a chronic, ongoing state of things.

> He *be* at the office, by 9. (He is always at the office by 9.)
> He *been* with her since forever.

5. Zero copula: Always eliminate the verb *to be* whenever it would combine with another verb, in Standard English.

> S.E.: She is going out with him.
> B.E.: She going out with him.

6. Eliminate *do* as in:

> S.E.: What do you think? What do you want?
> B.E.: What you think? What you want?

Rules number 3, 4, 5, and 6 provide for the use of the minimal number of verbs per idea and, therefore, greater accuracy in the choice of verb.
7. In general, if you wish to say something really positive, try to formulate the idea using emphatic negative structure.

> S.E.: He's fabulous.
> B.E.: He bad.

8. Use double or triple negatives for dramatic emphasis.

> S.E.: Tina Turner sings out of this world.
> B.E.: Ain nobody sing like Tina.

9. Never use the *-ed* suffix to indicate the past tense of a verb.

> S.E.: She closed the door.
> B.E.: She close the door. Or, she have close the door.

10. Regardless of intentional verb time, only use the third person singular, present indicative, for use of the verb to *have*, as an auxiliary.

> S.E.: He had his wallet then he lost it.
> B.E.: He have him wallet then he lose it.
> S.E.: He had seen that movie.
> B.E.: We seen that movie. Or, we have see that movie.

11. Observe a minimal inflection of verbs. Particularly, never change from the first person singular forms to the third person singular.

> S.E.: Present Tense Forms: He goes to the store.
> B.E.: He go to the store.

S.E.: Past Tense Forms: He went to the store.
B.E.: He go to the store. Or, he gone to the store. Or, he been to the
    store.

12. The possessive case scarcely ever appears in Black English. Never use an apostrophe ('s) construction. If you wander into a possessive case component of an idea, then keep logically consistent: *ours, his, theirs, mines.* But, most likely, if you bump into such a component, you have wandered outside the underlying world-view of Black English.

S.E.: He will take their car tomorrow.
B.E.: He taking they car tomorrow.

13. Plurality: Logical consistency, continued: If the modifier indicates plurality then the noun remains in the singular case.

S.E.: He ate twelve doughnuts.
B.E.: He eat twelve doughnut.
S.E.: She has many books.
B.E.: She have many book.

14. Listen for, or invent, special Black English forms of the past tense, such as: "He losted it. That what she felted." If they are clear and readily understood, then use them.
15. Do not hesitate to play with words, sometimes inventing them: e.g. "astropotomous" means huge like a hippo plus astronomical and, therefore, signifies real big.
16. In Black English, unless you keenly want to underscore the past tense nature of an action, stay in the present tense and rely on the overall context of your ideas for the conveyance of time and sequence.
17. Never use the suffix -*ly* form of an adverb in Black English.

S.E.: The rain came down rather quickly.
B.E.: The rain come down pretty quick.

18. Never use the indefinite article *an* in Black English.

S.E.: He wanted to ride an elephant.
B.E.: He want to ride him a elephant.

19. Invarient syntax: in correct Black English it is possible to formulate an imperative, an interrogative, and a simple declarative idea with the same syntax:

B.E.: You going to the store?
    You going to the store.
    You going to the store!

Where was Willie Jordan? We'd reached the mid-term of the semester. Students had formulated Black English guidelines, by consensus, and they were now writing with remarkable beauty, purpose, and enjoyment:

I ain hardly speakin for everybody but myself so understan that."
–Kim Parks

Samples from student writings:
"Janie have a great big ole hole inside her. Tea Cake the only thing that
fit that hole. . .

"That pear tree beautiful to Janie, especial when bees fiddlin with the
blossomin pear there growin large and lovely. But personal speakin, the love
she get from starin at that tree ain the love what starin back at her in them
relationship." (Monica Morris)

"Love is a big theme in, *They Eye Was Watching God.* Love show people
new corners inside theyself. It pull out good stuff and stuff back bad stuff. . .
Joe worship the doing uh his own hand and need other people to worship him
too. But he ain't think about Janie that she a person and ought to live like
anybody common do. Queen life not for Janie." (Monica Morris)

"In both life and writin, Black womens have varietous experience of love
that be cold like a iceberg or fiery like a inferno. Passion got for the other
partner involve, man or woman, seem as shallow, ankle-deep water or the
most profoundest abyss." (Constance Evans)

"Family love another bond that ain't never break under no pressure."
(Constance Evans)

"You know it really cold/When the friend you/Always get out the fire/Act
like they don't know you/When you in the heat." (Constance Evans)

"Big classroom discussion bout love at this time. I never take no class
where us have any long arguin for and against for two or three day. New to
me and great. I find the class time talkin a million time more interestin than
detail bout the book." (Kathy Esseks)

As these examples suggest, Black English no longer limited the students,
in any way. In fact, one of them, Philip Garfield, would shortly "translate" a
pivotal scene from Ibsen's *Doll House*, as his final term paper:

Nora: I didn't gived no shit. I thinked you a asshole back then, too,
you make it so hard for me save mines husband life.
Krogstad: Girl, it clear you ain't any idea what you done. You done
exact what once done, and I losed my reputation over it.
Nora: You asks me believe you once act brave save you wife life?
Krogstad: Law care less why you done it.
Nora: Law must suck.
Krogstad: Suck or no, if I wants, judge screw you wid dis paper.
Nora: No way, man. (Philip Garfield)

But where was Willie? Compulsively punctual, and always thoroughly
prepared with neatly typed compositions, he had disappeared. He failed to
show up for our regularly scheduled conference, and I received neither a note
nor a phone call of explanation. A whole week went by. I wondered if Willie
had finally been captured by the extremely current happenings in South
Africa: passage of a new constitution that did not enfranchise the Black

majority, and militant Black South African reaction to that affront. I wondered if he'd been hurt, somewhere. I wondered if the serious workload of weekly readings and writings had overwhelmed him and changed his mind about independent study. Where was Willie Jordan?

One week after the first conference that Willie missed, he called: "Hello, Professor Jordan? This is Willie. I'm sorry I wasn't there last week. But something has come up and I'm pretty upset. I'm sorry but I really can't deal right now."

I asked Willie to drop by my office and just let me see that he was okay. He agreed to do that. When I saw him I knew something hideous had happened. Something had hurt him and scared him to the marrow. He was all agitated and stammering and terse and incoherent. At last, his sadly jumbled account let me surmise, as follows: Brooklyn police had murdered his unarmed, twenty-five year old brother, Reggie Jordan. Neither Willie nor his elderly parents knew what to do about it. Nobody from the press was interested. His folks had no money. Police ran his family around and around, to no point. And Reggie was really dead. And Willie wanted to fight, but he felt helpless.

With Willie's permission I began to try to secure legal counsel for the Jordan family. Unfortunately Black victims of police violence are truly numerous while the resources available to prosecute their killers are truly scarce. A friend of mine at the Center for Constitutional Rights estimated that just the preparatory costs for bringing the cops into court normally approaches $180,000. Unless the execution of Reggie Jordan became a major community cause for organizing, and protest, his murder would simply become a statistical item.

Again, with Willie's permission, I contacted every newspaper and media person I could think of. But the William Bastone feature article in *The Village Voice* was the only result from that canvassing.

Again, with Willie's permission, I presented the case to my class in Black English. We had talked about the politics of language. We had talked about love and sex and child abuse and and men and women. But the murder of Reggie Jordan broke like a hurricane across the room.

There are few "issues" as endemic to Black life as police violence. Most of the students knew and respected and liked Jordan. Many of them came from the very neighborhood where the murder had occurred. All of the students had known somebody close to them who had been killed by police, or had known frightening moments of gratuitous confrontation with the cops. They wanted to do everything at once to avenge death. Number One: They decided to compose personal statements of condolence to Willie Jordan and his family, written in Black English. Number Two: They decided to compose individual messages to the police, in Black English. These should be prefaced by an explanatory paragraph composed by the entire group. Number Three: These individual messages, with their lead paragraph, should be sent to

Newsday.

The morning after we agreed on these objectives, one of the young women students appeared with an unidentified visitor, who sat through the class, smiling in a peculiar, comfortable way.

Now we had to make more tactical decisions. Because we wanted the messages published, and because we thought it imperative that our outrage be known by the police, the tactical question was this: Should the opening, group paragraph be written in Black English or Standard English?

I have seldom been privy to a discussion with so much heart at the dead heat of it. I will never forget the eloquence, the sudden haltings of speech, the fierce struggle against tears, the furious throwaway, and useless explosions that this question elicited.

That one question contained several others, each of them extraordinarily painful to even contemplate. How best to serve the memory of Reggie Jordan? Should we use the language of the killers—Standard English—in order to make our ideas acceptable to those controlling the killers? But wouldn't what we had to say be rejected, summarily, if we said it in our own language, the language of the victim, Reggie Jordan? But if we sought to express ourselves by abandoning our language wouldn't that mean our suicide on top of Reggie's murder? But if we expressed ourselves in our own language wouldn't that be suicidal to the wish to communicate with those who, evidently, did not give a damn about us/Reggie/police violence in the Black community?

At the end of one of the longest, most difficult hours of my own life, the students voted, unanimously, to preface their individual messages with a paragraph composed in the language of Reggie Jordan. *"At least we don't give up nothing else. At least we stick to the truth: Be who we been. And stay all the way with Reggie."*

It was heartbreaking to proceed, from that point. Everyone in the room realized that our decision in favor of Black English had doomed our writings, even as the distinctive reality of our Black lives always has doomed our efforts to "be who we been" in this country.

I went to the blackboard and took down this paragraph, dictated by the class:

"...YOU COPS!
WE THE BROTHER AND SISTER OF WILLIE JORDAN, A FELLOW STONY BROOK STUDENT WHO THE BROTHER OF THE DEAD REGGIE JORDAN. REGGIE, LIKE MANY BROTHER AND SISTER, HE A VICTIM OF BRUTAL RACIST POLICE, OCTOBER 25, 1984. US APPALL, FED UP, BECAUSE THAT ANOTHER SENSELESS DEATH WHAT OCCUR IN OUR COMMUNITY. THIS WHAT WE FEEL, THIS, FROM OUR HEART, FOR WE AIN'T STAYIN' SILENT NO MORE:"

With the completion of this introduction, nobody said anything. I asked for comments. At this invitation, the unidentified visitor, a young Black man, ceaselessly smiling, raised his hand. He was, it so happens, a rookie cop. He had just joined the force in September and, he said, he thought he should clarify a few things. So he came forward and sprawled easily into a posture of bar-room, or fireside, nostalgia:

"See," Officer Charles enlightened us, "Most times when you out on the street and something come down you do one of two things. Over-react or under-react. Now, if you under-react then you can get yourself kilt. And if you over-react then maybe you kill somebody. Fortunately it's about nine times out of ten and you will over-react. So the brother got kilt. And I'm sorry about that, believe me. But what you have to understand is what kilt him: Over-reaction. That's all. Now you talk about Black people and white police but see, now, I'm a cop myself. And (big smile) I'm Black. And just a couple months ago I was on the other side. But see it's the same for me. You a cop, you the ultimate authority: the Ultimate Authority. And you on the street, most of the time you can only do one of two things: over-react or under-react. That's all it is with the brother: Over-reaction. Didn't have nothing to do with race."

That morning Officer Charles had the good fortune to escape without being boiled alive. But barely. And I remember the pride of his smile when I read about the fate of Black policemen and other collaborators, in South Africa. I remember him, and I remember the shock and palpable feeling of shame that filled the room. It was as though that foolish, and deadly, young man had just relieved himself of his foolish, and deadly, explanation, face to face with the grief of Reggie Jordan's father and Reggie Jordan's mother. Class ended quietly. I copied the paragraph from the blackboard, collected the individual messages and left to type them up.

Newsday rejected the piece.

The Village Voice could not find room in their "Letters" section to print the individual messages from the students to the police.

None of the tv news reporters picked up the story.

Nobody raised $180,000 to prosecute the murder of Reggie Jordan.

Reggie Jordan is really dead.

I asked Willie Jordan to write an essay pulling together everything important to him from that semester. He was still deeply beside himself with frustration and amazement and loss. This is what he wrote, un-edited, and in its entirety:

"Throughout the course of this semester I have been researching the effects of oppression and exploitation along racial lines in South Africa and its neighboring countries. I have become aware of South African police brutalization of native Africans beyond the extent of the law, even though the laws themselves are catalyst affliction upon Black men, women and children. Many Africans die each year as a result of the deliberate use of police force to protect the white power structure.

"Social control agents in South Africa, such as policemen, are also used to force compliance among citizens through both overt and covert tactics. It is not uncommon to find bold-faced coercion and cold-blooded killings of

Blacks by South African police for undetermined and/or inadequate reasons. Perhaps the truth is that the only reasons for this heinous treatment of Blacks rests in racial differences. We should also understand that what is conveyed through the media is not always accurate and may sometimes be construed as the tip of the iceberg at best.

"I recently received a painful reminder that racism, poverty, and the abuse of power are global problems which are by no means unique to South Africa. On October 25, 1984 at approximately 3:00 p.m. my brother, Mr. Reginald Jordan, was shot and killed by two New York City policemen from the 75th precinct in the East New York section of Brooklyn. His life ended at the age of twenty-five. Even up to this current point in time the Police Department has failed to provide my family, which consists of five brothers, eight sisters, and two parents, with a plausible reason for Reggie's death. Out of the many stories that were given to my family by the Police Department, not one of them seems to hold water. In fact, I honestly believe that the Police Department's assessment of my brother's murder is nothing short of ABSOLUTE BULLSHIT, and thus far no evidence had been produced to alter perception of the situation.

Furthermore, I believe that one of three cases may have occurred in this incident. First, Reggie's death may have been the desired outcome of the police officer's action, in which case the killing was premeditated. Or, it was a case of mistaken identity, which clarifies the fact that the two officers who killed my brother and their commanding parties are all grossly incompetent. Or, both of the above cases are correct, i.e., Reggie's murderers intended to kill him and the Police Department behaved insubordinately.

Part of the argument of the officers who shot Reggie was that he had attacked one of them and took his gun. This was their major claim. They also said that only one of them had actually shot Reggie. The facts, however, speak for themselves. According to the Death Certificate and autopsy report, Reggie was shot eight times from point-blank range. The Doctor who performed the autopsy told me himself that two bullets entered the side of my brother's head, four bullets were sprayed into his back, and two bullets struck him in the back of the his legs. It is obvious that unnecessary force was used by the police and that it is extremely difficult to shoot someone in his back when he is attacking or approaching you.

After experiencing a situation like this and researching South Africa I believe that to a large degree, justice may only exist as rhetoric. I find it difficult to talk of true justice when the oppression of my people both at home and abroad attests to the fact that inequality and injustice are serious problems whereby Blacks and Third World people are perpetually short-changed by society. Something has to be done about the way in which this world is set up. Although it is a difficult task, we do have the power to make a change."

–Willie J. Jordan Jr.
EGL 487, Section 58, November 14, 1984

It is my privilege to dedicate this book to the future life of Willie J. Jordan Jr.
August 8, 1985

Voice as Juice: Some Reservations about Evangelic Composition

by I. Hashimoto

> They hear a voice on every wind,
> And snatch a fearful joy.
> —Thomas Gray

When teachers talk about the good qualities of student writing, one of their favorite terms is "voice." Good student writing has it; bad student writing doesn't. "Voice" is sometimes a sign of control, of "ethos," of "style." It is often associated with "persona" or "mask." But it is also often associated with something Peter Elbow in *Writing with Power* calls "juice"—a combination of *"magic potion, mother's milk,* and *electricity"* (286). When we read writing that has this "juice," we "feel the pulse" of a writer "churning over the facts the world presents" (Ruszkiewicz, *Well Bound Words* 67); we sense the "energy, humor, individuality, music, rhythm, pace, flow, surprise, believability" (Murray, *Write to Learn* 144); we "hear the voice of a real person speaking to real people" (Lannon, *The Writing Process* 14). And while this "voice-as-juice" seems to have gained a considerable amount of respectability lately, it brings with it a kind of evangelical zeal that may not do us any good at all.

Juice and the Evangelical Tradition

Much of the power of evangelism comes from fear: fear of death, fear of failure, fear of the unknown, fear of one's sinful thoughts. Robert Schuller, founder of the Walk-In-Drive-In Church, asks:

Are you   limping when you could be walking strong, whimpering when you could be whistling, crying when you could be laughing?

Are you   being defeated by your problems, facing frustrations that are discouraging you, heartaches that are depressing you?

Reprinted from *College Composition and Communication* (February 1987). Copyright 1989 by the National Council of Teachers of English. Reprinted with permission.

Are you	bored with life, tired of living, lacking zest and excitement?
Are you	watching somebody make a great success of an opportunity you turned down?
Are your	projects and dreams struggling when they could be thriving, shrinking when they could be growing, failing when they could be succeeding? (13)

The answer to this attitude that "produces doubt, stimulates fear, and generates a mental climate of pessimism and fatigue" (15) is "possibility thinking"—belief that "God keeps His promises. 'He that has begun a good work in you will complete it' . . . If you have faith as a grain of mustard seed you can say to this mountain move—and nothing shall be impossible unto you" (36).

In the classroom, composition teachers often capitalize on the same kinds of fear: fear of limping and whimpering instead of "walking strong," fear of depression and frustration, fear of being boring, lacking "zest and excitement," and "shrinking" instead of "growing." Donald C. Stewart asks in *The Versatile Writer:*

> . . . do you think of yourself as a happy person, one who brings warmth and laughter to any group you join? But do others think of you that way? How would you feel if someone told you that your sense of humor was a bit sarcastic and painful to others? How smart are you? Have you discovered that the percentage of good students is much higher in college than in high school? How do you rank among this new group of peers? Do you feel put down by that knowledge—or are you challenged? How do you really feel about racial injustice and ethnic prejudice in our country? Have you ever really been in love? Do you see yourself as suave and sophisticated, or as a nerd? How do you know? (8)

Peter Elbow addresses *Writing with Power* to "that person inside everyone who has ever written or tried to write: that someone who has wrestled with words, who seeks power in words, who has often gotten discouraged, but who also senses the possibility of achieving real writing power" (6). Elbow wants to help those of us who "are tied in knots by trying to be creative and critical at the same time" and so write "wretchedly" (9). He wants to help those who have a "fear of badness" that holds them back from developing "power" (302). James E. Miller, Jr. and Stephen Judy set out to help students who find their writing "dead . . . inhibited and restrained, and frequently dehumanized and unreadable" *(Writing in Reality* 7). Ken Macrorie sets off to help the "whining boys crawling like snails unwillingly to school" *(Uptaught* 3).

One reason "voice" fits in so well with evangelism is that "voice" has strong Biblical roots. Elijah heard a "still small voice." John the Baptist had a voice that cried out in the wilderness. God told St. John the Divine, "Behold, I stand at the door, and knock: if any man hear my voice, and open the door,

I will come in to him, and will sup with him, and he with me" (Rev. 4.20). And St. John beheld a door that opened into heaven and heard a voice like a trumpet talking to him. And he heard voices and thunderings and saw beasts with wings crying "Holy, holy, holy, Lord God Almighty, which was, and is, and is to come."

And "voice" in writing carries with it some of the same Biblical feel, the sense of mystery and music that comes to true believers. Sheridan Baker and Robert Yarber tell students, "You should bear yourself as a member of humankind, knowing that we are all sinners, all redundant, and all too fond of big words" *(The Practical Stylist* 3). Stewart calls the "authentic voice" students discover through "self-discovery" "a kind of revelation in which you not only begin to see yourself through the eyes of others, but also acquire a fundamental sense of individuality, which transcends the roles you play in life" (8). Ken Macrorie tells students to "speak the truth" *(Searching Writing* 28) because in doing so, we "lose ourselves and our egos." He concludes, "It's a positive miracle, and we might as well profit from it" (32). And underlying all of this is the fundamental faith we must have to recognize our "real voices":

> Look for real voice and realize it is there in everyone waiting to be used. Yet remember, too, that you are looking for something myste-rious and hidden. There are no outward linguistic characteristics to point to in writing with real voice. Resonance or impact on readers is all there is . . . You have to be willing to work in the dark, not be in a hurry, and have faith. (Elbow 312)

Composition teachers are also quick to capitalize on the power of the simple evangelical message: heaven or hell. Students who discover their "voices" are saved from damnation—eternal dullness, spiritual death, death by technology. "Writing with no voice," says Elbow, "is dead, mechanical, faceless" (287). Writing without "authentic voice," says Maxine Hairston, seems "fake or canned or put together by formula"; writing with "authentic voice" is "distinctive and original" *(Successful Writing* 19). "Voice separates writing that is not read from writing that is read," says Donald M. Murray *(Write to Learn* 144). Good writers, says Roger Garrison, are "honest," "sincere," and "human"—bad writers are "phony" and fall victims to the "tides of phony, posturing, pretentious, tired, imprecise, slovenly language, which both suffocate and corrupt the mind" (Coles and Vopat 273). Good writing, say Baker and Yarber, "should have a voice, and the voice should be unmistakably your own" (6); bad writing has "dullness," "anonymity," the "monotone of official prose," and "academic mildew" (3). "Bad prose," says Leo Hamalian in "The Visible Voice," "sounds as though it had been ground out by a sausage machine or produced with labor pains," but "good prose" almost always contains a "personal voice" (227). "Nothing," says Harvey Daniels, "is more central to all good writing than this authentic personal voice, this sound of a genuine, deeply engaged author at work finding out what she thinks":

This authenticity naturally pays off at the end of a writing project, when the strong, unique voice draws the reader into the piece and propels him along. But even from the beginning, the excitement that comes from real commitment to a job of thinking and writing moves the work along, makes the writer want to get it right, motivates close revision and editing, instills care and pride in the whole process. (Coles and Vopat 261)

"Voice" makes people whole, allows them to be born again. "Voice" gives the saved "power" and returns to them their essential humanity. And, perhaps most importantly, "voice" provides *immediate salvation* if sinners renounce complexity and the evils of over-intellectualizing, return to simple black-and-white ideals, and embrace their primitive, emotive, human selves.

Certain aspects here are worth emphasizing. One is the importance of *emotion* to all of this. Those without "voice" are coldly rational, calculating; those with "voice" are warm, full of spirit and energy, outgoing, capable of enjoying fun in the sun and roses in the spring. Metaphors for "voice" such as "juice," "mother's milk," "magic," and "electricity" evoke emotion long before they evoke understanding. Elbow tells us, "Sometimes I fear I will never be clear about what I mean by voice" (286), but we are not supposed to "understand" voice—rather, we are supposed to *experience* it, perhaps as the Lord's voice came out of the fire and brightness and entered the prophet Ezekiel. And despite his attempts to "work this thing out more fully and rationally" (287), Elbow only succeeds in underscoring the non-rational nature of "voice." He tells us that writing with no "voice" is "dead, mechanical, faceless," but he is unable to explain exactly what he means by "dull" or "mechanical" or "faceless." He points out that people with "voice" have "a sound or texture—the sound of 'them'" (288), but can't really explain what such a "sound" really is. And the more he writes, the more he fuzzes the issue up: "Real voice" has "power and resonance" and "reality" (292). In "real voice," "the words somehow issue from the writer's center—even if in a slippery way—and produce resonance which gets the words more powerfully to a reader's center" (298).

"Voice," then, is something we can't discuss and analyze but can only *feel or participate in* as the words "bore through" (Elbow 313). Elbow tells us, "I seem to talk, in short, as though what's important is not the set of words on the page—the only thing that the reader ever encounters—but rather something *not* on the page, something the reader never encounters, namely the writer's mental/spiritual/characterological condition or the *way* she wrote down the words" (357). "Blessed indeed," says Paul Tournier in *The Adventure of Living*, "are those who hear God's voice or who can recognize his inspiration in some thought that comes into their minds, and who still retain the humble prudence dictated by our always uncertain human condition" (187).

The advantage of such vague, emotive description is that salvation becomes a very *personal* affair. "Each individual plays the card he holds," says Paul Tournier, "and that is his adventure"—an adventure that links him to God:

> What I am concerned to point out is the vital need felt by every human being to express himself, to manifest his person to the outside world—and in the most personal manner possible. And what a joy this is to him! (87)

Likewise, Donald C. Stewart tells us:

> Your authentic voice is that authorial voice which sets you apart from every other living human being despite the number of common or shared experiences you have with others; it is not a copy of someone else's way of speaking or of perceiving the world. It is your way . . . The closer you come to rendering your particular perception of your world in your words, the closer you will come to finding your authentic voice. (9)

"Voice," like the humanity it comes from, gives *everyone* access to salvation—the halt, the lame, the troubled masses. Elbow tells us that one thing is more important than anything else: "everyone, however inexperienced or unskilled, has real voice available; everyone can write with power."

> Nothing stops you from writing right now, today, words that people will want to read and even want to publish. Nothing stops you, that is, but your fear or unwillingness or lack of familiarity with what I am calling your real voice. (304)

Murray tells us, "Voice is the quality, more than any other, that allows us to recognize excellent writing" (A *Writer Teaches Writing* 21). And, while the concept is "sophisticated, abstract, and theoretical," he emphasizes, "everyone already recognizes voice and makes use of it" (22).

The Consequences of Zeal

If the major problem here were simply adapting the evangelic method to composition instruction and cashing in on the emotional spirit that accompanies conversion, there would be no problem. We could all use exuberant, highly spirited students, especially at two o'clock on Friday afternoons. But the limitations may far outweigh the advantages. First, such evangelical exhortation may not be appropriate for all students. Not everyone watches Jimmy Swaggart on Sunday mornings—and not everyone needs the same kind of spiritual comfort, feels existential pain, needs a week-end soul-boost to carry him/her through the rest of the week. Likewise, not all students come to composition class stunned, in pain, feeling the frustration of writing dead prose, experiencing the loneliness of the unvoiced, the depersonalized, the mechanical. Not all of them see the power of writing coming from "voice." (Some, in fact, want to write voiceless academic prose, get their transitions right, their introductions direct and straightforward, their message clear.) And, consequently, not all of them need the immediate success of discovering their own "voices," the sense of discovery they experience from discovering their own, real selves.

Furthermore, such evangelical exhortation may not be appropriate for all kinds of writing. Certainly, it may work well when students are working on personal narratives and projects that ask them to turn inward to probe their feelings, motivations, commitments. Yet not all writing is so personal. Not all writing requires a commitment to self. Take, for example, the following passage from the President's Commission on the Assassination of President Kennedy:

> Lee Harvey Oswald spent almost all of the last 48 hours of his life in the Police and Courts Building, a gray stone structure in downtown Dallas that housed the headquarters of the Dallas Police Department and the city jail. Following his arrest early Friday afternoon, Oswald was brought immediately to this building and remained there until Sunday morning, November 24, when he was scheduled to be transferred to the county jail. At 11:21 that morning, in full view of millions of people watching on television, Oswald was fatally wounded by Jack Ruby, who emerged suddenly from the crowd of newsmen and policemen witnessing the transfer and fired a single shot at Oswald. (184)

The most obvious problem is that this piece was written by a *committee*—and, like all such collaborations, does not—cannot—have a single, "personal voice" at all. Yet more important is whether personal "voice" is essential at all in writing used to convey information and establish facts—or whether "voice" as self-discovery or "juice" or "electricity" may *detract* from or clutter the facts, hide important details, and, consequently, affect *content* in inappropriate ways. Certainly, to call such writing "dull" or "dead" or "mechanical" or "voiceless" doesn't seem to make any sense. We could, for instance, try to add some juice by tinkering with point-of-view:

> Police and Courts Building. City jail. Gray stone in downtown Dallas. Lee Harvey Oswald, the killer of the President, his mind on the secrets he'll never be able to tell. We feel the cold and sense his impending death as deep inside, he imagines the fates in balance— tipping now one way, now the other until . . . click. A key turns. And someone grabs his arms roughly, dragging him back to the ugly present . . . footsteps down the cool corridor and through several doors and into the light and people! People everywhere and someone has thrust a camera high over the crowd and . . . oh! my God! Someone in a dark hat lunges before the television cameras and a small (pop!) an oh! my God! they've shot me! Someone has shot me! Jack Ruby . . . the television cameras roll; the world rushes down, down and the bare concrete and . . . and Oswald lies dying, the truth clenched tight between his teeth.

Or we might try to juice up a tough but introspective narrator:

> Lee Harvey Oswald spent the last 48 hours of his punk's life in the Police and Courts Building, in downtown Dallas. The President down, Connally wounded, the world had been slugged in the gut, and the dirty little bastard knew it. We knew it, and he had to have, sitting there, his twisted demented, soulless mind on the glory that he thought was now his. They booked the skinny little Russian sympathizer in City Jail and were shipping him off to prison, but while we were watching, a cheap nightclub hood named Jack Ruby stepped out of the crowd and shot him dead, at first sending a wave of relief through our souls but leaving a lingering sense of doubt, of loss, of emptiness.

But while such tinkerings might increase the concentration of juice, they don't seem to increase the *historical value* of the original manuscript at all.

Indeed, because the whole notion of "voice" is so mystical and abstract, the term "voice" may have become nothing more than a vague phrase conjured up by English teachers to impress and motivate the masses to write more, confess more, and be happy. Peter Elbow himself has even expressed some doubt about the reality of this juice:

> As I've been trying to work and rework my thoughts about voice these last four years, I have been nervous about the charge that what I am calling "real voice" is just writing that happens to tickle my feelings or my unconscious concerns and has nothing to do with the words' relationship to the writer. The charge is plausible: if I experience resonance, surely it's more likely to reflect a good fit between the words and *my* self than a good fit between the words and the writer's self; after all, my self is right here, in contact with the words on the page, while the writer's self is nowhere to be found. (300)

Elbow, of course, concludes that he "cannot disprove the charge" but goes on anyway, suggesting that the "hypothesis" is still worth investigating because despite his doubts, he has "trust" in his own taste and, ultimately, trust in his own ability as a good reader to recognize voice when it occurs.

But this trust or faith in "good reading" does nothing for those who see reading as some kind of *transaction* between reader and text, who suggest that *all* good readers—no matter how spiritually enlightened—bring their own biases, preconceptions, and experiences to what they read, and, in doing so, *change* the text, affect the "juice" of the text itself. Here, for instance, is a passage on cheerleading by Roberta David:

> There you are—out on the field—in front of the crowd! Your team rushes out—the air rings with cheers! The big game is about to start.
>
> Is this the most exciting moment in your life? You bet it is. You are the object of everyone's attention—you are a cheerleader!
>
> What an honor you have earned! You are in charge of sparking

the enthusiasm of a large crowd. Along with the other cheerleaders in the squad, you will take your position, raise up your arms, and lead hundreds of voices in the team cheer. Your cheerleading at the big game, or any other game, is important—just as cheerleading is a major function in schools throughout America. (9)

Does this writing have "juice"? Does it lack "juice"? If it has "juice" (and I'm not sure it does), is that "juice" enough to make the passage good writing? In fact, even if Davis became more fully juiced through some kind of inner revelation and commitment, would the passage be any better? The problem here may not necessarily be "juice" at all but *content and context*. Do we care enough about cheerleading to read about it? Would certain teenagers find the passage exciting and important simply because Davis addresses their wishes and desires? If so, would they need to feel Davis's "juice" at all? Would others find the whole affair stupid and meaningless and ridiculous no matter how much "juice" it contained?

The same problem, of course, occurs whenever we have to deal with ideas, feelings, or experiences we don't especially like or agree with. How many teachers, for instance, could suspend their feelings to "hear" the "voice" of a neo-Nazi advocating further extermination of the Jews? A confessed pornographer writing explicit descriptions of orgies? A child rapist describing the joys of youth? Indeed, to believe in "voice," we have to believe that texts *contain* voices that somehow get activated by eye-contact, or contain something like pixie dust that creates voices in our heads or bodies when we read. And we have to believe that biases, preconceptions, and expectations in no way alter or affect a good reader's ability to feel or participate objectively in those voices.

Finally, and perhaps most importantly, this evangelical approach to "voice" and the firm belief that everyone can be "saved" by discovering his/ her "voice" may have *anti-intellectual consequences*. The great 19th century evangelist Dwight L. Moody once said, "I would rather have zeal without knowledge; and there is a good deal of knowledge without zeal" (Hofstadter 108). In the early 20th century, Billy Sunday told people, "Thousands of college graduates are going as fast as they can straight to hell. If I had a million dollars I'd give $999,999 to the church and $1 to education" (Hofstadter 122). Billy Graham tells worshippers, "We are a nation of empty people. Our heads are crammed full of knowledge, but within our souls is a spiritual vacuum" (7). And by telling the masses not to worry about intellectual matters, interpretation of texts, and development of philosophic arguments, preachers like Moody and Sunday and Graham can save three or four times as many sinners than more intellectual brethren—and in a fraction of the time.

The temptation to use anti-intellectual, evangelical appeals for "voice" in composition teaching may often be motivated by similar concern for saving as many sinners as possible in the most efficient, practical manner possible. Certainly at a time when deans are worrying about the attrition rate from required courses and declining enrollments in the humanities, voice evangelism offers simple salvation to many: increased enrollments and happy, complacent students. Self-centered, passive students can wait for revelation without the pain and frustration associated with intellectual pursuits and confusion or disorientation from unaccustomed methods of thought. To succeed, they can forego external research, shelve new ideas, and devaluate facts. Indeed, whereas students might go through four or more years of college and become more and more frustrated with how little they know, students who spend their time learning about themselves and discovering their authentic "voices" can take a short-cut to excellence, can perhaps, if they believe Peter Elbow, even become published in a relatively short period of time.

The problem, of course, is that writing is an intellectual endeavor and the more students are exhorted to pursue spiritual goals of zeal, "electricity" and personal salvation, the more "voice" appears to be short-sighted and inappropriate. At the end of his chapter on "the writer's attitude," for instance, Donald C. Stewart supplies a sample student essay in which the student concludes that children who receive the "routine answers of science and logic" are somehow damaged for life:

> As the child continues to question, he continues to receive those same scientific answers, dished up for him by people who accept them passively, people who no longer wonder themselves. The child may come to believe them or not, but he probably will stop asking his questions, for they appear naive in his maturing world. If Americans believe in anything as firmly as they believe in money, it is the power of science to explain all and cure all. With this belief, there is no need to keep wondering about the mysterious qualities of snow or cows; there is no need to wonder at all. This natural curiosity in the child will be snuffed out, and he will passively accept the answers he is given. (33)

Stewart is apparently willing to let readers take such sentiment seriously. He makes no comment in either his text or the accompanying teacher's manual about the problems of defining "natural curiosity" (are scientists naturally curious?), "wonder" (is there scientific "wonder"?), and "maturing world" (is there a conflict between "wonder" and "maturity"?). He also apparently finds nothing strange about the causal relationships the writer of this sample sets up between "scientific answers," "logic," "natural curiosity," and maturation. And while the essay seems to support very well Stewart's notion that good writing comes from the gut, that "the closer you come to rendering your particular perception of your world in your words, the closer you will come to finding your authentic voice" (9), I would doubt that many good scientists—or good thinkers in any academic discipline for that matter—could take it seriously.

Many voice evangelists apparently like to snipe at the work of "academics"—who evidently are sinful because they make things needlessly complex or confusing or cause unnecessary busy-work. Yet such sniping only further underscores the limitations of overzealous appeals to "voice." Stewart tells readers, "Students are always writing exams, term papers, reports, short papers—anything a teacher can think of for them to do" (5). Yet certainly many teachers are not just groping around for anything they can think to burden students with. Roger Garrison suggests that readers need to "hear an honest, human voice," and concludes: "Academics haven't helped honest writing much, either. If I read 'outcome,' 'cognitive,' 'interact,' 'heuristic,' or 'viable' many more times, I shall throw up" (Coles and Vopat 273). And while students may *like* to believe that honest human voices do not reveal themselves in academic terminology, certainly very little scholarly work of much value could go on without such terminology.

In a book called *Sometimes You Just Have to Stand Naked,* David Bartholomy relates "voice" to "natural style" and tells students:

> Once you've found your natural writing style, repaired its flaws, begun developing it . . . and become comfortable with it . . . you won't be afraid to write for anyone, not even the strictest teacher. And you'll be able to adapt it to any writing situation, from the least to the most formal. (47)

Apparently, with a natural voice, students need not worry about content at all. Bartholomy tells them, "If there's no personality in your writing, it's dead. If it's not *your* personality, you're dead. Bang, bang" (48). Notice also how teachers become "strict"—evidently representatives of a mindless, dead, academic community that is more interested in nit-picking than it is in learning.

I would emphasize that I am *not* arguing here that all those who advocate "voice" are necessarily anti-intellectual themselves. I *am,* however, suggesting that many advocates use such anti-intellectual appeals for motivational reasons—and in doing so, they undercut their own intellectual enterprises and undermine the importance of teaching composition at all on the college level.

Conclusion

The term "voice" has many uses and I'm not suggesting that we abandon it completely. I am suggesting, though, that we ought to be *careful* when we tell students that we "can't hear" their "voices" or when we tell them that "good" writing always has a "voice" and bad writing is "voiceless." We should watch out when we slip into easy generalizations about everyone having a "voice" and about "voice" being more important than anything else in writing. We ought to be careful about using vague, metaphoric language simply because we can't quite put our fingers on something more specific. There may be room for magic and non-rational thinking in writing, but we probably shouldn't fall too easily into a tradition that has strong and uncomfortably anti-intellectual roots and consequences.

Some may say that I am an alarmist, that I am making too much of this "voice," and surely we can be "positively" evangelic within limits. Yet I suspect that the more we insist that writing is "mystery," that evaluation has something to do with spiritual vibrations generated by texts themselves, that writing either has or doesn't have some "voice" that we can feel in our spirits—the more we begin to overstep our bounds and begin to abandon teaching for preaching.

Works Cited

Baker, Sheridan and Robert E. Yarber. *The Practical Stylist with Readings.* 6th ed. New York: Harper, 1986.

Bartholomy, David. *Sometimes You Just Have to Stand Naked: A Guide to Interesting Writing.* Englewood Cliffs, NJ: Prentice-Hall, 1983.

Coles, William E., Jr. and James Vopat. *What Makes Writing Good: A Multiperspective.* Lexington, MA: Heath, 1985.

Davis, Roberta, Harriette Behringer and Doris Wheelus. *Cheerleading and Baton Twirling.* New York: Grosset, 1972.

Elbow, Peter. *Writing with Power: Techniques for Mastering the Writing Process.* New York: Oxford, 1981.

Graham, Billy. *Peace With God.* Old Tappan, NJ: Fleming H. Revell, 1968.

Hairston, Maxine C. *Successful Writing.* 2nd ed. New York: Norton, 1986.

Hamalian, Leo. "The Visible Voice: An Approach to Writing." *The English Journal* 59 (1970): 227-230.

Hofstadter, Richard. *Anti-Intellectualism in American Life.* New York: Knopf, 1970.

Lannon, John M. *The Writing Process: A Concise Rhetoric.* 2nd ed. Boston: Little, 1986.

Macrorie, Ken. *Searching Writing: A Contextbook.* Rochelle Park, NJ: Hayden, 1980.

_____. *Uptaught.* New York: Hayden, 1970.

Miller, James E., Jr. and Stephen N. Judy. *Writing in Reality.* New York: Harper, 1978.

Murray, Donald M. *A Writer Teaches Writing.* 2nd ed. Boston: Houghton, 1985.

_____. *Write to Learn.* New York: Holt, 1984.

President's Commission on the Assassination of President Kennedy. *Report of the Warren Commission on the Assassination of President Kennedy.* New York: McGraw-Hill, 1964.

Ruszkiewicz, John J. *Well-Bound Words: A Rhetoric.* Glenview, IL: Scott, Foresman, 1981.

Schuller, Robert H. *Move Ahead with Possibility Thinking.* Old Tappan, NJ: Fleming H. Revell, 1967.

Stewart, Donald C. *The Versatile Writer.* Lexington, MA: Heath, 1986.

Tournier, Paul. *The Adventure of Living.* Trans. Edwin Hudson. New York: Harper, 1965.

Ethos Versus Persona

Self-Representation in Written Discourse

by Roger D. Cherry

Audience has received a great deal of attention in research on writing.[1] Several recent studies (e.g., Ede & Lunsford, 1984; Elbow, 1987; Kroll, 1984; Park, 1986; Roth, 1987) suggest that writers employ a wide range of strategies in conceiving and portraying their audience when writing. A new lexicon has emerged for describing how writers represent audience, both to themselves during composing and in final written texts. Oppositions such as "audience addressed versus audience invoked" and "intended audience versus imagined audience," as well as terms such as *implied audience, unknown audience, extended audience,* and *universal audience*, have been used to describe the creativity and flexibility that go into audience construction.

Although numerous studies have begun to explore the complexity of audience representation in writing, no corresponding literature on self-representation in written discourse has yet emerged. Composition textbooks often refer to "persona," or sometimes to *ethos*, and the notion of "voice" is prevalent in the composition literature, but these terms and the concepts behind them have not been subjected to careful examination in either composition theory or composition research. Neglect of self-representation in the study of writing is curious given the almost universal significance attached to the self-as-speaker or self-as-writer by rhetoricians and discourse theorists.

The present essay focuses on self-representation in rhetorical theory and in literary critical theory in an effort to provide a useful starting point for future studies of self-portrayal in written discourse. I will argue that, like audience representation, self-representation in writing is a subtle and complex multidimensional phenomenon that skilled writers control and manipulate to their rhetorical advantage. Decisions about self-portrayal are not independent, but vary according to the way in which writers characterize their audience and other facets of the rhetorical situation. A better understanding of self-representation in written texts can thus contribute to a more complete understanding of how writers construct rhetorical situations in the act of composing.

Reprinted from *Written Communication* 5 (July 1988): 251-76. Used with permission.
[1] See Ede (1984) for a review of recent work on audience.

Two terms for describing self-representation—*ethos* and *persona*—are commonly conflated, despite the fact that there are good historical and conceptual grounds for maintaining a distinction between them. A historical examination of the two terms shows that *ethos* and persona derive from different traditions and therefore provide different (but complementary) perspectives on self-representation in written discourse. Distinguishing between *ethos* and persona will enable us to refine our critical vocabulary for describing and analyzing self-portrayal in writing, which in turn will allow us to conduct research that is more sensitive to how writers actually project themselves into written text.

The remainder of the essay is organized as follows: The first two sections explore the historical background and meaning of *ethos* and persona, respectively. In the next section I consider some of the reasons they have often been conflated. The fourth section of the essay suggests some of the ways in which maintaining a distinction between *ethos* and persona might be helpful for literary criticism, as well as for rhetorical theory and research on writing. In the concluding section I explore some limitations of implementing the *ethos*/persona distinction in both theory and practice.

Ethos

Although the concept of *ethos* can be discerned in earlier discussions of rhetoric, Aristotle provides the earliest surviving detailed analysis of the ethical argument.[2] In the *Rhetoric* Aristotle (1954, p. 1356a) describes three *pisteis*, or means of securing persuasion. *Pathos* involves arousing an appropriate emotional response in the audience, *logos* has to do with principles of sound argumentation, and *ethos* is concerned with the character of the speaker as portrayed in the speech itself. *Ethos* refers to the need for rhetors to portray themselves in their speeches as having a good moral character, "practical wisdom," and a concern for the audience in order to achieve credibility and thereby secure persuasion.

Aristotle maintains that since rhetoric is concerned with matters that are contingent rather than absolute (i.e., since rhetoric is based on probability rather than on necessity), the character of the speaker is especially important in securing assent. He also contends that the persuasive appeal of the speaker's character must be seen as based on the speech itself, not on prior reputation.

In Book II of the *Rhetoric*, Aristotle (1954, p. 1377b) reemphasizes the importance of the ethical and pathetic arguments and suggests that *ethos* is especially important in deliberative rhetoric. He analyzes the ethical argument in greater detail by identifying the characteristics that lend credibility to the

---

[2] For a historical treatment of *ethos* from the pre-Socratics through Whately, see Sattler (1941). Sattler (1947) is based on the earlier work and focuses on *ethos* in classical rhetoric. More recent general discussions of *ethos* are those of Rosenthal (1966), Yoos (1979), Halloran (1982), and Johnson (1984).

speaker (p. 1378a): *phronesis* (practical wisdom), *arete* (good moral character), and *eunoia* (goodwill toward the audience).

Phronesis is usually translated as "practical wisdom" or "good sense."[3] In the *Nicomachean Ethics,* Aristotle describes *phronesis* as the intellectual virtue that enables one to adapt theoretical principles to practical circumstances, to select appropriate means for achieving desired ends in particular situations.[4] As Aristotle (1925, p. 1144a) puts it in the *Nicomachean Ethics,* "the work of man is achieved only in accordance with practial wisdom [i.e., *phronesis*] as well as with moral virtue; for virtue makes us aim at the right mark, and practical wisdom makes us take the right means." As the virtue concerned with wisdom in action, *phronesis* enables one to judge the suitability of specific actions in the search for moral excellence.

The second component of *ethos,* according to Aristotle, is *arete.*[5] The term itself presents some difficulty because of the wide variety of meanings it carries at different times and in different contexts in Greek thought. This difficulty is mirrored in modern translations of the *Rhetoric.* Freese renders *arete,* as it appears in Aristotle's discussion of the three components of the ethical argument (p. 1378a), as "virtue." Roberts, on the other hand, translates the term in the same context as "good moral character." Freese's translation is the more literal of the two, but Roberts captures the broader meaning of the term.

Aristotle uses the word *arete* in several different senses. When he describes the various moral or intellectual virtues in the *Nicomachean Ethics,* he uses *arete* (or the plural *aretai*). He uses *arete* in a similar sense at times in the *Rhetoric* as well. In Book III, for example, Aristotle speaks of four "virtues" of style. It is this sense of the word *arete* that is often translated "excellence" rather than "virtue." How, then, in Aristotle's description of the components of *ethos* in the *Rhetoric,* does *arete* come to be rendered as "moral character" by translators such as Roberts.

The etymology of *ethos* sheds some light on the connection between *ethos* and moral virtue. The rhetorical term *ethos* (ἦθος) is derived from another, closely related Greek word (ἔθος), meaning "custom or habit." The connection between (ἦθος) and (ἔθος) can be established by examining another word (ἠθική), the Greek term for moral or ethical virtue, which shares the same stem as *ethos.* In Book II of the *Nichomachean Ethics,* Aristotle offers the following derivation of (ἦθος)

Moral virtue . . . is formed by habit, [ἔθος], and its name, [ἠθική], is

---

[3] Self (1979) provides a useful general discussion of *phronesis.*
[4] In the *Nicomachean Ethics,* intellectual virtues are distinguished from moral virtues. The former are closer to what we would call "capacities" or "mental faculties" than to what we would normally describe as "virtues." Aristotle's concept of moral virtue is closer to our everyday notion of a virtue as a desirable character trait. As an intellectual virtue, *phronesis* enables one to select appropriate means for achieving a given end, for example, to choose virtuous acts in order to achieve moral virtue (*arete*).
[5] For a historical discussion of *arete,* see Jaeger (1945).

therefore derived, by a slight variation from [ἔθος]. (p. 1103a; trans. Ostwald)

Because (ἦθος) and (ἠθική) share the same stem, it can reasonably be assumed that both terms derive from (ἔθος) (Corts, 1968; Miller, 1974).

Aristotle argues in the *Nichomachean Ethics* that individuals are not predisposed at birth to be either virtuous or morally depraved. Instead, a disposition for moral goodness (i.e., moral character) is acquired through the habitual exercise of virtue. As one of the components of rhetorical *ethos*, *arete* refers to the disposition or character that results from the exercise of moral and intellectual virtues, as well as the virtues of style. In effect, the use of the word *arete* to designate one of the components of *ethos* is intended to unite both senses of *arete*—both the exercise of virtue and the morally good character that results from habituation. Hence the frequent rendering of *ethos* as "moral character."

The final personal characteristic upon which the successful ethical appeal depends is *eunoia*, or goodwill toward the audience. In a discussion of Isocrates' use of the concept of *eunoia* in his political thinking, de Romilly (1958, p. 91) observes that "eunoia, in Greek, is something more than good will: it means approval, sympathy, and readiness to help." De Romilly suggests that Isocrates' concept of *eunoia* accords well with his overall approach to rhetoric and philosophy, an approach that mediates between the widely divergent approaches of Plato and the sophists.[6]

Eunoia is emphasized in the *Rhetoric* in connection with deliberative rhetoric (p. 1366a). For Aristotle, an important aspect of *ethos* involves assessing the characteristics of an audience and constructing the discourse in such a way as to portray oneself as embodying those same characteristics. He suggests that "people always think well of speeches adapted to and reflecting their own character: and we can now see how to compose our speeches so as to adapt them and ourselves to our audience" (p. 1390a, trans. Roberts).

Aristotle's concept of *ethos* has not been passed down unchanged through the history of rhetoric.[7] Cicero, for example, does not use the term *ethos*; the closest he comes to the term itself is to discuss the adjectival form *ethikon*, which he contrasts with *pathetikon* (Cicero, 1939, p. 128; see Enos & McClaran, 1978, p. 102; Sattler, 1941, p. 140, n. 1). These two "topics," as Cicero calls them, result in different styles of speech and thus different effects on the audience. According to Cicero, *ethikon* is "courteous and agreeable, adapted to win goodwill," while *pathetikon* is "violent, hot and impassioned" (p. 128). Quintilian suggests that there is no exact equivalent in Latin for *ethos*, but that *mores* (an individual's moral constitution) probably comes

---

[6] Plato insists that rhetoric, if practiced at all, must have a philosophical basis; the sophists emphasized the pragmatic benefits of rhetoric and maintained that rhetoric must be found on a practical understanding of the workings of persuasion in everyday life. Isocrates' position, very much in line with Aristotle's (at least on this point), is that rhetoric must accommodate both philosophy and practical affairs.

[7] See Sattler (1941) for a detailed treatment of these changes.

closest (see Enos & McClaran, 1978, p. 102; Sattler, 1941, pp. 141-143). He goes on to contrast *ethos* and *pathos* along Ciceronian lines (*Instituto Oratoria*, pp. 421-423).

Although Cicero and Quintilian do not follow Aristotle step-for-step in their treatments of *ethos*, the basic concept is of obvious importance in their rhetorical treatises. Cicero associates *ethikon* with *lenitas*, a restrained style that helps to make apparent an orator's moral character. He also identifies *dignitas* and *auctoritas* as desirable qualities in an orator. According to Enos and McClaran (1978, p. 102),

> Cicero considered *dignitas* the mark of a man's breeding, an idealistic quality associated with virtuous conduct and pristine values. . . .
> Similar to *dignitas, auctoritas* was associated with an orator's morality and public image; it was a type of long-range *ethos*.

Quintilian's insistence that the orator be morally upstanding reveals a heavy reliance on the basic concept of *ethos* as well. Although they do not adopt wholesale Aristotle's analysis of *ethos*, the Roman rhetoricians, if anything, place more emphasis on *ethos* than did Aristotle through their focus on the *vir bonus* (see Brinton, 1983; Craig, 1981; Grant, 1943; MacKendrick, 1948).

As would be expected, *ethos* is handled somewhat differently by various rhetorical theorists throughout the history of rhetoric. Yet Aristotle's systematic analysis of *ethos*, as well as most treatments of the ethical argument throughout the rhetorical tradition, focus on credibility, on the speaker's securing the trust and respect of an audience by representing him-or herself in the speech as knowledgeable, intelligent, competent, and concerned for the welfare of the audience.[8]

Persona

It would be convenient if Roman rhetoricians had simply substituted the term *persona* for *ethos*. *Persona* would then have picked up where *ethos* left off and we could assume that the two terms should be considered synonymous. The problem, however, is that *persona* has come down to us not through a rhetorical tradition, but through a literary tradition.[9] In order to

---

[8] Although the rhetorical tradition has focused primarily on spoken discourse, it is reasonable to assume that rhetorical concepts such as *ethos* play an essential role in written discourse as well.

[9] Cicero does use the term *persona*, but the context in which he does so makes it clear that he is not using the term as a substitute for *ethos*. In the passage below, Cicero describes the importance of role playing in preparing clients and their cases for court:

> It is my own practice to take care that every client personally instructs me on his affairs . . . and to argue his opponent's case to him, so that he may argue his own and openly declare whatever he has thought of his position. Then, when he has departed, I play three characters [*tres personas*], myself, my opponent, and the arbitrator. . . . In this way I gain the advantage of reflecting first on what to say and saying it later. (*De Oratore*, p. 102)

The notion of persona at work here clearly has to do with play acting a role, that is, assuming a *dramatis persona* or "mask." As will become apparent momentarily, this idea of persona is consonant with what is known of the origins of the term.

understand something of the history and meaning of *persona*, we must turn to literary criticism, where the term has been used most extensively.[10]

Elliott (1982, p. 21) points out that the etymology of the word *persona* is mired in difficulty:

> *Persona* has one of the most complex histories known to philologists, a history full of contradiction, controversy, enigma. Sober German philologists have been known to go into raptures over the obscure provenance and tangled permutations of the word. No one is certain even of its origin.

Elliott reviews what is known about the etymology of *persona* and concludes that, although the precise history of the word cannot be pinned down, "there is no question that, in Latin, *persona* refers originally to a device of transformation and concealment on the theatrical stage" (p. 21). The term *persona* gradually acquired other meanings beyond its initial meaning of "theatrical mask," among them the notion of "role," both in a dramaturgical sense and in the broader sense of a social role.

The poetry (e.g., Pound's *Personae*) and the literary criticism from the early part of this century show an awareness of the basic critical concept of the persona, but it was not until the late 1940s that the term itself came into widespread use among literary critics. In critical theory, the notion of the persona has been employed to account for the disjunction between an author and the author's presence in the literary text. Critics have debated the legitimacy and usefulness of the persona as a critical concept, focusing on whether or not (and if so, to what extent) personae should be identified with their creators. According to Elliott,

> the word *persona* is used by literary interpreters in an effort to clarify the relationship between the writer—the historical person—and the characters the writer creates. That relationship is never simple . . . but it is made more difficult when the writer uses the first person singular pronoun, when he writes "I." (p. x)

After considering a wide range of texts from a number of historical periods, particularly works that employ a first-person narrator or speaker and clearly call into question the relationship between the historical author and the voice or persona that emerges from the text, Elliott suggests that the notion of the persona is necessary in critical approaches even to so-called confessional poetry that overtly attempts to minimize the distance between historical and textual author, such as Robert Lowell's *Life Studies*.

---

[10]Self-representation in written discourse has been addressed from a number of different perspectives in literary critical theory. An interesting early treatment of the issue is that of Tillyard and Lewis (1939), who consider the problem in rather broad terms in connection with biographical criticism (see also Cherniss, 1943). The question of sincerity (see Abrams, 1958; Ball, 1964; Davie, 1968; Trilling, 1972) and the problem of "international fallacy" (see Wimsatt & Beardsley, 1967) also touch on issues that bear on self-representation in literary discourse.

Use of the persona as a critical tool has been commonplace for several decades, but even from the beginning there was serious opposition to the very idea of the persona (Elliott, 1982, pp. 3-17). Some critics argue that authors can never really be said to be present in the literary text, that it is essential to distinguish between the voice or persona of the literary work and the historical author who created it. Others maintain that the notion of the persona erects an unnecessary obstacle between author and reader that obscures rather than clarifies critical inquiry. Wright (1960, p. 8), for example, argues that

> however accustomed we may be to the more direct lyric in which the thoughts or feelings of the poet, or of the characters he presents, are stated with unambiguous explicitness, art is formal, and there must always be a distance, minimized or emphasized, between the maker of the poem and the persons in the poem. Poetry, dramatic or lyric, does not present fragments of human experience, but formalized versions of it. The actions represented do not really take place; the persons, including the "I," do not exist outside the poem, or at least do not exist in the same way.

Other critics maintain that the concept of the persona has been overworked and applied in situations where it is clearly not appropriate. Ehrenpreis (1974), for example, contends that

> inevitably, the term [persona] implies that a genuine person does exist, could reveal himself, but chooses not to. (p 52)

> In didactic or lyric poetry, as in the reflective or polemical essay, the author must be regarded as the speaker. He may talk ironically; he may imitate a man he despises; he may ask you to sneer at the fool he is copying; he may in mockery talk like his foolish audience. But unless we treat the material as indicating, however indirectly, what the author believes and is, we do not discover the meaning of the work. (p. 60)

At the heart of this debate over the persona is the matter of authorial presence.[11] Nearly all the critics who take a position on the appropriateness or worth of the persona ask the question, "To what extent and in what ways can the author be said to participate or represent him- or herself in the literary text?" The question—although usually not formulated explicitly—has to do with how directly the text provides access to the historical author.

Proponents of the need to examine personae in literary texts often imply that the persona is merely a necessary mask for the author, that the mask is

---

[11] Ehrenpreis's statement raised something of a stir when it appeared—enough, anyway, to prompt responses from some 18 critics in a symposium titled "The Concept of the Persona in Satire" in the *Satire Newsletter* (see, for example, Efron, 1966; Feinberg, 1966). The critics lined up on both sides of the issue, some rejecting Ehrenpreis's argument, in part on the basis of problems in the argument itself, and others prepared to defend it all costs.

needed for the author to set him- or herself in the right posture toward a particular subject matter for a particular audience. They maintain, however, that, in the last analysis, the mask—when properly understood and interpreted—allows access to the opinions of the author. In their view, the author is mediated through the persona; the author is accessible, but only indirectly. Opponents of the notion of the persona counter that if the persona is merely a mask for the author—if indeed, as is often the case, the persona can be taken to represent the author him- or herself—then the persona becomes merely a cumbersome and unnecessary critical obstacle. They maintain that the author *is* the persona, and therefore is directly accessible.

Although they appear to be at odds, these positions on authorial presence and the persona are not necessarily mutually exclusive. Critics taking one or the other of these positions are often talking past one another, not because of any substantive disagreement—indeed they're sometimes trying to say precisely the same thing—but because of an inadequate definition of the concept over which they are arguing (see Elliott, 1982, p. 18). There is an element of truth to both positions. On one hand, there is a sense in which the author does not, indeed cannot, appear directly in the literary text. On the other hand, there is a sense in which the author is in fact present. In my view, the theorists who have taken extreme views on authorial presence have done so at least in part because of a failure to distinguish between the *ethos* of the historical author and the persona he or she may adopt in the literary text. Critics of the persona such as Ehrenpreis implicitly invoke a notion of *ethos* as part of their concern that the historical author not be exiled from the text. At the same time, those who argue for the persona seem drawn toward *ethos* when they attempt to explain reader response. Maintaining a distinction between *ethos* and persona might have helped to render these exchanges on authorial presence at least clearer, if not more productive.

The Conflation of Ethos *and Persona in* Rhetorical and Literary Theory

Ethos is one of three major *pisteis*, or means of persuasion, treated by Aristotle in the *Rhetoric*. It refers to the need for rhetors to portray themselves in their speeches as having a good moral character, "practical wisdom," and a concern for the audience in order to achieve credibility and thereby secure persuasion. *Persona*, on the other hand, has its origins in Roman drama and has been employed in literary critical theory to refer to an intentional "mask" a writer adopts in the written text.

Even on the surface the two concepts seem quite distinct. And yet *ethos* and persona have come to be considered virtually synonymous, or at least interchangeable. Gibson (1969, p. xi), in a book entitled *Persona: A Style Study for Readers and Writers*, implicitly suggests that *ethos* and persona are equivalent:

If one thinks of Aristotle's three rhetorical means of persuasion—the character of the speaker, the audience, the argument itself—it will be apparent that this book takes its hint from the first of these.

Although he does not use the Greek terms, Gibson is clearly referring to *ethos*, *pathos*, and *logos* and identifying the first with persona. Other studies simply use the two terms interchangeably without making an explicit connection between them (e.g., Myers, 1985; Odell & Goswami, 1982; Odell, Goswami, Herrington, & Quick, 1983).

The failure to distinguish between *ethos* and persona is apparent in literary criticism as well, particularly in the work of those influenced by the so-called Chicago school. Mack (1982), one of the first critics to suggest the importance of the persona, cites with approval a "reemergence of rhetoric" in critical approaches to literature and argues that satire is heavily dependent on *ethos* to establish the credibility of "the satirist." According to Mack,

> For the satirist especially, the establishment of an authoritative *ethos* is imperative. If he is to be effective . . . he must be accepted by his audience as a fundamentally virtuous and tolerant man, who challenges the doings of other men not whenever he happens to feel vindictive, but whenever they deserve it. On this account, the satirist's *apologia* for his satire is one of the stock subjects of both the classical writers and Pope: the audience must be assured that its censor is a man of good will, who has been, as it were, *forced* into action. (p. 59; emphasis in original)

It is not clear from Mack's discussion, however, whether he means by "the satirist" the historical author or the persona that emerges in the literary text.[12] Whatever Mack might have intended, subsequent critics used the term *ethos* to describe the persona, not realizing that the rhetorical term was being used in a way that was potentially problematic, at least for the question of the relationship between author and speaker in the literary text (see, e.g., Clifford, 1965; Efron, 1966; Feinberg, 1966).[13]

To some extent, Wayne Booth's (1961) *The Rhetoric of Fiction* takes a helpful step toward avoiding a confound between *ethos* and persona in narrative fiction. Booth argues for an "implied author" in the literary text that must be distinguished from the persona. According to Booth, the author

> as he writes . . . creates not simply an ideal, impersonal "man in general" but an implied version of "himself." (p. 70)

---

[12]Space does not permit examination of other passages that would support the claim that Mack's use of the term "the satirist" is equivocal.

[13]Ehrenpreis (1963) probably has Mack in mind when he observes that the terms *persona* and *ethos* had become synonymous in the critical literature on satire:

> For almost a quarter-century, the concept [of separation between historical author and authorial presence in the literary text] . . . has been finding wider and wider employment in research dealing with Swift, Pope, and their contemporaries. . . . Most scholars call it "persona" or "mask," but other labels are to be found. Rhetoricians speak of "ethical judgment" or "ethos." (p. 26)

> The "implied author" chooses, consciously or unconsciously, what we
> read; we infer him as an ideal, literary, created version of the real
> man. (pp. 73-74)

At first glance an "ideal, literary, created version of the real man" emerging
from the literary text would seem an apt description of Aristotle's notion of
ethos. In fact, this is how McKeon (1982) construes the implied author. She
argues that *The Rhetoric of Fiction* is "the first critical study to use Aristotle's
rhetorical concept of the ethical proof, the persuasive function of the orator's
character as it is projected in the speech; for clearly, that is precisely what
Booth's implied author is" (p. 11).

Although McKeon's suggestion at first appears sound, closer examination
reveals that identifying Booth's implied author with the *ethos* of the historical
author potentially results in a confounding of *ethos* and persona. Although
Booth argues for a distinction between the "I" or "narrator" of the literary text
and the implied author, he does not maintain the distinction consistently.
Booth clouds the distinction between the implied author and the persona when
he uses the term "second self" to refer at times to the implied author and at
other times to the persona.

On one hand Booth clearly marks a distinction between the implied
author and the persona when he maintains that

> it is a curious fact that we have no terms either for this created
> "second self" [i.e., the implied author] or our relationship with him.
> None of our terms for various aspects of the narrator is quite accurate.
> "Persona," "mask," and "narrator" are sometimes used, but they more
> commonly refer to the speaker in the work who is after all only one
> of the elements created by the implied author and who may be
> separated from him by large ironies. "Narrator" is usually taken to
> mean the "I" of the work, but the "I" is seldom if ever identical with
> the implied image of the artist. (p. 73)

On the other hand, Booth observes that there are times when "the second self
is given an overt, speaking role in the story" (p. 71). If, as the longer
quotation above suggests, one of the ways of distinguishing between the
implied author and the persona is to reserve the term *persona* to "refer to the
speaker in the work," then the basis for the distinction breaks down if it is
assumed that the implied author is sometimes "given an overt, speaking role
in the story." The potential confound between implied author and persona
becomes even more apparent with Booth's suggestion that "the art of
constructing reliable narrators is largely that of mastering all of oneself in
order to project the *persona*, the second self, that really belongs in the book"
(p. 83). The concept of the implied author, then, has a way of shifting ground;
in one instance it refers to the impression of the historical author formed by
the reader, while in another it refers to the narrative voice (or persona) that
presents characters and events to the reader.

Whereas McKeon holds that the implied author and *ethos* are equivalent, others have identified the implied author with the persona. Black (1970, p. 111), for example, refers to *The Rhetoric of Fiction* and suggests that "we have learned to keep continuously before us the possibility, and in some cases the probability, that the author implied by the discourse is an artificial creation: a persona, but not necessarily a person." The logical conclusion of accepting both McKeon's and Black's analyses would be that *ethos* and persona are equivalent (i.e., if *ethos* = implied author and if implied author persona, then *ethos* = persona).

The concept of the implied author is an important critical tool because, as Booth puts it, the implied author is "capable of calling attention to [the] work as the product of a choosing, evaluating person rather than as a self-existing thing" (p. 74). Booth's insistence on distinguishing between the historical author and the implied author, however, militates against the assumption that *ethos* and the implied author should be collapsed.

The notion of the implied author is most helpful if it is regarded as occupying a middle ground between the *ethos* of the historical author and the literary persona. It is precisely because the implied author serves to mediate between *ethos* and persona that the concept shifts so easily in Booth's discussion and has been drawn toward one side or the other in subsequent commentary. Maintaining a distinction between *ethos* and persona helps to clarify the nature and function of the implied author to preserve its integrity as a useful critical concept.

Distinguishing Between Ethos *and Persona*

In Literary Discourse

Distinguishing the *ethos* of the historical author from both the implied author and the persona provides a means of identifying varying degrees of mimetic representation in the literary text. The relationships among *ethos*, implied author, and persona in terms of their mimetic "distance" from the historical author might be represented on a continuum, as in Figure 1.[14]

Booth suggests that the distinction between the implied author and the persona or narrator rests on the fact that the implied author can be perceived as the guiding intelligence behind the creation of the persona. The implied

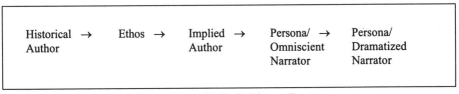

Figure 1. Degrees of Mimetic Self-Representation in the Literary Text

---

[14]Crutwell (1959/1960) also proposes such a continuum, but he does not distinguish between *ethos* and persona, and his categories and what they include are rather different from those proposed here; see also Friedman (1955) and Highet (1974).

author is a form of authorial presence that is omniscient and omnipotent within the confines of the imaginary world posited by the literary text. The persona, on the other hand, is a stylized mask confined to the role of narrator and is intended to have an imaginative life—literally a personality—of its own.

Because the implied author is itself a creation of the historical author, a distinction similar to the one Booth posits between the implied author and the persona should be maintained between the implied author and the *ethos* of the historical author. The question of *ethos* in the literary text should focus on the image of the historical author that emerges from the text itself. The question must turn on the extent to which, in creating the implied author and other aspects of the literary text, the historical author manifests those qualities upon which the successful ethical appeal depends.[15]

The implied author marks an intermediate position between the *ethos* of the author and the persona of the literary text. In fact, this seems to be the intention behind Booth's formulation of the concept in the first place. Collapsing the implied author into either *ethos* or persona destroys the value of Booth's initial insight—that there is a distinctive mode of self-representation in literary discourse that looks at one and the same time toward both the historical author and the persona. This Januslike quality of the implied author gives us a way of describing the fuzzy area of overlap in literary discourse in which *ethos* reaches toward persona and persona toward *ethos*. At the very least, preserving the autonomy of the implied author helps to maintain the distinction between *ethos* and persona.

In Nonliterary Discourse

Distinguishing between *ethos* and persona is important not only for literary discourse, but for other types of written discourse as well. The

---

[15]For Aristotle, of course, these qualities were *phronesis*, *arete*, and *eunoia*. Whether the concept of *ethos* might be modernized and specialized for contemporary theories of literary response is an open question, and one that could serve as the focus of some interesting research. My point here is simply that readers make judgments about the historical author on the basis of the literary text, and these judgments inevitably figure in one way or another into critical assessment. The concept of rhetorical *ethos* might serve as a useful starting point for characterizing the nature of the judgments that are made about the historical author. At least one explicit argument has been made for maintaining a distinction between *ethos* and persona in the literary text. Gerber (1967, p. 357) observes:

> One of the basic principles of rhetoric is that the ethos of the writer must engage the reader if the work is to fulfill its purposes. . . . But ever since Henry James and Percy Lubbock we have been primarily concerned with the persona the author employs, and not the ethos of the author himself. [The persona] was an important concept that was of incalculable value in helping us to discern the intrinsic values of a work. But it did something else too. It diverted our attention from the author as a totality who stood behind the mask.

> Rhetoric here is a corrective because it reminds us that it is the ethos of the author and not Huck that must finally engage use if Twain's ultimate purposes are to be served. Our concept of point of view thus becomes more comprehensive and sophisticated, as it should, since it now includes both the fictive narrator and the pervasive presence of the real author. The one enables us to assess the values within the book; the other challenges our beliefs outside the book and asks for our approval.

Although he refers to *The Rhetoric of Fiction*, Gerber does not comment on whether (or how) the implied author might be accommodated by the distinction between *ethos* and persona.

question of self-representation in the written text is most fruitfully approached as part of the larger question of how writers define and portray rhetorical situations in the texts they produce. The way in which the variables that constitute a rhetorical situation are perceived determines the "problem" that speakers or writers pose for themselves to solve through discourse. Previous research suggests that effective representation of a rhetorical problem is a first step toward creating written discourse that will function as a successful solution to the problem (Flower & Hayers, 1980).

The question of how speakers or writers characterize rhetorical situations has been the subject of some debate among rhetorical theorists. Bitzer (1968) maintains that situations call forth a rhetorical response, that persuasive discourse comes into being as an attempt to influence a given set of circumstances. Vatz (1973), on the other hand, argues that Bitzer's framework is too rigid and that participants in a rhetorical situation define the situation for themselves through the language they use to describe it. According to Vatz, "meaning is not discovered in situations, but *created* by rhetors" (p. 157; emphasis in original).

Of the various elements considered to be important in the rhetorical situation, audience has received the most attention in research on writing. Long (1980), for example, draws on the work of Ong (1975) in arguing that the audience for a piece of writing is most accurately regarded as a creation of the writer. Although he leans toward the notion of "audience-as-fiction," Park (1982) argues for a balanced view of audience that moves toward a reconciliation of the opposing perspectives of Bitzer and Vatz:

> However real the readers are outside the text, the writer writing must represent an audience to consciousness in some fashion; and the results of that "fiction" appear in what the text appears to assume about the knowledge and attitudes of its readers and about their relationship to the writer and the subject matter. (p. 249)

> To some extent, then, the task of analyzing audience is a matter of identifying the nature of the contexts that are already given by some aspect of the occasion . . . and of understanding the relationship between those that are given and those that must be more explicitly defined within the discourse itself. (p. 253)

Minot (1981) and Ede and Lunsford (1984) offer a similar perspective on audience in written texts. Ede and Lunsford label the notion of audience as a known, fixed entity "audience addressed" and the view of audience as a fictional creation "audience invoked." They argue that an appreciation of both types of audience representation is necessary for a complete understanding of the "wide and shifting range of roles for both addressed and invoked audiences" in written discourse (p. 169). In my view, Ede and Lunsford are correct in suggesting that audience must be regarded as playing a "fluid, shifting role" in the production of written text and in their insistence that audience must be considered in relation to other elements of the rhetorical situation.

Figure 2. Continuum of Writer and Audience Representation in Written Discourse

Self-representation in written discourse must be regarded in a similar light since self-portrayal will vary according to the way in which audience and other factors of the rhetorical situation are characterized. This variation can be described as taking place along a continuum analogous to the one Ede and Lunsford suggest is anchored by "audience addressed" and "audience invoked," with *ethos* representing the writer's "real" self at one end and persona representing the writer's "fictional" self at the other, as depicted in Figure 2.

Both poles on the writer side of the continuum illustrated in Figure 2 represent modes of self-representation confined to the written text, or different "textual selves." Still, these poles represent different dimensions of self-portrayal in written discourse. At the *ethos* end of the continuum, writers garner credibility by identifying themselves as holding a certain position or having particular kinds of knowledge or experience, as well as by demonstrating their "practical wisdom" and showing a concern for the audience. At the persona end of the continuum, writers exercise their ability to portray the elements of the rhetorical situation to their advantage by fulfilling or creating a certain role (or roles) in the discourse community in which they are operating. Some examples will help to demonstrate the potential value of rethinking self-representation in written text in terms of the *ethos*-persona continuum.[16]

Distinguishing between *ethos* and persona might be useful in the analysis of referential discourse (Kinneavy, 1971). Recent work in the social construction of knowledge and the sociology of science, as well as a body of work in rhetorical theory that explores the notion of "rhetoric-as-epistemic," have helped to establish the view that scientific and technical discourse are inherently rhetorical.[17] The basic idea of this perspective on scientific and technical discourse is that scientific facts or knowledge are not "discovered" by individuals in isolation but established through consensus-building

---

[16]I have dropped the implied author from this continuum because it does not seem necessary or appropriate to maintain the notion of the implied author for nonliterary discourse. The idea of the implied author does have a distinct "literary" quality about it, as Booth's (1961) initial definition suggests: "We infer him as an ideal, *literary*, created version of the real man" (pp. 73-74; emphasis added).
[17]See Toulmin (1972) for the social construction of knowledge, and Ziman (1968) and Gilbert and Mulkay (1984) for the sociology of science. Leff (1978) provides a helpful review of the literature on epistemic approaches to rhetoric.

discourse in scientific communities.[18]

If scientific and technical writing are fundamentally rhetorical, then we would expect self-portrayal to play a significant role in texts that fall into this general discourse type.[19] Two recent studies of scientific and technical writing—one a general theoretical essay, the other a detailed analysis of specific texts—suggest the potential value of distinguishing between *ethos* and persona in referential discourse. Corbett (1981, p. 217) observes that

> it would be a mistake to conclude that the *ethos* of the writer does not play a crucial role in technical writing. In technical writing, writers must exert their *ethos* much more skillfully and subtly than writers of other kinds of prose do. The encoder of the technical report must strike a delicate balance between rigorous anonymity and obtrusive personality, for some measure of *ethos* must be present in the document. . . . Although an image of the writer must come through to the readers, the technical report is not the place for a "loud" personality. The personalities of Richard Selzer and Carl Sagan are probably too obtrusive in their writings; the personalities of Lewis Thomas and Jeremey Bernstein seem to strike the appropriate balance.

In these remarks Corbett seems to be distinguishing (albeit implicitly) between establishing credibility and creating a persona in scientific or technical discourse. Although we may not agree with Corbett's judgment of particular authors, and, more important, although we may not want to limit our notion of the persona to a consideration of "personality," it does seem as though something like the *ethos*/persona distinction is at work in his discussion. Corbett's examples raise the possibility that the relative weight of *ethos* and persona in a particular text could be in part conditioned by a concern for the intended audience—that is, specialist versus popular (see Fahnestock, 1986). Distinguishing between *ethos* and persona might be a helpful first step in understanding this phenomenon and provide a useful terminology for describing it.

Similarly, in Myers's (1985) treatment of "The Social Construction of Two Biologists' Proposals," there seems to be room for the *ethos*/persona distinction. Myers suggests that decisions about self-representation form a central concern for both of the scientists he studied; they are acutely aware that how they portray themselves in the text will have an effect on whether funding is granted for their proposals. Yet, as Myers notes, self-representation is problematic in rather different directions. On one hand, they must

---

[18]See Overington (1977), Miller (1979), and Bruffee (1986) for useful discussions of the implications of this view.

[19]This is essentially the position taken by Campbell (1975) in his treatment of "The *Personae* of Scientific Discourse." The trouble with Campbell's discussion, however, is that, because he is concerned almost exclusively with the ethics of scientific inquiry and the ways in which writers establish credibility in scientific discourse, his remarks are really more germane to a discussion of *ethos* than they are to a treatment of persona. Unfortunately, Campbell never mentions *ethos*.

demonstrate their competence as practitioners of science; they must show that previous experience renders them qualified to perform the work they are proposing. On the other hand, they must present themselves and the proposed work as innovative, capable of producing valuable new knowledge, and therefore worthy of funding. Some of Myers's remarks on self-portrayal seem clearly concerned with *ethos*:

> For David Bloch, a Professor of Botany, the main problem of the proposal was to demonstrate his competence in a speciality different from that for which he had been funded in the past. (p. 223)

> The tone of almost every sentence of a proposal can be revised to show that one is cautiously but competently scientific. (p. 227)

> Clearly both authors are concerned with sounding scientific as well as being scientific. (p. 228)

Others of Myers's comments seem directed toward a rather different dimension of self-representation the biologists are trying to accommodate:

> The process of writing a proposal is largely a process of presenting—or creating—in text one's role in the scientific community. (p. 221)

> The researcher who wants to verify his model of the origin of life presents himself as the skeptical servant of the mountains of data printed out by his computer program. The researcher who wants to spend five more years in painstaking studies of snakes and lizards presents himself as a theoretician studying a new conceptual framework. (p. 237)

Whereas the first three observations seem to describe the writers' concern for *ethos*, the latter two seem to describe their attention to persona. Myers's insightful analysis of the proposals makes it clear that he is well aware of the tension between these two dimensions of self-portrayal. Distinguishing between *ethos* and persona might give us a useful way of analyzing and describing this tension and thereby yield insights into the decisions writers must make about self-representation in scientific and technical discourse.

A final, and very different, example of the *ethos*/persona distinction may help to make clearer still the nature and potential value of the distinction. Writing tasks used for evaluating composing skills are often constructed in such a way that the writer is placed in a simulated rhetorical situation and given a certain role or persona (see, for example, Faigley, Cherry, Jolliffe, & Skinner, 1985; Lloyd-Jones, 1977; Mellon, 1975). An assumption behind such tasks appears to be that a fully delineated rhetorical situation provides a degree of realism that is necessary for giving students the best opportunity to demonstrate their writing abilities.

While the validity of this assumption is still being investigated in research on writing evaluation, the *ethos*/persona distinction gives us a way of thinking about the complexity of evaluation tasks that call upon students to produce discourse in response to hypothetical rhetorical situations. Consider, for example, a writing evaluation topic that calls upon a student to assume the identity of a fictional personage and create a text appropriate for that individual in a given situation. The student must create a *persona* appropriate for the fictional rhetorical situation, but at the same time must create an *ethos* that is appropriate for the *real* (i.e., evaluative) rhetorical situation. The writer must construct a multilevel representation of the rhetorical problem with a fictional rhetorical situation embedded within the larger (real) evaluation context and then accommodate the different demands for self-representation successfully. Because of the light it sheds on the inherent complexity of certain types of writing evaluation tasks, the distinction between *ethos* and persona could prove useful for an emerging theory of writing evaluation.[20]

Conclusion

It is useful in literary and rhetorical theory, as well as in the analysis of written discourse, to distinguish between the two vehicles of self-portrayal represented by *ethos* and persona. Because the two concepts have come down to us through different traditions, *ethos* and persona provide different perspectives on self-representation in written text. With its roots in the rhetorical tradition, *ethos* refers to a set of characteristics that, if attributed to a writer on the basis of textual evidence, will enhance the writer's credibility. Persona, on the other hand, traces its roots through literature and literary criticism and provides a way of describing the roles authors create for themselves in written discourse given their representation of audience, subject matter, and other elements of context. Just as skilled writers employ a wide range of strategies in conceiving and portraying their audience, so do they command linguistic resources that enable them to portray themselves in written text a way that contributes to the optimum effectiveness of a given text.

But even though it is useful to distinguish between *ethos* and persona, it would be overzealous to characterize the distinction in terms of binary opposition. *Ethos* and persona are not mutually exclusive but interact with one another in rather complex ways. Distinctions between the two modes of self-representation will be more pronounced in some cases than in others, and since they are both concerned with textual representation of the self, *ethos*, and persona do approach one another and in many cases no doubt overlap.

In fact, if Aristotle's concept of *ethos* was fully rejuvenated, it would serve some of the function I have ascribed to the persona. Technically, *ethos* is the more robust of the two concepts, and, on the *ethos*/persona continuum

---

[20]It is interesting to note that, in a recent discussion of essay topics, Hoetker and Brossell (1986) argue that the instructions given to students in writing evaluation tasks should be "brief and simple and should honestly and succinctly describe the real rhetorical occasion—i.e., the student is being asked to write a piece of examination prose that several readers (English teachers) are going to evaluate in such and such a way—rather than prescribing fictional voices and audiences" (p. 329).

proposed earlier, a full-fledged Aristotelian notion of *ethos* would reach farther toward persona than would persona toward *ethos*. Because the components of *ethos*—*phronesis, arete,* and *eunoia*—are socially determined, and because *ethos* involves adapting discourse to audiences, thinking of *ethos* in terms of "role," either in a discourse community or in a larger social sense, can be justified. Even so, *ethos* would never fully absorb persona, largely because literary artifice is so strongly associated with persona. Rhetorical theory has operated for some time now with a "reduced" notion of *ethos* that limits the concept basically to credibility. By proposing an *ethos*/persona continuum, I am trying to work within modern assumptions about *ethos* and persona and to take advantage of differences between the two concepts that can be discerned in the ways the two terms are currently used (when they are not conflated). It could be argued that perpetuating a truncated notion of *ethos* does a disservice to Aristotle, and this possibility does make me somewhat uneasy, but I think the prospect of advancing our understanding of self-representation in written discourse is worth the risk of offending Aristotle or Aristotelians.

It is only by discriminating among different dimensions of self-portrayal that we can be sensitive to how these dimensions interact with one another. When we approach self-representation starting with *ethos*, we assume a real author and look for the transformations the author will undergo as a result of appearing in print. When we begin with persona, we assume a degree of artifice or transformation and search for the real author. From either perspective, maintaining a distinction between *ethos* and persona can sharpen both rhetorical and literary criticism by giving us a means of differentiating and describing the multiple selves we project into written discourse and the changes in self-representation that might occur within a single written text.

Distinguishing between *ethos* and persona need not imply that we should reserve *ethos* for describing authorial presence in nonliterary texts and persona for treating authorial presence in literary texts. To the contrary, both notions may well be necessary for describing both types of discourse. While it is important to distinguish among them, the rhetorical concept of *ethos* and the (essentially) literary concepts of the persona and the implied author can complement and enrich one another. In literary discourse, *ethos* can be accompanied by other forms of self-portrayal best described in terms of persona. The relative prominence (and proportion) of *ethos* and persona in a given text will depend not only on the general discourse type but on the writer's representation of key elements in the rhetorical situation—that is, audience, subject matter, exigence, and the writer him- or herself.[21]

---

[21]Two additional caveats: (1) While it can be useful, the distinction between *ethos* and persona should not be rigidly applied in the study of written texts or, worse, applied merely for its own sake. I do not intend to make—and I am not suggesting that anyone else should make—an industry out of distinguishing between *ethos* and persona. Like all tools (conceptual and otherwise), the distinction should be applied where it is useful or necessary, not merely for the sake of applying the tool. (2) Although it may be a necessary addition to a theory of writing evaluation, the distinction between *ethos* and persona may well be too subtle to be immediately applicable to writing pedagogy.

Future inquiries to determine whether (and if so, how) writers and readers employ something such as the *ethos*/persona distinction in producing and comprehending written text are no doubt in order.[22] Judgments about writers play a key role in our evaluations of written discourse, and these judgments are not one dimensional. When we evaluate a writer's intelligence, integrity, and competence, we evaluate his or her basic character and credibility by assessing qualities that fall under the rubric of *ethos*. At the same time, when we make judgments about "voice" or "tone" and consider the role or roles the writer creates for him- or herself in the text, we evaluate qualities that fall under the rubric of persona.

My hope is that future studies will reveal in greater depth and detail the dynamics of self-representation in writing. I have been concerned in the present essay simply to identify some key issues in self-representation in written text and to clarify those issues by discriminating among concepts advanced in previous discussions of self-portrayal in rhetorical and literary theory. The essay has shown, I believe, that maintaining a distinction between *ethos* and persona is an important first step in investigating both the choices writers make and the judgments readers make about self-representation in written discourse.

---

[22]*Ethos* has been the subject of a great deal of research in speech communication; see Andersen and Clevenger (1963), McCroskey and Young (1981). It will be interesting to see the extent to which research findings in *ethos* in written discourse parallel the findings for spoken discourse.

References

Abrams, M. H. (1958). *The mirror and the lamp: Romantic theory and the critical tradition.* New York: W. W. Norton.

Andersen, K., & Clevenger, T., Jr. (1963). A summary of experimental research in ethos. *Speech Monographs, 30,* 59-78.

Aristotle. (1925). *The Nicomachean ethics* (D. Ross, Trans.). Oxford: Oxford University Press.

Aristotle. (1926). *The "art" of rhetoric* (J. H. Freese, Trans.). Cambridge, MA: Harvard University Press.

Aristotle. (1954). *Rhetoric* (W. R. Roberts, Trans.). New York: Random House.

Aristotle. (1962). *Nicomachean ethics* (M. Ostwald, Trans.). Indianapolis: Bobbs-Merrill.

Ball, P. M. (1964). Sincerity: The rise and fall of a critical term. *Modern Language Review, 59,* 1-11.

Bitzer, L. (1968). The rhetorical situation. *Philosophy and Rhetoric, 1,* 1-14.

Black, E. (1970). The second persona. *Quarterly Journal of Speech, 56,* 109-19.

Booth, W. C. (1961). *The rhetoric of fiction.* Chicago: University of Chicago Press.

Brinton, A. (1983). Quintilian, Plato, and the *vir bonus. Philosophy and Rhetoric, 16,* 167-184.

Bruffee, K. A. (1986). Social construction, language, and the authority of knowledge: A bibliographical essay. *College English, 48,* 773-790.

Campbell, P. N. (1975). The *personae* of scientific discourse. *Quarterly Journal of Speech, 61,* 391-405.

Cherniss, H. (1943). The biographical fashion in literary criticism. *University of California Publications in Classical Philology, 12,* 279-291.

Cicero. (1939). *Orator* (H. M. Hubbell, Trans.). Cambridge, MA: Harvard University Press.

Cicero. (1942). *De Orators* (E. W. Sutton & H. Rackham, Trans.). Cambridge, MA: Harvard University Press.

Clifford, J. L. (1965). The eighteenth century. *Modern Language Newsletter, 3,* 89-153.

Corbett, E. P. J. (1981). A rhetorician looks at technical writing. In J. C. Mathes & T. E. Pinelli (Eds.), *Technical communication: Perspectives for the eighties* (pp. 213-218). Washington, DC: NASA.

Corts, T. E. (1968). The derivation of ethos. *Speech Monographs, 35,* 201-202.

Craig, C. P. (1981). The *accusator* as *amicus*: An original Roman tactic of ethical argumentation. *Transactions of the American Philological Association, 111,* 31-37.

Crutwell, P. (1959/1960). Makers and persons. *Hudson Review, 12,* 487-507.

Davie, D. (1968). On sincerity: From Wordsworth to Ginsberg. *Encounter, 31,* 61-66.

Ede, L. (1984). Audience: An introduction to research. *College Composition and Communication, 35,* 140-154.

Ede, L., & Lunsford, A. (1984). Audience addressed/audience invoked: The role of audience in composition theory and pedagogy. *College Composition and Communication, 35,* 155-171.

Efron, A. (1966). Untitled statement in The concept of the persona in satire: A symposium. *Satire Newsletter, 3,* 100-108.

Ehrenpreis, I. (1963). Personae. In C. Camden (Ed.), *Restoration and eighteenth-century literature: Studies in honor of Alan Dugald McKillop* (pp. 25-37). Chicago: University of Chicago Press.

Elbow, P. (1987). Closing my eyes as I speak: An argument for ignoring audience. *College English, 49,* 50-69.

Elliott, R. C. (1982). *The literary persona.* Chicago: University of Chicago Press.

Enos, R. L, & McClaran, J. (1978). Audience and image in Ciceronian Rome: Creation and constraints of the *vir bonus* personality. *Central States Speech Journal, 29,* 98-106.

Fahnestock, J. (1986). Accommodating science: The rhetorical life of scientific facts. *Written Communication, 3,* 275-296.

Faigley, L., Cherry, R. D., Jolliffe, D. A., & Skinner, A. M. (1985). *Assessing writers' knowledge and processes of composing.* Norwood, NJ: Ablex.

Feinberg, L. (1966). Untitled statement in The concept of the persona in satire: A symposium. *Satire Newsletter, 3,* 108-111.

Flower, L., & Hayes, J. R. (1980). The cognition of discovery: Defining a rhetorical problem. *College Composition and Communication, 31,* 21-32.

Friedman, N. (1955). Point of view in fiction: The development of a critical concept. *Publications of the Modern Language Association, 70,* 1160-1184.

Gerber, J. C. (1967). Literature: Our untamable discipline. *College English, 28,* 351-358.

Gibson, W. (1969). *Persona: A style study for readers and writers.* New York: Random House.

Gilbert, G. N., & Mulkay, M. (1984). *Opening Pandora's box: A sociological analysis of scientists' discourse.* Cambridge: Cambridge University Press.

Grant, W. L. (1943). Cicero on the moral character of the orator. *Classical Journal, 38,* 472-478.

Halloran, S. M. (1982). Aristotle's concept of ethos, or if not his somebody else's. *Rhetoric Review, 1,* 58-63.

Highet, G. (1974). Masks and faces in satire. *Hermes, 102,* 321-337.

Hoetker, J., & Brossell, G. (1986). A procedure for writing content-fair essay examination topics for large-scale writing assessments. *College Composition and Communication, 37,* 328-335.

Jaeger, W. (1945). *Paideia: The ideals of Greek culture* (Vol. 1, 2nd ed.) (G. Highet, Trans.). New York: Oxford University Press.

Johnson, N. (1984). Ethos and the aims of rhetoric. In R. J. Connors, L. S. Ede, & A. A. Lunsford (Eds.), *Essays on classical rhetoric and modern discourse* (pp. 98-114). Carbondale: Southern Illinois University Press.

Kinneavy, J. L. (1971). *A theory of discourse.* Englewood Cliffs, NJ: Prentice-Hall.

Kroll, B. (1984). Writing for readers: Three perspectives on audience. *College Composition and Communication, 35,* 172-185.

Leff, M. C. (1978). In search of Ariadne's thread: A review of the recent literature on rhetorical theory. *Central States Speech Journal, 29,* 73-91.

Lloyd-Jones, R. (1977). Primary trail scoring. In C. R. Cooper & L. Odell (Eds.), *Evaluating writing* (pp. 33-66). Urbana: National Council of Teachers of English.

Long, R. C. (1980). Writer-audience relationships: Analysis or invention? *College Composition and Communication, 31,* 221-226.

Mack, M. (1982). The muse of satire. In M. Mack (Ed.), *Collected in himself: Essays critical, biographical, and bibliographical on Pope and some of his contemporaries* (pp. 55-64). Newark: University of Delaware Press.

MacKendrick, P. (1948). Cicero's ideal orator: Truth and propaganda. *Classical Journal, 43,* 339-347.

McCroskey, J., & Young, T. J. (1981). Ethos and credibility: The construct and its measurement after three decades. *Central States Speech Journal, 32,* 24-34.

McKeon, Z. K. (1982). *Novels and arguments: Inventing rhetorical criticism.* Chicago: University of Chicago Press.

Mellon, J. C. (1975). *National assessment and the teaching of English.* Urbana: National Council of Teachers of English.

Miller, A. B. (1974). Aristotle on habit (ἔθος) and character (ἦθος): Implications for the *Rhetoric. Speech Monographs, 41,* 309-316.

Miller, C. R. (1979). A humanistic rationale for technical writing. *College English, 40,* 610-17.

Minot, W. (1981). Response to Russell C. Long, "Writer-audience relationships: Analysis or invention?" *College Composition and Communication, 32,* 335-337.

Myers, G. (1985). The social construction of two biologists' proposals. *Written Communication, 2,* 219-245.

Odell, L., & Goswami, D. (1982). Writing in a non-academic setting. *Research in the Teaching of English, 16,* 201-223.

Odell, L., Goswami, D., Herrington, A., & Quick, D. (1983). Studying writing in non-academic settings. In P. V. Anderson, R. J. Brockmann, & C. R. Miller (Eds.), *New essays in technical and scientific communication* (pp. 17-40). Farmingdale, NY: Baywood.

Ong, W. J. (1975). The writer's audience is always a fiction. *Publications of the Modern Language Association, 90,* 9-21.

Overington, M. A. (1977). The scientific community as audience: Toward a rhetorical analysis of science. *Philosophy and Rhetoric, 10,* 143-164.

Park, D. B. (1986). Analyzing audience. *College Composition and Communication, 37,* 478-488.

Park, D. B. (1982). The meanings of "audience." *College English, 44,* 247-257.

Romilly, J. de. (1958). Eunoia in Isocrates or the political importance of creating good will. *Journal of Hellenic Studies, 78,* 92-101.

Rosenthal, P. I. (1966). The concept of ethos and the structure of persuasion. *Speech Monographs, 33,* 114-126.

Roth, R. G. (1987). The evolving audience: Alternatives to audience accommodation. *College Composition and Communication, 38,* 47-55.

Sattler, W. M. (1941). *Conceptions of ethos in rhetoric.* Unpublished doctoral dissertation, Northwestern University.

Sattler, W. M. (1947). Conceptions of *ethos* in ancient rhetoric. *Speech Monographs, 14,* 55-65.

Self, L. (1979). Rhetoric and *phronesis:* The Aristotelian ideal. *Philosophy and Rhetoric, 12,* 130-145.

Tillyard, E. M. W., & Lewis, C. S. (1939). *The personal heresy: A controversy.* London: Oxford University Press.

Toulmin, S. (1972). *Human understanding.* Princeton, NJ: Princeton University Press.

Trilling, L. (1972). *Sincerity and authenticity.* Cambridge, MA: Harvard University Press.

Vatz, R. E. (1973). The myth of the rhetorical situation. *Philosophy and Rhetoric, 6,* 154-161.

Wimsatt, W. K., Jr., & Beardsley, M. C. (1967). The intentional fallacy. In *The verbal icon.* Lexington: University of Kentucky Press.

Wright, G. T. (1960). *The poet in the poem: The personae of Eliot, Yeats, and Pound.* Berkeley: University of California Press.

Yoos, G. (1979). A revision of the concept of ethical appeal. *Philosophy and Rhetoric, 12,* 41-58.

Ziman, J. (1968). *Public knowledge: The social dimension of science.* Cambridge: Cambridge University Press.

Judging Writing, Judging Selves

by Lester Faigley

One of the effects of the writing-as-process movement has been to change the way many teachers evaluate student writing. While most teachers of writing still assign grades to papers at some point in the course of instruction, the emphasis has shifted from summative to formative evaluation, or, in the language of process advocates, from a teacher's role as judge to one of coach. Nancy Sommers and others have taught us that evaluative comments on students' texts should serve as aids in revising rather than as justifications of particular grades. While many of us have been influenced by these discussions, the literature on writing evaluation restricts the process of evaluation to the *means* of evaluation, largely teachers' and peers' responses to student writing. This literature tends to assume that a broad consensus exists about what constitutes good writing and that we can recognize good writing when we see it.

Absent from most current discussions of evaluation is an older notion of process reflected in the etymology of the term. The Latin roots of *evaluation* are *ex* + VALUE—to be "out of" or "from" value. Each judgment of value is made from some notion of value, usually a notion that is widely shared within a culture. College writing research in the disciplinary period which began, roughly, in the mid 1960s has not told us much about exactly what it is that teachers value in student writing. Researchers who have used statistical methodologies to address this question have thrown little light on the issue. The only consistent finding has been that the length of essays is associated with judgments of quality.[1] Textbooks, by and large, are of little help because they speak of good writing in general terms such as those Michael Adelstein and Jean Pival use to define good writing: "clear," "concise," "effective," "interesting," and projecting "the authentic voice of the writer" (6). And

---

Reprinted from *College Composition and Communication* (December 1989). Copyright 1989 by the National Council of Teachers of English. Reprinted with permission.

[1] See Diederich for further discussion. Statistical analyses of text features in student writing that predict readers' judgments of quality have not produced striking results. For example, Kerek, Daiker, and Morenberg found that papers written by college freshmen who were taught sentence combining for one semester were rated higher in quality than those of a group taught by a traditional method. The students taught sentence combining also increased significantly in the syntactic measures of clause and T-unit length. But when the researchers analyzed the extent to which syntactic factors of clause and T-unit length influenced readers' judgments, they found that the measures were almost unrelated to the assessments of writing quality. In other words, the readers of these papers were not bowled over by the sentence combiners' syntactic dexterity; indeed, they hardly noticed it.

guidelines published by English departments—at least at places where I've taught—are even less specific. An "A" paper is one that "displays unusual competence"; hence, an "A" paper is an "A" paper.

One explanation of why definitions of good writing are either circular or absent altogether is that in recent decades we have been using the wrong criteria to explain our judgments. If we look at the history of writing instruction in America, we find that writing teachers have been as much or more interested in *who* they want their students to be as in *what* they want their students to write.[2] To examine assumptions about selves in writing evaluation, I will contrast a report reviewing a 1929 test in English that was used for making college admissions decisions with a recent collection of "best" student essays, Coles and Vopat's *What Makes Writing Good*, a collection that is especially valuable for this project because it includes commentary from the teachers who nominated the student examples. But before I proceed to these analyses, I want to discuss briefly some recent theorizing about the self in discourse.

Constructing Selves in Discourse

One of the most troubling ideas for the humanities and the social sciences in the last two decades is the "decentering" of the individual subject from the atomic, rational consciousness of Descartes to a socially constructed self located in networks of discourses. The unified, individual consciousness coterminous with the physical body turns out not to be the "natural" self but a Western version with specific historical and economic origins. Members of English departments know this critique of individual consciousness largely through the work of European theorists labeled "structuralists" and "poststructuralists" and through secondary applications, but there have been other critiques of Western notions of individualism. For example, Takeo Doi spends an entire book trying to explain the Japanese concept of *amae,* which is an emotional concept of the self that extends beyond the individual to encompass others. Doi discusses how this non-Western concept of self leads to what Westerners perceive as contradictions in Japanese society: "Only a mentality rooted in *amae* could produce a people at once so unrealistic yet so clearsighted as to the basic human condition; so compassionate and so self-centered; so spiritual and so materialistic; so forebearing and so wilful; so docile and so violent—a people, in short, that from its own point of view is preeminently normal and human in every respect" (9-10). Doi gets at why

---

[2] From the early national period through most of the nineteenth century, literacy was associated with Protestant and nationalistic values (Heath, Spring). By the turn of the century justifications for the teaching of literacy as well as the materials themselves had become more secular in character (Applebee). See Trachsel for an excellent review of the vast literature on writing assessment that arose along with the growth of college English departments and the use of essay examinations for college admissions in the first decades of the twentieth century.

conceptions of self are difficult to describe from within a culture: they appear obvious and natural to insiders.

The notion of a socially constructed self has been discussed in anthropology for several decades. In 1938 Marcell Mauss argued that the idea of the individual self is uniquely Western. A great deal of ethnographic evidence has been gathered that supports Mauss' position, and more recently anthropologists have examined the ways in which languages embody notions of the self. One reason why the idea of the self as an autonomous, individual consciousness is plausible in the West is that the grammars of European languages are compatible with notions of individualism. In European languages the fact that "I" or "*yo*" or "*je*" or '*ich*" refers indexically to the speaker of the utterance suggests that the speaker possesses an autonomous consciousness and at the same time is aware of that consciousness. But in certain non-European languages the "I" can in some circumstances refer to others as well as the speaker. Greg Urban has found that in Shokleng, a Brazilian Amerindian language, "I" can point both to the speaker's physical self and to an imaginary self that maintains reference with third-person forms. The subjectivity constructed in Shokleng discourse, therefore, can extend beyond the individual body to assume multiple voices, constituting a self that is distinctly cultural.

How selves are constructed in discourse has also been the focus of much recent literary theory, especially in British poststructuralism. A useful introduction to British poststructuralism is Catherine Belsey's *Critical Practice*. Belsey describes two metaphors for language that have dominated during the nineteenth and twentieth centuries: one the empiricist metaphor of language as the transparent window on reality, the other the expressivist metaphor of language as the vehicle for projecting the thoughts and emotions of the individual (also see Morgan). She shows how these seemingly contradictory metaphors both assume that language originates within the minds of individuals. Belsey calls the merger of the two metaphors "expressive realism." While different versions of expressive realism may privilege the individual pysche over perceived reality or vice versa, all versions share the assumptions that language exists outside of history and is innocent of politics.

Realism from classical Greece onward assumes that language can transmit directly what is signified. With the Romantics came the belief that emotions could be transmitted as well; hence literature and art became both mimetic and expressive. The task of the author, poet, or artist was seen as twofold: the artist must represent reality accurately and convey to the viewer the heightened emotions that the artist has experienced. This theory treats the experience of reading as unproblematic. The universal "truths" contained in great art and literature are available to anyone with adequate facilities to discern them. That readers might be from different cultures, of different genders, and from different social classes does not matter because reading is perceived as the one-way flow from one autonomous mind to another, and the text is a self-contained object for passive consumption. While the implications of expressive realism for the reading of literature have been widely studied in the 1980s, the consequences for the teaching of writing have only begun to be investigated.

High and Solitary Minds

Assumptions from expressive realism were commonplace in college English pedagogy before World War II, both in writing and in literature courses. In the period between the world wars several approaches to the teaching of writing competed—a few of them quite innovative—but as Berlin notes, an Arnoldian view of English studies dominated during this period. The writing courses at Eastern colleges in particular were based on reading and responding to great works of literature. The student subject was elevated by the experiences of reading great literature and drew moral lessons from those experiences. A broad explication of these assumptions can be found in *Examining the Examination in English,* a 1931 report of an external review of the College Entrance Examination Board's 1929 examination in English.

Authentic Voices

The assumptions underlying the evaluation of the writing of college students today would seem much more complex than in 1931. In a nation where over half of those who graduate from high school go on to college, distinctions made among students according to their responses to canonical literature have become much less relevant; indeed, the teaching of canonical literature as the primary subject matter for writing courses has diminished considerably since World War II, leaving no single model of writing instruction to replace it. Given the resulting multiplicity of approaches to the teaching of writing, the relationships between assumptions about "good" writing and the privileging of particular selves among our students would seem more difficult to analyze than ever. But if we should not expect to locate a well-articulated set of assumptions such as Ruskin's and Arnold's statements on expressive realism, neither should we pretend that current assumptions cannot be identified. Stephen North describes current assumptions about teaching writing as a "House of Lore," a sprawling collection of rooms built from a variety of materials without a blueprint or regard for the coherence of the overall structure. North's house-of-lore metaphor is in some ways similar to recent efforts to explain the workings of ideology, which likewise is constructed without overall design and contains many contradictions. But contemporary theorists (e.g., Therborn, Thompson) understand ideology as a fluid process rather than a structure of ideas, constantly being renegotiated and, at the same time, reconstituting those who are subjected to an ideology. The means of constructing subjectivities within an ideology is through discourses such as those of expressive realism. In Althusser's influential critique, discourses interpellate human beings by offering them an array of subject positions that people recognize, just as when a person turns when someone shouts "hey, you." The term *subject* contains a pun. People are *subjected* to dominant ideologies, but because they recognize themselves in the subject positions that discourses provide, they believe they are *subjects* of their own actions. The recognition, therefore, is a misrecognition because people fail to see that the subject positions they occupy are historically produced, and they imagine that they are freely choosing for themselves. Theorists following Althusser analyze the self in discourse as neither the personality of the speaker/writer nor the rhetorical notion of *persona* but as a composite of subject positions and active in the reproduction of those positions (e.g., Easthope, Weedon).

For a description of the selves that writing teachers now privilege in "good" writing, William Coles and James Vopat's *What Makes Writing Good* is an extremely valuable source of data. Coles and Vopat describe the idea for the book as coming in a conversation following Coles' presentation at the 1981 Wyoming Conference on Freshman and Sophomore English. After Coles had discussed what he considered the best student paper he had ever received, the editors speculated on what sorts of writing other teachers might select. They asked 48 teachers to contribute one example of student writing that "in some way demonstrates excellence," along with the writing assignment and a commentary explaining how the example is distinguished. It's hard to imagine a broader range of contributors, extending from distinguished theorists (e.g., Wayne Booth, James Britton, Edward Corbett), to empirical researchers (e.g., Linda Flower, Andrea Lunsford), to technical writing teachers (e.g., Paul Anderson, Carolyn Miller), to linguists (e.g., James Sledd, Joseph Williams), to practicing writers (e.g., Donald Murray, Roger Sale), and representing diverse viewpoints (e.g., Donald Stewart, Frank D'Angelo, William Irmscher, Richard Young, Walker Gibson, David Bleich, Richard Ohmann). But the range of contributors is not matched by a similar range of student writing. By my count at least 30 of the examples in the collection are personal experience essays—20 of them autobiographical narratives—and several of the remaining 18 include writing about the writer. Only four examples are in the genres of professional writing (two letters and two reports). Four examples discuss briefly works of literature, but there is no literary analysis paper of the kind described in rhetoric texts. Only two essays present sustained analyses of other texts. One of them is an essay nominated by James Vopat on Studs Terkel's *Working,* and the other, nominated by Joseph Williams, contrasts the first two speeches in Thucydides' *History of the Peloponnesian War.* Not one essay resembles the frequently assigned "research paper."

I have no simple explanation for the strong preference for autobiographical essays. Perhaps it is because, as Michael Holzman suggests in commenting on the narrative he nominated, our students "have some highly unusual stories to tell" (156). But the commentaries on the autobiographical narratives suggest something more is involved than their engaging quality. Several teachers mention that while the particular example they discuss is flawed (spelling and mechanical errors are reproduced), the student achieves excellence because he or she is either "honest" (James Britton, Roger Garrison, Larry Levy, Erika Lindemann), writes in an "authentic voice"

(Harvey Daniels, Leo Rockas), or possesses "integrity" (Walker Gibson). For example, Erika Lindemann says, "Good writing is most effective when we tell the truth about who we are and what we think. What makes Norma's [the student writer] paper, 'At the Beach,' so powerful is that she is honest about her feelings toward her parents" (161). Norma Bennett's paper is a narrative of a summer vacation spent with her two divorced parents who now go to different resorts. Her mother wears her PTL jacket (in the days before Jim and Tammy's fall) and spends much of the day either sleeping or sobbing. Her potbellied father also spends much of the day sleeping—passed out drunk on the beach with a 25-year-old woman in a white string bikini while the writer babysits the woman's young child. I have a great deal of sympathy for students like Norma Bennett, who must cope with difficult family situations as well as the pressures of college, but why is writing about potentially embarrassing and painful aspects of one's life considered more honest than, say, the efforts of Joe Williams' student, Greg Shaefer, who tries to figure out what Thucydides was up to in writing about the Peloponnesian War?

James Britton and his colleague, Steve Seaton, make comments similar to Lindemann's about a student narrating her parents' reactions to her boyfriends: "In our view, a principal virtue of Maggie's writing is in its *honesty;* one reads it with a continuing sense of the writer's struggle to say what she means and mean what she says" (79; emphasis in original). Britton and Seaton claim "that for her to write with such honesty on the topic of family relationships betokens an unusual trust in the reader she has in mind, her teacher. Such a relationship of trust must be the outcome of successful teaching of this class over a period of time—something that must be *earned,* can't be *demanded"* (79; emphasis in original). I don't understand why, as Britton and Seaton suggest, receiving such papers from students is a benchmark of successful writing instruction. I have read narratives written for large-scale writing assessments that deal with intense personal events such as the experience of being raped, yet the writer had no knowledge of who would read the paper or what would become of it.

Several of the commentaries on the autobiographical narratives imply that autobiographical writing is more "truthful" than nonautobiographical writing. Larry Levy says, "I wanted students to develop a response beyond stereotype and mass culture to their own questions" (125). Stephen Tchudi says, "I hope to engage students in writing from their own experience. I also want to push my freshmen away from writing the standard 'five paragraph' freshman theme, with its canned openings, wooden organizational structures, obligatory endings" (175). Roger Garrison declares, "Good writing is inevitably honest writing. Every writer, beginner or not, needs what Hemingway called 'a built-in crap detector.' All of us, like it or not, are daily immersed in tides of phony, posturing, pretentious, tired, imprecise, slovenly language, which both suffocate and corrupt the mind" (273). I don't doubt these teachers' claims that assigning autobiographical narratives often produces a freshness of insight that students might not achieve with typical transactional forms of student writing such as the standard research paper. As Harvey Daniels wryly observes, autobiographical papers can be "a welcome burst of enjoyment amid the often dreary and endless process of evaluating student work" (260).

In several of the commentaries on the autobiographical narratives, however, is an assumption that individuals possess an identifiable "true" self and that the true self can be expressed in discourse. This same assumption even carries into the student essays. Peggy Bloxam, James Vopat's student who writes about degradation in Studs Terkel's *Working,* summarizes the stories the workers tell about their jobs:

> These people all feel degraded, and no wonder. They are lowering their moral and intellectual standards to meet the demands of a job. In a sense, they are denying their true selves and imposing over it a false self. (351)

Bloxam then cleverly equates writing about degradation to the workers' degradation:

> I sit and stare at a piece of paper when I could be writing a paper for a different class. These are degrading circumstances because they are limiting the real potential of the worker. Here, too, a false self possessing characteristics totally divorced from those of the real self has taken over. (351)

Bloxam's distinction sounds like and perhaps even draws on the traditional Marxist concept of ideology as "false consciousness," a distorting lens imposed on the working class concealing their true selves. The question which remains for both traditional Marxists and "authentic voice" proponents is how do we distinguish the true self?

One of the autobiographical narratives in *What Makes Writing Good* offers a good example for analyzing notions of the self because the teacher, Rebecca Faery, speaks of the student's essay as a way "to lay claim to the self she is in the process of becoming" (334). Below is the essay that the student, Lindsay Lankford, wrote:

> My post office box is empty today, as it is almost every day. To peer inside is always an afterthought, seldom rewarded. Once a month, though, I'm assured of mail. C & P Telephone Company loves me, and sends me nice long bills, each call marked in minutes and money owed. These bills, and the stubs in my checkbook from their payment, are all that remain of past communications. The telephone, however, is fast and easy to use. Letters can take days, sometimes weeks to reach their destination. Furthermore, writing letters involves a great deal of time and effort; yet letters have some very real advantages.
>
> I spent a year in Paris and quickly discovered that transatlantic phone calls were not within my budget. So I was left with that most archaic mode of communication, the letter. And I loved it. Every Sunday morning was devoted to my weekly letter home, a letter which often took all morning. I'd go through the whole week in memory, and re-live it. I'd go to the *tabac,* and remember how

pleased I was when the little man with his dirty black apron complimented my slowly improving French. Or I'd be in the Jeu de Paume, and feel again the excitement I felt when I finally learned to love Cezanne. I'd recall how bitterly and miserably cold I was last Thursday, and how really good the coffee tasted in that cafe near Sacre Coeur. I'd remember walking out of Notre Dame at seven p.m., after an hour of warm and rich Vivaldi, and finding Paris dusted with snow, glinting and sparkling in the streetlights. Or summer nights in the Latin Quarter, drinking *vin ordinaire* in outdoor cafes, talking too much about Life and Art and the Future, subjects that are always and can only be discussed after too much wine.

My Sunday letters were the times when I put these vignettes together, and made my memories concrete and coherent. Mama has kept these letters for me, in a manila folder in the top drawer of her Louis XV desk. And whenever I want them, whenever I want to remember, they are there for me. For although I addressed them to Mama and Daddy, they were always written essentially to myself. Mama and Daddy saw Europe through my eyes, with my perceptions and impressions. My letters were unselfconscious and utterly honest, for the time and space lag between letters made intimacy easier. My parents learned more about me from a year of letters than they had in nineteen years of personal interaction.

I loved their letters to me, too. They were never filled with earth-shattering news, but they revealed a lot. Actually, most people's lives are dull; it's the way they perceive their lives that is interesting. My sister Allison lives in the Negev Desert, in a tiny trailer. Her world consists of her husband, their two small children, and very little else. Her letters were always wrinkled, smeared with something sticky, covered in crayons and written over extended periods of time. They were a mess: descriptions of the gingerbread village Allison had made for the Christmas party, their plans for moving back to the States, Lauren's latest word, and details of Elizabeth's third birthday party. Allison's letters were disjointed, but ebullient. Living on an army base in the Israeli desert would seem a barren existence, yet Allison's letters describe a busy and happy, if somewhat chaotic, life.

I saw Mama's world through her letters. With her eyes and her words, I saw the spring I was missing in Birmingham, how bright the azaleas were, how she'd never seen so many dogwoods in bloom. I realized how acute her perceptions are, how she notices the little details. She wrote of the garden, of the ever-growing, never-ending crop of green beans. Of the squirrel without a tail, how well he had adapted. From her letters, I knew how empty the house felt when Daddy was away on business, and then how cozy it was when he returned and they made great pots of seafood gumbo together. Mama's sphere is small: her house, her friends and her husband. Yet her letters taught me that her deep awareness of her world gave it its richness.

Daddy didn't write much, but his few letters were remarkable for what they revealed. Daddy is sixty-two and still passionate about learning. Daddy, who had one year of French in college and that forty years ago, wrote to me in French. My mental image of Daddy in his office, surrounded by French dictionary and grammar book, is very precious. I treasure the idea of Daddy as the student, instead of the one who knows all. And what Daddy can't say in English, he can write in French: *Je t'aime* ended every letter.

My post office box is empty today, and very likely to remain so tomorrow. For we've all slipped back into old patterns, old ways of communicating. Sometimes, we still find time to send little notes, notes written in haste and without much pleasure. These new letters are little more than abbreviations of the details we once vividly described. I think we all miss our old letters, although we neither discuss nor write them anymore. The barriers are back up. We're careful again, wary of the reckless revelations we once shared. The physical distances between us are less now; cautiously, we distance ourselves in spirit.

I've still got those old letters. They are priceless to me. For writing deals harshly with the banal, the superficial. The things we say to each other can seldom survive on paper. The things we dare to write are those we really mean. (330-32)

Lankford shows an awareness of the essay as a form, beginning with phone bills and check stubs as images of writing in our culture, juxtaposing scenes of intercontinental letter writing, then deftly returning to the empty post office box at the end. She wrote the essay in an advanced expository writing class, a course where Faery says, "I am most attracted by the idea of exposition as an act that, at best, *exposes* or *reveals* the truth about something" (332; emphasis in original). The truth Faery finds in Lankford's essay is "a harsh one, because she passes an unmerciful judgment on our era, which has dispensed with the practice of writing as a way of developing a picture of the world and of forming connections and relationships which make people feel at home in it and not alone" (335).

I too am touched by this essay. I enjoy getting long letters from overseas, and I would like to imagine my children writing long letters to me someday. I don't doubt Lankford's sincerity about the disappointment of going to the mailbox after a year of receiving letters from family and friends on other continents. At the same time, I'm struck by how similar student and teacher sound. Lankford plays teacher/critic when she describes her sister's letters as "disjointed but ebullient," praises her mother's inclusion of "little details," and lauds her father's efforts at brushing up his French. I'm also struck by how closely the description of Paris matches the one I formed from images in films and novels before I visited the multicultural city. From Vivaldi at Notre Dame to the value of writing, the truths "exposed" and "revealed" in the essay are a series of recognitions for a college English teacher. What else did she see in Paris?

Let me put it a different way. Could Lankford have written a similar essay if she had visited a place unfamiliar to us? Within a mile of my house in Austin, Texas, immigrant Mexican families have lived temporarily in storm sewers. What if Lankford had gone to live with them? Could she have written in the same way about her elation when they complimented her slowly improving Spanish? Would the warmth of their fire have felt as good as the warmth of coffee in the cafe near Sacre Coeur? Would her mother have written to her about the blooming dogwoods and the squirrel without a tail? Would her father have closed by saying *Te quiero* instead of *Je t'aime?* Most of all, would Lankford have discovered the value of letter writing as a means of calling attention to the plight of the immigrants and getting help for them?

I'm not advocating that our students adopt 1930s Soviet-style social realism as their model. The point is that Lankford's skill is demonstrated in assembling a series of subject positions. By bringing the essay effectively to closure at the end, she creates the illusion of a unified and knowing self that overviews the world around it. The epigrammatic conclusion reaffirms that she is the source of her language, that as she puts it, "The things we dare to write are those we really mean." Lankford agrees with "authentic voice" proponents that language transparently reveals what is going on in our consciousness. Because the self Lankford constructs is sensible and knowing, we trust her perceptions of reality—the characterizations of her father as the executive who continues to study, her mother as the homemaker who misses her father when he is away, and her sister as the busy mother of two small children. We "recognize" these people because they occupy familiar positions in middle-class nuclear families. It is the very ease of these recognitions— their natural and common-sense quality—that troubles many feminist scholars. Lankford's mother and sister may well be happy in, as Lankford puts it, their small spheres. Many other women, however, have sought to expand their own small spheres only to be confronted with patriarchal discourses that define a woman's chief concerns in relation to men and her family.

Not all of the student writers attempt to smooth over the contradictions inherent in the concept of a self. Coles' own "best" essay—the one he offered at the Wyoming Conference and the one that inspired the volume—is also an autobiographical narrative, written in response to the question "What is the proper metaphor with which to define a university so far as you are concerned?" Unlike most of the other autobiographical narratives in the Coles and Vopat collection, it does not present a unified subject position nor does it finally decide on a single metaphor for the university. The student writer, George Humphrey, weaves together several conflicting discourses and images that college students experience without attempting to resolve the conflicts. Here are the last three paragraphs of Humphrey's twelve-paragraph essay:

> I used to have conversations about D. H. Lawrence with a friend in the elevator. It started one day when I noticed a copy of *The*

Rainbow under his arm, and he noticed a copy under mine. The conversations did not last long—just long enough for the elevator to get from the 6th floor to the lobby, but now the only time I see my friend is in a class we have together. We say hello, but that is about all we say.

My wife has started to read Lawrence, though, and I talk with her about him.

Sometimes in our apartment we're conscious of the Rapid going by; sometimes we're not. (325)

Coles says of the paper, "the proper metaphor for the university then, this writer suggests, is whatever meaning a university student can make at any given moment of the many kinds of self-consciousness a university is designed to promote" (327). Coles apparently comes to this insight by way of psychoanalytic theory. If one grants the possibility of an unconscious mind, then the question of insincerity becomes moot. How can one possibly express one's *full* self, including the unconscious part? And what if one is sincerely expressing one's conscious self but unconsciously repressing something that remains unexpressed? Is the writer sincere or insincere?

A defender of Coles, Joseph Harris, says the problem with defining good writing as honest writing "is that it reduces writing to a simple test of integrity. Either your guts are out there on the page or they're not. It's easy to see, then, why so many students are baffled or intimidated when we ask them to write about what they really know. For what do they really know?" (161). To ask students to write authentically about the self assumes that a rational consciousness can be laid out on the page. That the self must be interpellated through language is denied. It is no wonder, then, that the selves many students try to appropriate in their writing are voices of authority, and when they exhaust their resources of analysis, they revert to moral lesson, adopting, as Bartholomae has noted, a parental voice making cliched pronouncements where we expect ideas to be extended.

If Harris is right in claiming that Coles has been widely misunderstood within the profession, perhaps it is because recognizing the sources of contradictory and incompatible discourses in student writing runs squarely against both the expressivist and rationalist traditions of teaching writing that deny the role of language in constructing selves. Those who encourage "authentic voices" in student writing often speak of giving students "ownership" of a text or "empowering" students. The former conflates the capitalist notion of property rights (as when my creative writing colleagues down the hall talk about selling the movie rights to their books) with autobiographical writing. The latter notion sounds like something we all support (for who among us would "disempower" students?), but it avoids the question of how exactly teachers are to give students power. Is it in self-expression or is it in earning power? The freedom students are given in some classes to choose and adapt autobiographical assignments hides the fact that these same students will be judged by the teachers' unstated cultural definitions of the self.

These definitions have changed significantly since 1931 when *Examining the Examination in English* was published, but certain assumptions have lingered. While we no longer hold that the experience of reading literature will directly lead students to a position of heightened awareness, judging from many of the essays in *What Makes Writing Good*, teachers of college writing are still very much concerned with the self. I am not suggesting that a single notion of self is shared by those who speak of an "authentic voice," but the assumptions can be traced historically. Modern American notions of individual self derive in part from nineteenth-century liberalism and utilitarianism, which in turn drew on Thomas Hobbes' theory of the atomic, self-interested self. The blend of economics and psychology in these notions of self remains evident in writing pedagogy. The ease with which writing textbooks tout the economic advantages of writing indicates the extent to which the Hobbsian concept of self-interest endures. Sheridan Baker begins *The Practical Stylist* with a section titled "Writing for Your Share." Baker advises students: "Your composition course prepares you for the challenges not only of college but of the business of life ahead, whether in the executive suite or the courtroom, the hospital or the consulate, the legislature or the press room" (2). For Baker "the business of life" is life in business.

Nevertheless, economic explanations do not account fully for the reproduction of notions of individualism in writing instruction. Marcel Mauss's historical study of the idea of self gives us some indication of the depth and scope of the concept. Mauss found that the concept of self arose in medieval Christianity but that the self as a discrete philosophical category developed in the seventeenth and eighteenth centuries culminating in the work of Kant and Fichte, where every action is the act of individual consciousness. Mauss recognized that Western notions of self make other notions opaque or invisible. What has been added since 1938 to Mauss' theory of the social construction of the self are theories of how notions of the self are interpellated in particular discourses. For example, the often quoted beginning of Foucault's "The Discourse on Language" alludes to how institutions persuade reluctant writers and speakers to believe that there is a place and voice for everyone in official discourses.

The self in student autobiographies, then, is not one that emerges like a butterfly from a chrysalis as Faery implies when she names the subject position in Lankford's essay as "the self she is becoming," but one that is discursively produced and discursively bounded. The student selves we encounter in *What Makes Writing Good* are predominantly selves that achieve rationality and unity by characterizing former selves as objects for analysis, hence the emphasis on writing about past experience rather than confronting the contradictions of present experience as does Coles' student George Humphrey. The teachers' commentaries on the narratives of past experience imply that success in teaching depends on making a student aware of the desired subject position she will occupy. Wayne Booth's student, Michael Fitzgerald, says of himself: "I know that I have a long way to go, but I want to get there" (292), and Booth ends his comment with the sentence, "He is on his way" (297). But where is he going? It is this notion of the student writer as a developing rational consciousness that makes most talk of *empowerment* so confused. Even though the ability to write in certain discourses is highly valued in technologically advanced nations, power is exercised in a network of social relations and reconstituted in each act of communicating. No matter how well we teach our students, we cannot confer power as an essential quality of their makeup. We can, however, teach our students to analyze cultural definitions of the self, to understand how historically these definitions are created in discourse, and to recognize how definitions of the self are involved in the configuration of relations of power.

Works Cited

Adelstein, Michael E., and Jean G. Pival. *The Writing Commitment.* 4th ed. San Diego: Harcourt, 1988.

Althusser, Louis. "Ideology and Ideological State Apparatuses." *Lenin and Philosophy and other Essays.* Trans. Ben Brewster. London: New Left Books, 1971. 121-73.

Applebee, Arthur. *Tradition and Reform in the Teaching of English: A History.* Urbana: NCTE, 1974.

Baker, Sheridan. *The Practical Stylist.* 6th ed. New York: Harper, 1985.

Bartholomae, David. "Inventing the University." *When A Writer Can't Write.* Ed. Mike Rose. New York: Guilford, 1985. 134-65.

Belsey, Catherine. *Critical Practice.* London: Methuen, 1980.

Berlin, James A. *Rhetoric and Reality: Writing Instruction in American Colleges, 1900-1945.* Carbondale: Southern Illinois UP, 1987.

Bourdieu, Pierre. *Distinction: A Social Critique of the Judgement of Taste.* Trans. Richard Nice. Cambridge: Harvard UP, 1984.

Coles, William E., Jr., and James Vopat. *What Makes Writing Good.* Lexington: Heath, 1985.

Commission on English. *Examining the Examination in English: A Report to the College Entrance Examination Board.* Cambridge: Harvard UP, 1931.

Diederich, Paul B. *Measuring Growth in English.* Urbana: NCTE, 1974.

Doi, Takeo. *The Anatomy of Dependence.* Trans. John Brewster. Tokyo: Kodansha, 1973.

Easthope, Anthony. *British Post-Structuralism.* London: Routledge and Kegan Paul, 1988.

Foucault, Michel. "The Discourse on Language." *The Archaeology of Knowledge.* Trans. A. M. Sheridan Smith. New York: Harper & Row, 1976. 215-37.

Harris, Joseph. "The Plural Text/The Plural Self: Roland Barthes and William Coles." College *English* 49 (February 1987): 158-70.

Heath, Shirley Brice. "Toward an Ethnohistory of Writing in American Education." *Writing: The Nature, Development, and Teaching of Written Communication.* Vol. 1. Ed. Marcia Farr Whiteman. Hillsdale: Erlbaum, 1981. 25-45.

Kerek, Andrew, Don Daiker, and Max Morenberg. "Sentence Combining and College Composition." Perceptual *and Motor Skills: Monograph Supplement* 51 (1980): 1059-1157.

Mauss, Marcel. "A Category of the Human Mind: The Notion of Person; The Notion of Self." Trans. W. D. Halls. *The Category of the Person: Anthropology, Philosophy, History.* Ed. Michael Carrithers, Steven Collins, and Steven Lukes. Cambridge: Cambridge UP, 1985. 1-25. Trans. of "Une Catégorie de l'Esprit Humain: La Notion de Personne, Celle de 'Moi.'" 1938.

Morgan, Bob. "Three Dreams of Language; Or, No Longer Immured in the Bastille of the Humanist Word." *College English* 49 (April 1987): 449-58.

North, Stephen M. *The Making of Knowledge in Composition: Portrait of an Emerging Field.* Upper Montclair: Boynton/Cook, 1987.

Sommers, Nancy. "Responding to Student Writing." *College Composition and Communication* 33 (May 1982): 148-56.

Spring, Joel. *The American School: 1642-1985.* New York: Longman, 1986.

Therborn, Göran. *The Ideology of Power and the Power of Ideology.* London: Verso, 1980.

Thompson, John B. *Studies in the Theory of Ideology.* Cambridge: Polity, 1984.

Trachsel, Mary. "The History of College Entrance Examinations in English: A Record of Academic Assumptions about Literacy." Diss. U of Texas, 1987.

Urban, Greg. "The 'I' of Discourse." *Semiotics, Self, and Society.* Ed. Benjamin Lee and Greg Urban. Berlin: Mouton de Gruyter, in press.

Weedon, Chris. *Feminist Practice and Poststructuralist Theory.* London: Basil Blackwell, 1987.

Parentheticals
and Personal Voice

by Arthur L. Palacas

Personal voice in writing, a lively and controversial topic among compositionists, is an important proving ground for composition research. The question lurks whether compositionists can transcend the subjectivity surrounding their field, and Hashimoto (1987) warns against excessive subjectivity lest those who advocate voice "undercut their own intellectual enterprises" (p. 79). The challenge is clear. Can personal voice in writing be described objectively? Is it, in fact, a coherent concept? Can it be taught? Or is this aspect of composition studies ultimately consigned to the world of opinion and mere emotional advocacy? With a view to some hopeful answers, I explore here the nature of personal voice in writing, applying linguistic method to secure needed objectivity.

I do not directly argue the virtues of voice, the value of teaching voice in writing, nor the role of voice in different types of writing. I simply assume that some types of writing invite a more personal style, others a more objective one, and that writers need to be aware of the differences. This is not to deny the importance of these issues nor their reality, but the fact is that while voice has its many proponents, the concept is not universally valued or encouraged in student writing. The concept of personal voice is not even mentioned as such in the index of the typical college composition handbook, where voice refers only to grammatical voice, the opposition between active and passive sentence structure.

Of more direct concern is the very basic question: What is personal voice in writing? Many compositionists and composition teachers hope to steer their students away from "school writing," "themewriting," or "Engfish," and to help them find their own writing voice. But the concept is not well-understood, and it is doubtful whether readers would always agree when a written piece actually displayed voice. Even more doubtful is whether all teachers would agree how to teach voice or just what to teach about it.

What do compositionists say voice is? Among the proponents of personal voice in student writing, Coles (1978) claims that writing with voice is writing with "the sound of honesty" (p. 95), writing that shows the "mind in the act of working" (p. 127), creating "the illusion of some one's handling

---

Reprinted from *Written Communication*, 6.4 (October 1989): 506-27. Reprinted with permission.

[the material]" (p. 249). For Elbow (1981), "Voice, in writing, implies words that capture the sound of an individual on the page" (p. 287), writing with "that fluency, rhythm, and liveliness that exist naturally in the speech of most people when they are enjoying a conversation" (p. 299). Daniels (1985) says that an authentic personal voice has the "sound of a genuine, deeply engaged author at work finding out what she thinks" (p. 261), and for Donald Murray (1973) voice is "the force which drives a piece of writing forward. It is an expression of the writer's authority and concern" (p. 70). The authors of these and other such descriptions, in their attempts to capture realities they perceive, have rightly drawn the attention of the composition world to the phenomenon of voice and have undoubtedly prompted fruitful pedagogical changes in some classrooms.

Yet, as subjective and impressionistic as these descriptions are, they do not give a clear picture of what voice actually "looks like" on the page, and they ultimately fall short as a universal source of practical advice to the writing student. Elbow (1981), though an advocate of "real" voice, even denies voice any objective reality, claiming that "there are no outward linguistic characteristics to point to in writing with real voice. Resonance or impact on the reader is all there is" (p. 312). It is in response to such statements that Hashimoto (1987) calls for greater objectivity for the sake of composition studies.

Examples do, in fact, exist of writing we might all agree actually projects a voice, as seen below. How honest such writing is, there is no objective way to tell. And whether such writing mimics spoken language, and how it does so, are at least debatable questions; advising students to simply mimic speech—without providing clear limits and guidelines—would seem quite inadequate. At this level of discussion, where such key, pre-theoretic notions as "honest writing" and "the life and rhythms of spoken language" are not well understood, little is gained in terms of reproducible information—that is, in terms of communicable knowledge of discourse patterns that capture what compositionists mean by voice. Attaining such knowledge as transcends private interpretation requires an approach that is explicit and testable.

A Linguistic Worlds Framework

Voice can be better understood in terms of a linguistic theory that accounts for the syntactic, semantic, and lexical character of the actual linguistic material observed on the page, the stuff that causes the perception of voice.

The theoretical framework I assume, but can only briefly touch on here, is a model of discourse semantics in which each and every meaning expressed in a (spoken or written) text is assigned to a *linguistic world*—an abstract discourse unit comprised of a set of propositions identified with a particular propositional attitude of a particular person at a particular reference time (Palacas, 1989). The term *propositional attitude*, used here somewhat more broadly than the semanticist's traditional use, includes such mental orientations, or mentalities, as factive, desiderative, hypothetical, ironical, imaginary, belief, dream, and perhaps a few others. The linguistic worlds model is intended to capture intuitions about such discourse notions as someone's dream world, hypothetical world, or past real world, as expressed in a text.

In reference to single-speaker texts, in general, the speaker is ultimately responsible, of course, for all the meanings expressed. The primary world of a text is the speaker's present time factive world, the world of speaker-facts, to which meanings are attributed when there is no call to do otherwise. But meanings expressed by the text may also be attributed to other worlds, as well. For example, some meanings expressed in a text might be attributed to a subordinate, past dream of a person other than the speaker. In the sentence, "Ben dreamed that steak would be served for breakfast," the meanings in the subordinate clause are attributed to the subordinate world of Ben's past dream. The meaning of the entire sentence is assigned to the present factive world of the speaker, who reveals the (to him) fact of the dream. But within this world is another, subordinate world, Ben's past dream world—not a firsthand dream, but one reported secondhand by the speaker. To understand the sentence is to attribute meanings to two worlds, one contained within the other, both worlds being constructions by the speaker. The empirical nature of this framework is evident in its demand for rules that assign to linguistic worlds all meanings expressed in a text in a way that mirrors the way readers actually attribute meanings.

The World of the Reflective Mentality

Linguistic worlds give us a way of talking about voice. I propose that personal voice is the interacting product of two worlds—the speaker/author's present time *factive* world and the speaker/author's present time *reflective*, or evaluative, world—two speaker/author real worlds distinguished solely by the opposition between the factive mentality and a reflective mentality. (The complicated question of reference time is not germane to this discussion and it is not pursued further.) Meanings associated with the factive mentality have the sense of factually presented truths; these are first-order, and in terms of the text, unevaluated meanings. Meanings associated with the reflective mentality are reflections—second-order thoughts about, or evaluations of, other presented meanings; typically these are reflections on first-order, factive meanings, but may be reflections on any presented meanings, including other second-order reflections. By its nature, the reflective mentality is the more self-conscious and is the key to voice.

This view holds that the phenomenon of voice is inherently heteroglossic, to use Bakhtin's term, and at a minimum diglossic. On the production side, voice springs from the writer's juggling between a factive voice and a reflective voice—between factively expressed meanings and reflectively expressed meanings (in some ways related to Emig's (1971) "extensive" and "reflexive" modes of composing). On the perception side, the reader correspondingly attributes some meanings to the writer's factive world, and other meanings to the writer's reflective world, to his more "private" thoughts, as the text gives impetus to do so. Quite parallel to dramatic asides that give the audience the secret thoughts of a character, the (apparently) inner world of the writer's reflections is exposed, giving the reader a sense of privileged personal access to the writer's self.

But when is an author expressing factive meanings and when reflective meanings? How can the text help us know when the writer is speaking from his factive world and when from his reflective world? The ability to answer this question is obviously crucial for the view being proposed. The more deeply one looks, the more complex the answer may become. Assuming that there is such an increasingly complex road to travel, clear examples are needed to begin the quest.

Parentheticals and Voice

The clearest examples of a linguistic strategy for projecting the reflective mentality come from the use of parentheticals and appositives, henceforth simply parentheticals. The investigation in this article is limited to parentheticals as prototypical means for causing the perception of a personal voice in written discourse. The field of voice is vast, and rather than survey it, I attempt to make some initial substantive inroads by a narrow focus on parentheticals in the belief that the results will be useful in themselves and will lead to further research. Consequently, I omit discussion of many elements of subjective language that can contribute to the perception of a personal voice, such as first and second person pronouns, deictic expressions, evaluative adjectival and adverbial modifiers, quotation marks, colloquialisms, fragments, speech acts, and stylistic shifts, all of which require independent investigation. Some of these have been discussed elsewhere in terms relevant for stylistic study, for example, Williams (1981) and Banfield (1982).

Many interesting-to-read passages contain sentences that are, in traditional terms, undiagrammable, poorly diagrammable, or diagrammable with total lack of insight—because of the variety of parenthetical structures sprinkled throughout them. By virtue of their structure, these sentences project a personal voice. A number of examples are given in (1) to (12) below, including several from William Coles, whose own style is conveniently amenable to analysis. In each example, the added italics mark portions that clearly seem to be associated with the personal voice in the sentence.

(1) The order the writer makes of the assignments, *I think,* would have been fuller, *of more final value to him as a student,* had he made the one final turn to see himself as his most important reader, and writing, *therefore,* a means of self clarification. (Coles, 1978, p. 267)

(2) The paper is marred by generality, *I think,* but *for me* it's saved, *maybe just saved,* by voice. (Coles, 1978, p. 264)

(3) That way, *with "point" talk—isn't that a nice pun he has in his final sentence?*—I become a point, *a point on a line, just as he says.* (Coles, 1978, p. 211)

(4) Perhaps more important than anything else, *at least to me,* is the way in which the paper as a gesture—*one in which rejection and acceptance become adjuncts of each other*—enacts the most meaningful paradox of teaching and learning. (Coles, 1978, p. 270)

(5) The syntax permits, *encourages,* the voice to help. (Lanham, 1979, p. 11)

(6) A collage consists not of a single perfectly connected train of explicit thinking or narrating but rather of fragments: arranged *how shall we say*—poetically? rhetorically? randomly? (Elbow, 1981, p. 148)

(7) It does not mean some, *any,* political theory or principle. (Erickson, 1985, p. 90)

(8) One day—*his parents did not learn this until about two years later*—having had enough of the teacher's meanness, he just got up from his desk and without saying a word, walked out of the room and went home. (Holt, 1984, p. 410)

(9) They seem to believe that schools are better, *more honorable* places than the world outside—*what friends of mine at Harvard once called "museums of virtue."* (Holt, 1984, p. 415)

(10) But many newspapers will die—*many already have*—and even the ones that live are unlikely to cause young boys to stand on the street corner in reverie. (Greene, 1984, p. 322)

(11) . . . but never did they seem so generically weak, *so fragile.* . . . (Greene, 1984, p. 322)

(12) We are supposed to be fairly glib when it comes to any other subject—*newspaper men, it is said, can write about cats or kings*—but we stumble around when we try to explain what all of this is doing to us. (Greene, 1984, p. 327)

The italicized portions are all parentheticals and all do, it appears, project a reflective voice, the voice of a reflecting self, the author, reflecting on what he is saying. Each italicized portion has a recognizably self-editing function, wherein the author has self-consciously paused to evaluate what he has just expressed and offers a personal comment on it—an edit. To overstate the case, it is as if the author wrote something down, stopped momentarily to take stock of what he had written, then offered the editorial comment or elaboration represented in the italicized portion. Sometimes the comment is perceived as an afterthought. In this type of reflective writing, the reflections of the author about his own words are a matter of record, with both the preedited and edited versions existing side by side. In more objective-style, nonreflective writing, that is, in writing that does not project a reflecting self, such editing is done *off the record*, so to speak, and we see only the final product. Of course, the reality is that skillful reflective writing is itself a written product that has undergone the usual unseen editing that precedes product. Thus, this style of writing can become a strategy for projecting a sense of self-consciousness.

Linguistic Characteristics of Parentheticals

The potential number of examples like (1) to (12) above is boundless. The apparent systematicity of such examples suggests that there are linguistic rules underlying their construction and raises the natural question: What are the linguistic properties of the parenthetical structures in such sentences? Or, in terms more pertinent to composition, what linguistic properties correlate with the projection of a reflective voice in such sentences?

Phonologically, parenthetical material in general forms its own "separate intonation-group" (Cruttenden, 1986, p. 78). As can be observed, the italicized portions are normally read with "comma intonation"—with a pause before and after, accompanied by a shift in intonational contour relative to the remainder of the sentence, or by a deliberate repetition of the intonational contour of the preceding phrase.

A shift in intonational contour may be to a lower level of pitch and stress, or to a higher level of pitch and stress, the two patterns pictured here:

Downward Shift Pattern

basic intonation level

lowered intonation level

Upward Shift Pattern

raised intonation level

basic intonation level

Such phonological shifting gives the effect of a temporary removal from the more basic intonational pattern of the sentence.

The shift to a *lowered* pattern can be illustrated by the usual reading of the first parenthetical in example (2):

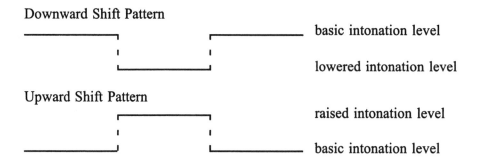

The paper is marred by generality   but for me it's saved. . .

I think

The *raised* intonational pattern can be illustrated by example (5), where the second verb, "encourages," is read with emphasis:

encourages

The syntax permits | | the voice to help.

A *repeated* intonational pattern is illustrated by what is probably the usual reading of the portion from example (3) in (13), with the phrase "a point on a line" having the same intonation pattern as the preceding phrase, "a point"—the same terminal prominence and rising-falling tone with proclaiming-function (Brazil, 1985)—thus forming a parallel structure with it (Cruttenden, 1986, p. 78). (The capitalization of "point" and "line" in (13) indicates the phonetic prominence, and the arrow indicates the tonal modulation.)

(13) I become a POINT, a point on a LINE, just as he says.

Such physical pauses, intonation shifts—literal shifts of the voice—and repeated intonation patterns signal an associated mental shift to a reflective world, which we can equate with a reflective voice. All parentheticals share the functional property of signaling a shift to the reflective mentality.

The signal, itself, indicates the disconnectedness of the parenthetical from the contiguous parts of the sentence, not just phonetically but also syntactically and semantically. Syntactically, parentheticals share a distinctively loose structural connection in the sentence, verging on the absence of any structural connection. In fact, the total lack of structural connection is exactly what Rotenberg (1978) argues,[1] and what McCawley (1989) suggests as a possibility since "parentheticals and vocatives can be argued to enter into discontinuous constituent structure and indeed do not even clearly combine into a syntactic unit with the sentence they interrupt." This lack of structural connection is the point of view adopted here. Likewise, semantically, parentheticals appear not to be part of the same assertion as the clauses into which they are interposed; each represents a separate, additional assertion. Hooper and Thompson (1973) argue convincingly for the separate assertional character of appositive relatives, a conclusion recalling the traditional (and overstated) intuition that nonrestrictive clauses are "not necessary to the meaning of the sentence and may be omitted" (Hodges & Whitten, 1986: p. 517). Givon (1980) suggests, in general, that loosely connected clausal structures represent meanings that are not part of the

---

[1] This reference was pointed out to me by Arnold Zwicky.

assertion made in the main clause (p. 372).

These phonological, syntactic, and semantic characteristics of parentheticals support the functional position presented here, namely, that linguistic phenomena of various sorts are signs of a shift to a second-order reflective, evaluative, commentative mentality—a shift of worlds. Parentheticals, in particular, with their alien structural relationship to the structures they modify, signal just such a shift. An author adds parentheticals into a sentence under construction, as second-order reflections, to clarify, correct, hedge, or otherwise *comment* (Jackendorff, 1977, p. 94) on what he has just said or what he is saying in the sentence. (Or, as suggested earlier, an author might use this *add-in* syntactic strategy to project thoughtfulness and/or concern for the reader.)

A Functional Syntax of Parentheticals

What I propose, then, is that sentences such as those in (1) through (12) are functionally bipartite, projecting two levels of thought. As a beginning step toward developing what might be called the *grammar of voice*, I take seriously the earlier mentioned idea that parentheticals are structurally unattached and are added into a sentence from outside; the two levels of thought correlate with two levels of syntax in these sentences, the syntax of the *basic sentence*, and the syntax of *paragrammatic constructions*. The *basic sentence* is a sentence of any degree of complexity devoid of parentheticals; the grammar of basic sentences will be referred to as the *basic grammar*. (Basic sentences are not to be confused with traditional simple sentences, nor with the kernel sentences of transformational grammar, which are also simple sentences.) *Paragrammatic structures* include parentheticals (and possibly other constructions)—words, phrases, or clauses grammatical in their own right and inserted into the basic sentence but not integral to the grammar of the basic sentence itself. Basic grammar is to be contrasted with *paragrammar*, which is to be thought of as the system for superimposing paragrammatic structures onto basic sentences. Paragrammar is essentially the grammar of the reflective mentality.

In the production of parentheticals, a break occurs in the construction of the basic sentence, during which principles of paragrammar are applied to interpose paragrammatic material into the basic structure. After the paragrammatic construction is completed, the construction of the basic sentence resumes. Such interruption and resumption of the basic structure may occur many times within a sentence. Each of the twelve example sentences contains interposed into it one or more second-level, *paragrammatic* structures. To illustrate with example sentence (1), repeated here,

    (1)   The order the writer makes of the assignments, *I think*, would have been fuller, *of more final value to him as a student*, had he made the one final turn to see himself as his most important

reader, and writing, *therefore*, *a* means of self clarification.

omission of the italicized paragrammatic material yields the basic sentence (1a):

> (1a) The order the writer makes of the assignments would have been fuller had he made the one final turn to see himself as his most important reader, and writing a means of self clarification.

Sentence (1a) is a standard, no frills grammatical sentence expressed straightforwardly in the writer's *objective*, or *factive* voice; other things being equal, the structure of the sentence signals no shift to the author's reflective world, projects no sense of a personal, subjective self.[2] However, the parenthetical insertion of the mental verb *think* with its first-person subject adds a paragrammatical dimension to the sentence. With this one addition, sentence (1) becomes (1b):

> (1b) The order the writer makes of the assignments, *I think,* would have been fuller had he made the one final turn to see himself as his most important reader, and writing a means of self clarification.

This addition projects a second voice (note the physical change of voice in the oral reading of the sentence), this time the reflective voice of the writer, who uses this paragrammatic structure to qualify an otherwise too dogmatic speculation—perhaps as a strategy to under-cut an objection by his reader. Or perhaps the strategy was to give a sense of personal flexibility and open-mindedness, or simply to make the writing more personal and engaging. Whatever the strategy, the reflective voice implies a self, a first person, expressing reflections for the benefit of the implied second-person listener/reader, thus drawing the latter into the communicative event.

A second paragrammatic addition to the sentence, the phrase, "of more final value to him as a student," clarifies the meaning of "fuller"; and a third paragrammatic addition, the transitional conjunctive adverb, "therefore," clarifies the logical connections between the parts of the sentence. Each of these additions, too, projects the second-level reflective voice of the writer, as do the underlined paragrammatic portions of all the examples shown.

Syntactic and Functional Types of Parentheticals

Heretofore, we have not distinguished between types of parentheticals, except to note that they vary grammatically from a single word to an entire sentence, and so we might ask what types there are and whether they correlate

---

[2] In this reading the comma before the final phrase clarifies the sentence structure so that the reader will not accidentally conjoin "reader and writing." In this interpretation, the sentence reads with equal force with or without the comma. My comments apply to this reading, not to the reading in which the comma indicates that what follows is an afterthought.

with particular types of reflections. Although investigating their syntax exhaustively is beyond the scope of this article, we can make a useful beginning by observing that parentheticals exemplified in (1) to (12) fall into three categories that we can describe informally as *displacements, equivalents,* and *interruptives.*

Displacements and equivalents can be understood in relation to basic grammar. Displacements are paragrammatic expressions related to expressions that have a standard, factive-style role in the basic grammar but are located in a structural position not defined for them by the basic grammar. The expression "I think" in (1) is a displacement, simply inserted into the sentence in a clearly nonbasic position. The basic position of an expression like "I think," a verb of propositional attitude, is at the head of the complement clause it introduces. As can readily be observed, using the expression "I think" in its basic (nondisplaced) grammatical position, as in (1c), strips it of its structurally defined reflective voice:

> (1c) *I think that*[3] the order the writer makes of the assignments would have been fuller had he made the one final turn to see himself as his most important reader, and writing a means of self clarification.

Other examples of displacements are found in sentences (2) and (12). Sentence (2) has the same "I think" as sentence (1), and sentence (12) has the displaced "it is said," a paragrammatic structure within a paragrammatic structure. These examples, and many others like them—"I am sure," "without a doubt," "wouldn't it be nice to believe," "we might suspect," "there can be no question," "it is possible to imagine," "I have just discovered"—weaken or strengthen a statement in a particular way by asserting a propositional attitude toward it as commentary and revealing the nature of the author's authority to make the statement. Although displacements can be composed of other types of constructions and used for other purposes as well, their use for paragrammatic insertion of a propositional attitude is an important and common one.

An equivalent is a paragrammatic structure that duplicates the grammatical role of and offers an equivalent to, elaboration on, or replacement for the immediately preceding structure. In sentence (1), the expression "of more final value to him as a student" is a paragrammatic equivalent of "fuller." The construction "fuller" belongs to the basic sentence and plays the grammatical role of a subjective complement, the subject it modifies being "the order the writer makes of the assignment." But the construction "of more final value to him as a student," though it does not belong to the basic sentence, plays exactly the same grammatical role as "fuller"—it is a duplicate subjective

---

[3] Sandra Thompson, in forthcoming work, proposes that the absence of the subordinating particle "that" makes this construction functionally equivalent to its use in other positions in the sentence. This suggests that omitting the subordinator is sufficient to make a displacement of this construction.

complement. Having two (noncoordinate) subjective complements is impossible in a basic sentence. But it is possible to have a second subjective complement as a paragrammatic equivalent; in this case, the second instance, a paragrammatic addition to the sentence, represents the author's considered revised version of the first, as if the sentence had read: "... the assignment would have been fuller, *that is*, of more final value to the student ..." The revision is shown in process, so to speak, with the preedited version and its edited equivalent side by side. Actual physical replacement of the preedited version would complete the edit, masking the editing process, and would yield (1d), a basic sentence in which the revision is no longer shown paragrammatically and no longer projects a reflective voice:

> (1d) I think that the order the writer makes of the assignments would have been *of more final value to the student* had he made the one final turn to see himself as his most important reader, and writing a means of self clarification.

Such paragrammatic equivalents seem responsible especially for the repeated intonational pattern mentioned earlier, which signals the second-order intention to equate in some way the parenthetical and what it modifies.

The example sentences contain numerous additional instances of paragrammatic equivalents. To mention a few examples, in sentence (3), the paragrammatic occurrence of "with 'point' talk" can be seen as an equivalent to or revised version of the adverbial phrase "that way"; and "a point on a line" can be seen as a similar revised version of the immediately preceding "a point." In (5), the paragrammatic "encourages" revises the main verb "permits"; in (7), the adjectival "any" can be seen as an emphatic revision for "some"; in (9), "more honorable" is the equivalent of "better," and "what a friend of mine at Harvard once called 'museums of virtue' " is offered as the equivalent of "better, more honorable places than the world outside."

Besides displacements and equivalents, the example sentences illustrate yet another paragrammatic type—interruptives—a category not so easily described in terms of the basic grammar. In sentences (3), (6), and (8), for example, each shows an entire clause simply dropped into the basic structure; but these inserted clauses play no definable grammatical role relative to the basic sentence. And, in sentence (4), the phrase "at least to me" seems also not to have any natural grammatical place within basic sentence structure. Such structures, lacking a role definable in terms of the natural categories of basic sentence grammar, are the paragrammatic interruptives. These structures seem even more loosely related to the sentence than other paragrammatic structures, but they nevertheless play the same functionally relevant role of offering an authorial comment on other material in the sentence. The existence of nonclausal interruptives, in particular—such as "that is," "namely," the "at least" of "at least to me," and the "no" of "no, I mean such and such"—suggests that paragrammar may possess elements with special, second-order discursive function that are entirely independent of basic sentence grammar.

In conformity with this last suggestion, adverbial conjuncts, such as "therefore," "nevertheless," or "in addition," may in some contexts be viewed as interruptives, because they appear not to play an integral grammatical role in the basic clause. This treatment would analogize adverbial conjuncts to sentence-initial subordinate clauses as discussed in Matthiessen and Thompson (1988), where the relevant subordinate clauses are seen as "hypotactic." Hypotactic clauses sit next to a main clause, and "although the [main and hypotactic] clauses are interdependent and stand in a head-dependent relation to one another at some level, there is no sense in which one is a part of the other." Adverbial conjuncts in their normal sentence-initial location may have this same "hypotactic" lack of syntactic connection to a main clause and therefore act as interruptives. Such might be the case, for example, in a sentence like, "Moreover, writing causes consternation," where the adverbial "moreover" is pronounced somewhat separately from the main clause. However, in (1), the adverbial conjunct "therefore" is in the second of two conjoined phrases and seems to carry reflectional power only in its displaced location, not in the normal position it would have at the beginning of the conjoined phrase (or clause). Its medial insertion into the conjoined phrase results in the cleaving of the latter, with accompanying comma intonation and the projection of a reflective voice.[4] Restoring the adverbial conjunct of (1) to its normal position results in (1e), a sentence very like (1) except that it is totally stripped of any structurally defined reflective voice:

> (1e) I think that the order the writer makes of the assignments would have been of more final value to the student had he made the one final turn to see himself as his most important reader and therefore writing a means of self clarification.

Interestingly, (except for the absence of "fuller"), sentence (1e), with its "normalized" version of the paragrammatic structures in sentence (1), has the same propositional content as (1). Yet, normalizing the paragrammatic structures—by restoring "I think" to its normal grammatical role, by physically replacing "fuller" with its paragrammatic equivalent, and by extracting the interruptive "therefore" from its interposed position—has effectively removed the reflective voice of (1), and has made the reading of the sentence less personally engaging. It does seem, then, that paragrammar is a clear signal of a shift to the reflective world of the author—to the author's reflective voice.

One more parenthetical subtype not yet exemplified but with far-reaching implications can be mentioned here. No example has been given of what might be called a paragrammatic *overlap*, a more subtle case where the paragrammatic structure looks exactly like its minimal-pair basic structure. A

---

[4] In example sentence (8), the participial phrase "having had enough of the teacher's meanness" fits this description of an interruptive, and it does seem to project a personal voice. But the nature of this voice, possibly reconstructing the voice of the student the passage is about, raises complications that would take us far afield.

sentence like (14),

> (14) As such, composition has been deemed—by many faculty in English and other departments, students, parents, the media, a host of linguistic guardians, and whoever else is interested in joining the conversation—a service course. (Samuelson, 1988)

with the agentive phrase, "by . . . ," between dashes, is quite different in voice from the same sentence in (15) with the dashes and accompanying intonational shift removed:

> (15) As such, composition has been deemed by many faculty in English and other departments, students, parents, the media, a host of linguistic guardians, and whoever else is interested in joining the conversation a service course.

Although the agentive phrase of (15) is generated by the basic grammar, the same phrase in (14) is not. As a parenthetical expression, it has only a loose syntactic connection to the sentence, perhaps no connection, as discussed earlier, and is added paragrammatically. The parenthetical usage, indicated by the written dashes and represented in speech by comma intonation, signals a shift to the speaker's reflective world, evidencing the writer's change of mind, perhaps, as to whether the reader would readily grasp the intent of the agentive phrase without its having been explicitly mentioned. Whatever the exact reflectional intent of the writer, the shift in structure has signaled a shift to the reflective mentality, showing yet another, albeit more subtle, syntactic type for signaling such shifts.

Paragrammatic overlaps may have implications for other, apparently nonparenthetical structures that may evidence the reflective voice. All semantically nonrestrictive elements that appear to be integrated into the syntax of the basic sentence, such as certain uses of adjectives and certain elements of meaning in nouns, might be viewed as reflective overlays onto a factive base. Accounting for these may require a theory of multiple attachment of constituents, such as found in McCawley (1989), with one attachment in the basic sentence and another, paralleling the attachment of overlap structures, outside the basic sentence, tying up with the reflective world. Perhaps reflective elements with more pragmatic than syntactic or lexical origins would also receive similar treatment.

Paragrammar and Syntactic Theory

Whatever the exact rules for or constraints on paragrammar, a variety of syntactic types appears to be available for paragrammatic interposition of linguistic material into a sentence and for the projection of a reflective voice. The functional approach of paragrammar, it should be emphasized, may be quite distinct from the perspective of formal syntactic theory. With the focus of syntactic theory exclusively on *form*, the sentence is viewed as an already constructed formal object whose structural pattern is compared to the pattern of other already constructed sentences in order to discover overall patterns and pattern parallels. The functional approach is meant to be more closely related to matters of production. The contrast is most starkly seen in relation to Emonds's transformational approach to parentheticals. In Emonds's (1979, 1985) theory, example sentence (1), repeated here for convenience, might be derived from (1f) by certain rules of rearrangement and ellipsis; (1f) would be seen as the "Deep Structure," the underlying, grammatical "source" of (1):

(1)   The order the writer makes of the assignments, *I think*, would have been fuller, *of more final value to him as a student*, had he made the one final turn to see himself as his most important reader, and writing, *therefore*, a means of self clarification.

(1f) The order the writer makes of the assignments would have been fuller or the order the writer makes of the assignments would have been *of more final value to the student* had he made the one final turn to see himself as his most important reader and *therefore* he had made the one final turn to see writing as a means of self clarification or so *I think*. (Commas purposely omitted.)[5]

In this analysis, in which sentences are viewed as completed objects, the full grammatical content of the derived sentence is available in the source sentence.

But in "on-line" paragrammatic terms, a paragrammatic sentence is not a transformational manipulation of a Deep Structure containing paragrammatic material in potential form. An entirely different situation obtains. In "on-line" terms, the paragrammatic constructions in (1) are not shifted from theoretical basic locations to their paragrammatic locations. Instead, sentence (1) is derived during the left-to-right construction of the basic sentence (1a), also repeated here.:

(1a) The order the writer makes of the assignments would have been fuller had he made the one final turn to see himself as his most important reader, and writing a means of self clarification.

As a basic sentence, (1a) contains no paragrammatic items and no potential paragrammatic items. But during its left-to-right construction, the author, for commentative purposes, superimposes the paragrammatic expressions of (1) onto this basic structure.

All twelve example sentences are derived in the same way. To give three more illustrations, sentences (2), (3), and (4), repeated here, are derived from (2a), (3a), and (4a), respectively during their left-to-right production:

---

[5] I have taken certain what I believe are minor liberties in suggesting (1f) as the underlying structure of (1), made necessary here because of the greater complexity of this example than the ones dealt with in Emonds.

(2)   The paper is marred by generality, *I think,* but *for me* it's saved, *maybe just saved,* by voice.

(2a) The paper is marred by generality, but it's saved by voice.

(3)   That way, *with "point" talk—isn't that a nice pun he has in his final sentence?*—I become a point, a *point on a line, just as he says.*

(3a) That way I become a point.

(4)   Perhaps more important than anything else, *at least to me,* is the way in which the paper as a gesture—*one in which rejection and acceptance become adjuncts of each other*—enacts the most meaningful paradox of teaching and learning.

(4a) Perhaps more important than anything else is the way in which the paper as a gesture enacts the most meaningful paradox of teaching and learning.

As a final comment on the examples, note that there can be more than one level of reflection. In sentence (3), a first level of reflection is displayed by the paragrammatic phrase "with 'point' talk," which clarifies the introductory phrase "That way." In a second level of reflection, the inserted sentence, "isn't that a nice pun he has in his final sentence," comments on the quoted word "point" in the first paragrammatic insertion. Hence, we have a reflection on a reflection. Similarly, in sentence (12), the displacement, "it is said," is a reflection on the reflection that "newspaper men can write about cats and kings."

To conclude this discussion of the grammar of voice, we have seen that in at least one manifestation, the phenomenon of a reflective voice can be captured by a functional theory of paragrammar in which paragrammatic structures are objective correlates of a reflective voice. As authorial reflections on what the author is expressing, they are metaconstructions, language on language. If this analysis is correct, then—echoing Bakhtin—one clear meaning of *voice* is actually a construction of *multiple voices,* including an objective-style voice and one or more pragmatically motivated subjective-style, reflective voices. Bakhtin (1925) saw that "(i)n the verbal medium, in each utterance, however trivial it may be, a living dialectical synthesis is constantly taking place between the inner and outer" (p. 433). Furthermore, reflective voices, as comments, imply a definite *I–you* relationship between writer and reader in which the writer reveals inner thoughts to the reader, and thus personally engages them. It is this power of language to transcend the typical information-transmitting communication model and to invite a relationship between people that, I believe, makes voice so important to compositionists. The structural approach taken here is not the whole story on voice, by any means, but it does offer a more concrete, if still partial, understanding than has hitherto been available and a starting place for further exploration. It provides an objective way of describing voice and of pursuing it as a coherent notion. It may also provide new ways to think about the teaching of voice.

Pedagogical Comments

Pedagogically, the separation between the factive and the reflective levels of sentence structure has potential for the teaching of voice. It gives substance to the notion, encouraging more concrete discussion and, for those so inclined, even making the construction of exercises possible; it has the potential of turning voice into a technique to be skillfully and artfully practiced. (Of course, this does not mean that reflective voice is to be taught by teaching the technical concepts of paragrammar any more than it was ever wise to directly teach students transformational grammar. Good pedagogy comes from the ingenuity of good teachers, the way the best sentence-combining exercises came about. Though the latter were inspired by elements of a transformational grammar, they are not a form of transformational grammar itself.) The phonological effects of paragrammatic structures, too, with their raised, lowered, and deliberately repeated intonational patterns, like theatrical "asides," might be used with good effect to dramatize the reflective nature of paragrammatic additions and their audience appeal. Also, attention to paragrammar has the potential for helping beginning writers become more fluent by allowing some of the writing process to become part of the written record, part of the product. The tension between conflicting, partial thoughts and well-formed, perfected writing can be resolved, to an extent, by allowing that tension to be expressed through paragrammatic structures that clarify, qualify, restate, meet objections, pose alternatives, or, in general, that comment on the current topic. Indeed, since paragrammar is a device for writers to display selectively their ongoing thoughts, might not working with paragrammar even encourage beginning writers to think more reflectively about their writing as they write?

Conclusion

Perhaps the theory of paragrammar introduced here captures, to an extent, what Coles means by "honest writing" and writing that shows "the mind in the act of working", and what Elbow means by writing with the "fluency, rhythm, and liveliness" of speech. Paragrammatic constructions of the sort exemplified project a reflective consciousness and give the impression of a writer present with the reader and in the process of rethinking and revising, taking his own words quite seriously. Revision is characteristic of honest effort and of conversation. Paragrammatic attention to such pragmatic purposes as clarifying, hedging, correcting and commenting, by their nature, show the thoughtful involvement of a writer in his subject, but it also engages a reader because it takes the reader into account, again paralleling conversational language, which by its nature takes the listener into account. Paragrammatic style is also like speech in one more way. In both speech and paragrammatic-style writing, editing is on record, whether in the hearing of listeners or in the written record. This distinguishes the paragrammatic writing style from the objective style, where all editing is "off the record." Thus, although paragrammatic writing may not necessarily be honest and may not actually reflect speech in every way, it does have properties that are characteristic of both.

Finally, in these initial steps toward a grammar of voice, I hope I have given a reasonable demonstration of the importance of explicitness in matters of composition that touch on language form. And I hope I have, by implication, also shown that the particular language interests of compositionists can lead to new understandings about grammar and the relationship between language form and language use—between linguistic competence and performance—understandings that may help our teaching of writing. Compositionists, with their sensitivities to the nuances of particular language in the discursive setting, will have an intuitive feel for matters regarding which other students of language may show lack of awareness or interest. Significant new ground can be gained as compositionists formulate their intuitions into empirically explicit statements—statements that can influence the theoretical picture of language emerging in our times.

References

Bakhtin, M. M. (1925). *The dialogic imagination.* (M. Holquist, Trans. & Ed.). Austin: University of Texas.

Banfield, A. (1982). *Unspeakable sentences.* Boston: Routledge & Kegan Paul.

Brazil, D. (1985). Phonology: Intonation in discourse. In T. van Dijk (Ed.), *Handbook of discourse analysis*, Vol. 2. London: Academic Press.

Coles, W. E., Jr. (1978). *The Plural I.* New York: Holt, Rinehart & Winston.

Cruttenden, A. (1986). *Intonation.* New York: Cambridge University Press.

Daniels, H. (1985). Harvey Daniels's assignment. In W. E. Coles, Jr., & J. Vopat (Eds.), *What makes good writing.* Lexington, MA: Heath.

Elbow, P. (1981). *Writing with power: Techniques for mastering the writing process.* New York: Oxford University Press.

Emig, J. (1971). *The composing processes of twelfth graders.* Urbana, IL: National Council of Teachers of English.

Emonds, J. E. (1979). Appositive relatives have no properties. *Linguistic Inquiry, 10,* 211-243.

Emonds, J. E. (1985). *A unified theory of syntactic categories.* Cinnaminson, NJ: Foris.

Erickson, E. E., Jr. (1985). Norms regained. *University Bookman,* Summer.

Givon, T. (1980). The binding hierarchy and the typology of complements. *Studies in Language, 4,* 333-377.

Greene, B. (1984). Paper boy. In G. Levin (Ed.), *Prose Models*, 6th Ed. New York: Harcourt Brace Jovanovich.

Hashimoto I. (1987). Voice as juice: Some reservations about evangelical composition. *College Composition and Communication, 38,* 70-79.

Holt, J. (1984). The right to control one's learning. In G. Levin (Ed.), *Prose Models,* 6th Ed. New York: Harcourt Brace Jovanovich.

Hodges, J. C., & Whitten, M. E. (1986). *Harbrace College Handbook,* 10th Ed. New York: Harcourt Brace Jovanovich.

Hooper, J., & Thompson, S. A. (1973). On the applicability of root transformations. *Linguistic Inquiry, 4,* 465-497.

Jackendorff, R. (1977). *X-bar syntax: A study of phrase structure.* Cambridge, MA: M.I.T. Press.

Lanham, R. A. (1979). *Reviewing prose.* New York: Scribner's.

Matthiessen, C., & Thompson, S. A. (1988). The structure of discourse and "subordination." In J. Haiman & S. Thompson (Eds.), *Clause combining in discourse and grammar.* Amsterdam: John Benjamins.

McCawley, J. D. (1982). Parentheticals and discontinuous constituent structure. *Linguistic Inquiry, 13,* 91-106.

McCawley, J. D. (1989). Individuation in and of syntactic structures. In M. Baltin and A. Kroch (Eds.), *Alternative conceptions of phrase structure.* Chicago: University of Chicago Press.

Murray, D. (1973). The maker's eye: Revising your own manuscripts. *Learning by teaching: Selected articles on writing and teaching* by Donald Murray. Revision of original in *The Writer,* October, 1973.

Palacas, A. L. (1989). *Linguistic worlds and first person indirect discourse.* Unpublished manuscript.

Rotenberg, J. (1978). *The Syntax of Phonology.* Unpublished doctoral dissertation, Massachusetts Institute of Technology.

Samuelson, J. (1988). *Rethinking composition as a service course.* Unpublished manuscript.

Williams, J. M. (1981). Literary style: The personal voice. In T. Shopen & J. M. Williams (Eds.), *Variables in English.* Cambridge, MA: Winthrop.

Talking Back to the Speaker

by Clara Claiborne Park

Let's suppose I have something to say. And I fool around with it, and write it again, and try it another way, and another, because even though it's saying what I want it to it's not saying it right. And suppose it finally comes to me that the trouble (part of the trouble) is the *voice*: that I'm writing it for *The Hudson Review* when it should be for *PMLA*. Or vice versa. So I rewrite it one more time and send it in. If it's published, and if (just suppose) it's talked about, its thesis, its illustrations, its attitudes, its arguments, will not be attributed to a speaker. They will be attributed to me.

I have, of course, a number of voices. I want to juggle two of them here: one loose, a bit anecdotal, appropriate to personal history, the other appropriate to the chase through texts. The texts will show how small can be the beginnings of a major change in the conditions of literary perception, and how inconspicuously it can achieve authority. I'll use the other voice to insinuate what I think.

"It has become traditional," explains J. Paul Hunter in the poetry volume of *The Norton Introduction to Literature*,

> to distinguish between the person who wrote the poem and the person who speaks in a poem, for an author often chooses to speak through a character quite different from his or her real self.

Traditional: what everybody knows, without knowing how we know it; the universal practice which has come to seem right. Hunter, with his "often," is a pretty low-key expositor of the tradition, willingly conceding that "in many poems the speaker is very like the author, or [there's a catch] very like what the author wishes to think he or she is like," and that "between the speaker who is a fully distinct character and the author speaking honestly and directly, are many degrees of detachment." Written not for freshmen but for us, M.H. Abrams' *Glossary of Literary Terms* is considerably more categorical:

> In recent literary discussion "persona" is often applied to the first-person narrator, the "I", of a narrative poem or novel, or the lyric speaker whose voice we listen to in a lyric poem. Examples of personae are . . . the first-person narrator of Milton's *Paradise Lost* (who in the opening passages of various books discourses at some

Reprinted from *Hudson Review* 42.1 (Spring 1989): 21-44. Reprinted with permission.

length about himself); the Gulliver who tells us about his misadventures in *Gulliver's Travels*; . . . the speaker who talks first to himself, then to his sister, in Wordsworth's "Tintern Abbey"; the speaker who utters Keats's "Ode to a Nightingale". . . . ; and the Duke who tells the emissary about his former wife in Browning's "My Last Duchess." By calling these speakers "personae" . . . we stress the fact that they are all part of the fiction, characters invented for a particular artistic purpose. That the "I" in each of these works is not the author as he exists in his everyday life is obvious enough in the case of Swift's Gulliver and Browning's Duke, less obvious in the case of Milton. . . . , and does not seem obvious at all to an unsophisticated reader of the lyric poems of Wordsworth and Keats.

For "recent literary discussion" Hunter's "degrees of detachment" are only a function of the reader's naiveté. That every literary "I" is fictional is "a fact." "We stress" it. It takes only a single pronoun to embody a tradition.

Now an anecdote. I've told it elsewhere so I'll keep it short:

It's twenty-five years ago. You can tell, because I'm teaching Great Books, and in a community college, and to pretty much everyone who comes in off the street. We're reading the *Inferno*; a student, not one of the smart ones, raises his hand. He hasn't spoken before, but today he has a question. "We've read what Homer says about the afterlife, and what Plato says, and now we're reading what Dante says, and they're all different. Mrs. Park. *Which of them is true?*"

The good students rustle and smirk; already they know (how?) that this isn't a question you ask in English class. A bit of irony will reinforce them and solace me; they're on my side, I need them, teaching isn't easy. Or I can drop irony for sympathetic explanation, summon I. A. Richards out of the air in which he is unquestionably hovering, and say something to the effect that "the statements which appear in the poetry are there for the sake of their effects upon feelings, not for their own sake," and that "to question whether they deserve serious attention as *statements claiming truth* is to mistake their function." I catch myself just in time. Who is closer to Plato and Dante, I and my little band of sophisticates, or this earnest questioner? Which of us is reading as they expected to be read?

That happened long ago. Today we have a more elaborate armamentarium against the profound demands of naiveté. Today I could explain to my student that Plato told his myths of the afterlife through a speaker who though called Socrates was only a fiction invented for a particular artistic purpose. I could involve him in distinctions between Dante the narrator and Dante the poet. I could invoke spectres, an "implied author," a ghostly "authorial presence." I could raise wall after glass wall between him and these vanished human voices he had come to think had something to say directly to him. If I really worked at it, I could bring even such a student to believe what my smart students of a generation ago already suspected; that in English class, what's relevant is what's interesting, not what, if anything, is true.

Actually, I don't get many students like that any more. I'm teaching in a different place, and time, too, alters curriculum and consumers. Great Books aren't being taught much these days: teachers have doubts about "the canon"; students' interests in literature seldom reach back past 1900. Not that they're not smart. Most of the students in my sections of Introduction to Literature don't need Hunter's explanation; some wouldn't even be surprised by Abrams'. The preppies and the kids from suburban high schools already know what you are supposed to do when you talk about a poem; the others will find out the first week that you say "the speaker" and not "Frost says," that it's not Shakespeare who's worried he's growing old, not Donne who's saying good-bye to his lover, not Keats who talks to a vase. Soon the locution of detachment will become second nature. A class on *Channel Firing* will clue in the laggards, since the others have already had *My Last Duchess*. Next step "The Turn of the Screw," or if that's too familiar, *The Good Soldier*. That'll learn 'em who to trust.

The speaker. The narrator. I want here to trace something of the history of this innocent locution, since there was within living memory a time when it wasn't traditional, when the distinction between "the person who writes" and "the person who speaks" went unmade, except, of course, when poems like Browning's enforced it. Did reading feel different then? If language conditions experience—and certainly to think *that* has become traditional—so pervasive a change in the way we talk about poems and stories must matter; must affect as well as reflect the way they are taught and encountered—not to say written. Does critical and pedagogic practice enact an idea of progress, of gain uncompensated by loss? What should we conclude about a time when professors and critics were more unsophisticated than today's freshmen, when everybody said "the poet says," or "Milton," or "Keats" as if it was the most natural thing in the world? For memory informs me, and my coevals confirm, that it was possible as recently as the forties to take courses from the likes of Austin Warren and F.O. Matthiessen and emerge innocent of the distinction. Back then, when Yeats wrote that his heart was driven wild, we assumed that—masks or no masks—he meant it.

It happened that between the forties and the sixties I was out of the academic world, and when I got back into it, the tradition was in place. My colleagues taught *My Last Duchess* and *Channel Firing*; they said "the speaker"; they talked about voice and tone. One likes to do the done thing; soon I was doing it too. I do it to this day, off and on, at least when I'm teaching Introduction to Literature. But because I didn't grow up with it, because I encountered the ideas not as an exciting corrective but as a fact accomplished, I still view it as an outsider. It is as an outsider that I interrogate the nagging discomfort I feel when I hear the words, or read them, or say them. It's small, but in twenty-five years it hasn't gone away. It is out of that discomfort that I chase down the history of the phrase and ponder its implications.

If I can remember a time before the speaker, I can remember too how we read poetry in the olden days. By the time I was eighteen, I had read hundreds of poems, thousands of lines, hitting the high spots, sieving out phrases that fitted my sense of life, ignoring the rest; drunk on eloquence, sometimes merely on sound, on Abanah and Pharphar, on silken Samarcand and cedared Lebanon—reading like a child, if that conveys any meaning today when it's a rare child that grows up on poetry. We were still reading like that in college; the word "impressionistic" was made for us. We didn't know you *could* analyze a poem. I remember the exams—marvelous, expansive essay topics, tempered by "spot questions," previously unseen passages whose period and author we must identify merely by style, by the way the words went. We got quite good at this, so we must have learned something, but nevertheless it was a revelation to take Matthiessen's course and pay *attention* to poems, to watch meaning emerge from the scrutiny of syntax and symbol and structure. Imagine it, you could write a whole paper on one poem. Unbeknownst, we were being introduced to "close reading," to the New Criticism, as yet hardly christened. But not to "the speaker."

People had written about poetry (if we begin with Plato) for more than two millennia without feeling the need for such a phrase. Where should I start my chase? Not with Johnson; champion of the common reader, his sense of the poet's relation to his utterance would be as direct as Sidney's a century and a half before. Shelley wouldn't use it, nor Wordsworth, nor Arnold. Though Chambers' Victorian *Cyclopedia* recognized the "mysterious, misanthropic personage who tells the story of Tennyson's *Maud*," or the possibility that some of Shakespeare's sonnets were "written in a feigned character," there was no word of a speaker. Maybe Eliot? For our generation of readers, everything started with him.

How the years telescope our past! Revisited, Eliot sounded a lot closer to Arnold than to Cleanth Brooks; he didn't do close reading, found it "very tiring" when other people did, had, apparently, no need for "the speaker." I. A. Richards? That seemed more likely. He had given us poetry as pseudo-statement, and one good distancing mechanism deserves another. I took out *Practical Criticism*.

Cambridge students in the twenties, apparently, read no better than our freshmen do today. (But how much better they wrote! How wide their vocabularies! How complex their sentence structure! How much they seemed to know about prosody, about literary history, even though it only seemed to get in their way!) They read, in fact, much as I had twenty years later, and Richards had found out what to do about it. By the simple but original expedient of presenting them with unattributed poems, he deprived them of their hard-learned stereotypes and, sentence by sentence, insisted that they attend to what the poet was saying. In 1943, I hadn't really thought that poems came in sentences, like prose; I'd thought they were a different kind of thing altogether.

Since Richards had literally eliminated the poet from his students' experience of reading, I was ready momentarily to encounter the poet's surrogate, the speaker. And so I did, first in a trivial example (quoted from a rather obtuse student who had evidently reached for the phrase lacking the poet's name), then used by Richards himself.

> Furthermore, the speaker . . . chooses or arranges his words differently
> as his audience varies. . . . Finally, apart from what he says (Sense),
> his attitude to what he is talking about (Feeling), and his attitude to
> his listener (Tone) there is the speaker's intention, his aim, . . . the
> effect he is endeavouring to promote.

Had I already located the *ur*-persona? Not so fast. The book was half over.
Richards had considered thirteen poems without mentioning a speaker; he was
now embarking on a general discussion, not of poetry, but of "human
utterances," of speech itself. Naturally speech implied a speaker. This one,
like most others, had aims and intentions, endeavoured to promote effects;
"We speak," Richards informed us, "to say something." His *we* was inclusive.
Here was no mask, no "voice," no Duke of Ferrara, not even necessarily a
writer. Richards' speaker was only ourselves talking. I kept on reading, but in
185 more pages the speaker did not reappear.

Might he show up in Richards' star pupil? William Empson's *Seven Types
of Ambiguity* appeared in 1930, the year after *Practical Criticism.* It gave us a
word we couldn't do without, and taught us, more than any other single book,
how much could be teased out of a poem. (Eliot was later to refer to "the
lemon-squeezer school of criticism.") But it did not distinguish poet and
speaker. The single time Empson used the term was to make clear, in
discussing Herbert's *The Sacrifice,* that "the speaker is Jesus." The phrase was
available at need, but normal usage remained, to use Abrams' word,
"unsophisticated." It did not occur to Empson to render anonymous that
"speaker who talks first to himself, then to his sister" in *Tintern Abbey*, or to
attenuate Wordsworth's relation to what, in Empson's straightforward words,
"he wants to make a statement about."

> Wordsworth seems to have believed in his own doctrines and wanted
> people to know what they were. It is reasonable, then, to try to extract
> from this passage definite opinions on the relations of God, man, and
> nature.

> Wordsworth may . . . *have felt a something far more deeply infused*
> than the *presence* that *disturbed* him.

> He talks as if he owned a creed.

When Empson writes of Shelley's Skylark that "the poet is rapt into an
ecstasy which purifies itself into nescience," it might be Matthew Arnold.

Five years later, in R. P. Blackmur's *The Double Agent,* the speaker's
voice is still inaudible, even in the chapter on "The Masks of Ezra Pound,"
where Blackmur explains, for readers to whom it is evidently unfamiliar, a
term that neither Richards nor Empson had used:

> *Persona,* etymologically, was something through which sounds were
> heard, and thus a mask. . . . Mr. Pound's work has been to make
> *personae*, to become . . . in this special sense . . . a person through

which what has most interested him . . . might be given voice.

Yet Blackmur talking about poets was no more sophisticated than Empson. For him too poets spoke to say something, and in general the poem was what they said: "An apple, Mr. Stevens says [in *Le Monocle de Mon Oncle*], is as good as any skull to read." It might be "says," or something stronger: "For Keats, the Nightingale . . . let him pour himself forth." In any case, Keats uttered the ode, not a speaker.

By 1935, then, speaker and persona had made their appearance, but separately and very inconspicuously. Clearly, they had not yet made their way into critical practice, let alone theory.

It wasn't until I rounded up an old copy of Brooks and Warren that I found what I was looking for. I should have looked there first. Here were the terms I had found in place in the mid-sixties: Richards' *tone,* and with it, the speaker as we have come to know him. For the first time? Who can say? Literary critics have not as yet earned a concordance, and the teacher, as someone once remarked, sculpts in snow.

Cleanth Brooks and Robert Penn Warren's *Understanding Poetry* was first published in 1938, and its fourth edition is in print today—an astonishing record of pedagogical influence. Brooks and Warren brought the principles of neo-critical reading within the compass of teachers in every college, then in every high school. Revisiting it today, it's hard to appreciate the originality of his modestly titled "Anthology for College Students." The poems were accompanied by the explanations, questions, and exercises of a conventional textbook. Certainly the selection was new; metaphysical and modern poems were generously interspersed among the nineteenth-century favorites. But it was their arrangement that most plainly proclaimed a new agenda. They were not in chronological order, nor were they grouped by author nor by theme. A long "Letter to the Teacher" made the priorities clear: "Study of biographical and historical materials," served by chronological and authorial ordering, and "inspirational and didactic interpretation," invited by thematic grouping, were mere substitutes for the proper "object for study," "the poem in itself."

The poem in itself was now inherently dramatic (as Blackmur had said it sometimes but not always was). As a little drama, it had acquired a speaker. "What does section four [of *Ode to the West Wind*] tell us about the speaker? Does the poem sufficiently present his situation? Or do you need to consult a life of Shelley in order for the passage to gain full significance?" The answer was not far to seek.

Though Richards had not doubted that a poet, like other human utterers, had aims and intentions, he had denied him the truth-value of what he said. Poetry was different from philosophy, from all expository prose; it made pseudo-statements. (Eliot concurred, then demurred when he became a Christian.) Brooks and Warren made the application clear: there should be no "confusion between scientific and poetic communication." Poetry's pleasure and profit should be sought, not as of old in particular beauties or isolable *sententiae*, but in the poem as "an organic system of relationships," "object for study," objet d'art. In his *Principles*, Richards had named "message hunting." Brooks and Warren introduced the phrase to a generation of teachers and students—and poets—who learned from it not only how poetry should not be read but what it should not be.

And how does "the speaker" function to deter message-hunting? *Mrs. Park, which of them is true?* Why should the speaker speak truly? The Duke of Ferrara did not. Once the poet was dissolved in the persona, his poems scattered under new rubrics like "tone" and "imagery," a student was no longer in a position to ask questions about the attitudes and convictions of a single human being. *We* speak to say something; "the speaker" might say something different in every poem. And though the poet-as-speaker might retain his aims and intentions, the student must experience them with some loss of urgency. The danger of "inspirational or didactic interpretation" is markedly reduced when the unacknowledged legislators of mankind speak at one remove. Only a fool trusts a man in a mask.

Yet again, not so fast. If any such implications existed, they were still in embryo. Brooks and Warren might say "the speaker," but they were far from saying it consistently. And they certainly did not think of their new phrase as a possible focus of critical or pedagogic attention. Their Glossary contained no entry for "speaker" or "persona," and in their single explanatory sentence the poet came first. "Every poem implies a speaker of the poem, either the poet writing in his own person or someone into whose mouth the poem is put." The authors themselves shifted between speaker and poet almost at random.

> [Of *A Slumber Did My Spirit Seal*] Is the speaker saying that his loved one seemed so thoroughly immortal that he simply was asleep to the possibility that she could ever die?

> [Of *The Scholar Gypsy*] The poet says that his own age is confused by doubts.

There is, of course, a distinction to be made between the poet insofar as he speaks to say something, and the poet *qua* poet, shaping, ordering, choosing, and now and then the authors seemed to have it in mind: "Does the poet succeed in dramatizing the suggestion that the daffodils accept the speaker as a companion?" But the distinction collapses in practice. Back to the *Nightingale*: "This poem is obviously a reverie induced by the poet's listening to the song of the nightingale," not the poet as craftsman, but "the poet . . . just sinking into the reverie," the poet who "wishes for a dissolution of himself," and "breaks out of his reverie" in the last stanza. "Poet" melts imperceptibly into "speaker" as the discussion progresses, the total number of occurrences of each holding equal at eleven. In the book as a whole the usage is almost entirely fluid: if "the speaker" of the *Nightingale* has an "attitude toward death," it's "the poet" who has an "attitude toward fate" in Marvell's *The Definition of Love*. Sometimes the likely distinction is actually reversed: for *Among School Children* it's "the speaker himself and . . . the woman he loves," yet for *Two Songs from a Play*, so much less personal and circumstantial, it's "Yeats believes." Brooks and Warren are not yet committed to the speaker. "Is Johnson actually pointing a moral?" they ask of *The Vanity of Human Wishes*; when push comes to shove, as it generally does with the Doctor, it's back to the poet. Even an inspirational or didactic interpretation may get by if you agree with it: for *Shine, Perishing Republic*, the questions are "Does this poet hate America? Is he trying to admonish his country?"

Brooks was no more consistent when writing alone and for grown-ups, and only slightly more conscious. In *Modern Poetry and the Tradition* (1939), written, presumably, while he was working on *Understanding Poetry*, we hear much more from poets than from speakers: "Marvell . . . compares himself and his mistress to parallel lines"; "Donne may argue as in 'The Nocturnal on St. Lucy's Day' that he is nothing." Speaker and poet comfortably coexist: of *Ode to the Confederate Dead*: "The world which the dead soldiers possessed is not available to the speaker of the poem. . . . Moreover, the poet is honest: the leaves, for him, are merely leaves." Eight years later, in *The Well Wrought Urn*, the smokeless air over Westminster Bridge still "reveals a city the poet did not know existed," and it is "the poet" who begins the Immortality Ode "by saying he has lost something." By the next page, however, there has been a silent metamorphosis into "what the speaker has lost," and soon the usage is hopelessly confused: "Wordsworth says that the rainbow and the rose are beautiful": "the moon is treated as if she were the speaker himself"; "the poet cannot see the gleam." Practice has not yet hardened into consistency, still less into precept. Elton's *Glossary of the New Criticism*, published the next year, glossed "tone" and "irony," but not "persona."

Brooks came closest to making the distinction explicit in the chapter on Gray's Elegy, where he reproved Empson for failing to realize that "we are not dealing with Gray's political ideas," but with "what the Elegy says," with "the *speaker's* choice." The emphasis is Brooks's own; we can imagine him underlining the word. The issue resurfaced only in an appendix, where Donald Stauffer was criticized for confounding "the protagonist of the poem with the poet, and the experience of the poem as an aesthetic situation with the author's personal opinion." But Brooks was only working toward such aesthetic purity; in the body of the book he had not yet attained it. Old simplicities die hard.

It was not until 1951, in Reuben Brower's *The Fields of Light*, that we were told straight out that a poem is not merely a drama, but "a dramatic fiction," and that "its speaker, like a character in a play, is no less a creation of the words on the printed page." Brower's first chapter is titled "The Speaking Voice"; its first heading is "The Speaker." It is indeed an *ur*-text for persona, cited as such in Abrams' bibliography. Here the space allotted to "the poet writing in his own person" has visibly contracted; Brower is considerably farther along the road to the Universal Speaker.

> The voice we hear in a lyric, however piercingly real, is not Keats's or Shakespeare's; or if it seems to be . . . we are embarrassed and thrown off as if an actor had stopped and spoken to the audience in

his own person.

Description hardens into prescription. Poets may seem to speak in their own voices, perhaps they even do so in fact, but they shouldn't. Brower can accept it when Shelley in *Ode to the West Wind* comes on in "his familiar character of priest-prophet," but with "I fall upon the thorns of life! I bleed!," "the dramatic fiction slips disturbingly: the allegory refers us too directly to Shelley's biography," though Brower concedes it is "only after the poem's high commotion is past that we feel the lapse." But however compelling the theatrical metaphor, those of us who remember how entirely, in the forties, we had learned to condescend to Shelley may suspect that it was less the slippage of the mask that embarrassed than the sentiment. There seems no reason, after all, why a priest-prophet in his familiar character can't feel sorry for himself. The unobtrusiveness of the human author has become a criterion, in poetry and in the novel as well; Brower reproves E. M. Forster for "somewhat portentous observations" which "in their unironic solemnity . . . are not altogether in character for the narrator of *A Passage to India*."

James would have committed no such gaffe. Four years later, Brooks and Wimsatt would identify the novelist's "problem of securing impersonality for his art," and ask, "How does the narrator avoid introducing himself into the work?" How? He does so by joining the speaker on stage. There sock and buskin conveniently separate him from authorial temptations to say what he thinks or feels, and readerly temptations to experience his statements unprotected by irony. Mechanisms of detachment tend to cluster.

Yet actual critical practice continues to resist such aesthetic austerity. In Brower's verbs, poets still speak for themselves. As he compares sonnets by Donne and Hopkins, "Hopkins calls directly on God for help"; "Donne . . . for all his queries, [is] certain of his close and passionate relation to Christ," while "Hopkins [is] tortured at the very center of his faith." There are no apologies for his near-lapse into biography. Though Brower asserts a distinction between speaker and poet, he makes it only when need compels, as it does in his discussion of *Love III*, where his use of "story-teller," "narrator," "sinner," and "guest" (not, however, "speaker") only underlines the difference between Herbert's dramatized and universalized encounter with divinity and Donne's and Hopkins' direct and personal address.

Brower was far too good a reader to sacrifice that difference to a theory; writing naturally of "the intimacy of Donne's prayer" in Holy Sonnet X, he reserved "the speaker" for the overtly dramatized situation of *The Ecstasie*. In fact, Brower seldom used the term. It appears in a discussion of the *Essay on Riches*, to be immediately cancelled by a reference to "Pope's ridicule." It is notably missing in the extended treatments of *Absalom and Achitophel*, of Yeats's *Two Songs*, even of *Surprised by Joy*, though a footnote is there to admonish us that "a biographical reading, which the usual footnote to the poem invites, is altogether misleading and singularly unprofitable." Brower's transitional location between past naiveté and future rigor is marked by the doubled noun with which he concludes his discussion of the speaking voice:

"the poet-speaker."

T.S. Eliot's "The Three Voices of Poetry," first published in 1953, is also cited as an *ur*-text for Persona. Actually to consult it, however, is to experience the retroactive power of an idea to compel us to misunderstand a text, indeed to reverse its meaning. Eliot in 1953 was writing plays, and far from making the dramatic voice the type of all poetic speaking, he was particularly concerned to distinguish it. He explicitly restricts the poet as persona to the third of his three voices, that actually to be heard on a stage. In the first voice, "the voice of private meditation," the poet is "talking to himself—or to nobody"; in the second, he is "talking to other people." Only in the third does the poet create "a dramatic character speaking in verse." Devotees of the universal persona may be startled to realize that by this Eliot does not mean dramatic monologue but actual drama, in which the poet is "saying . . . only what he can say within the limits of one imaginary character addressing another imaginary character," characters who have "equal claims" upon him, and whom, therefore, "he cannot wholly identify . . . with himself." In dramatic monologue, however, "it is surely the second voice, the voice of the poet talking to other people, that is dominant." Though metaphorically "he has put on costume and makeup," he hasn't really.

> Dramatic monologue cannot create a character. When we listen to a play by Shakespeare, we listen not to Shakespeare but to his characters; when we read a dramatic monologue by Browning, we cannot suppose we are listening to any other voice than that of Browning himself.

To the author of *Prufrock* it couldn't be clearer: "What we normally hear . . . in the dramatic monologue is the voice of the poet." Even in the play *The Rock*, the chorus was "speaking directly for me," speaking, moreover, in the second voice, the voice that Brooks and Brower found so off-putting but which Eliot here claimed as his own: "The voice heard in all poetry that has a conscious social purpose—poetry intended to amuse or instruct, poetry that preaches or points a moral"—that invites a reader, among other things, to consider whether what it says might be true. No wonder Eliot didn't say "the speaker."

But for all his influence, Eliot was not teaching English in American colleges. Brooks and Warren were; it is from their second edition, published in 1950, that I have quoted, and the memories of fifties graduates confirm that it was in that decade that the speaker permeated the diction of the English class. And as the decade progressed, critics became more aware of what they were doing; for their 1960 edition, Brooks and Warren revised their Nightingale section to eliminate those eleven occurrences of "the poet." They were less aware of why they were doing it. Though the invocation of "the speaker" harmonized with New Critical de-emphasis of biography and "conscious social purpose," the association was never explicit. Even in 1960 Brooks and Warren did not completely banish the poet; though Keats was speakerized, Marvell and Yeats were left alone.

Poems vary, however, in the insistence with which they solicit interest in their poet. Shakespeare's sonnets are notorious for inveigling critics into biographical lapses, and their treatment in what for convenience I will call the Brooks and Warren years demonstrates how consistently the use of "the speaker" correlates with the critic's biographical stance.

When Empson wrote in *Seven Types* that "Shakespeare is being abandoned by Mr. W. H. and stiffly apologizing for not having been servile to him," he was only continuing a tradition already well established when Wordsworth, or someone very like him, said that "with this key / Shakespeare unlocked his heart." (Naturally it was Browning who replied, "If so, the less Shakespeare he.") Even in 1941, in *The New Criticism* itself, John Crowe Ransom, trying to cool down Empson's "overreading" of Sonnet 73, was quite comfortable writing things like

> At this stage in the sequence, Shakespeare is melancholy. He finds the world evil and would like to die. His health is probably bad, for he refers to the likelihood of death.

Ten years later, Edward Hubler and Wilson Knight were still reading the sonnets as the expression of Shakespeare's personal concerns; neither used "the speaker." But by 1963 the speaker is claiming an authority critics cannot ignore, though they vary in how consciously they recognize it. In Hilton Landry's *Interpretation in Shakespeare's Sonnets,* the speaker takes over, imperceptibly to the author, but before the reader's eyes.

As to biography, Landry is a fence-sitter. Though he applauds critical "efforts to dispose of the biographical school of sonnet criticism," he "cannot agree . . . that the poet's interests are not deeply involved," especially in view of Sonnets 40 and 41. And for the first half of his book the ancient locution comes naturally, as he writes of "Shakespeare's reluctance to blame a friend directly," of "Shakespeare asking the handsome youth, 'What is your substance, whereof are you made?'" "The sonnets which open the sequence urge the patron repeatedly to marry . . . but that was before Shakespeare's own dark lady seduced the patron." On page 63, however, the speaker makes a silent entrance; Sonnets 40, 41, and 42 now become "a trio of poems in which the speaker comments on aspects of a sexual triangle." For some ten pages thereafter poet and speaker coexist freely, in relation to the same poems and sometimes in the same paragraph. Then the balance tips. References to "the poet" and "Shakespeare" diminish, then disappear. By the end of Landry's book the speaker commands the field, with 27 instances in 24 pages. There has been no discussion of voice or persona, but the poet has slipped away.

The next year, when Murray Krieger came to the Sonnets, he not only said "speaker," but could be explicit about it: "Shakespeare presents us with a true lover . . . as his poet-persona." Poet-persona, lover, and Shakespeare are distinguishable, though still close; both Shakespeare and the speaker are poets, after all, so "the poet" can be written with something of the old ease. They may even both be lovers; once Krieger even slips into writing not that the speaker but "Shakespeare calls upon his friend" to accept "the blessing of parenthood." But for the rest his usage is both consistent and aware. How satisfyingly—and unexpectedly—the textual chase confirms personal history! It must have been just about 1964 that I got the news that poems were now to be talked about in a new way.

By 1968, the avowal of biographical interest has taken on a distinctly defensive coloration. Brent Stirling must confess on the first page of *The Shakespeare Sonnet Order* that "unlike some readers," he "would like to have some of the answers to the biographical mysteries." Stirling still feels easy saying "Shakespeare." So does Barbara Hernnstein Smith in her 1969 teaching edition: "The nature of Shakespeare's relation to the young man is addressed in many of the sonnets." James Winny, however, whose *The Master-Mistress* was published the same year, uses every argument he can think of to exclude a biographical reading, including the moral one (Shakespeare wouldn't have confessed anything so discreditable), and except when such references as "eternal lines" and "black ink" validate "the poet," he is careful to say "speaker."

In his 1969 *Essay on Shakespeare's Sonnets* and his 1977 edition of the poems, Stephen Booth has achieved full theoretical and practical consistency. Cooler than Winny, he jokes away any lingering biographical impurities. "Shakespeare was almost certainly homosexual, bisexual, or heterosexual. The sonnets provide no evidence on the matter." Since Booth's interest is in linguistic rather than human events, he does not often refer to whoever it is that utters the poems, but when he does, as in the discussion of Sonnet 35, the entity who "blames himself" is "the speaker."

Hallett Smith's 1981 book on the sonnets is perhaps the best illustration of the newly traditional diction of detachment. He too thinks he hears Eliot's Voices; he begins *The Tension of the Lyre* by quoting the first one, "the poet talking to himself." Invisibly and immediately, however, it is transmogrified, paraphrased into "poems in which the poet seems to be talking to himself." That "seems" sums up the speaker's forty-year progress toward universal imperium. For Smith, "the focus is on the feeling of the speaker," "the speaker's love is like a fever"; "there is little evidence in the first seventeen sonnets that the speaker feels love for the person addressed." And it's not only the speaker who's grown dim in the aesthetic distance, he's taken his friend with him, "the audience of the poem, fictional though it probably is." Pluralized, fictionalized, reduced to an It—what a fate for "the person addressed"! When at length Smith "must now consider the character of the poet (or speaker)," the parenthetical addition must disinfect so intimate a contact, and we are at once admonished to restrict our interest. "The 'I' of the sonnets . . . may or may not bear a close resemblance to William Shakespeare, but he is a *persona* with identifiable traits." We can guess which we are to prefer. Art's impersonality is more manageable than the untidy spectacle of poets who claim to look into their hearts and write. When Smith is momentarily brought "very close to the conclusion that the speaker in the Dark Lady sonnets is a man named Will, and that we are to take that person as William Shakespeare," his only recourse is to change the subject.

Poets tend to view things differently. Eliot had insisted his verse spoke for him. John Berryman added his own emphasis: "One thing that critics not themselves writers of poetry occasionally forget is that poetry is composed by actual human beings. . . . When Shakespeare wrote, 'Two loves I have,' reader, he was *not kidding*." A qualification followed—it was 1962, and the tradition was hardening: "Of course the speaker can never be the actual writer, who is a person with an address" and other impedimenta he can't carry into the poem. Distinguishing person and persona, Berryman quoted Ransom's phrase, "the highly compounded authorial 'I'." But all he seemed to mean was that a poet (he was talking about Lowell's highly personal *Skunk Hour*) may speak for others besides himself. It may even be the persona that makes the speaking possible: in a few years, Berryman would be writing the *Dream Songs*. When Robert Pinsky, poet as well as critic, identified the distancing persona as one of modern poetry's "strategies for retaining or recovering . . . the tones of the forbidden language of Arnold or Tennyson," Berryman was his premier example of how a poet through a persona "can use the style which annoys or embarrasses him, but which for some purposes he needs—needs more or less for its original, affirmative purposes." Needs as we all do; driven, we use irony to bypass irony. Reader, Henry was *not kidding*.

Only occasionally did critics join poets to retard the speaker's progress. Irvin Ehrenpreis resisted his invasion of eighteenth-century studies; in 1963 (the year of Landry's silent shift) his brief essay, "Personae" insisted on what had never before required insistence, that the fictive work is written by "the real person," and "if he tells a story, we must ask what he (not his emanation) means by the story. "But common sense appearing in an obscure festschrift and limiting its examples to Swift and Pope was not about to stop the tradition. Pinsky noted (in the mid-seventies) that speaking through a persona might "to a seventeenth-century reader . . . seem a bizarre way of writing poems of personal feeling"; he might have added that it might seem a bizarre way of talking about them. Indeed C. L. Barber, reviewing in 1978 Booth's books on the Sonnets, demurred briefly but explicitly from "those manuals of New Criticism" that "neatly separat[e] a 'speaker,' a dramatized presence, from the poet who mimes him," and argued gently that the "formalism" of Booth's interpretation ignored "human motives," "human gestures in the poems . . . that must reflect actual, . . . if somewhat obscure, personal relationships." Barber offered alternative interpretations which not only used the old locutions—as in "the poet's relation to the young man"—but depended on them. But these critical voices, eminent as they were, did not carry far. By 1981, the speaker's hegemony was so complete that John Reichert was impelled to ask, in a little-read but trenchant essay, "Do Poets Ever Mean What They Say?"

And it was in 1981 that my chase started, with the unyielding explanation of "Persona" I have quoted from the fourth edition of Abrams' *Glossary*—carried over unchanged, I was to find, from the third edition of ten years before. I had to take it as Abrams' own view; other entries made it clear enough when he disagreed with the ideas he summarized. Yet doubt nagged;

could the critic I remembered really practice the antiseptic sophistication he seemed to mandate? I must find out how Abrams himself had been talking in the years when critics were learning to say "the speaker." Textual chases never end, but every chase at last must have a stop. Mine would stop here.

By now dates had become evidence; I did not expect to find a speaker in *The Mirror and the Lamp.* That marvelous book was published in 1953 and begun much earlier; I had read it as an unpublished doctoral dissertation in 1944. I checked; in it, Young, Boileau, and Pope (for a sample) came right out and "said" what they said in their poems; MacLeish made "a poetic statement"; Cowley even "sang," as poets were erstwhile wont to do. And so it was even in 1963; in the essay "Romanticism and the Spirit of the Age," Abrams regularly introduced poetic quotations by the simple "says" (Collins, Coleridge); Blake "complained to the Muses," and Wordsworth not only said and described, but insisted, dismissed, claimed and proclaimed, plainly pointed out, and bade farewell. Not for long, however. I could almost have predicted the date; if 1963 was for Landry the year of the speaker, for Abrams it was 1965. In "Structure and Style in the Greater Romantic Lyric" we hear for the first time of "a determinate speaker . . . whom we overhear as he carries on . . . a sustained colloquy, sometime with himself or with the outer scene, but more frequently with a silent human auditor, present or absent."

The verbs are now all the speaker's—it is he who "achieves an insight, faces up to a tragic loss, comes to a moral decision, or resolves an emotional problem." In *Frost at Midnight,* the Coleridge who said things so readily only two years before has become "the meditative mind," "the solitary and wakeful speaker"; to the speaker, too, is attributed the childhood under review. Abrams' account of the *Ode on a Distant Prospect of Eton College* is equally fastidious: the poem "evokes in memory the lost self of the speaker's youth," and not Gray but the speaker "watches the heedless schoolboys at their games." When it's not the speaker who gets the verb, it's by a common alternate strategy, the poem itself, as "Keats's first long poem of consequence . . . represents what he saw, then thought, while he 'stood tiptoe upon a little hill.' " And no sooner has Abrams quoted William Lisle Bowes's clear statement that his sonnets "describe his personal feelings," than he rephrases it with the familiar dubiety; the sonnets "present a determinate speaker, whom we are invited to identify with the author himself." The word "persona" makes its expected appearance two pages later. The tradition is, it would seem, firmly in place.

And yet within the year Abrams' own speaker had returned to the limbo whence he came. In the 1966 essay, "Coleridge, Baudelaire, and Modernist Poetics," Wordsworth (in *The Prelude*) is describing, and without intermediary, "how, 'inspired by the sweet breath of heaven,' he assumed the prophet's sacred mission," and "calling on his fellow poet, Coleridge . . . to carry on with him 'as joint labourers in the work.' " Coleridge himself has reclaimed the right to say; the essay closes with him talking. " 'Joy,' he says . . . 'is the spirit and the power, / Which, wedding Nature to us, gives in dower, / A new Earth and new Heaven.' "

Though his *Glossary* explanation appeared for the first time in 1971, by 1972 Abrams' own poets had got back all their verbs. In *Natural Supernaturalism,* Shelley remarks and diagnoses; Coleridge dismisses, reveals, and reviews his life; Arnold asks; Eliot remarks, Auden makes a wry comment, Plath testifies, and Stevens enquires, rejects, and says, all in verse, and all *in propria,* as we used to say, *persona.* Wordsworth himself explains, announces (repeatedly), says, goes on to say, goes on to *pray,* puts it, feels, proclaims, and cries. Though Abrams of course recognizes when his poet speaks "through the medium of an invented character," and though he more than once discusses *Tintern Abbey,* there is no word of "the speaker who talks first to himself, then to his sister." When his sister is mentioned, in fact, the "his" refers directly to an antecedent "Wordsworth." Nor should we be surprised that Abrams couldn't keep his distance; that speaker is hardly consonant with the rich and humane contextuality of a critic the entire tenor of whose work opposes what he identified (in 1966, in "Coleridge, Baudelaire, and Modern Poetics") as "an aesthetic of an otherwordly, self-sufficient poem." It is characteristic, though odd, that when Abrams returned briefly to the idea of persona (in "Two Roads to Wordsworth," published like *Natural Supernaturalism,* in 1972), it was to praise it as an antidote to too much New Criticism, a concept which can "rehumanize poetry by viewing the poet, in Wordsworth's phrase, 'as a man speaking to men.'" But the reference to persona, though appreciative, is momentary. As with Brower, subject and verb tell the story, and through the seventies Abrams's speaker does not revive. Abrams's own *Norton Anthology* briskly returns to Coleridge the childhood he lost in 1965 as businesslike notes to *Frost at Midnight* inform the student that "The scene is Coleridge's cottage at Nether Stowey," "The infant in line 7 is his son Hartley," "The 'stern preceptor' . . . the Reverend James Boyer," and the "sister beloved" his sister Ann. And in an essay written as recently as 1983, Coleridge says, Wordsworth proclaims, and to provide the grand coda: "Shelley announced that

> The world's great age begins anew,
> The golden years return."

And they yet may, if common sense keeps breaking in. But it's a long road back to innocence. I don't teach Great Books anymore, worse luck, but sometimes I teach Dante. This year, in a paper entitled "Textual Cocktails," I read that "the interplay of Dante-as-poet (as opposed to Dante-as-pilgrim, both poetic constructs of Dante-as-author), textualizes the Inferno." The young man who wrote that is a marvelous student and a marvelous person, brilliant, excitable, and excited about ideas. But I fear he has almost lost the capacity to ask naive questions. I miss my community college students. Though they weren't used to literature, they were, some of them, perhaps for that very reason, ready to take it into their lives with an astonishing, hungry directness. I learned from them what I won't forget. Newly born Renaissance readers, they were coming into their heritage, reading for the reasons Horace and Sidney knew, for profit and delight. For them art could still hold the mirror up to nature. I learned to value that prelapsarian trust, to doubt that any paradise I could promise within The Poem Itself would be happier far. Could I sniff, farther down the road, an even newer criticism, one in which author, history, truth, meaning itself would dissolve, an insubstantial pageant faded? Subversion, as an activity, is overrated; the community college showed me that I did not want, and do not want, to undermine the assumption of very young people that great authors speak great words, and that great words proffer wisdom. Abrams would be the last to disagree that although we should not hunt messages, we should be willing to recognize and honor them when they are found.

Of course the speaker is often a useful concept, sometimes a necessary one. The pervasive attention to voice has increased the subtlety with which we are able to read literary texts as well as the length at which we can write about them, articulating nuances before undiscussed, if not therefore unapprehended or unfelt. But let's be sensible. Here, for example, is a new book attributing to Emily Dickinson "a voice, which though it is surely not hers, is so intimately defined by her habits of mind that it encourages friendship, familiarity, even affection." I'm told it's not hers, but I'm never told why. I'm supposed to know. Well, I don't know. Of course, as Abrams explained in the *Glossary*, "the I . . . is not the author as he exists in his everyday life," and "in each of the major lyricists the nature of the persona alters, sometimes subtly and sometimes radically, from one of his lyrics to the next." But do we really need to be told that the poet in everyday life never tasted a liquor never brewed, or wandered where the Muses haunt, especially since in the latter case the poet actually *was* with darkness and with dangers compast round? Our gain in subtlety is a loss in human community if we succeed in detaching the utterance from the uttering tongue and mind and heart, not occasionally and provisionally but as a matter of course. For we are all utterers—teachers, critics, poets, people—and at issue is the fullness of human commitment not merely to literature but to language, and language's commitment to what as human beings we think and believe and want and need to say. As to altering from one utterance to the next, everybody does that all the time, as any collection of letters—Flannery O'Connor's, say—will confirm. You'd have to be pretty unsophisticated to believe that "the speaker who utters Keats's *Ode to a Nightingale*" is the author as he exists in his everyday life, but you'd have to be more sophisticated than I care to be to believe he's not Keats at all. I would prefer my students to recognize that poets are just like folks, arted up a bit, perhaps, but still doing for the most part the same sort of thing their teachers do when they write an article, that they themselves do when without thinking they alter their tone for a parent or an employer or a friend. And although it is certainly possible to draw therefrom the conclusion that every voice is fictional, I do not care to press the point. It seems unnecessary for students to question the coherence of their own personalities because they write differently for the College newspaper and for me. Unleashed, the idea of the speaker takes on a terrifying applicability.

From that speaker it is only a step to the "novelistic, irretrievable, irresponsible figure" conjured up by Roland Barthes, "the Author himself— that somewhat decrepit deity of the old criticism," who plays at seeing himself as "a being on paper and his life as a *bio-graphy* . . . a writing without referent," "a text like any other." Or Foucault: "It would be as false to seek the author in relation to the actual writer as to the fictional narrator; the 'author function' arises out of their scission—in the division and distance of the two." So quotation marks break out all over, as Derrida tells us that "it would be frivolous to think that 'Descartes,' 'Leibniz,' 'Rousseau,' 'Hegel,' etc. are the names of authors," and adds that the "indicative value" he attributes to them is only "the name of a problem." A problem indeed; a problem at once frivolous and dire, an intellectual heresy, a *trahison des clercs.* A concept that can assimilate the Milton who in darkness implored celestial light to shine inward to Lemuel Gulliver is a concept that devalues human personhood and human pain.

My voice has slipped; these notes have changed too much to tragic. Critics still use the names of poets naturally. Heartening inconsistencies still challenge critical rigor. Biography is back, albeit too often tricked out in such psychometaphysical garments as to obscure the human form divine rather than reveal it. If poets should reclaim the right (I quote Pinsky) "to make an interesting remark or speak of profundities, with all the liberty given to the newspaper editorial, a conversation, a philosopher, or any speaker whatever," even the inspirational and didactic may return: a recent issue of *The Hudson Review* contains an article on "the moral authority of poetry." And students, thank God, are ever virgin; each generation must be taught anew the mechanisms of detachment, or, as I'm told it's now called, distantiation. Left alone, it is no more possible to distance them from the human statement, from what Archibald MacLeish called "the human voice humanly speaking," than Brecht's epic gimmicks could insulate his audiences from Mother Courage.

Reading, rightly understood, is a relationship; we read, Auden said, "to break bread with the dead." "All methods of criticism and teaching are bad," wrote Northrop Frye, "if they encourage the persistent separation of student and literary work"; our job as teachers is to try our best to "weaken those tendencies within criticism which keep the literary work objective and separated from the reader." I would rather have students too naive than not naive enough. Distrust exacts a price, as when children are taught to refuse rides from strangers. We pay it as criticism metastasizes, as we read more and more cleverly, first looking behind masks, then discerning masks where no masks are, then persuading ourselves that the eyeholes are empty. Cleverness excludes, and distrust privatizes. Distrust of the text opens the way to elaborated and idiosyncratic readings, and to a criticism that legitimizes them, even as it delegitimizes the common and accessible experience it stigmatizes as naive. I want my students to hear voices, to recognize ambiguities—even, in moderation, ironies. I want them to experience the literary work as a thing well wrought. Yet I am conscious of the price. The "object for study" all too easily becomes "objective" in Frye's sense, a problem to be solved, not an utterance like our own.

In this process, I believe the speaker has played an unobtrusive but influential part. I have for my last years as a teacher my own project of subversion, my target the sophistication that compasses me round. Fortunately it's not impossible, if you're confidently old-fashioned enough, to reactivate a nineteen-year-old's naivete. Dante, as ever, is a great help, Dante all tangled in biography and history, Dante the author, Dante the pilgrim, Dante the poet of many voices, who in Canto XX of the *Inferno* uses his own to tell us how to read a poem:

> *Se Dio ti lasci, lettor, prender frutto*
> *di tua lezione, or pensa per te stesso*
> *com' io potea tener lo viso asciutto . . .*

"Reader, so may God grant you to gather fruit of your reading, think now for yourself how I could keep my cheeks dry. . . ." Do we think it was only the poet's emanation that wept? Think of the poet's emotion, reader, so you can share it. If you want to gather the fruit of your reading, take care how you interpose with poetic constructs, especially those you yourself have constructed. Listen very carefully to what Dante is saying. Consider, even, that it might be in some sense true.

Looking and Listening for My Voice

by Toby Fulwiler

Just before the roundtable began, in Seattle, my friend John Trimbur asked me something about "foundationalism." When I asked did he mean Ford, Carnegie, or Rockefeller, John said, patiently, that I really ought to read more of the current literature on discourse communities. I responded, a bit defensively, that I had tried but couldn't get past the counter-hegemonic language. When Min Lu heard that, she raised her eyebrows, Pat Bizzell looked suspicious, Lil Brannon said "Really?" and Joe Harris wondered, no doubt, what I was doing on the panel in the first place. I explained that I really couldn't read some of that stuff any more than I could write or speak it, and if that meant the revolution would have to go on without me, that was OK. These words among friends were not, in any way, angry—and probably didn't even happen, though they seemed to.

Whether the conversation was real or not, it makes a good introduction to the following query into the nature of my own written voice: where it came from, what distinguishes it, and where it fits in our profession. In part, my search arises from recent CCCC discussions of the metaphorical notion of voice in writing—some identifying tone or timbre that makes us conscious of the author's presence, that lets us *hear* the person behind the sentences.

The prevailing *social constructionist* view focuses on the limited degree to which authors determine or control the major features (style, structure, topic, attitude) of their voices. Writers such as Ken Bruffee and David Bartholomae argue persuasively that writers *speak* primarily with the language of the specific discourse community to which they necessarily belong. Bruffee explains that "language and its products, such as thought and the self, are social artifacts constituted by social communities" ("Collaborative Learning and the Conversation of Mankind," *College English* 46 [Nov. 1984]: 641). Bartholomae concurs, suggesting in "Inventing the University" that writers "write in a history that is not of the writer's own invention" (*When a Writer Can't Write*, Ed. Mike Rose, Guilford, 1985, 143). In other words, our voices are determined largely outside of our selves, according to where we live and work, what we read, and with whom we interact.

Reprinted from *College Composition and Communication* (May 1990). Copyright 1990 by the National Council of Teachers of English. Reprinted with permission.

But did you ever try and locate your own voice? It's a tricky business. Even as I began the quest, I knew that I could no more identify all the determiners of my voice than I could all the beliefs and emotions that create my self. However, as the apparent author of my own writing, perhaps I could shed some light on the verbal constructions associated with *my own name*, that apparently present me—re-present me—for good or ill, to the rest of the world.

What do people mean when they tell me that they hear *me* in my published writing? "That really sounds like you" or "I really heard *you* in that piece"—I infer these to be statements about "voice." ("Yes, that really sounds like Toby's voice.") Are they saying something about my voice—hence my values and beliefs—or are they saying something more superficial about style? ("Yes, that really looks like the style in which Toby writes"—formal, informal, blunt, pretentious, whatever.)

If people hear me as a voice somehow distinct from the discourse community to which I obviously belong, what does that mean? Where, how, and why does my voice distinguish itself from the others who also dwell in my community? If I look closely at samples of my own writing, will *I* find the uniqueness that others tell me they find? And, more importantly, will that uniqueness be a telling or a trivial difference?

In the past I have not pressed these friendly voice-finders on the origins of their knowledge about my voice, but now I wish that I had, as I have become curious, myself, to know *where* or *how*, exactly, my voice is to be found. Is it in the skillful use of particular verbal constructions—say noun clusters, prepositional phrases, or appositives? Or the frequency of more dubious constructions such as split infinitives, dangling modifiers, or mixed metaphors? Am *I* characterized once and for all by a truly unholy number of fragments, dashes, and contractions? Or because I don't use enough active verbs, coordinating conjunctions, or semicolons? Could my voice be found in more elusive features—in rhythm, balance, scale, or symmetry? Or in more structural features—say in airtight logic, clever transitions, or cogent conclusions? Or in my choice of topics—like this one investigating personal voice? Or in a predictable attitude toward these topics—as in "A personal voice, along with truth, justice, and beauty, is a good thing to have."

I am having some fun picking at the particular features of what some of us would call "voice"—and others call "style." Nevertheless, I am genuinely interested in some relatively difficult questions: do I have an authentic voice (or more than one)? Where can I find it (them)? What does it (they) actually look like? How much does it (they) vary according to circumstances? And how much conscious control do I exert over it (them)?

My Private Voice

I began looking for evidence of my own voice where I expected most unequivocally to find it, the pages of my personal journals (kept on and off now since I was a sophomore at the University of Wisconsin in 1962). The following sample was selected with as much scientific methodology as I could muster—a quick flip to a random page in my current journal. Here is the resulting sample, taken from an entry dated 2/29/88:

> Laura's out with Carol at her book group; Meg's out after work w/ friends; Anna's upstairs with Allison, mad because I banned the telephone tonight. I have spent all afternoon on catch-up writing tasks—until I really *am* caught up! (Even got the *CCC* review done in a record two days!) The reason for a lot of this blocking out of small stuff is to allow me to concentrate tomorrow on the VOICE piece for CCCC—as yet just in the discovery stages. Too, I'd like to get the piece with Hank up and off the computer & sent to the *Chronicle* . . . why have I been so slow here?

What are the elements, if any, that reveal my authentic voice in this piece? Let's look.

Topic: You see me here reflecting on the current state of my professional life, taking stock of where I am, checking on what projects are finished, what still to be done, and in general writing to warm up, mark time, and perhaps begin some formal writing shortly. In all these ways, this is typical of what I do with private writing in my journal, including the casual and digressive comments about family and friends.

Context-Bound References: I refer to people you cannot be expected to know unless I provide you with a key: i.e., Laura is my wife, Carol a teacher friend of hers, Megan my seventeen-year-old daughter, Anna my thirteen-year-old, Allison her fourteen-year-old friend, Hank a colleague in history at the University of Vermont.

Informal Language: Many features here suggest language in an informal or colloquial mode—the language James Britton calls "expressive." Look, for example, at the frequent contractions and abbreviations (& and w/), a parenthetical construction, a variety of marks denoting special emphasis (underlining, capitalization, exclamation marks), vague words ("stuff," "a lot"), and something that's either a fragment or a run-on sentence (or both combined) at the very end.

Punctuation: We see, in addition to commas and periods, a whole range, from those marks considered especially informal (dashes) to those especially formal (semicolons), to those misused (an ellipsis for a dash, capitalization to italicize), to those that imply emphasis (exclamation marks, underlining), digression (parentheses), and questioning (?).

Rather than continue in this particular analytical vein, let me summarize my own impression of the personal voice found in my journal: it has all the features identifiable as private language, not intended to go very far away from the self—abbreviations, contractions, digressions, fragments, casual punctuation, and imprecise diction. In other words, my so-called most personal and private language is so typical of many others' personal and private language that it's been categorized and labeled—Britton calls it "expressive," Janet Emig calls it "reflexive," and Arthur Applebee calls it "personal." So much for the uniqueness of my voice in this authentic, private sample—which, by the way, is a very typical entry from my journal.

My Public Voice

The other most obvious place I looked for evidence of my authentically-me voice was in my published writing, for it is there, not in my journal, that people say they have actually heard me speaking. From "Writing Across the Curriculum: Implications for Teaching Literature" (*ADE Bulletin*, 88 [Winter 1987]: 35–40), I selected a short passage that seemed appropriately representative and looked at it to find evidence of the *I* that sounds like me. In the following passage, I was setting up an argument in favor of more in-class writing as a route to more active learning:

> THE MONOLOGUE IN THE CLASSROOM. The dominant mode of instruction in American colleges and universities—especially the larger ones—is top down and one way. Walk down the halls and look into the classrooms and what you most commonly see is an instructor standing in front of a class talking and rows of students sitting, listening, and copying. Sometimes these classes number in the hundreds, making other modes of instruction difficult—but not impossible—to conceive. Even in smaller classes of twenty-five and thirty the lecture/copy mode often prevails. In such classrooms it is the teacher, not the students, who practices and explores her language skills. This is the mode of education which Brazilian educator, Paulo Freire, aptly describes as "banking"—depositing knowledge in people as you do money in savings accounts. (36)

We see no context-bound references here. The only proper noun, the name of Paulo Freire, is briefly labeled ("Brazilian educator"). Though I use dashes three times, a lot in one paragraph, each is used conventionally—as is all the other punctuation. There is little of the variety or imprecision found in the journal entry. The diction, too, is more formal, with no contractions, abbreviations, first-person pronouns, or colloquial words. In other words, the features here are less varied and more conventional, suggesting language aimed at readers who do not know me personally—readers to whom I want to appear conventional and respectable.

(At this point the enormity of the task begins to dawn on me: I realize that the only convincing way to locate "me" in my own prose will be to locate a significant number of "not me's" in other people's prose. Voices against which my voice might be tested for distinction. In other words, to hear authenticity in my voice I will need to know in-authenticity when I see it. (This is getting progressively more complicated (I have now constructed in this paper a parenthetical within a parenthetical within yet another parenthetical.)))

However, while this published passage from the *ADE Bulletin* is more conventional in terms of identifiable features, there remain elements of timbre, of rhythm, of balance, of directness, of concreteness, and maybe of simplicity that I believe sound like me. I notice, too, that the language doesn't sound very sophisticated, but may be clear to the ear of even college freshmen. What explains how it got that way? My unique individual development? My membership in a particular discourse community?

Actually, I think I know at least part of the answer.

My Eighteen-Year-Old Self

When I look at the identifiable features of my public writing voice, I see a composite that I have created and continue to create, but that, at least until now, I have not been aware of creating. I do not remember sitting down and deliberately deciding to find a certain rhythm or tone or timbre or con- creteness—yet I know that as I write and revise I am continually reading back to myself my sentences to see if they sound right, to see if they are clear *to me*, and to see if they sound *like me*—the one I would like to have heard. No matter even that I am writing this essay for *College Composition and Communication* rather than *Language Arts* or *The Journal of Teaching Writing*—well, some matter—but before I risk sending it to this editor or that reviewer, I make sure it is intelligible, reasonable, and readable to this reviewer (me) first. My first audience remains the one in my own head—an argument made fifteen years ago by Walter Ong and more recently by Peter Elbow and Don Murray.

But to what audience in my own head—there are several—do I write? My eighteen-year-old self. I'm not sure that I can prove this, but I believe the me to whom I read back my prose is less my current full-professor self and more my first-year-college-student self. In reading Bartholomae's "Inventing the University," I recalled just how much I had in common with the first-year student struggling to join a university community whose governing rules seemed arcane and mysterious. Bartholomae explains that in order to write successfully for him, his students must figure out "what I know and how I know what I know . . . they have to learn how I write and offer some approximation of that discourse" (140).

Of course. And that was exactly my problem as a semi-serious college student of eighteen at the University of Wisconsin in 1961. Unlike many of my classmates who intended to become engineers, businessmen, doctors, and lawyers, I was not sure why I was in college in the first place. I struggled to write coherently in all my subjects that year, especially in French, and ended the year on probation. (I also smashed up my 1953 Studebaker, lost my girlfriend, and made sort of a general mess out of my life.) The reason I recall this now is that I was forced to make decisions that year about changing my habits (of mind as well as body) or dropping out of the academic game altogether. So I began to change my habits, began to look, deliberately, for the first time, for entry points into a community I did not well understand. That self-conscious knock at the door remains indelibly etched in my mind. I knew so little, wanted to know so much, and began the long apprenticeship of trial and error, replicating the discourse of the masters, that eventually gets English majors into graduate school.

My eighteen-year-old self belonged to discourse communities whose values were shaped largely by local conditions—white, protestant, middle-class, Midwest, suburban, high school—which resulted in values that were generally materialistic, conservative, apolitical, anti-academic, and so on. The community that I currently inhabit includes values generally associated with liberal-arts universities and English department writing programs; the resulting values might generally be described as intellectual, relatively leftist, a-religious, though still very middle-class, and so on. When I look at the former community in light of my current personal and professional identity, it can best be described as virtually "pre-academic" and "pre-disciplinary." Yet I am ascribing to it great powers in determining my current public voice.

I still carry around in my head that eighteen-year-old self for whom the world of intellectual ideas, historical contexts, and multi-syllabic words were puzzles of enormous proportions. Consequently—I think—I have always tried hard to make my own writing intelligible to that confused kid who wanted *in* nearly thirty years ago. If I can make my current voice clear to that earlier self I generally figure I can communicate with anybody. In fact, I credit that eighteen-year-old self—for whom nothing could be assumed, for whom everything had to be explained—with whatever successes I've had in teaching both "first-year composition classes" and "interdisciplinary writing work-shops," since both eighteen-year-olds and faculty members outside of English need modern rhetorical scholarship explained in the most elemental language possible.

Observations

It is not the nature or within the scope of this investigation to conduct an elaborate analysis of my voice print. I will, however, sketch out some of the propositions I have come to believe in writing this paper.

1. *If there is such a thing as an authentic voice, it is protean and shifty.* Even the most authentic voice—if it is mature—clearly changes so much, according to who is listening and why, that "authenticity" is hard to establish. (This is evident even in the two brief passages I selected for examination.)
2. *Most published voices are carefully constructed.* They are composed, revised, and edited to present the self in particular ways, conveying as best they can an image on paper that corresponds to a self-image in the author's head. (In my own case, at least in the *ADE* piece, I fuss over words, ideas, and especially rhythms in my writing to portray a writer who is at once democratic and scholarly, fair and committed, serious and ironic, etc.—all at the same time.)
3. *Authenticity can best be found by looking at whole pieces of discourse, preferably more than one.* It also helps to examine pieces written for different audiences and purposes. (In other words, in any given sentence or paragraph I'm likely to sound authoritarian, Republican, or silly—impressions that

subsequent paragraphs would surely correct.)

4. *When people hear a voice in writing, what they most likely hear is a tone conveyed through an aggregate of smaller discourse features characteristic of the writer's public persona.* (For example, in writing I commonly use parentheses to suggest an ironic perspective on my own discourse—which in turn parallels a similar perspective on my life—something a writing teacher in a literature department surely needs.)

5. *The structure of a whole piece of writing contributes significantly to the image of rationality in a writer's voice.* For this reason, journal entries, where paragraphs are few and digressions frequent, may convey a more scattered image of the writer.

6. *Distinctive writing voices commonly depend on language features associated with creative or imaginative writing.* In *An Alternate Style* (Hayden, 1980), Winston Weathers identifies these as features of Grammar B. These include deft description, apt analogies, careful crots, and frequent figures of speech (such as alliteration which you see me working hard at here).

7. *The writing topic itself contributes to the sense of voice.* Most of us choose to write about only a very limited number of the world's possible topics, and we do so for a reason. In other words, the topic—along with one's attitude toward it—may be a stronger determiner of what I would call "voice" than any specific linguistic trait. (All my published writing is about writing—in favor of more and certain kinds of it, for instance—so it is unlikely you would find *my* voice in a piece about computer chips, monetary reform, or grizzly bears.)

8. *Published voices are more distinctive than private voices.* My public voice, the one that others hear as "me," is, in fact, a carefully constructed artifact, designed to accomplish exactly what it does—sound like the me I want to appear to be. (As you read this paper, I hope that you can actually *hear* this voice—assertive, ironic, comic, balanced, conversational, whatever.) This public voice is carefully worked and crafted. But the work and craft are mine. My voice speaks from principles in which I believe and is shaped according to revision strategies I have learned. It is "authentic," in that it is honest, sincere, and trustworthy, but it is self-consciously so.

9. *My own voice is determined, to a significant extent, by a discourse community long thought left behind.* It is that thirty-year-earlier self that helps shape my current voice: conversational, simplistic, and fairly democratic (small "d"). (This stance is very tricky here, as I am aware of the sophisticated readership of *CCC*, yet don't want to violate the principles of voice just identified.).

10. *Writers' private, expressive language conveys less sense of voice than their transactional language.* This is at least true in my own case as I believe the linguistic features of my expressive language may actually resemble other private voices more than my own "authentic" public voice. Whether people actually hear the public "me" in my journal will be a hit-or-miss proposition. However, I would say it differs stylistically rather than substantially, as I often

write about the same things in both modes. While my expressive language is "authentic," it is not distinctive. (I actually believe that I am more interesting, lively, and socially aware than my private voice suggests. But more boring, dull, and self-centered than my published voice reveals.)

A Conclusion of Sorts

In the process of writing this paper, I have come to believe that I have a recognizable public voice, both embedded within and yet distinctly apart from others who inhabit the same community that I do. At the same time, its pitch, tone, and register can vary according to where it is directed. Though I can, on occasion, feign and adopt other voices—as when I'm writing obligatory memos, grant proposals, and other kinds of fiction—those more alien voices are difficult for me to maintain for any length of time.

It is clear to me that I write from within and, at the same time, from without an identifiable discourse community. Though this community almost always determines the topic of my writing, it does not necessarily determine its stance and style. Lately, these features of my voice seem to be at odds with the norm within my own community—which, like all academic communities, has adopted a specialized discourse that makes it difficult for eighteen-year-olds to enter and participate. The most identifiable features of my public voice are constructed to resist what I see as the exclusionary use of language by my own discourse community. (Sorry, John.)

Consequently, I believe that my own historical development—and the trials and errors contained therein—has made me forever uncomfortable within the discourse community to which I otherwise belong. It is my own paradoxical need to be within and yet write against it that most determines the total shape of my voice. If I am correct, you will find that same voice in this piece as well.

In Praise of Sound

by Don Ihde

The beginning of man is in the midst of *word*.

And the center of word is in breath and sound, in listening and speaking. In the ancient mythologies the word for soul was often related to the word for breath. In the biblical myth of the creation, God breathes life into Adam, and that breath is both life and word.

Today mythical thought is still repeated in other ways. We know that we live immersed in a vast but invisible ocean of air which surrounds us and permeates us and without which our life must necessarily escape us. For even when we humans wander far from the surface of the earth to that of the moon or deep into the sea, we must take with us packaged envelopes of air which we inhale and exhale. But in the words about breath there lurk ancient significances by which we take in the haleness or health of the air which for the ancients was spirit. From breath and the submersion in air also comes *in-spire*, "to take in spirit," and upon a final *ex-halation* we ex-(s)pire, and the spirit leaves us without life. Thus still with us, hidden in our language, is something of the ontology of Anaximenes who, concerning the air, thought, "As our souls, being air, hold us together, so breath and air embrace the entire universe."[1]

But the air which is breathed is not neutral or lifeless, for it has its life in *sound* and *voice*. Its sound ranges from the barely or not-at-all noticed background of our own breathing to the noises of the world and the singing of word and song among humans. The silence of the invisible comes to life in sound. For the human listener there is a multiplicity of senses in which *there is word in the wind*.

From a thoroughly contemporary source the importance of soundful significance may be discerned today as well. This new interest arises from various fronts of the contemporary sciences and philosophies. In philosophy there can be no doubt that questions of language and speech have been of great if not dominant importance in current philosophy. If on the one side that interest has been primarily in logic and syntax, as is the case with the Anglo-American philosophies, and on the other the interest has been the birth of meaning in speech in Continental thought, the question of word has been a

---

Reprinted from *Listening and Voice: A Phenomenology of Sound*. Athens, OH: Ohio UP, 1976: 3-16. Used with permission.
[1] Philip Wheelwright, *The Presocratics* (New York: Odyssey Press, 1966), p. 60.

central concern of the twentieth century. There has also arisen and flourished a whole series of linguistic sciences which relate to the question of word: phonetics, semiology, structural and generative linguistics, and the diverse schools of semantics.

Yet after the critical thinker has studied and read through these disciplines with their admittedly brilliant advances, there can remain a doubt that everything essential has been noted. For there appears in the very proliferation of disciplines addressed to the question of word a division which leaves word disincarnate. On the one side are the disciplines which address the structure, the form, the mechanics of language. Its surface and depth rules which produce significances are conceived of almost without the sense of enactment by a speaker in what may be termed a mechanics of language. The philosopher, concerned with comprehensiveness, must eventually call for attention to the *word as soundful*. On the other side the sciences which attend to the soundful, from phonetics to acoustics, do so as if the sound were bare and empty of significance in a physics of the soundful. And the philosopher, concerned with the roots of reflection in human experience, must eventually also listen to the *sounds as meaningful*.

There is a third source of the contemporary interest in sound and listening which, while so familiar as to be taken for granted, includes within it a subtle and profound transformation of experience itself as our capacities for listening are changed by technological culture. Its roots lie in the birth of the electronic communications revolution. Through this revolution we have learned to listen farther than any previous human generation. The telephone, the radio, and even the radio telescope have extended the range of our hearing as never before. It has also made technologically produced sound pervasive, as the Beatles and Beethoven alike blare forth from the living-room stereo.

But above all, the electronic communications revolution has made us aware that once silent realms are in fact realms of sound and noise. The ocean now resounds with whale songs and shrimp percussion made possible by the extension of listening through electronic amplification. The distant stars, which perhaps are not so thoroughly in a "harmony of the spheres" of the Pythagoreans, nevertheless sputter in the static of radio-astronomy. In our urban environments noise pollution threatens the peace of mind which we now wishfully dream of in terms of quieter eras.

It is not merely that the world has suddenly become noisier, or that we can hear farther, or even that sound is somehow demandingly pervasive in a technological culture. It is rather that by living with electronic instruments our experience of listening itself is being transformed, and included in this transformation are the ideas we have about the world and ourselves.

If we grant that the origins of science lie with the Greeks, aided by the sense of mastery implied in the human role of cocreator with the Hebrew God, there remains a distinct distance from both Greek science and Hebrew theology in the rise of technology. Contemporary science is *experienced* as embodied in and through instruments. Instruments are the "body" which extend and transform the perceptions of the users of the instruments. This phenomenon may be considered apart from the usual considerations of the logic of the sciences, of the inner language of science in mathematics, and it may be investigated in terms of the experience through technology of the world, others and myself.[2]

What is of special interest to the thoughtful listener is then the way instruments, particularly those of the electronic era, introduce ways of listening not previously available. If one playfully turns to a speculative consideration of the role of instrumentation as a means of embodied experience in relation to the rise of modern science, a hypothesis suggests itself. Whether by historical accident or a long-held and traditional preoccupation with vision, the new scientific *view* of the world began with equally new instrumental contexts made possible by the emerging technologies of lens grinding and a concern with optics. Galileo's moons, never before seen, are *experienced through* the embodying and extending instrument of the telescope. The universe comes into view, is *observed* in its ever-extending macrocosm, through the instrument. Nor does it make any essential difference in the phenomenon of the transformed experience whether the discovery follows and confirms a speculation or initiates and inaugurates a new view of things. In either case what was previously unseen occurs within experience itself. The same occurs under the gaze of the microscope. A miniworld never before seen even if its existence had been suspected unfolds with a wealth and richness of animals, plants, cells, and microbes not dreamed of in the theoretical imagination which preceded the perception. Thus with increasingly passionate excitement humankind became more and more entranced with this extension of its vision.

Subtly, however, the extension of vision not only transformed but *reduced* humankind's experience of its newly found domains. For the picture of the world which began to unfold through the new instrumentation was essentially a *silent* world. The macrocosmic explosions of the stars and the microcosmic noise of insects and even of cells had not yet reached the human ear. If today we know that this silence was not a part of the extended but reduced world of early modern science, it is in part due to the later development of another means of embodiment through electronic instruments. What was first seen was later given *voice*.

In the gap between optics and electronics in this speculation, the sense of the world moved from the once silent Galilean and Newtonian universe to the noisy and demanding universe of today. But almost by rebound the intrusion of sound perhaps reveals something about our previous way of thinking, a thinking which was a viewing, a *worldview*. We have discovered a latent, presupposed, and dominant visualism to our understanding of experience. If on the popular front it has taken those concerned with media, such as

---

[2] See Patrick Heelan, "Horizon, Objectivity and Reality in the Physical Sciences," *International Philosophical Quarterly* 7 (1967): 375-412. Also, Don Ihde, "The Experience of Technology," *Cultural Hermeneutics* 2 (1974): 267-79.

Marshall McLuhan, and Walter J. Ong, to point this out for contemporary consciousness, it is because this visualism has long been there for us to see had we but the reflective power to discern it.

This visualism may be taken as a symptomatology of the history of thought. The use and often metaphorical development of vision becomes a variable which can be traced through various periods and high points of intellectual history to show how thinking under the influence of this variable takes shape.

The visualism which has dominated our thinking about reality and experience, however, is not something intrinsically simple. As a tradition it contains at least two interwoven factors. The first is more ancient and may be thought of as an implicit *reduction to vision* whose roots stem from the classic period of Greek philosophical thought. Its source lies not so much in a purposeful reduction of experience to the visual as in the glory of vision which already lay at the center of the Greek experience of reality.

In contemporary philosophy it has been Martin Heidegger who has made us most aware of the deeper roots of the vision of the Greeks. Through his radical analysis of the question of Being, Greek thinking itself emerges as the process of allowing Being to 'show forth' as the 'shining' of *physis*, of the 'manifestation' of Being as a 'clearing' all of which recalls the vibrant *vision* of Being. Nor is Heidegger alone in this recognition of the intimacy between vision and the ultimately real for Greek thought. Theodor Thass-Thienemann notes, "The Greek thinking was conceived in the world of light, in the Apollonian visual world. . . . The Greek language expresses this identification of 'seeing' and 'knowing' by a verb which means in the present *eidomai,* 'appear', 'shine', and in the past *oida,* 'I know', properly, 'I saw'. Thus the Greek 'knows' what he has 'seen'."[3] Even the Greek verb meaning "to live" is synonymous with "to behold light."[4] Before philosophy and deep in the past of Greek experience the world is one of vision. In this sense visualism is as old as our own cultural heritage.

But with the development of philosophy, more with its *establishment* in the Academy and the Lyceum, the preference for vision expressed in the wider culture begins to become more explicit. Visualism arises with a gradual distinguishing of the senses. One of the earliest examples lies in the enigmatic claim of Heraclitus that "eyes are more accurate witnesses than ears."[5] Not being given a context for the fragment, it is of course quite difficult to discern what Heraclitus meant. He could have meant that to see something happen in the flesh is more accurate than to hear of it through gossip. But even if this is not what he had in mind, the relation of sight and accuracy already appears to be established. Experientially it is not at all obvious that eyes are more discriminating than ears.

---

[3] Theodor Thass-Thienemann, *Symbolic Behavior* (New York: Washington Square Press, 1968), p. 147.
[4] F. David Martin, *Art and the Religious Experience* (Lewisberg, Pa.: Bucknell University Press, 1972), p. 236.
[5] Wheelwright, *The Presocratics*, p. 70.

Even the ordinary listener performs countless auditory tasks which call for great accuracy and discrimination. In physical terms the mosquito buzzing outside the window produces only one-quadrillionth of a watt of power; yet one hears him with annoyance, even if one can't see him. And the moment trained listening is considered, feats of discrimination become more impressive. The expert auto mechanic can often detect the difficulties in an engine by sound, although when it has been taken apart the play in the bearings may be difficult to see. And in the paradigm of disciplined listening, the musician demonstrates feats of hearing which call for minute accuracy. The listener to the subtlety of Indian music with its multiple microtones discovers an order of extremely fine auditory embroidery.

But whether or not Heraclitus stated a preference for vision which may already conceal a latent inattentiveness to listening, Aristotle, at the peak of academic philosophy, notes, "Above all we value sight . . . because *sight is the principle source of knowledge* and reveals many differences between one object and another."[6] Here is a clearer example of a preference for vision and emerging distinctions among the senses.

Several features of this text stand out. First, it is clear that Aristotle notes that the valuation of sight is already something common, taken for granted, a tradition already established. Second, there is again the association of sight with differences and distinctions which may be the clue to a latent inattentiveness to listening. But, third and most important, the main thrust of Aristotle's visualism lies in the relation between sight and *objects*. The preference for vision is tied to a metaphysics of objects. Vision already is on the way to being the "objective" sense.

Once attention to the latent visualist tradition of philosophy is made concerning the intimate relation between light imagery and knowledge, a flood of examples comes to mind. For visualism in this sense retains its force in English and in most related Indo-European languages. Only the briefest survey shows the presence of visual metaphors and meanings. When one solves a problem he has had the requisite *insight*. Reason is the *inner light*. There is a *mind's* "*eye*." We are *enlightened* when informed by an answer. Even the lightbulb going on in a cloud over the cartoon character's head continues the linkage of thought with vision.

Less obvious but equally pervasive are the terms which, while they have lost the immediacy of light imagery, retain it at the root meaning. *Intuition* comes from the Latin *in-tueri*, "to look at something." Even *perceive* is often implicitly restricted to a visual meaning. Vision becomes the root metaphor for thought, the paradigm which dominates our understanding of thinking in a reduction *to* vision.

Philosophy and its natural children, the sciences, have often blindly accepted this visualism and taken it for granted. It is not that this tradition has been unproductive: the praise of sight has indeed had a rich and varied

---

[6] Aristotle, *Metaphysics*, trans. John Warrington (London: J. M. Dent and Sons), p. 51 (italics mine).

history. The rationality of the West owes much to the *clarity* of its vision. But the simple preference for sight may also become, in its very richness, a source of the relative inattentiveness to the global fullness of experience and, in this case, to the equal richness of listening.

Even within the dominant traditions there have been warnings in the form of minority voices. Empedocles called for a democracy of the senses.

> Come now, with all your powers discern how each thing manifests itself, trusting no more to sight than to hearing, and no more to the echoing ear than to the tongue's taste; rejecting none of the body's parts that might be a means to knowledge, but attending to each particular manifestation.[7]

And from the very earliest stratum of Greek philosophical thought Xenophanes voiced the note that experience in its deepest form is global: "It is the whole that sees, the whole that thinks, the whole that hears".[8]

Were, then, the dominant visualism which has accompanied the history of thought a mere inattention to listening, the praise of sound which may begin in its own way in the twentieth century would be but a corrective addition to the richness of philosophical vision. And that itself would be a worthwhile task. But the latent reduction *to* vision became complicated within the history of thought by a second reduction, a reduction *of* vision.

The roots of the second reduction lie almost indiscernibly intertwined with those arising from the preference for vision; the reduction *of* vision is one which ultimately separates sense from significance, which arises out of doubt over perception itself. Its retrospective result, however, is to diminish the richness of every sense.

For the second reduction to occur there must be a division of experience itself. This division was anticipated by two of the Greeks, Plato and Democritus, who were opposed in substance but united formally in the origin of Western metaphysics. For both, the ultimately real was beyond sense, and thus for both, sense was diminished. Both "invented" metaphysics.

This invention was the invention of a perspective, a perspective which was ultimately *imaginative*, but which in its self-understanding was the creation of a "theoretical attitude," a stance in which a constructed or hypothesized entity *apart from all perceptual experience* begins to assume the value of the ultimately 'real'. With Democritus the occasion for the invention of metaphysics came with the idea of the *atom*. The atom is a thing reduced to an *object*. Rather than a thing which shows itself within experience in all its richness, the atom is an object which has 'primary' qualities to which are added as effects 'secondary' qualities which are 'caused by' the primary qualities. Thus, too, is *explanation* born. The task of metaphysics is to "explain" how the division it introduces into the thing is overcome by a

---

[7] Wheelwright, *The Presocratics*, p. 70.
[8] Ibid., p. 32.

theory of complex relations between the 'primary' and the 'secondary' qualities.

Democritus's atoms are no longer things, they are "objects" which, while they may *seem* to possess the richness of things, at base are "known" to be poorer than things. Democritus's atoms, according to Aristotle, possess only *shape, inclination* (direction of turning), and *arrangement*. But note what has happened to sense: "visually" the atoms are "really" colorless, and insofar as they are colorless in "reality" they are "beyond" sense *in principle*. This is a leap which propels Democritus onto a path prepared for but never taken by his predecessors. Anaxagoras's "seeds," which were the predecessors of atoms, were in *practice* invisible, because they were too small for our eyes to see. What was lacking was a means of bringing them into view. But even though our powers are limited, for Anaxagoras "appearances are a glimpse of the unseen."[9]

But with the Democritean atom which is *essentially* colorless, what sense "gives" is placed under an ultimate suspicion. For Democritus it is "by convention that color exists, by convention sweet, by convention bitter." Knowledge is divided into sense, and what is not yet named but which is essentially different from sense. "Of knowledge there are two types: the one genuine, the other obscure. Obscure knowledge includes everything that is given by sight, hearing, smell, taste, touch; whereas genuine knowledge is something quite distinct from this."[10] This momentous turning was not taken without some doubt. Democritus heard this doubt in a voice given to the senses, "Ah, wretched intellect, you get your evidence only as we give it to you, and yet you try to overthrow us. That overthrow will be your downfall."[11] Nor is it ever clear that the "overthrow" succeeded completely. Even the atom retained one, though diminished, *visual* attribute in its *shape*. The preliminary result of the "invention" of metaphysics was the diminution *of* vision in its essential possibilities.

Plato in his own way made the same "invention." But Plato's version of the "invention" of metaphysics was, if anything, more complete than Democritus's. If Democritus's atoms retained one visible predicate, Plato's ultimate "reality," the Idea of the Good, in itself contained none but was presumably known only to the mind or intelligence. There does remain an *analogy* with the sensible, and that analogy is again visual. The Idea of the Good is "like" the sun in the visible realm. "It was the Sun, then, that I meant when I spoke of that offspring which the Good has created in the visible world, to stand there in the same relation to vision and visible things as that which the Good itself bears in the intelligible world to intelligence and intelligible objects."[12] But Plato steadfastly maintained that this was merely an analogy: "light and vision were thought to be as like the Sun, but not identical

---

[9] Ibid., p. 160.
[10] Ibid., p. 182.
[11] Ibid., p. 182.
[12] Plato, *The Republic*, ed. Francis Cornford (London: Oxford University Press, 1945), p. 219.

with it . . . to identify either with the Good is wrong,"[13] because the distinction between the visible or sensible and the intelligible which founds the doctrine of forms of Ideas has already separated sense from reason. The sensible realm in its "likeness" or analogy to the purely intelligible realm of the Ideas becomes a "representation" which indicates what cannot be sensed. In the notion of imitation, mimesis, and representation lies the direction which is counter to that of the polymorphic embodiments of experience, and which lays the antique basis for the more modern forms of the dualism of experience which pervade the contemporary era. The ancient sources of the double reduction of experience in visualism did not become clear or mature until the opening of the modern era. Modern visualism as a compounded reduction of experience is clearly notable in the work of Descartes where both the Democritean and Platonic anticipations meet to form the basis of modern visualism. Descartes unites and preserves the ambiguities of the diminution of the senses in his praise of the *geometrical method*. For Descartes the light and visual imagery has become metaphorical in a rather perfunctory sense: "Having now ascertained certain principles of material things, which were sought, not by the prejudices of the senses, but by the *light* of reason, and which thus possess so great evidence that we cannot doubt their truth, it remains for us to consider whether from these *alone* we can deduce the explication of all the phenomena of nature."[14] Thus in the rise of modern metaphysics there is retained the echo of a distrust of the senses and a corresponding faith in reason as an invisible, imperceptible realm of truth.

With Descartes the progression of the diminution of sense continues, and the object is now reduced to its geometric attributes: he further reduces the Democritean atom. "The nature of the body consists not in weight, hardness, colour and the like, but in extension alone it is in its being a substance extended in length, breadth, and depth."[15] Here the Democritean anticipations of a doctrine of 'primary' and 'secondary' qualities take the form of being defined in geometric terms. Extension is 'primary' and all other qualities are 'secondary' or derived.

- -

This progressive march of reductionism in philosophy is more than a mere visualism which stands as its symptom. It is a tendency which lies more deeply in a certain self-understanding of philosophy. On a surface level, and again symptomatically, a visualism can be called into question by pointing up consequences which lead to the inattention to important dimensions of experience in other areas, here, in particular in an inattention to listening. Not only are sounds, in the metaphysical tradition, secondary, but the inattention to the sounding of things has led to the gradual loss of understanding whole

---

[13]Ibid., p. 220.
[14]René Descartes, *A Discourse on Method*, trans. John Veitch (London: Everyman's Library, 1969), p. 212 (italics mine).
[15]Ibid., p. 200.

ranges of phenomena which are there to be noted.

What is being called visualism here as a symptom is the whole reductionist tendency which in seeking to purify experiences belies its richness at the source. A turn to the *auditory dimension* is thus potentially more than a simple changing of variables. It begins as a deliberate decentering of a dominant tradition in order to discover what may be missing as a result of the traditional double reduction of vision as the main variable and metaphor. This deliberate change of emphasis from the visual to the auditory dimension at first symbolizes a hope to find material for a recovery of the richness of primary experience which is now forgotten or covered over in the too tightly interpreted visualist traditions.

It might even be preliminarily suspected that precisely some of the range of phenomena at present most difficult for a visualist tradition might yield more readily to an attention which is more concerned with listening. For example, symbolically, it is the *invisible* which poses a series of almost insurmountable problems for much contemporary philosophy. "Other minds" or persons who fail to disclose themselves in their "inner" invisibility; the "Gods" who remain hidden; my own "self" which constantly eludes a simple visual appearance; the whole realm of spoken and heard language must remain unsolvable so long as our seeing is not also a listening. *It is to the invisible that listening may attend.*

If these are some of the hopes of a philosophy of listening and voice, there remains within philosophy a strong resistance to such a task. For philosophy has not only indicated a preference for the visual and then reduced its vision from the glowing, shining presence of *physis* to its present status as the seeing of surfaces as combinations of atomized qualities, but it has harbored from its classic times a suspicion of the *voice*, particularly the sonorous voice. Although there may be a certain touch of irony in the *Republic* of Plato (who could be a more subtle rhetorician than Socrates?), the intimation of danger in poetry, dramatic recitation, and even in certain music remains. There is in philosophy a secret tendency toward a morality of sparseness which today is typified by a preference for desert landscapes. Socrates noted, "It strikes me, said I, that without noticing it, we have been purging our commonwealth of that luxurious excess we said it suffered from."[16]

In the wider Greek culture, however, the Apollonian love of light was balanced by the Marsyasian love of sound. The tragedies spoke in sonorous voices through the *persona,* or "masks," which later are held to mean also *per-sona* or "by sound." Nietzsche, who much later placed into a dialectic the Apollonian and the dark and furious Dionysian, affirmed that one must also accept a "god who dances" as well as the stability of Apollonian form. Yet in spite of the apparent domination of a new reduced Apollonian visualism, there is also another root of our Western culture which takes as primary a version

---

[16]Plato, *The Republic*, p. 87.

of a "god who dances" with the movement and rhythm of sound.

That tradition is not that of philosophy but that of the Hebrew theology of the imagery of word and sound. The primary presence of the God of the West has been as the God of Word, YHWH. "And God *said,* let there be—. . . . " The creative power of the Hebrew God is *word* which is spoken forth as power: *from word comes the world.* And although God may hide himself from the eyes, he reveals himself in word which is also event in spite of the invisibility of his being. Human life, too, as the word-breath which unites the human with others and the gods is a life in sound. But if the world is devocalized, then what becomes of listening? Such has been a theological question which has also pervaded our culture.

A theology is not a philosophy, and what is needed is not a revival of theology, not even a secular theology. For so long as the gods remain silent—and if they are dead they have fallen into the ultimate silence—no amount of noise will revive them. But if they speak they will be heard only by ears attuned to full listening. For what is needed is a *philosophy* of listening. But is this a possibility? If philosophy has its very roots intertwined with a secret vision of Being which has resulted in the present state of visualism, can it listen with equal profundity? What is called for is an ontology of the auditory. And if any first expression is a "singing of the world," as Merleau-Ponty puts it, then what begins here is a singing which begins in a turn to the auditory dimension.

But while such a symptomatology has its tactical uses, a deliberate decentering of visualism in order to point up the overlooked and the unheard, its ultimate aim is not to replace vision as such with listening as such. Its more profound aim is to move from the present with all its taken-for-granted beliefs about vision and experience and step by step, to move towards a radically different understanding of experience, one which has its roots in a *phenomenology* of auditory experience.

Section 2:
Two Recent Views

Letter to Readers, 1993

by Carol Gilligan

Of the many questions people have asked me in the years since *In a Different Voice* was published, three kinds come up frequently and go to the heart of my writing: questions about voice, questions about difference, and questions about women's and men's development. In thinking about these questions and learning from the work of other people, I have come to understand voice, difference, and development in ways that go beyond what I knew at the time when I wrote this book. I have also come to see more clearly the book's two-part structure: the relationship between psychological theory and women's psychological development, including the ways in which psychological theory becomes prescriptive. In the outer chapters (1, 2, and 6), I introduce a relational voice and develop its counterpoint with traditional ways of speaking about self, relationship, and morality, as well as the potentials for misunderstanding, conflict, and growth. In the inner chapters (3, 4, and 5), I reframe women's psychological development as centering on a struggle for connection rather than speaking about women in the way that psychologists have spoken about women—as having a problem in achieving separation.

I will begin with voice. The work of Kristin Linklater, one of theater's leading teachers of voice, has led me to a new understanding of voice and also to a far deeper understanding of my own work. Her analysis of the human voice has given me a physics for my psychology—a way of understanding how the voice works in the body, in language, and also psychologically, and therefore a way of explaining some of the psychological processes I have described. I have learned about resonance and come to a new way of understanding how the voice speaks in relationship—how it is expanded or constricted by relational ties—from Normi Noel, an actor, director, and voice teacher who builds on Linklater's work and that of Tina Packer. These women, all of whom work in the theater, have an understanding of voice which is physiological and cultural as well as deeply psychological. Linklater speaks of "freeing the natural voice," the title of her first book, and what she means is that you can hear the difference between a voice that is an open channel—connected physically with breath and sound, psychologically with feelings and thoughts, and culturally with a rich resource of language—and a voice that is impeded or blocked. Having worked with Linklater, I have

Reprinted from *In a Different Voice: Psychological Theory and Women's Development* (Cambridge, MA: Harvard UP, 1993): xv-xxvi. Reprinted with permission.

heard and experienced the differences she describes. I also have learned from working with Noel to pick up relational resonances and follow the changes in people's voices that occur when they speak in places where their voices are resonant with or resounded by others, and when their voices fall into a space where there is no resonance, or where the reverberations are frightening, where they begin to sound dead or flat.

With this dramatic expansion of the empirical base of my work, I find it easier to respond when people ask me what I mean by "voice." By voice I mean voice. Listen, I will say, thinking that in one sense the answer is simple. And then I will remember how it felt to speak when there was no resonance, how it was when I began writing, how it still is for many people, how it still is for me sometimes. To have a voice is to be human. To have something to say is to be a person. But speaking depends on listening and being heard; it is an intensely relational act.

When people ask me what I mean by voice and I think of the question more reflectively, I say that by voice I mean something like what people mean when they speak of the core of the self. Voice is natural and also cultural. It is composed of breath and sound, words, rhythm, and language. And voice is a powerful psychological instrument and channel, connecting inner and outer worlds. Speaking and listening are a form of psychic breathing. This ongoing relational exchange among people is mediated through language and culture, diversity and plurality. For these reasons, voice is a new key for understanding the psychological, social, and cultural order—a litmus test of relationships and a measure of psychological health.

In an introduction to *Love's Labour's Lost* in the Riverside edition of Shakespeare's plays, Anne Barton makes an observation about language which rings true in the current discussion of culture and voice: "Language cannot exist in a vacuum. Even on what may seem to be its most trivial and humorous levels, it is an instrument of communication between people which demands that the speaker should consider the nature and feelings of the hearer. In love above all, this is true—but it is also true in more ordinary relationships." In this play about love and language, heterosexual love requires a change in language, following the demonstration that the men do not know the women whom they say they love: "Gently, but firmly, the men are sent away to learn something that the women have known all along: how to accommodate speech to facts and to emotional realities, as opposed to using it as a means of evasion, idle amusement, or unthinking cruelty."

Elizabeth Harvey, in *Ventriloquized Voices,* explores the question of why and when men, in the English Renaissance and also at present, have chosen to create feminine voices or to speak through female bodies, to ventriloquize their voices in this way. I find her analysis extremely helpful because she is so clear about the difference between the epistemological question of whether a man can know what it is to be a woman and therefore can speak on women's behalf and the ethical and political questions: what are the ethics and politics of men speaking for women or creating a feminine voice? When I have spoken with women about experiences of conflict, many women have a hard time distinguishing the created or socially constructed feminine voice from a voice which they hear as their own. And yet women *can* hear the difference. To give up their voice is to give up on relationship and also to give up all that goes with making a choice. It was partly because of the link between voice and choice that the *Roe v. Wade* decision initiated or legitimized a process of psychological and political growth for many women and men.

Which brings me to the question of difference. In the early 1970s, when I was working with Lawrence Kohlberg as a research assistant, I found his argument very powerful: in the aftermath of the Holocaust and the Middle Passage, it is not tenable for psychologists or social scientists to adopt a position of ethical neutrality or cultural relativism—to say that one cannot say anything about values or that all values are culturally relative. Such a hands-off stance in the face of atrocity amounts to a kind of complicity. But the so-called objective position which Kohlberg and others espoused within the canon of traditional social science research was blind to the particularities of voice and the inevitable constructions that constitute point of view. However well-intentioned and provisionally useful it may have been, it was based on an inerrant neutrality which concealed power and falsified knowledge.

I have attempted to move the discussion of differences away from relativism to relationship, to see difference as a marker of the human condition rather than as a problem to be solved. Robert Alter, in *The Art of Biblical Narrative,* has observed that the ancient Hebrew writers developed a narrative art because only through narrative could they convey a view of human life as lived reflectively, "in the changing medium of time, inexorably and perplexingly in relationship with others." At present, I find that women writers, and especially African-American poets and novelists who draw on an oral/aural tradition and also on searing and complex experiences of difference, are taking the lead in voicing an art that responds to the question which now preoccupies many people: how to give voice to difference in a way that recasts our discussion of relationship and the telling of truth.

One problem in talking about difference and the consequent theorizing of "difference" lies in the readiness with which difference becomes deviance and deviance becomes sin in a society preoccupied with normality, in the thrall of statistics, and historically puritanical. Toni Morrison, in *The Bluest Eye,* shows how the choice of a Platonic standard of beauty, or an ideal type of "the mother" or "the father" or "the family," affects children whose bodies do not conform to the standard and whose parents or families do not fit the ideal. In this early novel, Morrison gives voice to a father who rapes his daughter, drawing the psychological line that makes it possible to understand and speak about how such a violation could happen not only from the point of view of the daughter but from the father's point of view as well. In *Beloved,* Morrison gives voice to a mother who has killed her daughter rather than see her be taken back into slavery, and in this way explores a psychological and ethical question that has eluded the literature on psychological and moral development: what does care mean, or what could it potentially mean or entail, for a woman who loves her children and is living in a racist and violent society—a society damaging to both women and men?

Where I find myself troubled by the current arguments about difference is where I find them unvoiced and hauntingly familiar—where it is not clear who is speaking, where those spoken about have no voice, where the conversation heads toward the endless circle of objectivism and relativism, veering off into the oldest philosophical or ontological question as to whether there is or is not an Archimedean position, whether or not there is a God. A friend, quoting Stendhal, remarked that "God's only excuse is that he doesn't exist," and even this conversation in contemporary circles leads back to gender and difference, dominance and power. I find the question of whether gender differences are biologically determined or socially constructed to be deeply disturbing. This way of posing the question implies that people, women and men alike, are either genetically determined or a product of socialization—that there is no voice—and without voice, there is no possibility for resistance, for creativity, or for a change whose wellsprings are psychological. At its most troubling, the present reduction of psychology either to sociology or biology or some combination of the two prepares the way for the kind of control that alarmed Hannah Arendt and George Orwell— the hand over the mouth and at the throat, the suffocation of voice and the deadening of language which ripen the conditions for fascism and totalitarian rule, the psychic numbing which is associated with that now curiously unspoken word "propaganda."

Moral problems are problems of human relations, and in tracing the development of an ethic of care, I explore the psychological grounds for nonviolent human relations. This relational ethic transcends the age-old opposition between selfishness and selflessness, which have been the staples of moral discourse. The search on the part of many people for a voice which transcends these false dichotomies represents an attempt to turn the tide of moral discussion from questions of how to achieve objectivity and detachment to how to engage responsively and with care. Albert Hirschman, the political economist and author of *Exit, Voice, and Loyalty,* contrasts the neatness of exit with the messiness and heartbreak of voice. It is easier to step out than to step in. Relationship then requires a kind of courage and emotional stamina which has long been a strength of women, insufficiently noted and valued.

Relationship requires connection. It depends not only on the capacity for empathy or the ability to listen to others and learn their language or take their point of view, but also on having a voice and having a language. The differences between women and men which I describe center on a tendency for women and men to make different relational errors—for men to think that if they know themselves, following Socrates' dictum, they will also know women, and for women to think that if only they know others, they will come to know themselves. Thus men and women tacitly collude in not voicing women's experiences and build relationships around a silence that is maintained by men's not knowing their disconnection from women and women's not knowing their dissociation from themselves. Much talk about relationships and about love carefully conceals these truths.

Current research on women's psychological development speaks directly to this problem. The Harvard Project on Women's Psychology and the Development of Girls, in its investigation of women's lives, moves backward through developmental time, from adulthood to adolescence, and from adolescence to childhood. Taking the voices of adult women as its starting point, including the women who speak in this book, we have now listened in depth to the voices of adolescent girls in girls' schools and to girls and boys in coeducational schools and after-school clubs. Once we found ourselves at home in the halls of adolescence, we moved with some measure of confidence and with new questions into the world of younger girls, initiating a five-year study of girls ages seven to eighteen and a three-year exploratory prevention project involving girls and women.

In the course of this research, Lyn Mikel Brown, Annie Rogers, and I came to a place where we heard a distinct shift in girls' voices and observed that this change in voice coincided with changes in girls' relationships and their sense of themselves. For example, we began to hear girls at the edge of adolescence describe impossible situations—psychological dilemmas in which they felt that if they said what they were feeling and thinking no one would want to be with them, and if they didn't say what they were thinking and feeling they would be all alone, no one would know what was happening to them. As one girl put it, "no one would want to be with me, my voice would be too loud." Hearing what she was saying, she compounded her conundrum by explaining, "But you have to have relationships."

Listening to these girls in relational impasse, we found ourselves rethinking psychological theory and listening anew to ourselves and other women. We were struck by the frankness and fearlessness of these young girls, their determination to speak truthfully, and their keen desire to remain in relationship. At the same time, we began to witness girls edging toward relinquishing what they know and what they have held fast to, as they come face to face with a social construction of reality that is at odds with their experience, so that some kind of dissociation becomes inevitable. Girls' initiation or passage into adulthood in a world psychologically rooted and historically anchored in the experiences of powerful men marks the beginning of self-doubt and the dawning of the realization, no matter how fleeting, that womanhood will require a dissociative split between experience and what is generally taken to be reality.

While our research provided evidence of girls' resistance to dissociation, it also documented the initiation of girls into the psychological divisions that are familiar to many women: the coming not to know what one knows, the difficulty in hearing or listening to one's voice, the disconnection between mind and body, thoughts and feelings, and the use of one's voice to cover rather than to convey one's inner world, so that relationships no longer provide channels for exploring the connections between one's inner life and the world of others.

Suddenly it became clear why Amy's voice in this book was so striking to so many women and also why it left some women with a profound sense of unease. Amy's phrase "it depends" has been repeated by many women who also resist formulaic solutions to complex human problems. But her very insistence on the limitations of such formulas for resolving human conflicts led some women to hear her voice as it was heard by conventional psychologists: as wishy-washy, as indecisive, as evasive, and naive. The psychologist who interviewed Amy knew that her responses to the questions she was asked would result in her being assessed as not very "developed"— as not having a clear sense of self, as not being very advanced in her capacity for abstract thinking or moral judgment—which is why she kept repeating the questions to Amy, to give her another chance.

At fifteen, Amy carried that doubtful voice within herself and consequently struggled between two voices which kept running in and out of one another. The interview at fifteen caught her in the midst of an active process of dissociation, of knowing and then not knowing what she knew. For example, she saw that there was something deeply troubling about saying that a person should steal medicine to save the life of someone who is poor and dying, when she knew that in the city where she lived, poor people were dying every day for lack of medicine and she had no intention of stealing medicine to save them. At eleven, she said simply that stealing was not a good solution to this problem, that in fact it was likely to compound the problem by leaving the sick person not only without medicine and dying but also potentially all alone, without relationship and possibly with diminished economic resources as well. At fifteen, however, she could see the logic in a way of speaking about moral conflicts that she also saw as threatening to relationships and out of touch with reality, a way of reasoning that required making a series of separations, that began to alter her relationship with herself and to cloud her sense of reality. Misremembering what she had said at eleven, swaying back and forth between one way of approaching the problem and another, Amy at fifteen was in the process of changing her mind.

This change of mind and also of heart, which we observed repeatedly among girls in adolescence, led my colleague Annie Rogers to speak of girls' losing their "ordinary courage," or finding that what had seemed ordinary— having a voice and being in relationship—had now become extraordinary, something to be experienced only in the safest and most private of relationships. This psychological seclusion of girls from the public world at the time of adolescence sets the stage for a kind of privatization of women's experience and impedes the development of women's political voice and presence in the public world. The dissociation of girls' voices from girls' experiences in adolescence, so that girls are not saying what they know and eventually not knowing it as well, is a prefiguring of many women's sense of having the rug of experience pulled out from under them, or of coming to experience their feelings and thoughts not as real but as a fabrication.

At the same time, by recording girls' strong and courageous voices and by documenting girls' search for good ways of maintaining their voices and their relationships, the research of the Harvard Project provides evidence that grounds the questions raised in this book in a new way. The ongoing human conversation about separation and connection, justice and care, rights and responsibilities, power and love, takes a new turn when it is joined to evidence of girls' resistance to entering the conversation in terms of these dichotomies at just the time when they are reaching maturity and in many societies also gaining a public voice or vote. Separations and detachments, which previously have been taken as the marks of development in adolescence and presented as psychological facts, no longer seem necessary or inevitable, natural or good. The road back from "selflessness" which many of the women in this book travel, often at great cost to themselves and to others, is no longer an inevitable journey. The disconnection in this book between the resistance and courage of eleven-year-old Amy and the more desultory voices of some of the teenagers in the abortion-decision study may well reflect a loss of relationship rather than a failure to develop relationships—the loss of relationship that becomes audible when women construct moral conflicts as choices between selfish and selfless behavior.

Joining this understanding of women's psychological development with theories of human development which turn out to be theories about men, I have arrived at the following working theory: that the relational crisis which men typically experience in early childhood occurs for women in adolescence, that this relational crisis in boys and girls involves a disconnection from women which is essential to the perpetuation of patriarchal societies, and that women's psychological development is potentially revolutionary not only because of women's situation but also because of girls' resistance. Girls struggle against losing voice and against creating an inner division or split, so that large parts of themselves are kept out of relationship. Because girls' resistance to culturally mandated separations occurs at a later time in their psychological development than that of boys, girls' resistance is more articulate and robust, more deeply voiced and therefore more resonant; it resonates with women's and men's desires for relationships, reopening old psychological wounds, raising new questions, new possibilities for relationship, new ways of living. As girls become the carriers of unvoiced desires and unrealized possibilities, they are inevitably placed at considerable risk and even in danger.

Coming to the study of women's psychological development from her vantage point as a psychiatrist and psychoanalyst working with women in therapy, Jean Baker Miller observes that girls and women in the course of their development, in their attempt to make and maintain relationships, paradoxically keep large parts of themselves out of relationship. Miller's formulation of this paradox is central to a new understanding of the psychology of women and leads to a powerful rethinking of psychological suffering and trouble.

Miller and I have been struck by the fact that although we have approached the study of women and girls from different directions and worked in different ways, we have arrived at much the same insight into the relationship between women's psychology and the prevailing social order. A new psychological theory in which girls and women are seen and heard is an inevitable challenge to a patriarchal order that can remain in place only through the continuing eclipse of women's experience. Bringing the experiences of women and girls to full light, although in one sense perfectly straightforward, becomes a radical endeavor. Staying in connection, then, with women and girls—in teaching, in research, in therapy, in friendship, in motherhood, in the course of daily living—is potentially revolutionary.

In the course of teaching psychology, I often read Freud's essay "Civilization and Its Discontents," the essay in which he asks the question, why have men created a culture in which they live with such discomfort? And I talk with students about the liar paradox—"Romans always lie, said the Roman"— which becomes fascinating to many people at adolescence, the time when Freud sees detachment from childhood relationships and opposition to the previous generation as necessary for the progress of civilization and when Piaget says that the hypothetical takes precedence over the real. It is only recently that I have come to hear this paradox differently. "Romans always lie, said the Roman," contains a factual truth about imperialism: that there is a lie at the center of any imperial order.

This is the point of Joseph Conrad's prophetic and controversial novel *Heart of Darkness*. As Marlow travels into the heart of what was then the Belgian Congo, he begins to search for Mr. Kurtz, who was sent by "the gang of virtue," the Europeans who saw themselves as bringing enlightenment and progress or civilization to the Africans. Marlow believes that Kurtz will restore his faith in the vision of enlightened imperialism that is at odds with the pervasive evidence of corruption, lethargy, violence, and disease. As he reaches the interior, Marlow learns that Kurtz is dying. And meeting the dying Mr. Kurtz, he discovers the ultimate corruption. At the bottom of the report which Kurtz has prepared to send back to the Company in Belgium along with his shipment of ivory, he has scrawled the words which were to be enacted repeatedly in the twentieth century: the final solution to the problem of difference—"Exterminate all the brutes." The dying Mr. Kurtz himself offers the commentary: his last words are, "The horror! The horror!"

Marlow says that he cannot bear a lie, that lies deaden the world, "like biting into something rotten." And yet at the end of the book he lies to the woman who was Mr. Kurtz's Intended, the nameless European woman who waits for Kurtz and keeps alive his image. When Marlow visits her in Belgium, to return her portrait which was among Kurtz's possessions, she asks about Kurtz's last words, and Marlow lies to her: "The last word he pronounced was—your name."

This white lie is literally a white lie, because it covers the presence of the black woman with whom Mr. Kurtz was living—the woman who was actually with him. This issue of racial difference in the body of a woman goes to the heart of what is currently one of the most painful and difficult differences between women: war crimes in which white women have been directly involved.

Over the past two years, I have been a member of a group composed of eleven women—five black, five white, and one Hispanic—to ask about our relationship to the future by asking about our relationships with girls. Where are we as black, white, and Hispanic women in relation to black, white, and Hispanic girls? How can we create and maintain connections that cross the lines of racial division and in this way move toward breaking rather than perpetuating the cycle of racial domination and violence?

In an extraordinary passage in Conrad's novel, Marlow justifies his lie to Kurtz's Intended—as much to himself as to the men on shipboard who are listening to his story while waiting for the tide to turn:

> I heard a light sigh and then my heart stood still, stopped dead short by an exulting and terrible cry, by the cry of inconceivable triumph and of unspeakable pain. "I knew it—I was sure!" . . . She knew. She was sure. I heard her weeping; she had hidden her face in her hands. It seemed to me that the house would collapse before I could escape, that the heavens would fall upon my head. But nothing happened. The heavens do not fall for such a trifle. Would they have fallen, I wonder, if I had rendered Kurtz that justice which was his due? Hadn't he said he wanted only justice? But I couldn't. I could not tell her. It would have been too dark—too dark altogether.

This intersection between race and gender, colonialism and masculine narratives, also marks the convergence between the liar paradox and the relationship paradox: the place where women's and men's lives join and "civilization" makes its iron grip felt. A lie about progress joins with a lie about relationship, trapping both women and men and obliterating relationships among women. It is this intersection which joins the two parts of this book—the lie in psychological theories which have taken men as representing all humans, and the lie in women's psychological development in which girls and women alter their voices to fit themselves into images of relationship and goodness carried by false feminine voices.

Voicing the Self: Toward a Pedagogy of Resistance in a Postmodern Age

by Randall R. Freisinger

Had I consciously tried, I don't think I could have assembled in one title four terms in composition studies that are very much more problematic, definitionally complex, and ideologically loaded than *voice*, *self*, *postmodernism*, and *resistance*. All four have undergone considerable scrutiny in recent years and have been the source at times of heated debate. In what follows, I want to explore each of these four terms, albeit necessarily in a summary fashion that omits much of the detail in the rich discourse surrounding them. At the same time I want to provide some links among these terms that might help restore certain pedagogical practices to a place of esteem. The terms *voice* and *self*, for example, I want to link together in the familiar phrase *authentic voice*, a concept we now associate with the 1960s and early 70s when such assignments as free writing and the personal, autobiographical essay were central to most writing curricula. I believe this personal writing pedagogy, for which Ken Macrorie, Donald Murray, James Britton, and Peter Elbow have been primarily responsible (and more lately attacked), has been a valuable but increasingly neglected tool for teaching students how to write, how to "voice" themselves, how to locate themselves within the complex network of surrounding institutions and culture. My central argument in what follows is that teachers of writing need to re-examine and revise the lessons of this Authentic Voice pedagogy and seek to incorporate them into the increasingly influential assumptions of postmodernism if schools are to provide students with a truly liberating education and society itself with a more equitable distribution of power.

The link between self and voice I stipulated above is certainly nothing new, and I felt the stipulation necessary only because both terms and the linkage itself have been severely interrogated, indeed dismissed, in the more recent postmodern climate of socially constructed selves and dialogic voices, a consequence I will take up later and one which needs to be reconsidered. If the Authentic Voice school seems naive and simplistic to many these days, such was not always the case. In the 1960s and early 70s, when the New

A similar version of this chapter will appear as "Voicing the Self: Toward a Pedagogy of Resistance in a Postmodern Age" in the forthcoming book *Voices on Voice: A (Written) Discussion*, edited by Kathleen Blake Yancey. Used here by permission of the copyright holder, The National Council of Teachers of English.

Criticism still held a steady course in my doctoral program and when governmental hypocrisy and institutional oppression, including that of the university, were as commonplace as the daily reports of atrocities in the Viet Nam war, I can well remember the names of Macrorie and Elbow being literally evoked in conspiratorial whispers by graduate students or raged against and/or mocked by professors in the faculty lounge. In an age of sham and cant, the very idea of authenticity, with its existential resonances, was vastly appealing to many of us who were just beginning our professional lives and who were just beginning to glimpse the possibility that teaching composition was not so clearly the trench work we had been brought up to believe. Furthermore, many of our students were extremely responsive to the simple idea that they could give voice in powerful words and images to what *they* thought really mattered, that in fact First-year English might not be a game of "psyche out the professor" after all but a legitimate opportunity to explore self and tell some long repressed truths. Many of us spent hours running from cubicle to cubicle, reading to each other the seemingly amazing things our once lip-locked students had suddenly blurted out. We all felt as if we had just witnessed the angel bid Caedmon sing or a little like Galileo staring at newly discovered planets.

And when, in the late 70s, I began my work in writing across the curriculum with Art Young and Toby Fulwiler at Michigan Tech, I read James Britton's *Language and Learning* and later his *The Development of Writing Abilities (11-18)* and immediately found in both texts corroboration for Macrorie and Elbow in Britton's central claims that what he called expressive writing—writing for the self—was the matrix out of which more formal modes of writing naturally evolved and that a writer had to "get it right with the self" before getting it right with his or her ultimate audience. Doing workshops for faculty at my own university and for groups at other universities around the country, I was constantly amazed at how threatening and controversial this notion of expressive writing was. Faculty, particularly those from English departments, regarded those of us who directed such workshops as subversives, although they were usually not quite certain why, except that we didn't have enough to say about mechanics and grammar and were somehow into "touchy-feely" stuff inappropriate to the rigors of a "real" university education.

As a way of proceeding, let me first examine three of the four terms I mentioned above—voice, self, and postmodernism—by briefly looking at the history of each and considering some of the problems each term raises for writing teachers. It will quickly become evident that it is impossible to separate these terms. They are, by now at least, in almost constant "dialogue" with one another, and to "voice" one of them inevitably prompts vocalizations from the others. Finally, I will try to unite these three terms in order to argue for a theory of education based on resistance and aspiring to bring about a more just society.

Self

To the traditionalist, this term seems commonsensical, a self-evident part of a long and honored tradition of humanistic learning existing at least since the Oracle at Delphi, over whose entryway was inscribed the famous imperative, "Know Thyself." From that point, through the trivium and quadrivium of the Greeks and Romans, through medieval scholasticism, Renaissance humanism, Romantic celebration of the ego, Arnoldian faith in the best that has been thought and said, right through T. S. Eliot's "tradition" and, most recently, in the renewed emphasis on acculturation sought by the Bennett-Bloom-Hirsch contingent, the Western liberal humanist tradition has accepted belief in a central core of stable, unified, transcendent, even transcultural self, a belief which served as a matrix out of which definitions of citizenship and ethical behavior and creativity are thought to evolve. Following the powerful assertion of individual selfhood accompanying the Enlightenment, nineteenth-century Romanticism made self the centerpiece of its philosophy. Poets in both England and America celebrated the personal over the universal, clearly manifested in these famous lines from Whitman's *Song of Myself*: "I celebrate myself, and sing myself, / And what I assume you shall assume / For every atom belonging to me, as good belongs to you." Whitman's celebration states a premise vital to Romantic theory and to neo-Romantic attitudes which resurfaced after the twentieth century break with Modernism. Contemporary American poet Galway Kinnell reiterates this theme in his essay "Poetry, Personality, and Death" when he says, "We [many American poets] move toward a theory in which the poet seeks an inner liberation by going so deeply into himself [sic]—into the worst of himself as well as the best—that he suddenly finds he is everyone" (p. 75). The personal is, in other words, ultimately universal. Poet Alberta Turner echoes Kinnell's claim when she says, in "Not Your Flat Tire, My Flat Tire: Transcending Self in Contemporary Poetry," that poets "are working on the same assumption that has always underlain both the making of fictional characters and the telling of autobiography—that the universally common experiences created by human psychology, physiology, and history insure that any cluster of specific, concrete details of any single human being's experience can be made to evoke similar responses from all human beings. . . . It is this problem of presenting the data of one unique self so that other unique selves will recognize it as their own that poses the chief artistic challenge to contemporary poets who probe their own selves for the sake of transcending the individual in order to reveal the universal self" (pp. 135-36).

It was not until Victorian times, with the rise of urban life and industrial capitalism, that faith in the universal or transcendent self—one that is firmly anchored and unchanging—began to waver. Matthew Arnold, ironically the avatar of a unitary culture founded on a stable concept of self, gives us one of the first serious signals of a destabilized self in his poem "The Buried Life": "But often, in the world's most crowded streets, / But often, in the din of strife, / There arises an unspeakable desire / After knowledge of our buried life; / A thirst to spend our fire and restless force / In tracking out our true, original course." But the desire, Arnold tells us, is nearly futile: "And many a man then in his own breast delves, / But deep enough, alas! none ever mines." We try, Arnold says, "in vain to speak and act / our hidden self," although finally he concedes that only in rare moments, through the transforming power of love, can we possibly discover our deeply embedded self. Arnold's fear is not so much that self doesn't exist, but rather that it rests beneath too many masks for us to have much success in reaching it.

When, a century later, John Barth opens his 1958 novel, *The End of the Road*, with his protagonist's equivocal introduction—"In a sense, I am Jacob Horner"—we know things have only worsened. Camus had already capped off a growing sense of alienation in modern times by telling us, in *The Myth of Sisyphus*, "Forever I shall be a stranger to myself and to the world" (p. 15). Wylie Sypher documented the results of this alienation in his 1962 study entitled *Loss of Self in Modern Literature and Art*, showing how the self had become anonymous, a victim of a collective, technological, vastly impersonal society. Shaken as the faith in self has been in our century's literature, this faith has never been entirely silenced. In American literature, especially in contemporary poetry, the self remains with us, sometimes a solace, sometimes a burden, but ultimately inescapable, even mythic, rooted in our very collective psyche. Consider, for example, Stephen Dobyns, whose voice through most of his major books of poems remains as recognizable as the concern for self in his poem "How You Are Linked," from his recent collection, *Body Traffic*. After beginning the poem on a note of estrangement—"There are days when you wake and your body / feels too long or too short, like a shirt shrunk in the wash . . ."—Dobyns tells us: "you decide / that the body you are wearing belongs to someone / you knew as a child. . . ." This child turns out to be someone the "you" of the poem abused repeatedly, and the imagined or real exchange of bodies serves as a form of atonement. In a dream the two meet, make amends, and the "you" awakes inside his own body again, and runs off joyously to repeat his same old mistakes until the world once again slams him into a stranger's body: "Who's this? you say, / as if it were some stray beauty, the seduced / victim of late night desire. But hidden within / this newcomer lurks only yourself: the monster, / the treasure, the curiosity you have passionately / tried to decipher for all the years of your life" (pp. 34-38). In the poetry of women, this quest for self has been especially strong. Citing the work of Sylvia Plath, Denise Levertov, Anne Sexton, Adrienne Rich, Diane Wakoski, Muriel Rukeyser, Gwendolyn Brooks, and Margaret Atwood, Sandra Gilbert, in a 1984 essay entitled "My Name is Darkness: The Poetry of Self Definition," argues that "the self-defining confessional genre, with its persistent assertions of identity and its emphasis on a central mythology of the self, may be (at least for our own time) a distinctively female poetic mode" (p. 99). The female poet, Gilbert says, "writes in the hope of discovering or defining a self, a certainty, a tradition, an ontology of selfhood, some irreducible and essential truth about her own nature" (pp. 100,102-03).

Voice

The concept of voice is so pervasive in our culture, either in its literal or its metaphoric sense, that it is easy enough not even to take note of it. At a recent lecture on my campus, Native American activist Donald Grinde, in providing an indigenous perspective on the Christopher Columbus myth, said toward the end of his speech that after the final defeat and humiliation at Wounded Knee, Indian peoples were *silenced*, that they became *voiceless*. A few weeks later, at the Episcopal church I attend, our priest was speaking of the plight of children in America, specifically the astonishing degree of hunger and poverty that afflict roughly one out of five children in one of the world's most materially rich societies. He urged us all to speak out, to write our elected officials, to bring an end to the relative silence in America on this subject. By so doing, he concluded, we would be lending our voices to those whose voice had been stilled. In a recent issue of *College English*, Barbara Henning, in an essay on basic writing instruction in the urban university, criticizes a number of pedagogical practices, including that of the Authentic Voice school, which has focused too much, Henning argues, on individualism. She characterizes basic writing students as "socially excluded, students who are 'selfless' and 'voiceless' because their experience and language do not allow them to construct a recognizable *mainstream* self and voice" (680). Feminists, after hundreds of years of being silenced, have acquired a voice, and the emerging men's movement is now seeking to help men regain their "real" voice, the one that allegedly lies beneath the false voices imposed by centuries of patriarchy. In short, the concept of voice saturates our public and private discourse, and, as writing teachers, we need not only to recognize this saturation but also to appropriate the best of the traditional aspects of this concept or create new perspectives if we are to adjust our curricula to fit a postmodern age. Let me begin with the notion of authentic voice, my ultimate aim being to recontextualize the concept, moving it out of its Romantic matrix and adapting it for our current needs.

Authentic voice is most likely an inheritance of our oral tradition and has long been regarded as a manifestation of this ontology of selfhood. As C. M. Bowra has demonstrated in his study of the origins of poetry, *Primitive Song*, ancient communities were held together by the power of this authentic voice reciting or singing the history and rituals of the tribe, and voice initially evoked an individual's mystical connection to the Divine or the Muse. That conception fell into disfavor in the rationalistic wake of the Enlightenment, but it came back with the advent of Romanticism in late Eighteenth-century Europe. Voice became closely linked metaphorically with breath itself, the breath of some transcendent Power playing upon the soul of the poet like wind on the strings of an aeolian harp, and the resulting music was truth spoken, as Wordsworth asserted in the famous Preface to his and Coleridge's *Lyrical Ballads*, in a natural voice to ordinary people who "convey their feelings and notions in simple and unelaborated expressions" (p. 735).

Under the combined influence of Modernism and the New Criticism, authentic voice again went, like Xanadu's sacred river Alph, underground for a while, only to surface again in the 1950s and early 60s in the spontaneous prose of Kerouac, Ginsberg's *Howl*, and Lowell's *Life Studies*. This was the beginning of the so-called Confessional movement (including the afore-mentioned poets such as Sexton and Plath), and much of the discourse dealing with the literature of the last four decades has been dominated by a commitment to voice. We know (or at least believe we know) a particular author by his or her distinctive voice. We read of prizes for "new voices." Young creative writers are told repeatedly that they must keep working at their craft until they "find their voice," which is regarded as a form of verbal equivalent for the physical presence of the author and as a lens to his or her authentic self. Poet and critic Jonathan Holden remarks in his *The Rhetoric of the Contemporary Lyric* that "the art of poetry consists mainly of the art of infusing feeling into language so that, without the aid of external devices such as the author's actual voice in performance, language on a silent page can attain the power and immediacy of a singing voice in the ear of the reader" (p. 135). And in *Style and Authenticity in Postmodern Poetry* Holden, locating the origin of the word "authenticity" in the Greek *authentes* ("one who does anything with his own hand"), concludes that our sense of value in a well-made poem "is intimately connected with our sense that it is not mass produced, not stamped out by machine, that the decisions which went into its shaping were not those of a committee, a corporation . . . but . . . of a single, passionate individual—the author—acting alone . . . us[ing] the best materials available: . . . human experience noticed in language . . . bear[ing] the un-mistakable mark of individual craftsmanship" (p. 184).

Contemporary literature quickly found an ally in the emerging discipline of composition studies, which in the 1960s and early 70s began to shift its emphasis from product to process, from the composed to the act of composing. Donald Stewart, in the Preface to his 1972 text *The Authentic Voice: A Pre-Writing Approach to Student Writing,* makes clear a pedagogical intent which had already begun to dominate writing instruction. Stewart asserts his conviction that "the primary goal of any writing course is self-discovery for the student and that the most visible indication of that self-discovery is the appearance, in the student's writing, of an authentic voice" (xii). In his Introduction he defines self-discovery as "the process of acquiring both a more objective and a psychologically deeper sense of the person you are . . . beyond the complex of roles you play in life" (p. 1). Authentic voice, he claims, "is a natural consequence of self-discovery" (p. 2). Stewart, along with many others, assumed, in other words, that each student had a unique self and voice, but exactly *how* these resources were to be tapped remained somewhat unclear, although a variety of pre-writing or invention strategies, including free writing and journals, were advanced as the best tools for helping students discover their authentic selves. One spin-off of this emerging philosophy was the "talk-write" school, which attempted to get students to draw upon the "natural resources" of speaking as they began to write. If students would bring *their* reality into the classroom and into their writing, readers would, according to Lou Kelly in *From Dialogue to Discourse: An Open Approach,* "hear a *voice,*—carried from speaker to listener by inanimate symbols, carried by words on a piece of paper . . . a very audible voice. A voice that is alive with the sound of you" (p. 145).

Probably the two most prominent of the Authentic Voice advocates have been Ken Macrorie and Peter Elbow, both of whose positions are so well known that I need touch only briefly upon them here. Macrorie's ideas came from a variety of publications that made many of us rethink our pedagogical legacy. Both *Uptaught* and *A Vulnerable Teacher* were strong influences on me personally, but probably the most widely influential, on both secondary and college writing teachers, was *Telling Writing,* which in effect outlined what seemed at the time a radical pedagogy based on free-writing, journals, "telling facts," and "fabulous realities." Throughout the text Macrorie insists on truth-telling and avoiding the poisonous bite of the "Engfish" (institutional language or language that conceals rather than reveals self). Early in the book, Macrorie asserts that "all good writers speak in honest voices and tell the truth" (p. 5). Not *the* truth, he admits ("whoever knows surely what that is" [p. 5]), "but some kind of truth" (p. 5). Later on in the book, Macrorie connects truth to voice, a linkage which is discovered in an almost Zen-like manner during free writing: "In free writing a person frequently finds that his pen or typewriter seems to have taken over the job of writing and he [sic] is sitting there watching the words go down on paper" (p. 148). "Finding the right voice," he tells the student reader, "will help you write better than you ever thought yourself capable of writing" (p. 149). Not only will voice reveal truth, Macrorie insists, but it will also provide unity and coherence to one's writing. Macrorie ends his discussion of voice by admitting (and anticipating later critiques) that, "[l]ike everyone else who has ever spoken a word . . . you have at your command a number of *different voices* [italics mine]. Use them" (p. 157).

The influence of Macrorie on Elbow was immediately apparent. At the end of the Preface to his by now classic text, *Writing Without Teachers,* Peter Elbow says that his book "wouldn't have been possible without the example and support of Ken Macrorie" (p. x), so we should rightly expect to find strong parallels and similar pedagogical principles, and of course we do. We also find an emphasis on the liberating power which authentic voice can make available to inexperienced writers. Elbow notes early in the book: "In your natural way of producing words there is a sound, a texture, a rhythm—a voice—which is the main source of power in your writing. I don't know how it works, but this voice is the force that will make a reader listen to you, the energy that drives the meaning through his [sic] skull. . . . [I]t's the only voice you've got. It's your only source of power" (pp. 6-7). During the course of Elbow's advocacy of free writing exercises and teacherless writing groups, the word "magic," or synonyms for it, occurs a number of times, and this is an echo of the telling statement in the just-quoted passage: "I don't know how it works." Authentic voice is, for most of those who advocate it, somehow natural, innate, magical, unavailable for empirical verification or rational explanation.

This theme is developed at greater length in Elbow's *Writing With Power: Techniques for Mastering the Writing Process*, a book held together by three themes: 1) That the composing process must be privileged and separated from the critical faculty; 2) That every person has innate skill with written language; and 3) That his "cookbook" strategies for improving writing should be followed by novice writers until these "recipes" have been so internalized that these writers can take charge of their own writing. Early in the text he admits that voice is hard to talk about and is probably best learned through consciously imitating a voice the writer finds compelling. But in a later chapter, Elbow tackles the issue head on, using metaphors drawn from music to try to articulate what he has already admitted may not be explainable: According to him, we each have a chest cavity unique in size and shape so that "each of us resonates to one pitch alone" (p. 282). A few people, he grants, "sing with ringing power, but no one seems to understand how they manage this, not even they. In this metaphorical world, then, even if we figure out the system, we are stuck. If we want to be heard we are limited to our single note. If we want to sing other notes, we will not be heard" (p. 282). It's important to notice how self and voice dovetail at this point for Elbow and the many teachers who have embraced his teaching philosophy, and it is equally important to attend to the assumption of a stable, unique self, an essence, that underlies this concept of voice. Elbow admits that writers may eventually be able to sing other notes after extensive practice, but they will only be able to do so if they are "willing to start off singing [their] own single tiresome pitch for a long time and in that way gradually teach the stiff cells of [their] bodies to vibrate and be flexible" (p. 282).

In a section entitled "How I Got Interested in Voice," Elbow chronicles his experience with student writing and his intuitive sense that some passages were somehow more "real." Furthermore, as he identified such passages to students and encouraged them to work more in that voice, their writing became more powerful and more connected to their sense of self. So Elbow decided he wanted to work out a "fuller theory of voice. For the power I am seeking, some people use words like *authenticity* or *authority*. Many people call it *sincerity*. . . ." Elbow himself prefers the word *juice* "because I'm trying to get at something mysterious and hard to define. 'Juice' combines the qualities of *magic potion*, *mother's milk*, and *electricity*. Sometimes I fear I will never be clear about what I mean by voice" (p. 286). At this point Elbow reproduces a note sent to him by Ellen Nold after he had apparently struggled to articulate his theory at a meeting of writing teachers. The note is telling and worth quoting in full, but I'll limit myself to her concluding sentences. After linking voice to notions of Quality found in Eastern thought, she advises: "Don't try to explain it to rationalistic people in rationalistic terms! It is something that ultimately cannot be explained to anyone who hasn't heard. And those who have heard will forgive you for the inadequacy of your words" (p. 287). Despite her advice, Elbow continues nevertheless, later pausing over the phrase "real self": "Real self. Real voice," he exclaims, "I

am on slippery ground here. There are layers and layers" (293). Perhaps
Elbow was already anticipating the first snipings of postmodernism, but these
snipings, which have now grown into a constant fusillade, have not deterred
Elbow. He has continued to explore the concept of voice and its relation to
power, an exploration in the face of considerable opposition for which, as I
shall finally argue, we should continue to be grateful.

Postmodernism

A very good analysis of the effects of postmodernism on the concept of
self is Kenneth Gergen's recent study, *The Saturated Self: Dilemmas of
Identity in Contemporary Life.*

In this postmodern world, Gergen claims, we are immersed in the
opinions and values of others by means of what he calls *the technologies of
social saturation* to the point that our self is ultimately erased, repopulated
with the multiple relationships we experience until there is finally the onset
of a multiphrenic condition "in which one begins to experience the vertigo of
unlimited multiplicity" (p. 49). These technologies of social saturation include
jet travel, photocopy and fax machines, computers, telephones, films,
television, VCRs, electronic mail, on-line information services, fiber optics,
and satellite communications leading to global linkages. Consequently, the
world shrinks. Our sense of time and place is altered. Everything is
accelerated. We are capable of many more and even nearly simultaneous
relationships. We begin to experience "a populating of the self, the acquisition
of multiple and disparate potentials for being." It is this process of self-
population for Gergen that "begins to undermine the traditional commitments
to both romanticist and modernist forms of being" (p. 69). "A multiphrenic
condition emerges," Gergen claims, "in which one swims in ever-shifting,
concatenating, and contentious currents of being. One bears the burden of an
increasing array of oughts, of self-doubts and irrationalities. . . . [T]he way is
open for the postmodern being" (p. 80).

Following a chapter on the erosion of Truth and the rise of relativism,
especially in the academy, Gergen turns to the emergence of postmodern
culture. He cites the breakdown of rational order, the challenge to all claims
to authority, the blurring of genres in architecture, literature, and music, the
free play in the visual arts. Traditional categories collapse, objective
knowledge seems illusionary, and the relativity of postmodernism leads to a
sense that all facets of culture and history are socially constructed, contingent
on the particularities of time and place. It is only a small move to seeing the
self as merely another example of the socially constructed. Finally, Gergen
concludes, "With postmodern consciousness begins the erasure of the category
of self. No longer can one securely determine what it is to be a specific kind
of person—male or female—or even a person at all. As the category of the
individual fades from view, consciousness of construction becomes focal. We
realize increasingly that who and what we are is not so much the result of our
'personal essence' (real feelings, deep beliefs, and the like), but of how we

are constructed in various social groups. . . . [O]ne acquires a pastiche-like personality. Coherence and contradiction cease to matter as one takes pleasure in the expanded possibilities of being in a socially saturated world" (p. 170).

I have barely done justice to this part of Gergen's analysis, but before I move on, a few words about the implications of Gergen's postmodern, saturated self on the notion of authentic voice. The word *voice* shows up a number of times in Gergen's treatment of self, but, as one might well expect, his sense of that word differs considerably from the meaning ascribed to it by the authentic voice theorists. The proliferation of communication technologies exposes us to a virtual host of other voices, many of which we consciously or unconsciously incorporate into our own. Thus it is *voices* Gergen stresses, not any single unique voice. In examining the academy's encounter with deconstruction, for example, Gergen makes the by now predictable critique of language which denies referentiality and makes language a system of differences. "Its structure pre-exists any single individual, and if sense is to be made, the individual must essentially participate in the communal conventions. Thus, individuals are not the intentional agents of their own words, creatively and privately converting thoughts to sounds or inscriptions. Rather, they gain their status as selves by taking a position within a preexisting form of language" (p. 110). There can be no *I*, only *we*, and the self perforce must exit, leaving behind a polyphony of voices. Pluralism predominates in the arts, and consciousness of unitary form is replaced by free play of mixed forms. Speaking of architecture, Gergen notes that "the postmodern building is designed to speak in multiple vernaculars" (p. 115), a reflection of the pastiche motif cited earlier. Later, underscoring the dramatic increase in relationships which one is able to maintain in a socially saturated world, Gergen observes, "In the case of 'Who am I?' it is a teeming world of provisional possibilities" (p. 139), not the stable sense of self implied by the imperative of the Oracle at Delphi. The intense competition of voices, Gergen maintains, challenges the notion of the thing (or person) in itself. We as individuals are an assemblage of voices, and "if each voice portrays the individual a little differently, then the very idea of an 'isolated self,' independent of the voices themselves, begins to teeter. . . . As the chorus of competitive voices builds, 'the person' as a reality beyond voice is lost. There is no voice now trusted to rescue the 'real person' from the sea of portrayals" (p. 140). In making his case for the positive side of postmodernism, Gergen notes the ways in which any language bears with it the traces or remnants of languages from subcultures and from previous historical eras, and he cites the *heteroglossia* of Russian literary theorist Mikhail Bakhtin to help him conclude, "In this sense, postmodernism invites a heteroglossia of being, a living out of the multiplicity of voices within the sphere of human possibility. There is little reason to suppress any voice. Rather, with each new vocabulary or form of expression, one appropriates the world in a different way, sensing aspects of existence in one that are hidden in another, opening capacities for relatedness in one modality that are otherwise hindered" (p. 247). It remains to be seen how accurate is Gergen's assessment of the positive potential in postmodernism. As we know, voices still are being silenced, despite the rose-tinted view Gergen provides us. Is it possible, within this multiplicity of voices, to empower those who yet have no voice? Postmodernism must allow for that liberation if it is to realize its full pedagogical potential.

So this postmodern critique of self and voice leaves us in a bit of a bind. On the one hand, the stable, transcendent self has been erased. On the other, postmodern theories posit a kind of lacuna, or empty space, at the center of the human organism, a space to be filled by language-mediated social experience and the agendas of ideological apparatuses. Such an either/or vision is, of course, oversimplified, reductive. The liberal humanist view *is* nostalgic, and it is seriously flawed by its inability to respond to the ideological critiques of Marxist and post-structuralist theory, e.g., that a stable self is illusory, that individuals are products of specific times and circumstances and unwittingly manipulated by powerful institutionalized interests beyond their control, that language cannot and never has been able to serve as a bridge between elusive subjective life and so-called objective reality. These latter theories, on the other hand, are incomplete because ultimately they are deterministic and pessimistic about human nature, reducing it to a passive and helpless entity and failing to posit a view of self (or human agency) which can allow for resistance to the repressive and dominatory mechanisms of economic, political, and educational systems. What we need is a theory of self which synthesizes these two theoretical extremes and offers hope for change, a kind of Archimedean notion of self which gives individuals a place to stand, a point of leverage by which they can move their world.

And it is this lack of such a point of leverage in current theory that makes this intensified attack on earlier versions of self matter to writing teachers who want to empower their students, not just in the sense of helping them get a job or enabling them to achieve upward social mobility, but in the more ambitious sense of equipping them to be active agents in the cause of social justice. A too-quick acceptance of poststructuralist theories is presently undermining useful pedagogical approaches prematurely, especially the expressive and personal writing most often associated with the Authentic Voice school. Consider, for example, the current challenge to personal writing resulting from postmodernist assumptions that have served to delegitimate the self. A useful illustration is James Berlin's 1988 *College English* article, "Rhetoric and Ideology in the Writing Class." As he has elsewhere, here Berlin classifies major rhetorical theories, identifies the ideological assumptions of each, and argues for his own preference. In this particular essay he identifies three current and competing rhetorical theories: Cognitive, Expressionistic, and Social-Epistemic. Using Goran Therborn's formulation of ideology as his framework, Berlin argues against Cognitive and Expressionistic theories in order to make a case for the Social-Epistemic.

I am interested here in his attack on Expressionistic rhetoric, because he lays the groundwork for subsequent challenges to personal writing and pedagogies seeking "authentic voice," the rhetoric, in other words, of Ken

Macrorie, Peter Elbow, Walker Gibson, William Coles, Jr., and Donald Murray. After tracing the roots of this rhetoric in the early years of this century, Berlin rejects it for its false epistemology, one located in a central self. For Expressionists, writing is valued as "an art, a creative act in which the process—the discovery of the true self—is as important as the product—the self discovered and expressed" (484). Berlin grants that, unlike the Cognitive school, Expressionistic rhetoric embraces as one of its primary aims a critique of a dominant and corrupt society. Unfortunately, Berlin concludes, the Expressionists' epistemology is its own worst enemy, defining resistance in purely individual rather than collaborative and social terms—this seems a valid critique and one I want to pursue later. Expressionists, according to Berlin, believe "[t]he only hope in a society working to destroy the uniqueness of the individual is for each of us to assert our individuality against the tyranny of the authoritarian corporation, state, and society. Strategies for doing so must of course be left to the individual, each lighting one small candle in order to create a brighter world" (487). This commitment to the epistemology of individual self, Berlin concludes, ironically allows the Expressionists to be co-opted by the very ideology they would subvert, an ideology rooted in "individualism, private initiative, the confidence for risk taking, the right to be contentious with authority (especially the state)" (487). Such private vision easily enough defers collective action, and self-expression is too often deflected into various forms of consumer behavior since the appeal to individuality lies at the heart of so much commodity advertising.

After making a case for Social-Epistemic rhetoric built in good measure on a social-constructionist epistemology, and after claiming for this rhetoric the power of critiquing the dominant culture without being co-opted, Berlin presents the pedagogy outlined in Ira Shor's *Critical Teaching and Everyday Life* as a model application of Social-Epistemic rhetoric. Oddly enough, Shor's practices are aimed, according to Berlin, at externalizing false consciousness and "changing students," Shor is quoted as saying, "from re-active objects into society-making subjects" (491). Unfortunately, the notion of "false consciousness," essentially Marxist in origin, has been problematic and ultimately rejected precisely because it has been interpreted as implying a true consciousness, a humanistic core self, underneath accumulated layers of capitalist-induced domination, a "full" or "true" consciousness which will surface when ideology disappears. Paul Smith, in *Discerning the Subject*, summarizes the Marxist perspective well for our purposes. "[H]is [Marx's] formulations take for granted that there *is* some essential humanity, but that it cannot yet be theorized since 'society does not consist of individuals, but expresses the sum of interrelations within which these individuals stand' [Smith is citing Marx here]. . . . Thus, concrete individuality does not exist in the current conditions of alienation but rather is smothered beneath the weight of these real conditions. In other words, subjectivity [or self] can currently have no force and no effect, and can only await its fulfillment, exactly, in the destruction of capitalism and the building of socialism/communism" (pp. 6-7). Smith goes on to note that Marx engages in a utopian ploy which "effectively deprivileges the very real existence experienced by the subject/individual only as a currently unrealized form of exactly that lure which has been offered by traditional notions ... Marxism looks forward to bringing about an 'individual,' exactly, whose unalienated activity 'will coincide with material life, which corresponds to the development of individuals into *complete* individuals' " (p. 7; again, Smith quotes Marx; the italics are Smith's). In fairness, the practices of Shor Berlin refers to do include a notable number of assignments that rely on personal, autobiographical, and expressive forms of writing. My purpose is not to devalue Shor's work but rather to point to an inconsistency in Berlin's argument. To Berlin's credit, he argues for a theory that *will* promote resistance, but his characterization of Expressionistic rhetoric seems, to me at least, oversimplified and incomplete, and his pedagogical solution seems tainted by the same epistemological problem that he says haunts the Expressionists.

Lester Faigley, in a recent *CCC* essay entitled "Judging Writing, Judging Selves," offers us another critique of personal or autobiographical writing, and, like Berlin, his attack is grounded in social constructionist assumptions about the way ideology operates to construct the social self. Faigley manages to avoid the predicament Berlin created for himself when the latter invoked the humanist Marxism of Ira Shor's pedagogy. Faigley does this mainly by relying on Louis Althusser's revisionist view of Marxism, a view which posits that "subjects" or selves are interpellated or summoned to play roles within an ideological structure and that this ideology never disappears; thus there can be no utopian future moment when false consciousness falls away and we live as full humans within an ideology-free society. Whether or not one would automatically live a "full" life in a society free of ideology, or whether the latter is even possible—both of these claims are debatable, but that seems to be the line of traditional Marxist logic. Faigley, like most commentators on Althusser, notes the pun inherent in Althusser's use of the term 'subject': "People are subjected to dominant ideologies, but because they recognize themselves in the subject positions that discourses provide, they believe they are subjects of their own actions ... people fail to see that the subject positions they occupy are historically produced, and they imagine that they are freely choosing for themselves" (403).

Faigley's real target is a 1985 book by William Coles, Jr. and James Vopat called *What Makes Writing Good*. For this book, forty-eight well-known teacher/scholars submitted pieces of student writing that they felt demonstrated excellence, along with a commentary explaining their choice. Faigley, puzzled by the high number of personal experience essays, observes, "I have no simple explanation for the strong preference for autobiographical essays" (404). In the commentaries, furthermore, he is troubled by the appearance of such characterizations as "honest," "authentic voice," and "integrity," and in both the commentaries and several of the student essays he detects the "assumption that individuals possess an identifiable 'true' self and that the true self can be expressed in discourse" (405). And Faigley goes on to say, borrowing heavily from current ideologically-based theory, "To ask students to write authentically about the self assumes that a rational consciousness can be laid out on the page. That the self must be interpellated through language is denied" (409-10). Faigley concludes that teachers of writing "are still very much concerned with the self" (410), a concern he clearly believes is inadvisable because it dupes students and teachers alike into believing that discovering authentic self is somehow empowering. "[We must]," he concludes, "teach our students to analyze cultural definitions of the self, to understand how historically these definitions are created in discourse, and to recognize how definitions of the self are involved in the configuration of relations of power" (411). I don't at all disagree with Faigley about *what* we must teach our students; the how is a different matter altogether. Furthermore, I believe the pedagogy he advocates is incomplete in that it fails to provide students with any point of Archimedean leverage. If we follow his pedagogy, we inform students of the ways in which ideology defines them and forces certain subject positions upon them, but we fail to provide them with any significant sense of self which might serve as ground for resistance and liberatory behavior. And in the process, by virtue of the way we locate ourselves with respect to them in terms of authority, we enact an ideology that further denies such a grounding to them.

Up to this point I have summarized briefly the concepts of self and voice in the Western tradition, both of which seem to have arrived at dead ends in postmodern versions of subjectivity. I have also asserted that the concept of self implicit in the Authentic Voice school, all but abandoned by composition theorists under the influence of postmodernism, still offers considerable potential sustenance to writing teachers who seek to design a liberatory pedagogy and work with their students to bring about a more just society. Let me now turn to theoretical work, some of it fairly "old" by this time and some of it still in process, that is beginning to map out a more positive view of knowledge and education and their potential for effecting social transformation.

To begin with, this positive view must be rooted in a concept of human agency. Human agency does not mean human "actor," for such a definition too easily reduces to a sense of assuming roles, much as an actor does. And that sense of the term shares too much in common with the concept of constructed or assigned parts in the social drama. At the heart of human agency is the ability to take action, sometimes in harmony with and sometimes against socially accepted values. Only when such action is possible is a theory of resistance feasible. For my purposes, human agency and self are roughly synonymous, though in what follows I intend to distinguish between these two roughly synonymous terms, on the one hand, and the traditional Romantic concept of self characterized earlier. Facets of the positive theory I advocated above have been available for some time in perspectives which have attempted to synthesize both the individual and social contributions of knowledge and to regard the link between the self and the social as interdependent or transactional. The work of Piaget, specifically his organic view of knowledge and the attendant theories of assimilation and accommodation, is one such facet. Piaget argues that organisms adapt to their environment by first assimilating the new and often frightening experience into their existing representation of the world and then by changing that representation to accommodate this new piece of information. For Piaget, this process of adaptation is ongoing and dynamic, not passive. We reconstruct ourselves in an ongoing transaction with our environment. Another facet can be found in economist Kenneth Boulding's 1956 monograph entitled *The Image: Knowledge in Life and Society*. Here Boulding outlines an epistemology that links the personal to the social but preserves the individuality of the self. Boulding argues for an image (or representation) of the world which feeds on and grows organically through the messages it receives, messages filtered through the individual history of each image or self. Louise Rosenblatt, in *Literature as Exploration* and *The Reader, the Text, the Poem*, has also made a powerful case, with particular respect to reading, for the transactional theory of knowledge, a theory strongly resembling Boulding's and Piaget's in its acknowledgment of both the personal and public dimensions of language and knowing. Rosenblatt insists on foregrounding the individual lived histories of students, and the way these lived histories shape student responses to literary texts. Janet Emig, in an essay entitled "Our Missing Theory," urges us to study learning theory, particularly what she describes as "Constructivism," emphasizing its personal dimension and characterizing it in terms that are consonant with the ideas of Boulding, Piaget, and Rosenblatt. "Through their private and their school encounters with text, their creation, comprehension, and interpretation, our students have built constructs about what reading and writing are and about what roles these processes serve, or do not serve, in *their* lives [italics mine]" (p. 92). We should begin with such personal knowledge, Emig argues, and one obvious way to do that, I would suggest, is through writing assignments that are personal and expressive in nature, at least in their initial phases, assignments that allow students to voice themselves and their location with respect to social authority and power in order to resist those forces which would explicitly or tacitly repress them.

Resistance

The fourth and final problematic term in my title—*resistance*—provides potential hope with regard to the subject, or self, and its capacity for liberatory struggle. If we can sensitize our students, make them aware of the ideology of the entrenched and empowered class and the way in which institutions often operate to maintain the status quo, we put these students in a position to fight back. Such retaliation might range from the minimal— essential recognition and articulation of their plight—to various forms of active resistance. We cannot, nor should we, choose for our students or pressure them into postures of resistance. Some, even after they recognize their disempowered condition, may prefer that condition to active resistance against it. To resist or not to resist: That choice is theirs alone. But if we can help them to recognize and voice their dominated condition, we will have served them well.

One way we might begin to raise the consciousness of our students is by rejecting the spatial metaphor of marginalization. Many of our students come to our classes feeling marginalized already, that is, out on the periphery, away from the center of power, so far out, in fact, that they bring with them attitudes of submission, helplessness, and indifference. The discourse of composition studies in recent times, as the discipline has become increasingly influenced by the ideological orientation of postmodernist theory, has been marked by a persistent reliance on the metaphors of marginalization and boundaries. Consider, for example, Mike Rose's excellent *Lives on the Boundary* (a moving and *personal* account of how educational and economic institutions made powerless him and the students he later worked with in literacy programs, and how sensitive teachers *can* make a difference). Consider, too, Carolyn Ericksen Hill's *Writing from the Margins: Power and Pedagogy for Teachers of Composition*. Both books intelligently characterize the way in which disempowered students can be kept that way by ideological forces. But much as I agree with the overall "rightness" of their respective conclusions, I worry that the metaphor each uses can send the wrong message to student and teacher alike. In fact, the disempowered are not somewhere "out there," at the edge, far removed. They are, rather, at the center of power's corrosive processes. Paulo Freire makes this point in his *The Politics of Education: Culture, Power and Liberation*: "In the light of such a concept [marginalization]," Freire argues, ". . . literacy programs can never be movements toward freedom. . . . These men [sic], illiterate or not, are not marginal. . . . They are not 'beings outside of'; they are 'beings for another.' Therefore the solution to their problem is to become, not 'beings inside of,' but men freeing themselves; for, in reality, they are not marginal to the structure, but oppressed men within it" (pp. 48-49). Illiteracy, for Freire, is a form of muteness in "the culture of silence" and literacy is tantamount to transformative action. If, he maintains, the illiterate can gain an awareness of how dominatory mechanisms work to oppress them, "they can 'have a voice,' that is, they [can] exercise the right to participate consciously in the sociohistorical transformation of their society" (p. 50). He insists that the literacy process "must relate *speaking the word* to *transforming reality*, and to man's role in this transformation. . . . [Such learners] will ultimately recognize a much greater right than that of being literate. They will recognize that . . . they have the right to have a voice" (p. 51). Freire clearly reinforces what I have been arguing in this essay about voice and human agency, but he is often too easily dismissed by critics who argue that the severe kind of illiteracy with which Freire has had to deal in third-world countries does not apply to conditions in this country. Though I agree with these critics in part, I suspect the conditions bear stronger similarities than most of us would like to admit. At any rate, let me turn to a few theoretical arguments that focus more directly on developed societies.

For those interested in the issues I have been exploring in this essay and
in a pedagogy with a liberatory agenda, Henry A. Giroux's *Theory &
Resistance in Education: A Pedagogy for the Opposition* is a good place to
begin. In this book, Giroux sets out to assay the history of radical educational
theory and its proponents—those who have regarded schools not merely as
sites of instruction but also as sites of political and cultural struggle—in order
to locate foundations upon which he might then construct a more
contemporary theory of educational resistance. Giroux maintains that all too
many of these educational critics are severely flawed because their theories do
not contain an adequate view of human agency that would enable students to
recognize and resist the sources of their domination. To supply what is
missing from most radical educational theory, Giroux turns to the critical
theory of the Frankfurt School—Adorno, Horkheimer, and Marcuse. "The
achievements of the critical theorists," Giroux stresses, "are their refusal to
abandon the dialectic of agency and structure [state apparatuses, etc.] . . . and
[their willingness to] treat seriously the claim that history can be changed,
that the potential for radical transformation exists" (p. 5). By human agency,
Giroux essentially means that human beings create history rather than merely
being prisoners of it. Students are not inevitably passive victims of prison-like
schools which invisibly reproduce the interests of the ruling class. Vital to
Giroux's outlook is that students are in some sense "selves," and that schools
are sites of struggle where resistance and change can occur. In too much
theory—educational or critical or literary—the concept of self has been
erased, so Giroux turns to those theorists who attempt to preserve self,
because, in one form or another, the capacity to resist depends on a theory of
self.

The Frankfurt School, Giroux maintains, rejected the positivist rationality
of science that had come to dominate in schools, and replaced it with the idea
of "dialectical thinking." He defines this by quoting Fredric Jameson's
definition: "[D]ialectical thinking is . . . thought about thinking itself, in which
the mind must deal with its own thought process just as much as with the
material it works on, in which both the particular content involved and the
style of thinking suited to it must be held together in the mind at the same
time" (p. 35). Such dialectical thought—which, I might add, echoes strongly
the ideas of James Britton—makes educators as well as students capable of
what Giroux calls "critique," or the ability to think oppositionally. Such
thinkers don't blindly accept the traditional narrative of progress and
historical continuity; instead, they seek "the breaks, discontinuities, and
tensions in history, all of which become valuable in that they highlight the
centrality of human agency and struggle while simultaneously revealing the
gap between society as it presently exists and society as it might be" (36).
The socially oppressed—and I want to supplement Giroux's listing of the
working class, women, Blacks, and other minorities by adding middle-class
students—need "to affirm their own histories through the use of a language, a
set of social conventions, and body of knowledge that critically reconstructs
and dignifies the cultural experiences that make up the tissue, texture, and

history of their daily lives (p. 37)." This is a matter of great importance, Giroux insists, because "once the affirmative nature of such a pedagogy is established, it becomes possible for students who have been traditionally voiceless in schools to learn the skills, knowledge, and modes of inquiry that will allow them to critically examine the role society has played in their own self-formation. . . . [I]t is important for students to come to grips with what a given society has made of them, how it is has incorporated them ideologically and materially into its rules and logic, and what it is they need to affirm and reject in order to begin the process of struggling for the conditions that will give them opportunities to lead a self-managed existence" (pp. 37-38). Here again we see Giroux's emphasis on human agency in the form of critique as pitted in dialectical fashion against a dominant culture. "[H]uman beings not only make history, they also make the constraints; and needless to say, they also unmake them . . . power is both an enabling as well as a constraining force" (p. 38).

After analyzing the concept of the "hidden curriculum"—"those unstated norms, values, and beliefs embedded in and transmitted to students through the underlying rules that structure the routines and social relationships in school and classroom life" (p. 47) in order to covertly undergird and reproduce the dominant society—Giroux insists that we must see schools as "sites of *both domination and contestation*" (pp. 62-63). Thus, we must recognize the dialectic tension between forces of reproduction, on the one hand, and the concrete, lived experiences of the students. Herein, Giroux suggests, lies a potent source of resistance, for the concrete histories of students, when brought to consciousness and placed in opposition to the cultural forces which have in part produced these concrete histories and which attempt to perpetuate the inequities there recorded, provide students with the necessary antecedent to resistance. Giroux ultimately says that the dialectic between the actual experience of students and the ideological agenda of schools is a far more complex matter than is generally granted by educational critics. Precisely because most of these critics omit any concern for human agency or self as a resisting entity, one of Giroux's most important contributions is his faith in the existence of human agency and his location of it in the concrete lives of students (as well as teachers). The self as Giroux conceives it may be ultimately socially constructed, but the product of this construction is not pure victim; it is a potent force for struggle, especially when the pedagogical environment is designed to explore the dialectic nature of education. Giroux's message is an affirmation of self and voicing as a tool for its growth. As such, it brings us closer to a mediation between post-modernist claims and the Authentic Voice pedagogy.

Another useful starting point is Paul Smith's *Discerning the Subject*. In this book-length study Smith also surveys a variety of social theories (the Frankfurt School, various Marxist perspectives, postmodernism) as well as individuals (Althusser, Adorno, Marcuse, Derrida), and he too finds them flawed for their failure to include a workable concept of human agency. He believes "the calls to resistance made by such educational theorists as Henry

Giroux are hampered by a view of subjectivity inherited from Fromm, Marcuse, and others" and he claims that an adequate theory of subjectivity and agency "must take account of what I call the mediating function of the unconscious in social life" (p. xxxi); thus he proposes that Lacan's theory of the unconscious could provide the missing piece in assembling a viable theory of resistance. One problem, he notes, is the philosophic tradition of dualism, which has split the world into subject (or perceiver, or consciousness) and object (the material world, that which is perceived). Both Marx and Freud, Smith claims, have aided postmodernism by problematizing an oversimplified concept of the self, the former by rooting self in material reality, the latter by locating "true" self in the murky regions of the unconscious. Another problem, Smith argues, is that the majority of poststructuralist theories deal with the idea of Self at such an abstract level (a process which Smith labels "cerning," that they produce, in his words, "a purely theoretical 'subject,' removed from the political and ethical realities in which human agents live," and he concludes that "a different concept of the 'subject' must be discerned" (p. xxix); that is, the central and privileged Western concept of the self or subject must be negated if a more rich and accurate theory is to emerge. He also argues against versions of a monolithic process of interpellation, insisting that resistance "can be glimpsed as soon as the 'subject' is no longer theorized as an abstract or cerned entity" (pp. xxx-xxxi).

Smith begins by establishing some definitions of terms, definitions useful for our purposes. He differentiates the terms "individual," "subject," and "agent." The individual, "that which is undivided and whole, and understood to be the source and agent of conscious action or meaning which is consistent with it," is essentially an illusion (xxxiii-xxxiv). The "subject" is not self-contained and is dominated by social formations, language, ideological apparatuses, and it is capable of many subject positions in a specific, lived life. "The term 'agent,' Smith says, "[marks] the idea of a form of subjectivity where, by virtue of the contradictions and disturbances in and among subject-positions, the possibility (indeed, the actuality) of resistance to ideological pressure is allowed for (even though that resistance too must be produced in an ideological context)" (p. xxxv). The main point in a sense is, as Smith notes, that "[a] person is not simply the actor who follows ideological scripts, but is also an agent who reads them in order to insert him/herself into them— or not" (pp. xxxiv-xxxv). In his concluding chapter, Smith reiterates "that the era of . . . poststructuralism has perhaps brought with it a tendency to problematize so much the 'subject's' relation to experience that it has become difficult to keep sight of the political necessity of being able to not only theorize but also *refer* to that experience" (159), and he contends that the specificity of experience—a rich source of resistance—has been severely debilitated by poststructuralist theories of language, representation, and subjectivity. "In other words," he says, "poststructuralism's skepticism, its radical doubt, about the availability of the referent has been canonized, even exaggerated, to the point that the real often disappears from consideration" (159).

After citing the failure of Marxism to provide an adequate account of the subject—mainly because this influential theory has, for the most part, ignored the individual dimension of the subject and stressed its collective nature— Smith poses what is the central issue for him and, to a certain degree, for Giroux as well: ". . . how and under what conditions subject/individuals simultaneously exist within and make purposive intervention into social formations" (p. 5). An individual's concrete experience and personal history are not, Smith insists, determined by what class one belongs to or what set of economic conditions one must accept. Smith stresses this point in a more focused manner when he characterizes the individual existence as always at one level *solitary*, not interpersonal or social; although we *are* socially constructed, this construction takes place within specific historical and personal conditions, and resistance is made possible by a dialectic tension between the interpellation of dominant institutions and the subject, which is always in a process of evolving. Smith is not willing to posit some "innate human capacity that could over-ride or transcend the very conditions of understanding and calculation—indeed of social existence. Resistance does take place, but it takes place only within a social context which has already constructed subject-positions for the human agent. The place of that resistance, has, then, to be glimpsed somewhere in the interstices of the subject-positions which are offered in any social formation. More precisely, resistance must be regarded as the by-product of contradictions in and among subject-positions" (p. 25). The personal history Smith repeatedly refers to as one half of the dialectic which makes resistance possible begins for him (and here he is influenced by Lacan) in one's engagement with language: "there is no such thing as a 'subject position' before the accession to language" (p. 31). This personal history is made up of an ongoing series of moments, "a continuing series of overlapping subject-positions which may or may not be present to consciousness at any given moment. . . . A person's lived history cannot be abstracted as subjectivity pure and simple, but must be conceived as a colligation of multifarious and multiform subject-positions" (p. 32). So the problem, as Smith sees it, is that theorists too often simplify and abstract the subject rather than recognize that each subject is the result of a compilation of moments which constitute singular histories. Despite the difficult language in Smith's analysis, the careful reader can begin to see connections between Smith's position and, for example, those of Giroux and Rosenblatt.

Disagreeing with Althusser that the subject is identical to the concept of individuality and at the same time the result of ideology, Smith argues that "the state of being a 'subject' is best conceived of in something akin to a temporal aspect—the 'subject' as only a moment in a lived life," the result being that interpellations don't automatically succeed. They can in fact fail, because what interpellation actually creates is contradictions, "and through a recognition of the contradictory and dialectical elements of subjectivity it may be possible to think a concept of the agent" (p. 37). "A singular history," Smith insists, "always mediates between the human agent and the interpellations directed at him/her . . . each of us necessarily negotiates the power of specific ideologies by means of our own personal history" (p. 37). "If this seems a platitude," Smith continues (in what I think is a key reminder), ". . . it bears reiteration . . . [because] of the emphasis that has been placed, in contemporary discourse, on the subjection of the 'subject,' usually to the detriment of any consideration of the human agent's own historical constitution" (p. 37).

There is more and yet richer ground to cover in trying to recapitulate Smith's subtle and at times difficult analysis of the failure of social and critical theory to provide an adequate concept of human agency which would make resistance possible. But I have, I think, given enough sense of Smith's work for us to see the major outlines of his argument. What is especially useful in both Giroux and Smith is that they recognize the importance of postmodern theory and are not attempting to discredit its contributions or argue for a return to a nostalgic theory of self. In fact, both seek to define self in more complex ways than either neo-Romantics or postmodernists have so far been willing to do. Both Giroux and Smith seek to locate or articulate a concept of self that allows for resistance, for opportunities for each of us to find our voice and enlist it in the struggle against oppressive forces. And as we have seen, both writers have explored new territory in this debate by their call for a more dialectical view of self. Before I conclude, I want to take a quick look at one final alternative to the limited concept of self against which I have arguing in this essay, an alternative found in what philosopher and political scientist Charles Taylor calls the *dialogical self.*

The very phrase itself, along with its opposite—*the monological self*— connects Taylor's perspective to the themes of voice and resistance I have been pursuing. Taylor considers the self to be essentially a modern and Western cultural phenomenon, at least in the sense that a concept of self goes beyond mere reflexivity, which earlier ages clearly possessed. It is a specific form of reflexivity that characterizes modern culture, a "radical reflexivity" that allows us to review and analyze our own thinking. Humans have always "devis[ed], or accept[ed], or have [had] thrust upon them descriptions of themselves, and these descriptions help to make them what they are" (p. 305). And Taylor stresses the moral or ethical dimension of many of these descriptions: "A human being exists inescapably in a space of ethical questions; she or he cannot avoid assessing himself or herself in relation to some standards" (p. 305). It is this sense of ethical space that truly defines our grasp of who we truly are, so our values serve as a compass for locating our selves in ethical space. This ethical space may be a defining feature of self, but the space itself changes; it is relative to one's time, place, and culture, and the "radical reflexivity" mentioned above Taylor cites as the central "ethical space" of the modern age. To do this, we "have had to discipline our thought to disengagement from embodied agency and social embedding. Each of us is called upon to become a responsible, thinking mind, self-reliant for his or her judgments" (p. 307). This disengaged first-person sigular "tends to see the human agent as primarily a subject of representations . . . about the world outside . . . [about] ends desired or feared" (p. 307). This subject is a "monological" one because it operates on the basis of its own inner representations. Such a subject lives in an inner space, in effect cut off or separated from others.

This "stripped-down view of the subject" (p. 307), this monological self, Taylor claims has permeated the social sciences and has been responsible for the privileging of individualism and rational choice-making. And the near-hegemony of this concept of self "stands in the way of a richer and more adequate understanding of what the human sense of self is really like, and hence of a proper understanding of the real variety of human culture, and hence of a knowledge of human beings" (p. 307). This monological view of self omits, says Taylor, two essential components of a fuller theory of self: the body and the other. Taylor notes that in the past two centuries some philosophers have tried to derive a fuller theory by conceiving of the human agent less in terms of a repository of representations and more in terms of someone engaged in practices, "as a being who acts in and on a world" (p. 308). To be sure, Taylor does not deny that humans frame representations which *do* inform their actions; but many of our actions are undertaken "unformulated." That is, they originate "from an understanding that is largely inarticulate" and which is always there, like a great ocean, reducing our representations "to islands in the sea of our unformulated practical grasp on the world" (p. 308).

This is where the body enters in. It doesn't simply execute our consciously framed goals; "[o]ur understanding itself is embodied. That is, our bodily know-how, and the way we act and move, can encode components of our understanding of self and world" (p. 309). Such understanding obviously affects the way we place ourselves in the physical world, but it is more than that: "My sense of myself, of the footing I am on with others, are in large part also" affected and shaped (p. 309). This bodily knowledge is not generally visible in our representations of the world and of others; it is most visible in our actions, which intuitively "sense" when they are appropriate or not. Here Taylor cites the work of Pierre Bourdieu, who has defined this tacit knowing as "habitus" (p. 309). Since our actions are not played out like soliloquies on a stage empty of all "actors" but that of the solitary self, the "other" must invariably come into play, and this brings us to the heart of the dialogic nature of this unarticulated knowledge. Acts of a solitary agent Taylor labels "monological" acts; those of more than one he calls "dialogical" acts. Shared agency is the key to dialogical acts, which may be seen as a form of collaboration. Taylor concludes: "We cannot understand human life merely in terms of individual subjects, who frame representations about and respond to others, because a great deal of human action happens only insofar as the agent understands and constitutes himself or herself as integrally part of a 'we'" (p. 311). Arguing against what he calls "a theory of introjection"—that is, the self is formed by simply internalizing the values and attitudes of others—Taylor rejects oversimplified theories of social construction because such theories leave no room for resistance. Indeed, suggests Taylor, the self draws from its social environment, but it must have within itself the capacity to say no, to refuse to conform, to set itself against the social world. Using conversation as his metaphor for the process he is advocating, Taylor says that the self "neither preexists all conversation, as in the old monological view; nor does it arise from an introjection of the interlocutor; but it arises within conversation, because this kind of dialogical action by its very nature marks a place for the new locutor who is being inducted into it" (p. 312). We find our voice, in other words, among the voices of others, in a dialogic relation with them. We are not passive or silent in the conversation, nor are we rendered impotent by it. We are in effect empowered by the dialogue, and our voice is capable of resisting when resistance is required. As Taylor observes, ". . . it is a matter of finding one's own voice as an interlocutor . . . [in a] dialogue at the very center of our understanding of human life, an indispensable key to its comprehension" (pp. 313-14). We need the theoretical direction provided by Bakhtin, Taylor concludes, because human beings "are constituted in conversation; and hence what gets internalized in the mature subject is not the reaction of the other, but the whole conversation, with the interanimation of its voices" (p. 314).

Conclusion and Questions for Further Study

We need to examine more deliberately the direction of composing pedagogy in light of what recent literary and social theory have claimed about language and knowing. It is obvious that we cannot simply cling to Romantic notions of self and Arnoldian concepts of culture and circle the wagons against Theorists, Philistines, and Barbarians. Nor should we, as it seems to me both Berlin and Faigley are inclined to do, sever our connections with teachers of the Authentic Voice school—teachers like Macrorie and Elbow and Coles—and the pedagogical practices they advocate and which have served us well. We might do well to listen to Peter Elbow when he says in a recent essay that "despite some recent critical theory, I'm not yet convinced we should give up talking in terms of selves and authors" (230).

Further study of the concept of self needs to be conducted. The extremes of the concept have been pretty well identified, but much remains to be settled about the way in which a self is constituted. The theory which derives from this further study will need to be a rich and more complex one, and it will need to continue to draw from a variety of disciplines for its evolving formulation. If we are to achieve the synthesis of old and new theory for which this essay has been arguing, we need to re-examine the pedagogical strategies associated with Expressionistic rhetoric and find ways of revising them in ways that will promote the dialectic and dialogic features which Giroux, Smith, and Taylor have been advocating. Some of this work has already begun to develop in the form of collaborative writing assignments, electronic writing classes (see Selfe), computer conferencing and group work, and conversations in the form of electronic journals. Additional momentum can be seen in the essay by Barbara Henning I cited earlier. To help basic writers, Henning has called for a dialogic pedagogy based on the work of Bakhtin, one which would involve "meeting and analyzing despair collectively, rather than accepting it as fate" (681). Such a pedagogy, she claims, can affect the consciousness of students and teachers "through rigorous dialogic interaction about issues of shared importance, and that small changes in consciousness (the internalized dialogue between human beings who are/were situated socially in worlds that are constantly changing) have the potential of affecting the society we live in" (681).

Additional work as well needs to be done in making students aware of the omnipresence of ideology, particularly in theories of language and in forms of writing instruction. Teacher/researchers need to use the personal or autobiographical essay to explore the potential for political awareness and transformation this genre possesses. As the philosopher Sam Keen says, we must all learn to tell our own stories or have them told for us. Too many students presently do not realize that they have a unique story to tell, and that in the telling they can come to see something about their location with respect to power that, in a variety of ways, serves to effectively silence them. Journals, expressive writing, I-Searches, personal essays—all can be made consonant with a revitalized and expanded theory of voice. Much is at stake here. As members of a professional community whose theory is at the same time its practice, we must neither blindly reject nor simply accept the precepts of postmodernism. The latter option, an uncritical acceptance, is dangerous, because, as Giroux has pointed out, "these perspectives are deeply pessimistic. By providing an 'air-tight' notion of domination and an equally reductionist notion of socialization, radical accounts provide little hope for social change or the promise of oppositional teaching within the schools. Consequently, they help to provide a blue-print for cynicism and despair, one that serves to reproduce the very mode of domination they claim to resist" (59). That, of course, is not what we want. If we are to find a way out of this impasse, we must negotiate the extremes of traditional views of self and voice and the tenets of social construction. We must preserve a theory of human agency so that our students as well as ourselves can, like Archimedes, seek a place to stand, a place from which to resist against a world so badly in need of change.

Works Cited

Berlin, James. "Rhetoric and Ideology in the Writing Class." *College English* 50 (1988): 477-94.

Boulding, Kenneth. *The Image: Knowledge in Life and Society*. Ann Arbor: University of Michigan Press, 1956.

Bowra, C. M. *Primitive Song*. New York: Mentor Books, 1963.

Britton, James. *Language and Learning*. Harmondsworth, Middlesex, England: Penguin, 1970.

Britton, James, Tony Burgess, Nancy Martin, Alex McLeod, and Harold Rosen. *The Development of Writing Abilities (11-18)*. London: Macmillan, 1975.

Camus, Albert. *The Myth of Sisyphus*. Translated by Justin O'Brien. New York: Vintage Books, 1955.

Connor, Steven. *Postmodernist Culture: An Introduction to Theories of the Contemporary*. Oxford, England: Basil Blackwell Ltd., 1989.

Dobyns, Stephen. *Body Traffic*. New York: Viking, 1990.

Elbow, Peter. *Writing With Power*. New York: Oxford University Press, 1981.

Elbow, Peter. *Writing Without Teachers*. London: Oxford University Press, 1973.

Elbow, Peter. "The Pleasures of Voice," in *Literary Nonfiction: Theory, Criticism, Pedagogy*. Ed. Chris Anderson. Carbondale, IL: Southern Illinois University Press, 1989, 211-234.

Emig, Janet. "Our Missing Theory," in *Conversations: Contemporary Critical Theory and the Teaching of Literature*. Eds. Charles Moran and Elizabeth F. Penfield. Urbana, IL: NCTE, 87-96.

Faigley, Lester. "Judging Writing, Judging Selves." *College Composition and Communication* 40 (1989): 395-412.

Freire, Paulo. *Pedagogy of the Oppressed*. New York: The Continuum Publishing Corporation, 1985.

Freire, Paulo. *The Politics of Education: Culture, Power, and Liberation*. New York: Bergin and Garvey, 1985.

Gergen, Kenneth J. *The Saturated Self: Dilemmas of Identity in Contemporary Life*. New York: Basic Books, 1991.

Gilbert, Sandra. "My Name is Darkness: The Poetry of Self-Definition," in *Poetics: Essays on the Art of Poetry*, Eds. Paul Mariani and George Murphy. A special issue of *Tendril*, 1984, pp. 98-110.

Giroux, Henry A. *Theory & Resistance in Education: A Pedagogy of the Opposition*. New York: Bergin & Garvey, 1983.

Henning, Barbara. "The World was Stone Cold: Basic Writing in an Urban University." *College English* 53 (1991): 674-685.

Hill, Carolyn Ericksen Hill. *Writing from the Margins: Power and Pedagogy for Teachers of Composition*. New York: Oxford University Press, 1990.

Holden, Jonathan. *Style and Authenticity in Postmodern Poetry*. Columbia, MO: University of Missouri Press, 1986.

Holden, Jonathan. *The Rhetoric of the Contemporary Lyric*. Bloomington, IN: Indiana University Press, 1980.

Kelly, Lou. *From Dialogue to Discourse: An Open Approach*. Glenview, IL: Scott, Foresman and Company, 1972.

Kinnell, Galway. "Poetry, Personality, and Death," in *Poetics: Essays on the Art of Poetry*, Eds. Paul Mariani and George Murphy. A special issue of *Tendril*, 1984, 67-84.

Macrorie, Ken. *A Vulnerable Teacher*. Rochelle Park, NJ: Hayden Book Company, 1974.

Macrorie, Ken. *Telling Writing*. Rochelle Park, NJ: Hayden, 1970.

Macrorie, Ken. *Uptaught.*. New York: Hayden, 1970.

Macrorie, Ken. *Writing to be Read*. Rochelle Park, NJ: Hayden, 1968.

Rose, Mike. *Lives on the Boundary*. New York: Penguin Books, 1989.

Roseblatt, Louise. *The Reader, the Text, the Poem: The Transactional Theory of the Literary Work*. Carbondale, IL: Southern Illinois University Press, 1978.

Rosenblatt, Louise. *Literature as Exploration*. New York: Appleton-Century-Crofts, 1938.

Smith, Paul. *Discerning the Subject*. Minneapolis: University of Minnesota Press, 1988.

Stewart, Donald. *The Authentic Voice: A Pre-Writing Approach to Student Writing*. Dubuque, IA: Wm. C. Brown Company, 1972.

Sypher, Wylie. *Loss of the Self in Modern Literature and Art*. New York: Random House, 1962.

Taylor, Charles. "The Dialogical Self," in *The Interpretive Turn*. Eds. David R. Hiley, James F. Bohman, and Richard Shusterman. Ithaca, NY. Cornell University Press, 1991, 304-14.

Turner, Alberta. "Not Your Flat Tire, My Flat Tire: Transcending the Self in Contemporary Poetry," in *A FIELD Guide to Contemporary Poetry and Poetics*, Eds. Stuart Friebert and David Young. New York: Longman, 1980, 135-146.

Whitman, Walt. "Song of Myself," in *Complete Poetry and Selected Prose of Walt Whitman*. Cambridge, MA: Houghton Mifflin, 1959.

Wordsworth, William. *The Poetical Works of Wordsworth*, Eds. Thomas Hutchinson and Ernest De Selincourt. New York: Oxford University Press, 1965.

Bibliography

Appelbaum, D. *Voice*. Albany: SUNY P, 1991.

Aristotle. *Rhetoric* [on ethos]. Trans. Rhys Roberts. *Aristotle: Rhetoric and Poetics*. New York: Random House, 1954.

Bakhtin, Mikhail. "Discourse in the Novel." *The Dialogic Imagination: Four Essays*. Ed. Michael Holquist. Trans. Caryl Emerson and Michael Holquist. Austin: U of Texas Press Slavic Series, no. 1, 1981. 259-422.

Barthes, Roland. "The Death of the Author." *Image, Music, Text*. Trans. Stephen Heath. New York: Hill and Wang, 1977. 142-48.

_____. "From Speech to Writing." *The Grain of Voice*. New York: Hill and Wang, 1985. 3-7.

_____. "The Grain of the Voice." *Image, Music, Text*. Trans. Stephen Heath. New York: Hill and Wang, 1977. 179-89.

Bedetti, Gabriella. "Interdisciplinary Approaches To Teaching Voice." *English Record* 36 (1985): 15-16.

Belenky, Mary Field, Blythe McVicker Clinchy, Nancy Rule Goldberger, Jill Mattuck Tarule. *Women's Ways of Knowing: The Development of Self, Voice, and Mind*. New York: Basic Books, 1986.

Bialostosky, Don H. "Liberal Education, Writing, and the Dialogic Self." *Contending with Words: Composition and Rhetoric in a Postmodern Age*. Eds. Patricia Harkin and John Schilb. New York: The Modern Language Association of America, 1991. 11-22.

Bolinger, Dwight. *Intonation and its Parts: Melody in Spoken English*. Stanford: Stanford UP, 1986.

Booth, Wayne. *The Rhetoric of Fiction*. Chicago: U of Chicago P, 1961.

Bowden, Betsy. *Chaucer Aloud: The Varieties of Textual Interpretation*. Philadelphia: U of Pennsylvania P, 1987.

Brandt, Deborah. *Literacy as Involvement: The Acts of Writers, Readers, and Texts*. Carbondale: Southern IL UP, 1990.

Brooke, Robert E. *Writing and Sense of Self Identity Negotiation in Writing Workshops*. Urbana, IL: National Council of Teachers of English, 1991.

Brooks, Phyllis. "Mimesis: Grammar and the Echoing Voice." *College English* 35 (Nov 1973): 161-68.

Brower, Reuben. "The Speaking Voice." *The Fields of Light: An Experiment in Critical Reading*. New York: Oxford, 1962.

Brown, Lyn Mikel and Carol Gilligan. "Listening for Self and Relational Voices: A Responsive/Resisting Reader's Guide." M. Franklin (Chair), *Literary Theory as a Guide to Psychological Analysis*. Symposium, A Psychological Association, Boston MA, 1990.

Brownmiller, Susan. "Voice." *Femininity*. New York: Fawcett Columbine, 1984.

Buber, Martin. *I and Thou*. New York: Charles Scribner, 1958.

Buley-Meissner, Mary Louise. "Rhetorics of the Self." *Balancing Acts: Essays on the Teaching of Writing in Honor of William F. Irmscher*. Eds. Virginia Chappell, Mary Louise Buley-Meissner, Chris Anderson. Carbondale: Southern IL UP, 1991.

Coles, William E. Jr. *The Plural I—And After*. Portsmouth NH: Boynton/Cook Heinemann, 1988.

Crismore, Avon. *Talking With Readers: Metadiscourse as Rhetorical Act*. New York: Peter Lang, 1989.

Crystal, David. *The English Tone of Voice: Essays in Intonation, Prosody, and Paralanguage*. London: Edward Arnold, 1975.

Dasenbrock, Reed Way. "Becoming Aware of the Myth of Presence." *Journal of Advanced Composition* 8 (1988): 1-11.

Donaghue, Denis. *Ferocious Alphabets*. New York: Columbia UP, 1984.

_____. "The Question of Voice." *ANTAEUS* 53 (Autumn 1984): 7-25.

Elbow, Peter. "The Pleasures of Voices in the Literary Essay: Explorations in the Prose of Gretel Ehrlich and Richard Selzer." *Literary Nonfiction: Theory, Criticism, Pedagogy*. Ed. Chris Anderson. Carbondale: Southern IL UP, 1989.

_____. "The Shifting Relationships Between Speech and Writing," *Conference on College Composition and Communication* 36.2 (October 1985): 283-303.

_____. "Voice in Literature." *Encyclopedia of English Studies and Language Arts*. Ed. Alan Purves. Urbana IL: NCTE, in press.

_____. "Writing and Voice" and "How to Get Power Through Voice" and "Magic in Writing." *Writing With Power*. New York: Oxford, 1981.

Eliot, T. S. "Three Voices of Poetry." *On Poetry and Poets*. New York: Farrar, Strauss and Cudahy, 1943. 96-112.

Ellsworth, Elizabeth. "Why Doesn't This Feel Empowering? Working Through the Repressive Myths of Critical Pedagogy." *Harvard Educational Review* 59.3 (August 1989): 297-323. (A critique of "voice as empowerment" teaching.)

Emerson, Caryl. "The Outer Word and Inner Speech: Bakhtin, Vygotsky, and the Internalization of Language." *Critical Inquiry* 10 (December 1983): 21-40.

Enos, Theresa. "Voice as Echo of Delivery, *Ethos* as Transforming Process." *Composition in Context: Essays in Honor of Donald C. Stewart*. Carbondale: Southern IL UP, 1992.

Evans, J. Claude. *Strategies of Deconstruction: Derrida and the Myth of the Voice*. Minneapolis: U of MN P, 1991.

Faludi, Susan. "Speak for Yourself." *New York Times Magazine,* 26 Jan 1992: 10.

Finke, Laurie. "Knowledge as Bait: Feminism, Voice, and the Pedagogical Unconscious." *College English* 54 (Jan 1993): 7-27.

Foucault, Michael. "What is an Author?" *Partisan Review* 42 (1975): 604-14. Reprinted in *Language, Counter-Memory, Practice*. Ed. Donald F. Bouchard. Trans. Donald F. Bouchard and Sherry Simon. Ithaca: Cornell UP, 1977.

Freedman, Sarah. "The Registers of Student and Professional Expository Writing: Influences on Teacher Responses." In *New Directions in Composition Research*. Ed. Richard Beach and Lillian Bridwell. New York: Guilford Press, 1984. 334-47.

Freire, Paolo. *The Pedagogy of the Oppressed*. Trans. Myra Bergman Ramos. New York: Seabury, 1968.

Frost, Robert. Introduction. *A Way Out*. New York: Seven Arts, 1917. In *Poetry and Prose*. Eds. Edward Connery Lathem and Lawrence Thompson. New York: Holt, 1972.

Gergen, Kenneth J. *The Saturated Self: Dilemmas of Identity in Contemporary Life*. New York: Harper Collins, 1991.

Gibson, Walker. "Authors, Speakers, Readers, and Mock Readers." *College English* 11 (Feb 1950): 265-69.

_____. *Persona: A Style Study for Readers and Writers*. New York: Random House, 1969.

_____. "The Voice of the Writer." *College Composition and Communication* 8.3 (Oct 1962): 10-13.

_____. *Tough, Sweet, and Stuffy: An Essay on Modern American Prose Styles*. Bloomington: Indiana UP, 1966.

Gilligan, Carol. *In A Different Voice: Psychological Theory and Women's Development*. Cambridge: Harvard UP, 1982. 2nd edition, 1993.

_____. "Joining the Resistance: Psychology, Politics, Girls and Women." *Michigan Quarterly Review* 29.4 (Fall 1990): 501-37.

Gilligan, Carol, Lyn Mikel Brown, and Annie G. Rogers. "Psyche Embedded: A Place for Body, Relationships, and Culture in Personality Theory." Henry Murray Lecture, Michigan SU, April 1988.

Gilyard, Keith. *Voices of the Self: A Study of Language Competence*. Detroit: Wayne State UP, 1991.

Giroux, Henry A. *Theory and Resistance in Education: A Pedagogy for the Opposition*. South Hadley, MA: Bergin and Garvey, 1983.

Goldberg, Jonathan. *Voice Terminal Echo: Postmodernism and English Renaissance Texts*. New York: Methuen, 1986.

Graddol, David and Joan Swann. *Gender Voices*. Oxford: Blackwell, 1989.

Griffin, Susan. "Shaftesbury's *Soliloquy*: The Development of Rhetorical Authority." *Rhetoric Review* 9.1 (1990): 94-106.

Gusdorf, Georges. *Speaking (La Parole)*. Trans Paul T. Brockelman. Evanston IL: Northwestern UP, 1965.

Hall, Donald. "Goatfoot, Milktongue, Twinbird: The Psychic Origins of Poetic Form." *Goatfoot Milktongue Twinbird: Interviews, Essays and Notes on Poetry, 1970-76*. Poets on Poetry Series. Ann Arbor: U of Michigan P, 1978.

Hanson, Melanie Sarra. *Developmental Concepts of Voice in Case Studies of College Students: The Owned Voice and Authoring*. Diss. Ann Arbor, Michigan: UMI, 1986.

Harris, Joseph. "The Plural Text/The Plural Self: Roland Barthes and William Coles." *College English* 49.2 (February 1987): 158-170.

_____. "Voice." *Contested Terms*. Unpublished MS.

Havelock, Eric. *The Muse Learns to Write: Reflections on Orality and Literacy from Antiquity to the Present*. New Haven: Yale UP, 1986.

_____. "Orality, Literacy, and Star Wars." *Written Communication* 3.4 (Oct 1986): 411-20.

Hawkes, John. "The Voice Project: An Idea for Innovation in the Teaching of Writing." *Writers as Teachers: Teachers as Writers*. New York: Holt Rinehart and Winston, 1970. 89-144. (Hawkes described the project at greater length in *Voice Project, Final Report*. Stanford: Stanford UP, 1967. ERIC ED 018 442.)

Hickey, Dona J. *Developing a Written Voice*. Mountain View, CA: Mayfield, 1993.

Hoddeson, David. "The Reviser's Voices." *Journal of Basic Writing* 3.3 (Fall/Winter 1981): 91-108.

Holquist, Michael. "Answering as Authoring: Mikhail Bakhtin's Trans-Linguistics." *Critical Inquiry* 10 (Dec 1983): 307-319.

hooks, bell. *Talking Back Thinking Feminist Thinking Black*. Boston: South End Press, 1989.

Ihde, Don. *Listening and Voice: A Phenomenology of Sound*. Athens OH: Ohio UP, 1976.

Irigaray, Luce "When our Lips Speak Together." *Signs* 6.1 (1980): 69-79.

Johnson, Barbara. "Metaphor, Metonymy, and Voice in Zora Neale Hurston's *Their Eyes Were Watching God*." Ed. Mary Ann Caws. *Textual Analysis: Some Readers Reading*. New York: MLA, 1986. 232-44.

Johnson, Nan. "Ethos and the Aims of Rhetoric." *Essays on Classical Rhetoric and Modern Discourse*. Ed. Robert J. Connors, Lisa Ede and Andrea Lunsford. Carbondale: Southern IL UP, 1984. 98-114.

Joos, Martin. *Five Clocks*. New York: Harcourt Brace, 1962.

Josipovici, Gabriel. *Text and Voice: Essays 1981 to 1991*. New York: St. Martin's, 1992.

_____. *Writing and the Body*, Princeton: Princeton UP, 1982 (can transform the physical body).

Katz, Steven. *The Epistemic Music of Rhetoric: The Temporal Dimension of Reader Response and Writing*. Carbondale: Southern IL UP, in press.

Keithley, Zoe. "My Own Voice: Students say it Unlocks the Writing Process." *Journal of Basic Writing* 11.2 (Fall 1992): 82-102.

Kennedy, George A. "Voice as Frame." *Classical Rhetoric and Its Christian and Secular Tradition from Ancient to Modern Times*. Chapel Hill: U of North Carolina P, 1980.

Kennedy, William J. "'Voice' and 'Address' in Literary Theory." *Oral Tradition* 2 (1987): 214-30.

Kneale, J. Douglas. "Wordsworth's Images of Language: Voice and Letter in *The Prelude*." *PMLA* 101.3 (May 1986): 351-61.

Kramarae, Cheris. *Technology and Women's Voices*. New York & London: Routledge and Kegan Paul, 1988.

Kristeva, Julia. "The System and the Speaking Subject." *The Kristeva Reader*. Ed. Toril Moi. New York: Columbia UP, 1986. 24-33.

Kroll, Barry, et al. *Exploring Speaking-Writing Relationships*. Urbana, IL: NCTE, 1981.

Larson, Richard L. "The Rhetoric of the Written Voice." *Rhetoric and Change*. Ed. William E. Tanner and J. Dean Bishop. Rev. ed. Arlington TX: Liberal Arts Press, 1985. 121-31. (Distributed by NCTE).

Leggo, Carl. "Questions I need to Ask before I Advise My Students to Write in Their Own Voices." *Rhetoric Review* 10.1 (Fall 1991): 143-52.

Lerman, Claire. "Dominant Discourse: The Institutional Voice and Control of Topic." In *Language, Image, and Media*. Ed. Howard Davis and Paul Walton. New York: St. Martin's, 1983. 75-103.

Liggett, Sarah. "The Relationship Between Speaking and Writing: An Annotated Bibliography." *College Composition and Communication* 35.3 (Oct 1984): 334-44.

Linklater, Kristin. *Freeing the Natural Voice*. New York: Drama Book Publishers, 1976.

Literacy/Orality Wars, special issue of *PRETEXT*.

Martin, Jacqueline. *Voice in Modern Theatre*. New York: Routledge, 1990.

McNeill, David. *Hand and Mind: What Gestures Reveal about Thought.* Chicago: U of Chicago P, 1992.

Miller, Alice. *The Drama of the Gifted Child: The Search for the True Self.* New York, Basic Books, 1981.

Moffett, James. "Liberating Inner Speech." *College Composition and Communication* 36.3 (Oct 1985): 304-8.

_____. "Writing, Inner Speech and Meditation." *Coming On Center.* Montclair NJ: Boynton Cook, 1981. 133-81.

Morson, Gary Saul, ed. *Bakhtin: Essays and Dialogues on His Work.* Chicago: U of Chicago P, 1986.

Murray, David, ed. *Forked Tongues: Speech, Writing and Representation in North American Indian Texts.* Bloomington: Indiana UP, 1991.

Olson, Charles. "Projective Verse." *Selected Writings.* Ed. Robert Creeley. New York: New Directions, 1966. 15-26.

Olson, David. R. "The Languages of Instruction: The Literate Bias of Schooling." Eds. R. C. Anderson, R. J. Siro, and W. E. Montague. *Schooling and the Acquisition of Knowledge.* Hillsdale, N.J.: Lawrence Erlbaum, 1977.

_____. "Writing: The Divorce of the Author from the Text." *Exploring Speaking-Writing Relationships: Connections and Contrasts.* Eds. B. M. Kroll and R. J. Vann. Urbana IL: NCTE, 1981. 99-110.

Ong, Walter. "From Mimesis to Irony: Writing and Print as Integuments of Voice." *Interfaces of the Word: Studies in the Evolution of Consciousness and Culture.* Ithaca: Cornell UP, 1977. 272-304.

_____. *Orality and Literacy: The Technologizing of the Word.* New York: Methuen, 1982.

_____. *Presence of the Word.* New Haven: Yale UP, 1967.

_____. "Voice as a Summons for Belief." *The Barbarian Within: and Other Fugitive Essays and Studies.* New York: Macmillan, 1962. 49-67.

Oral and Written Traditions in the Middle Ages. Special edition of *New Literary History: A Journal of Theory and Interpretation* 16.1 (Autumn 1984).

Peyre, Henri. *Literature and Sincerity.* New Haven: Yale UP, 1963.

Pritchard, William. "Ear Training." *Teaching What We Do.* Amherst College Faculty. Amherst MA: Amherst College P, 1991.

Randall, Margaret. "Reclaiming Voices: Notes on a New Female Practice in Journalism." *Walking to the Edge.* Boston: South End Press, 1991. 67-78.

Raymond, James C. "I-Dropping and Androgyny: The Authorial *I* in Scholarly Writing." *College English* 44.4 (1993): 478-83.

Ritchie, Joy S. "Beginning Writers: Diverse Voices and Individual Identity." *College Composition and Communication* 40 (May 1989): 152-73.

Safire, William. "The Take on Voice." *New York Times Magazine,* 28 June 1992: 14.

Scheurer, Erika. *"A Vice for Voices": Emily Dickinson's Dialogic Voice From the Borders.* Diss. U Mass Amherst, 1993.

Schueller, Malini Johar. *The Politics of Voice: Liberalism and Social Criticism from Franklin to Kingston.* Albany: SUNY Press, 1991.

Schultz, John. *Writing From Start to Finish: The Story Workshop Basic Forms Rhetoric Reader.* Portsmouth: Boynton/Cook Heinemann, 1982. Concise edition, 1990. See also his "The Story Workshop Method: Writing from Start to Finish." *College English* 39.4 (Dec 1977): 411-36. Also Shiflett, Betty. "Story Workshop as a Method of Teaching Writing." *College English* 35.2 (Nov 1973): 141-60.

Scott, Ralph. "Chaim Perelman: Persona and Accommodation in the New Rhetoric." *PreText* 5.2.

Silverman, Kaja. *The Acoustic Mirror: The Female Voice in Psychoanalysis and Cinema.* Bloomington: Indiana UP, 1988.

Sloan, Gary. "Why I Want My Students to Lose Their Voices." *English Journal* 72.4 (April 1982): 31-33.

Smith, Paul. *Discerning the Subject.* Minneapolis: U of Minn P, 1998.

Sommers, Jeffrey. *Model Voices: Finding a Writing Voice.* New York: McGraw Hill, 1989.

Stephens, Michael. *The Dramaturgy of Style: Voice in Short Fiction.* Carbondale: Southern IL UP, 1986.

Stewart, Garrett. *Reading Voices: Literature and the Phonotext.* Berkeley: U Cal P, 1990.

Stoehr, Taylor. "Tone and Voice." *College English* 30.2 (Nov 1968): 150-61.

Tannen, Deborah. "Oral and Literate Strategies in Spoken and Written Discourse." *Literacy for Life: The Demand for Reading and Writing.* Eds. Richard Bailey and Robin Fosheim. New York: MLA, 1983.

_____. *Talking Voices: Repetition, Dialogue, Imagery.* Cambridge: Cambridge UP, 1989.

Tavalin, Fern. *Voice.* Diss. U Mass Amherst, 1994.

Taylor, Charles. "The Dialogical Self." *The Interpretive Turn: Philosophy, Science, Culture.* Eds. David Hiley, James Bohman, and Richard Shusterman. Ithaca: Cornell UP, 1991. See also his *The Ethics of Authenticity.* (Harvard UP, 1991).

Tedlock, Dennis. *The Spoken Word and the Work of Interpretation.* Philadelphia: U of Pennsylvania P, 1983.

Trilling, Lionel. *Sincerity and Authenticity.* Cambridge, MA: Harvard UP, 1972.

Trimbur, John. "Beyond Cognition: The Voices in Inner Speech." *Rhetoric Review* 5 (Spring 1987): 211-21.

Varnum, Robin. *English 1-2 at Amherst College, 1938-66.* Urbana IL: NCTE, in press.

Vygotsky, Lev. *Thought and Language.* Trans. Eugenia Hanfman and Gertude Vakar. Cambridge: M.I.T. Press, 1962.

_____. *Mind in Society: The Development of Higher Psychological Processes.* Eds. M. Cole, V. John-Steiner, S. Scribner, and E. Souberman. Cambridge: Harvard UP, 1978.

Walkerdine, V. "On the Regulation of Speaking and Silence: Subjectivity, Class and Gender in Contemporary Schooling." Eds. C Steedman et al. *Language, Gender and Childhood.* London: Routledge, 1985. 203-41.

Welty, Eudora. "Finding a Voice." *One Writer's Beginning.* Cambridge: Harvard UP, 1984.

Wesling, Donald. "Difficulties of the Bardic: Literature and the Human Voice." *Critical Inquiry* (Autumn 1981): 69-81.

Williams, Joseph. "Literary Style: The Personal Voice." *Style and Variables in English.* Eds. T. Shopen & J. Williams. Cambridge MA: Winthrop Pubs Inc, 1981.

Yancey, Kathleen Blake, ed. *Voices on Voice: A (Written) Discussion.* Urbana IL: NCTE, 1994.

Zoellner, Robert. "Talk/Write: A Behavioral Pedagogy for Composition." *College English* 30.4 (Jan 1969). 267-320.

Zumthor, Paul. "The Text and the Voice." *New Literary History.* 16 (Autumn 1984): 67-92.

Zweig, Paul. "A Voice Speaking to No One." *In Praise of What Persists.* Ed. Stephen Berg. New York: Harper and Row, 1983. 281-89.

Index